DATE DUE

DEMCO 38-296

POPULAR BANDS AND PERFORMERS

by
Charles E. Claghorn

The Scarecrow Press, Inc.
Lanham, Md., & London

by Scarecrow Press, Inc.
4720 Boston Way, Lanham, Maryland 20706

4 Pleydell Gardens, Folkestone
Kent CT20 2DN, England

British Cataloging in Publication Information Available

Library of Congress Cataloging-in-Publication Data

Claghorn, Charles Eugene, 1911–
Popular bands & performers / by Charles E. Claghorn.
p.   cm.
1. Popular music—Dictionaries.   2. Musical groups—Dictionaries.
3. Musicians—Dictionaries.   I. Title.   II. Title: Popular bands
and performers.
ML102.P66C53   1995   781.63'03—dc20   94–42655

ISBN 0–8108–2976–2 (cloth : alk. paper)

Printed in the United States of America

 The paper used in this publication meets the minimum requirements of
American National Standard for Information Sciences—Permanence
of Paper for Printed Library Materials, ANSI Z39.48–1984.

CONTENTS

To My Dear Wife For Her Loving Support

PREFACE

There is great demand from the public for a handy reference work on modern music as evidenced by the success of Claghorn's *Biographical Dictionary of American Music* published in 1973 by Parker Publishing Company. This book went into five printings and sold 17,000 copies. The *Dictionary* contained concise biographies of 5,000 American composers, lyricists, and singers from the establishment of America to the date of publication.

This new book, intended as a 20-year update of the *Dictionary,* covers all the notable popular bands, musicians, singers, and songwriters of the 19th and 20th centuries with concise facts updated to 1994.

In the past twenty years there has been a musical explosion of popular bands and groups which are covered in this new book. Since there are already volumes of classical music and opera, this book covers only a few leaders in those fields. It specializes in modern music facts for young people, baby boomers, and folks who remember the love songs of the past.

This volume will be of special interest to libraries since reference librarians receive many requests for information on various musicians, bands, and singers.

All the new musicians and singers are included such as Paula Abdul, Garth Brooks, Jimmy Buffett, Billy Ray Cyrus, Hammer, Reba McEntyre, Bonnie Raitt, Bruce Springsteen, and the bands Guns 'N Roses, Ice Cube, Ice-T, Lush, Red Hot Chili Peppers and hundreds more. Foreign groups who have performed in the states are also included.

After reading through thousands of pages of books, magazines, and newspapers the author was able to locate the hard to find information contained in this book. It would take similar research to find the information contained in this one volume. This new book will thus be a handy reference work for the thousands of music fans all over the United States and the United Kingdom.

ACKNOWLEDGEMENTS

The author wishes to thank Lorraine Black and JoAnne MacIntosh, Reference Librarians at the Cocoa Beach Public Library, for obtaining magazines for reference. Thanks also to his brother, Don, and sister-in-law, Lynn Claghorn, owners of the Heritage Shoppe on the Ocean City, NJ boardwalk, for supplying old magazines.

HELPFUL HINTS

Songs are designated with double quotation marks such as "Jingle Bells." Albums, CDs, and videos are italicized such as *Spellbound.*

Where a musician or singer leaves a band or group and produces a solo album, he or she is designated with an asterisk (*), and the band is cross-referenced such as DR. DRE* and N.W.A.*.

If you have a favorite song or songs and wish information on the songwriters, consult Havlice: *Popular Song Index Third Supplement* 1989, Metuchen, N.J.: The Scarecrow Press, Inc.

Look up the name of the song in the *Popular Song Index* and find the songwriters. Consult Claghorn's book for information on the songwriters. Examples:

"Bei mir bist du schon." Sammy Cahn, Saul Chaplin & Sholom
  Secunda.
"By the light of the silvery moon." Ed Madden & Gus Edwards.
"Dixie." Daniel Emmett.
"I wonder who's kissing her now." Will Hough, Frank R. Adams,
  Joseph E. Howard, & Harold Orlob.
"In the good old summertime." George Evans & Ren Shields.
"Little Brown Jug." Joseph Eastburn Winner.
"Yes! we have no bananas." Frank Silver & Irving Cohn (Conn).

Claghorn's book will tell you the composer and the lyricist and supply some additional information.

Not all songwriters named in the *Popular Song Index* are included in this present volume: the author has attempted to indicate the composers and lyricists of the best known songs, especially the old-time favorites.

THE LISTINGS

A

AABERG, PHILIP
CD & album *High Plains,* album *Uptight.*

AARONSON, IRVING (1895–1963)
b. New York City, pianist/leader/songwriter. Leader of **The Commanders** in the 1930s, Aaronson wrote "Boo-Hoo," "The Song the Angels Sing."

ABBA
Norwegian/Swedish group. Benny Andersson, Annifred Lyng-stad-Fredriksson, Agetha Ulvaeus, Bjorn Ulvaeus. Hit singles "Dancing Queen" 1977, "Take a Chance on Me" 1978, album *Abba* 1980, *Video Music Performance* 1980. Annifred's solo album *Something's Going On* produced by Phil Collins 1982, *Again* 1983.

ABBADO, CLAUDIO (1933–)
Conductor. b. 6/26 Milan, Italy. American Bicentennial debut in 1976, album *New Year's Concert* 1991.

ABBOTT, GEORGE (1887–1995)
b. 6/25 Forestville, NY. Librettist for *Damn Yankees* 1955, *Fiorello* 1959, *Tenderloin* 1960, etc. Plans were made to celebrate his 105th birthday in NY City, but Abbott wasn't able to attend. He died February 1.

ABBOTT, GREGORY
CD & album *Shake You Down.*

ABC
Group from Sheffield, UK, Martin Fry, David Palmer, Stephen Singleton, Mark White. Debut album *Lexicon of Love* 1983, *Absolutely ABC, Alphabet City, How to be a Zillionaire*, video *Concert*.

ABDUL, PAULA (1962–)
b. 6/19 San Francisco, CA. Singer, multi-platinum music video *Straight Up* 1989. *Forever Your Girl* sold 10 million albums, top single "Cold Hearted Snake" on platinum album *Shut Up and Dance, Spellbound* 1991 sold 3 million albums, hit song "Rush Rush" 1991. Married actor Emilio Estevez on 4/12/92 in Santa Monica, CA.

ABDUL, RAOUL (1929–)
b. 11/7 Cleveland, Ohio. Organized chamber concerts in Harlem, NY City in 1958.

ABERCROMBIE, JOHN
Guitarist with **Directions,*** CDs & albums *Abercrombie/Johnson/Erskin, Animato, Current Events, Ecm Works, Getting There, Night*.

ACCEPT
CDs & albums *Eat the Heat, Metal Heart, Russian Roulette, Staying a Life*, etc.

AC/DC
Australian heavy metal band formed 1973 with Mark Evans, Brian Johnson, Phil Rudd, lead singer Bon Scott (deceased), guitarist Angus Young, Malcolm Young. No. 1 album *For Those About to Rock* 1981, music video *Fly on the Wall* 1986, platinum album *The Razor's Edge* 1990. Toured the world 1990/91, album *AC/DC LIVE* 1992. Three teens were crushed to death at their concert in Salt Lake County, Utah in January 1992. The band agreed to an undisclosed settlement with the families.

ACE
London pop/rock band with Fran Byrne, musician/singer Paul

Carrack, Tex Comer, Phil Harris, Alan King, hit single "How Long" 1973.

ACKERMAN, WILLIAM
CDs & albums *Childhood & Memory, Imaginary Roads, It Takes a Year, Passage, Past Light,* etc.

ACOUSTIC ALCHEMY
CDs & albums *Back on the Case, Blue Chip, Early Alchemy.*

ACTION RE ACTION
Group in Denmark led by drummer/percussionist Ed Thigpen in 1974.

ACUFF, ROY (1903–1992)
b. 9/15 Maynardville, TN. Singer & leader of the **Smokey Mountain Boys,** hit single "Wabash Cannonball," albums *Greatest Hits, The Best of Roy Acuff,* etc. A museum & library is being built in his honor in his hometown of Maynardville.

ADAM & THE ANTS
UK music group with Adam Ant*, Matthew Ashman, David Barbe, Chris Hughes, Terry Lee Miall, Kevin Mooney, Marco Pirroni, Gary Tibbs, Andrew Warren, 1977. Album *Kings of the Wild Frontier* 1981, hit single "Goody Two Shoes" 1982.

ADAMS, BRYAN (1959–   )
b. 11/5 Vancouver, Canada. Singer, hit singles "Lonely Nights" 1982, "Heaven" 1985, "There Will Never be Another Tonight" 1992.

ADAMS, EDIE (1929–   )
b. 4/16 Kingston, PA. Singer/actress appeared in *It's a Mad, Mad, Mad World* 1963. Married Ernie Kovacs.

ADAMS, FRANK R. (1883–1963)
b. Morrison, IL. Lyricist: together with Will M. Hough* and composers Joe E. Howard* and Harold Orlob* wrote "I Wonder Who's Kissing Her Now?" 1909.

ADAMS, GEORGE R. (1940–)
b. Covington, GA. Tenor saxist, albums *America* 1990, *Old Feeling* 1992.

ADAMS, JOHN
Composer/pianist won 1988 Grammy for contemporary composition *Adams: Nixon in China:* others *China Gates, Portraits, Shaker Loops, The Wound Dresser.* Opera *The Death of Klinghoffer* performed by the Opera de Lyon under Kent Nagano.

ADAMS, OLETA
Singer, *Circle of One,* song "Get Here" became a Desert Storm anthem 1991. "Don't Let the Sun go down on Me" track from *Two Rooms* 1992.

ADAMS, PARK "PEPPER" (1930–1986)
b. Highland Park, IL. Won *down beat* critics' poll as Baritone Saxist of 1980, CDs *Fat Tuesdays' Sessions, Mean What You Say, My One and Only Love.* Died 9/10 in New York City.

ADAMS, YOLANDA (1962–)
b. Houston, TX. Gospel singer/songwriter album *Just as I Am* on top ten gospel hits 1986. *Through the Storm* 1992. Sang at the Republican National Convention in Houston in 1992.

ADAMSON, HAROLD (1906–1980)
b. Greenville, NJ. Lyricist: with composer Jimmy Hugh wrote "It's a Most Unusual Day," with composer Victor Young* "Around the World I've Searched for You" 1956.

ADDERLEY, JULIAN E. "CANNONBALL" (1928–1975)
b. Tampa, FL. Alto saxist, formed the Cannonball Adderley Quintet with his brother Nat,* album *The Best of Cannonball Adderley.* Toured Europe & Japan. Died 8/8 in Gary, IN.

ADDERLEY, NATHANIEL "NAT" (1931–)
b. Tampa, FL. Cornetist/songwriter, composed "Work Song,"

"Jive Samba," etc. Performed at the Los Angeles Jazz Festival 1980.

ADDISON, ADELE (1925–)
b. 7/24 New York, NY. Soprano, debut role of Bess in *Porgy and Bess* 1958. Solo debut 1962.

ADE, KING SUNNY
CDs & albums *Aura, Ju Ju Music, Live Juju,* etc.

ADLER, KURT H. (1905–1988)
b. Vienna, Austria. Conductor of Spring Opera Theater of San Francisco 1961, founded Western Opera Theater 1966.

ADLER, RICHARD (1921–)
b. 8/3 New York, NY. Composer, wrote scores for *Damn Yankees* 1945 & *Pajama Game* 1954.

AEROSMITH
Heavy metal band formed 1970 with singer Steven Tyler, guitarist Joe Perry, Tom Hamilton, Joey Kramer, & Brad Whitford. Hit singles "Dream On" 1975, "Emotion" (on 1988 Top Ten Music Videos for *Aerosmith's Video Scrapbook)* & album *Permanent Vacation.* Platinum album *Pump* 1989, 1990 Grammy Group Vocal for "Janie's Got a Gun." Music video *Things that Go Pump in the Night* 1990, video *Love in an Elevator* 1992. Tyler & Perry joined Guns 'N Roses Paris concert in June 1992. American Music pop/rock & heavy metal/hard rock awards 1994. *Livin' on the Edge* Rock Group Grammy 1994.

AFTER 7
Singers Melvin Edmonds, Kevon Edmonds, Keith Mitchell, albums *After 7* 1989, *Takin My Time,* & *Ready or Not* 1992.

AGER, MILTON (1893–1979)
b. 10/6 Chicago. Composer wrote "Hard Hearted Hannah," "Ain't She Sweet." With lyricist Jack Yellen*: "Happy Days are Here Again" 1929 became campaign song for Franklin D. Roosevelt. Ager died 5/6 in Los Angeles, CA.

A-HA
CDs & albums *East of the Sun, West, Moon, Hunting High and Low, Stay on These Roads,* music video *Take on Me* 1992.

AHLERT, FRED E. (1892–1953)
b. New York, NY. Composer, with Bing Crosby* wrote "Where the Blue of the Night Meets the Gold of the Day" and with lyricist Joe Young* wrote "I'm Gonna Sit Right Down and Write Myself a Letter."

AIR
Ragtime jazz trio of saxist Henry Threadgill, bassist Fred Hopkins, and drummer Steve McCall formed in Chicago in 1971. Later tenor saxist Chico Freeman replaced Threadgill. Album *Air Lore.*

AIR SUPPLY
Australian pop/rock group formed 1976 with Russell Hitchcock & Graham Russell, hit single "The One that you Love" 1981, *Greatest Hits, Lost in Love, Love and Other Business, Now and Forever.*

AKERS, KAREN
CDs & albums *In a Very Pleasant Way, Presenting Karen Akers, Unchained Melodies,* video *On Stage at Wolf.*

AKIYOSHI JAZZ ORCHESTRA, TOSHIKO
Conductor of the Carnegie Hall Concert 1992, voted No. 1 in the Big Band Category by *down beat,* first woman in jazz history to be so honored.

AKST, HARRY (1894–1963)
b. New York, NY. Composer wrote "Laddie Boy" 1918, with lyricists Sam Lewis & Joe Young* "Dinah" 1925, with lyricist Lew Brown* the musical *Stand Up and Cheer* 1934.

ALABAMA
Country/rock group formed 1969 with Jeff Cook, Teddy Gentry, Mark Herndon, Randy Owen. Platinum album *Feels So Right*

1981, music video *Pass It on Down* 1990, hit single "Take a Little Trip" 1992, album *American Pride* 1992. Their June Jam held yearly in Fort Payne, Alabama. American Music Band award 1993, hit single "Once Upon a Lifetime" 1993. They are building a theater in Myrtle Beach, SC which opened in summer 1993. American Music Group award 1994.

ALBANY, JOSEPH "JOE" (1924–   )
b. Atlantic City, NJ. One of the first bebop pianists. With Lester Young* recorded "You're Driving Me Crazy," wrote songs for Anita Day, played at Carnegie Hall in NY City in June 1980.

ALBERT, STEPHEN JOEL (1941–1992)
b. 2/6 Brooklyn, NY City. Composer, *Symphony River Run* won the 1985 Pulitzer Prize. Had just finished his Symphony No. 2 for the NY Philharmonic when killed on December 27th in an auto accident on Cape Cod, MA. His Cello Concerto was performed by Yo-Yo Ma* with the NY Chamber Symphony in 1993.

ALBRIGHT, GERALD
Saxist, *Bermuda Nights, Dream Come True, Just Between Us, Live at Birdland.*

ALDEN, HAROLD
CDs & albums *13 Strings, Snowy Mountain Blues,* etc.

ALDEN, JOSEPH REED (1886–1951)
b. Grand Rapids, MI. Songwriter, with Richard A. Whiting* and Ange Lorenzo* wrote "Sleepy Time Gal" 1925.

ALEXANDER, ARTHUR (1940–1993)
Country/soul singer, hit "You Better Move On" 1962, album *Lonely Just like Me.* Died 6/9 in Nashville of heart failure.

ALEXANDER, ELMER "MOUSEY" (1922–1968)
b. Gary, IN. Drummer toured with Benny Goodman* & others. Suffered a heart attack and died 10/9 in Winter Park, FL.

ALEXANDER, MONTY
CDs & albums *Full Steam Ahead, Ivory and Steel, Triple Treat,* etc.

ALEXANDRIA, LORENZ (1929–)
b. Chicago, IL. Singer/conductor, *Harlem Butterfly, May I Come In?*, etc.

ALGIERS STOMPERS
Played at Preservation Hall in New Orleans in late 1970s.

ALI, RASHIED (1935–)
b. Philadelphia, PA. Drummer, led **Ali's Alley Orchestra** at his own night club in New York City in 1970s/80s.

ALICE IN CHAINS
Seattle, WA based rock/heavy metal band with Layne Staley, Jerry Cantrell, Mike Starr, & Sean Kenney, debut album *Facelift.* Appeared in film *Singles* 1992. Singer Staley broke his foot after a spill on a three-wheel all-terrain vehicle then performed on tour on crutches. Album *Dirt* 1992.

ALL
Singing/guitar group, *Allroy's Revenge, Breathe* 1992.

ALL-STARR BAND
Ringo Starr* of the **Beatles*,** Burton Cummings, Joe Walsh*, Timothy B. Schmidt, Dave Edmunds, Nils Lofgren*, Todd Rundgren*, & Tim Cappello, *Time Takes Time* 1992.

ALL STARS
Group led by guitarist Eddie Condon* included clarinetist/saxist Pee Wee Russell*, played at President Nixon's inaugural ball 1969.

ALLEN, DEBORAH (1935–)
b, 9/30 Memphis, TN. Singer/songwriter, wrote "Baby I Lied" 1983.

ALLEN, DUANE (1943–)
b. 4/29 Taylortown, TX. Guitarist/singer with the **Oak Ridge Boys*** country/pop group, hit single "Bobby Sue" 1982.

ALLEN, EDWARD "ED" (1897–1974)
b. Nashville, TN. Jazz trumpeter with Clarence Williams & others in 1920s, later played in NY City night clubs.

ALLEN, ELIZABETH (1934–)
b. 1/25 Jersey City, NJ. Singer/actress, hit "The Gay Life" 1962.

ALLEN, GEORGE NELSON (1812–1877)
b. Mansfield, MA. Composer & professor at Oberlin College, Ohio. With lyricist E. H. Chapin wrote "Bury Me Not in the Deep, Deep Sea" 1849. New words were written in 1907 by Wm. Jossey: "Bury Me Not On the Lone Prairie."

ALLEN, GERI
CDs & albums *In the Year of the Dragon, Twilight,* etc.

ALLEN, PETER W. (1944–1992)
b. 2/10 Tenterfield, Australia. Singer/songwriter, co-wrote "I Honestly Love You" 1974. Came to America, married Liza Minnelli*, later divorced. Wrote theme for *Arthur* 1981, video *Peter Allen and the Rockets,* sang at gay clubs like the Continental Baths. Died 6/18 of AIDS in San Diego, CA.

ALLISON, MOSE JOHN, JR. (1927–)
b. Tippo, MS. Pianist/singer/composer, *My Backyard, The Best of Mose Allison,* etc.

ALLMAN BROTHERS BAND
Formed 1968 in Macon, GA by Duane Allman, Greg Allman, Dicky Betts, Jaimoe "Jai Johnny" Johanson, Chuck Leavell, Berry Oakley, Butch Trucks (Claude Hudson), Lamar Williams. Later Warren Haynes*. Duane Allman died in a motorcycle accident in 1971. Classic album *At Fillmore East* 1971, *Ramblin' Man* 1973, *An Evening with the Allman Brothers* 1992, *Live at Great Woods* 1993, etc.

ALMEIDA, LAURINDO (1917–)
b. 9/2 Sao Paulo, Brazil. Jazz guitarist/composer toured Europe & U.S. with the **Modern Jazz Quartet***. Won five Grammys. *Chamber Jazz, Tango.*

ALMIGHTY, THE
CDs & albums *Blood, Fire and Love, Soul Destruction.*

ALPERT, HERB (1935–)
b. 3/31 Los Angeles, CA. Trumpeter/bandleader, led **Tijuana Brass,** hits "The Lonely Bull" 1962, 1965 Grammy winner "A Taste of Honey," "This Guy's in Love with You" 1968, "Rise" 1979. *Greatest Hits, Keep Your Eye on Me, Midnight Sun* 1992.

ALPHAVILLE
CDs & albums *Afternoon in Utopia, Forever Young, The Breathtaking Blue,* etc.

ALTER, LOUIS (1902–1980)
b. Haverhill, MA. Composed "Blue Shadows" 1927, "Manhattan Serenade" 1928, "Twilight on the Trail" (a favorite of President Franklin D. Roosevelt). Died 11/3 in New York City.

AMAZON
Group led by Thiago de Mello played in the Brazilian Jazz Festival at Jazzmania in New York City, June 1980.

AMBOY DUKES, THE
Ted Nugent*, Greg Arama, Cliff Davis, Rob Grange, Dave Palmer, Vic Mastrianni, Derck St. Holmes, Andy Solomon. Hit "Journey to the Center of Your Mind" 1968. "Meat Loaf" (Marvin Lee Aday) sang *Tooth, Fang and Claw* with the Amboy Dukes.

AMERICA
Gerry Beckley, Dewey Bunnell, Daniel Peek. Hit "A Horse with No Name" 1972, *America, Encore-More Greatest Hits.*

AMES BROTHERS
b. Boston, MA. Singers Ed (b. 1927), Gene, Joe, and Vic Ames (1925–1978). Surname was Urick. Hit singles "You, You, You" 1953, "Jolly Old St. Nicholas," album *Best of the Ames Brothers.*

AMMONS, EUGENE "JUG" (1925–1974)
b. 4/14 Chicago, IL. Tenor saxist son of Albert Ammons. The Chess Brothers cut his single "My Foolish Heart." Used the first echo chamber effect to enhance his sax by dangling a mike in the studio toilet. Died 8/6 in Chicago.

AMOS, TORI (1963–)
Singer/songwriter from North Carolina, now lives in London. Album *Little Earthquakes* 1992, *Under the Pink* 1994.

AMRAM, DAVID W. (1930–)
b. 11/17 Philadelphia, PA. Conductor/composer, led NY Shakespeare Festival 1956/57, National Symphony in Washington, D.C. 1972, toured Europe. Played French horn in New York clubs in 1970s.

AMSTERDAM, MOREY (1914–)
b. 12/14 Chicago, IL. Singer/songwriter, wrote lyrics for "Rum and Coca-Cola." See also Rupert Grant*.

ANDERSEN, ERIC (1943–)
b. 2/14 Pittsburgh, PA. Singer/composer, *Best of Eric Andersen, Ghosts upon the Road, Stages, The Last Album.*

ANDERSON, BILL (1937–)
b. 11/1 Columbia, SC. Country singer/songwriter, wrote "Walk Out Backward" 1962, "Strangers" 1965, CD *Best of Bill Anderson.*

ANDERSON, ERNESTINE (1928–)
b. Houston, TX. Jazz singer, *Be Mine Tonight, Big City, Live Concord to London, When the Sun Goes Down,* etc.

ANDERSON, JOHN (1954–)
b. 12/13 Apopka, FL. Country singer, hits "Swingin'" 1983, "Seminole Wind," "When It Comes to You," "Let Go of the Stone" 1993. *Greatest Hits, Too Tough to Tame.*

ANDERSON, LAURIE
CDs & albums *Big Science, Mister Heartbreak, Strange Angels,* etc. Videos *Collected Videos, Home of the Brave.*

ANDERSON, LEROY (1908–1975)
b. 6/29 Cambridge, MA. Composer/conductor, wrote "Blue Tango," "Bugler's Holiday," "Syncopated Clock," "Forgotten Dreams." Died 5/18 in Woodbury, CT.

ANDERSON, LYNN (1947–   )
b. 9/26 Grand Forks, ND. Country singer, "Rose Garden" won 1970 Emmy. *Greatest Hits, What She Does Best.* Married songwriter Glenn Sutton, later divorced. Named 1971 Vocalist of Year in Nashville, TN. Married Harold Stream III, divorced.

ANDERSON, MARIAN (1897–1993)
b. 2/17 Philadelphia, PA. Debut with Philadelphia Philharmonic 1925, first black soloist with Metropolitan Opera 1955, U.S. Delegate to the United Nations 1958, awarded Presidential Medal of Freedom 1963. Albums *Arias, Marian Anderson, Vol. 1.* Died 4/8 in Portland, Oregon.

ANDERSON, ROY
CDs *Blues Bred in the Bones, What Because, Wishbone,* etc.

ANDERSON, WILLIAM A. "CAT" (1916–1981)
b. 9/12 Greenville, SC. Jazz trumpeter, with Duke Ellington's* Band, recorded "Take the A Train." Died 4/30 in Norwalk, CA.

ANDREWS, JULIE (1935–   )
b. 10/1 Walton-on-Thames, UK. Singer/actress, lead in *My Fair Lady* 1956, *Camelot* 1960, *Mary Poppins* 1964, Oscar for *The Sound of Music* 1965. Sang with Ben Kingsley on album *The King and I* 1992, in NY show *Putting It Together* with music by Stephen Sondheim*, April 1993.

ANDREWS SISTERS
All born in Minneapolis, MN, LaVerne (1915–1967), Maxine (1918) & Patti (1920). Hits "Boogie-Woogie Bugle Boy from

Company B," "Don't Sit under the Apple Tree with Anyone but Me," "Beer Barrel Polka." Popular during World War II.

ANGER, DAVE
Albums *Live at Montreux '84, Tideline.*

ANIMALS, THE
British group with Eric Burdon, Bryan Chandler, Barry Jenkins, Alan Price, Dave Rowberry, John Steel, Hilton Valentine. Group came to the States in 1960s, "House of the Rising Sun," "Don't Let Me be Misunderstood," *Finally—Eric Burdon and the Animals.* Inducted into Rock & Roll Hall of Fame 1994.

ANKA, PAUL (1941–)
b. 7/30 Ottawa, Canada. Singer/songwriter, hits "My Way" 1967, "She's a Lady," "Lonely Boy," wrote *Tonight* show theme. 15 gold records, *21 Golden Hits, His Best,* video *An Evening with Paul Anka.*

ANOINTED PACE SISTERS
Nine-member gospel choir on The Stellar Awards TV show January 1993.

ANT, ADAM
CDs & albums *Antics in Forbidden Zone, Kings of the Wild Frontier, Prince Charming,* etc.

ANTHONY, RAY (1932–)
b. 1/20 Bentleyville, PA. Trumpeter/bandleader/songwriter, had own band after World War II, co-composed "The Bunny Hop" 1952, albums *Dream Dancing, Double Play, Sweet and Swinging.*

ANTHRAX
CDs & albums *Among the Living, Attack of the Killer B's, State of Euphoria,* video *Anthrax Through Time, Oldivnikufesin N.F.V.*

ANTON, SUSAN (1950–)
b. 10/12 Yuciapa, CA. Singer/actress had lead in film *Golden Girl* 1979.

A-1 ART BAND
Led by trombonist/composer Garrett List. Featured trumpeter Youseff Vancy, reedman Byard Lancaster, drummer J. R. Mitchell, singers Eugenia Sherman & Lillian Coleman at the Public Theater in New York City 1978.

APAKA, ALFRED
CDs & albums *Hawaiian Favorites, Hawaiian Wedding Song.*

APOLLO 18
Brooklyn duo of guitarist John Flansburgh and accordianist John Linnell, album *They Might be Giants.*

APOLLO STOMPERS
18 piece orchestra led by pianist Jaki Byard with trumpeter Nelson Bogart, bassist Ed Schuller, trombonists Gary Valente and Craig Harris at Ali's Alley in NY City 1978 & at New Jazz Concerts at Public Theater 1979. A second group at Michael's Pub in NY City.

APOSTLES
Los Angeles band hit "I Could be Anything" 1992.

APRIL WINE
Canadian group with Myles Goodwin, Brian Greenway, Steve Lang, Jerry Mercer, Gary Moffet. Platinum album *World's Goin' Crazy* 1976, *Harder Faster, Nature of the Beast,* etc.

ARC ANGELS
Rock & roll band with Charlie Sexton, guitarist Doyle Bramhall II, Tommy Shannon & Chris Layton, debut album *Arc Angels* 1992.

ARGENT
British group formed 1969 with singer/keyboardist Rodney Terence Argent, singer/guitarist Russell Ballard, John Grimaldi, Robert Henrit, John Verity, & Jim Rodford. Hit "Hold Your Head Up" 1972. Bassist Kinks joined the group 1978, album *Anthology/Greatest Hits.*

ARGENTO, DOMINICK
Composer won 1975 Pulitzer Prize for his composition *From the Diary of Virginia Woolf,* CD *Variations for Orchestra.*

ARKENSTONE, DAVID
CDs *Citizen of Time, In the Wake of the Wind, Island, Valley in the Clouds.*

ARLEN, HAROLD (1905–1986)
b. 2/15 Buffalo, NY. Pianist/composer with Ted Koehler* wrote "I Love a Parade," "Stormy Weather," with Johnny Mercer*: "That Old Black Magic," "Accentuate the Positive," "Over the Rainbow" for *The Wizard of Oz* 1939. Died 4/23 New York, NY.

ARMATRADING, JOAN (1950–   )
b. 12/9 St. Kitts, Nevis. Singer, *Hearts and Flowers, Show Some Emotion, Sleight of Hand, The Key, Walk Under Ladders.*

ARMSTRONG, LOUIS "SATCHMO" (1900–1971)
b. New Orleans, LA. Trumpeter/vocalist, played in honky-tonk clubs after 1914, married second wife Lil Hardin* in 1924, formed own band in 1927. Married Alpha Smith 1938, married Lucille Wilson 1942. His own band toured the world 1960s/70s. Dozens of his albums are available, video *Satchmo.* Died in New York City. A postage stamp was issued in his honor.

ARMY OF LOVERS
Chorus hit song "Crucified" from *Massive Luxury Overdose* 1992.

ARNAZ, DESI (1917–1986)
b. 3/2 Santiago, Cuba. Actor/singer/bandleader, called the "Mambo King." Married to Lucille Ball (1911–1989).

ARNAZ, LUCIE DESIREE (1951–   )
b. 7/17 Hollywood, CA. Actress/singer daughter of Lucille Ball & Desi Arnaz* starred in the film *The Jazz Singer* 1980 and on Broadway in *They're Playing Our Song.*

ARNDT, FELIX (1889–1918)
b. New York, NY. Pianist/composer wrote "Nola" 1915, words added in 1924 by James F. Burns.

ARNOLD, EDDIE (1918–)
b. 5/15 near Henderson, TN. Country singer/guitarist/songwriter known as the "Tennessee Plowboy." In Country Hall of Fame 1966, hit song "Make the World Go Away," album *Last of the Love Song Singers: Then & Now* 1993.

ARRESTED DEVELOPMENT
Atlanta funky/blues group led by Speech (Tod Thomas), Aerle Taree, D. J. Headliner, Rasa Don, & Montsho Eshe. Albums *People Everyday, 3 Years, 5 Months and 2 Days in the Life of Arrested Development* (the length of time to get their first recording produced 1992), on soundtrack for film *Malcolm X,* MTV video award for *Tennessee.* Toured 25 cities in 1992, Grammy as New Artist 1993. With electric bassist Foley on 1993 Lollapalooza Tour.

ARROYO, MARTINA (1940–)
b. 2/2 New York, NY. Soprano, debut at Metropolitan Opera in NY City 1965, leading soprano at the Met 1970/74, married violinist Emilio Poggoni.

ARTISTIC TRUTH
Group led by drummer Roy Brooks included singer Eddie Jefferson* 1973/75.

ASH, DANIEL
Albums *Get Out of Control, Foolish Thing Desire* 1993.

ASHFORD & SIMPSON
Nicholas Ashford b. 5/4/42 Fairfield, SC. wrote "Ain't No Mountain High Enough" recorded by the Supremes.* His wife Valerie Simpson, a singer/songwriter. Performed on Motown hits, album *Solid,* video *Ashford & Simpson.*

ASHMAN, HOWARD (1951–1991)

Lyricist, *Little Shop of Horrors, The Little Mermaid,* with Alan Menken* won 1990 Grammy (song in film) for *Under the sea,* with Menken *Beauty and the Beast* won Grammy (song in film) 1991.

ASHTON, SUSAN

Gospel singer *Angels of Mercy* 1992.

ASIA

Rock group formed 1981 with Geoffrey Downes, Steve Howe, drummer Carl Palmer, Greg Lake. Formerly Palmer was with **Emerson*, Lake & Palmer*** 1970/79. Hit "Heat of the Moment" 1983, album *Asia in Asdia* 1984, with singer/saxist John Payne *Aqua* 1992.

ASLEEP AT THE WHEEL

Won 1988 Grammy for Country Instrumental "Sugarfoot Rag" track from *Western Standard Time, Keeping Me Up Nights, Ten,* "Black & White Flag" on *Greatest Hits/Live & Kickin* 1992. *Red Wing* Country Instrumental Grammy 1994.

ASSOCIATION, THE

Pop/rock band with Gary Alexander, Ted Bluechel, Brian Cole, Russ Giguere, Terry Kirkman, Jim Yester. Gold records "Never My Love" 1967, "Cherish" 1968, albums *Greatest Hits, Songs Made Them Famous.*

ASSUNTO, FRANK JOSEPH (1932–1974)

b, New Orleans, LA, trumpeter/bandleader, led Dukes of Dixieland* 1949/60s. Died in New Orleans.

ASTLEY, RICK

1988 Top Ten Pop single for "Never Gonna Give You Up," albums *Free, Hold Me in Your Arms, Whenever You Need Somebody.*

A-STRINGS, THE

CD & album *Home for Christmas.*

ATKINS, CHESTER B. "CHET" (1924–)

b. 6/20 Luttrell, TN. Country singer/guitarist, joined Grand Ole Opry in Nashville, TN 1946, played in The White House for President & Mrs. Kennedy 1961, won 1990 Country Instrumental Grammy with Mark Knopfler for "So Soft, Your Goodbye," albums *Guitar for all Seasons, Stay Tuned, Steel Dreams*. With Jerry Reed *Sneakin' Around* won 1993 Grammy. Received Grammy Lifetime award in Feb. 1993.

ATLANTIC JAZZ

Albums *Avant Garde, Bishop, Fusion, Kansas City*, etc.

ATTERIDGE, R. HAROLD (1886–1936)

b. Lake Forest, IL. With composer Harry Carroll* wrote lyrics for "By the Beautiful Sea" 1913.

AUSTIN, GENE (1901–1972)

b. Gainesville, TX. Singer/songwriter, his theme song "My Blue Heaven" sold over 12 million records. Wrote "Those Wedding Bells Are Breaking Up That Old Gang of Mine."

AUSTIN LOUNGE LIZARDS

Albums *Creatures from the Black, Highway Cafe of the Damned*, etc.

AUSTIN, LOVIE (1887–1972)

Born Cora Calhoun in Chattanooga, TN. Pianist for Ma Rainey* (blues singer), recorded with Ida Cox*. Died in Chicago.

AUSTIN, PATTI (1948–)

b. 8/10 New York, NY, singer with James Ingram* had hit single "Baby Come to Me" (1982 theme song for *General Hospital*), albums *Carry On, Love is Gonna Getcha, The Real Me*, etc.

AUTOGRAPH

Albums *Loud and Clear, Sign In Please*.

AUTRY, GENE (1907–)

b. 9/29 Tioga, TX, actor/singing cowboy/songwriter. Wrote

"Here Comes Santa Claus" 1948 and over 250 songs. Owner of the California Angels (Los Angeles baseball team). Albums *Columbia Historic Edition, Country Music Hall of Fame.*

AVALON, FRANKIE (1939–)
b. Francis Thomas Avalone and 9/18 in Philadelphia, PA., actor/singer/trumpeter, hits "I'll Wait for You" 1958, "Venus," "A Boy without a Girl" 1959. Starred with Annette Funicello* in beach films. Albums *Stars of the Sixties* 1974, *Bobby Sox to Stockings* 1984.

AVERAGE WHITE BAND, THE
Scottish musicians who relocated to Los Angeles, CA in 1972. Lead vocalist/guitarist Hamish Stuart, vocalist/bassist Alan Ganie, guitarist Annie McIntyre, saxists Roger Ball & Malcolm Duncan, drummer Robbie McIntosh died of a heroin overdose at a Los Angeles party in Sept. 1974 & was replaced by Steve Verrone. Album *Average White Band.*

AWEKE, ASTER
Pop/Ethiopian singer, album *Aster,* CD *Kabu* (Sacred rock) 1992.

AX, EMANUEL
Pianist with cellist Yo Yo Ma* won a Chamber Music Grammy *Brahams' Sonatas for Cello and Piano* 1993.

AXTON, HOYT WAYNE (1938–)
b. 3/25 Duncan, OK, country music singer/songwriter.

AYER, NAT (1887–1952)
b. Boston, MA, composer, with words by Seymour Brown* wrote "Oh, You Beautiful Doll" 1911.

AYERS, ROY (1940–)
b. Los Angeles, CA. Vibraharpist, *Drive, Wake Up.*

AZYMUTH
Albums *Crazy Rhythm, Autobro, Telecommunications,* etc.

B

BABY FACE
Singer/songwriter, *Tender Lover* platinum album 1989, hit R&B single "Give U My Heart" 1992. With L. A. Reid & Daryl Simmons wrote "End of the Road" (Grammy winner) 1993.

BABYLON A.D.
Oakland, CA pop/metal band, *Babylon A.D., Desperate, Nothing Sacred,* toured US 1992.

BABYS, THE
British pop group with vocalist/drummer Tony Brock, Jonathan Cain, keyboardist/guitarist/vocalist Mike Corby, Ricky Phillips, Wally Stocker, singer/songwriter John Waits. Hits "Isn't It Time," "Head First," "Missing You" 1984, *Anthology, The Babys.*

BACHARACH, BURT (1929–)
b. 5/12 Kansas City, MO. Singer/composer, wrote "What's New Pussycat?" 1965, "Raindrops Keep Fallin' On My Head" (Oscar 1970 from *Butch Cassidy and the Sundance Kid*), "Walk on By," "What the World Needs Now is Love," CDs *25th Anniversary Album, Greatest Hits.*

BACHMAN-TURNER OVERDRIVE
Canadian heavy metal group formed **Guess Who*** 1963 & **Overdrive** 1972 with Chad Allen, Randy Bachman, Timothy Bachman, Jim Clench, Blair Thornton, C. F. Turner. Hit song "You Ain't Seen Nothin' Yet," *All Time Greatest Hits—Live, Not Fragile,* etc.

BAD BRAINS
Jazz/rock fusionists, *Bad Brains, Against 1, The Youth Are Getting Rest,* group toured US 1992/93.

BAD COMPANY
Lead singer Paul Rodgers, mid-70s rockers, "Can't Get Enough," "Feel Like Makin' Love," "Rock and Roll Fantasy," with

Mick Ralphs, Brian Howe, & Simon Kirke, *10 From 6, Bad Company, Dangerous Age, Holy Water, Here Comes Trouble* 1992.

BADALAMENTI, ANGELO
Composer, won 1990 Pop Instrumental Grammy for *Twin Peaks* theme.

BADFINGER
CDs & albums *Day after Day, Magic Christian Music,* etc.

BAER, ABEL (1893–1976)
b. Baltimore, MD. Composer, wrote "Lucky Lindy" 1927 to celebrate Lindbergh's flight across the Atlantic Ocean. Died 10/5 NY City.

BAEZ, JOAN (1941–)
b. 1/9 Staten Island, NY. Singer/songwriter/guitarist, sang "Joe Hill" at Woodstock Festival* 1969, crusader against the Vietnam War. With Bruce Springsteen* on 1988 top ten grossing concerts. *Speaking of Dreams* 1989, *Play Me Backwards* 1992.

BAGLEY, EDWIN E. (1857–1922)
Bandmaster/composer, wrote the "National Emblem March" 1906, tune used for "And the Monkey Wrapped Its Tail Around the Flagpole."

BAILEY, MILDRED (1907–1951)
Born Mildred Rinker, Tekoa, WA. Singer with Paul Whiteman* 1929/33, married Red Norvo* 1933/45 and sang in his band, then went solo. Album *Rockin' Chair.* Died in Poughkeepsie, NY.

BAILEY, PEARL (1918–1990)
b. 3/28 Newport News, VA. Singer, in Broadway show *Hello Dolly* 1967/69. Appointed US envoy to the United Nations by President Nixon, sang in The White House for President & Mrs. Reagan in September 1981. Album *16 Most Requested Songs.* Died 8/17 in Philadelphia, PA.

BAKER, ANITA (1957–)

b. 1/26 Toledo, OH. Singer, won 1988 R&B Vocalist Grammy for "Giving You the Best I've Got," won 1990 Grammy for "Compositions," platinum music video *One Night of Rapture* 1990, hit songs "My Funny Valentine" & "Sometimes I Wonder" 1992. Lives in Grosse Pointe Farms, Michigan.

BAKER, ARTHUR

Singer/songwriter, debut album with Al Green* on *Leave the Guns at Home* 1992.

BAKER, CHESNEY "CHET" (1929–1988)

b. 12/23 Yale, OK. Singer/trumpeter/jazz bandleader, album *Out of Nowhere* recorded 1982 & issued 1992. *Daybreak, Let's Get Lost,* etc., video *Candy.* Died 5/13 Amsterdam, Netherlands when he fell off a balcony.

BAKER, JOSEPHINE (1906–1975)

b. 6/3 St. Louis, MO. Sang in NY City night clubs then went to Paris in 1925, star in the Folies-Bergere, then became the toast of Paris. Died 4/12 in Paris.

BAKKER, TAMMY-FAYE

Singer & ex-wife of Jim Bakker, TV evangelist, sang on his TV programs.

BALFA, DEWEY (1927–1992)

Bayou fiddler, album *Louisiana Cajun.* Died 6/17 Eunice, LA.

BALL, ERNEST R. (1878–1927)

b. Cleveland, Ohio. Composer, with lyricist C. Olcott* wrote "Mother Machree" 1910, "When Irish Eyes are Smiling" 1912. With J. K. Brennan, "A little bit of heaven, sure they call it Ireland" 1914.

BALL, MARCIA

CDs & albums *Gatorhythms, Hot Tamale Baby, Soulful Dress.*

BALL, PATRICK
CDs & albums *Celtic Harp, O'Carolan's Dream, Secret Isles, From Distant Time*, etc.

BAND, THE
Rick Danko, Levon Helm, Garth Hudson, Richard Manuel, Robbie Robertson. Worked with Bob Dylan,* concert film *The Last Waltz* 1976, hit "The Weight," *Best of the Band, Music from Big Pink, Stage Fright*, etc., video *The Last Waltz* 1984. Inducted into Rock and Roll Hall of Fame 1994.

BANDY, MOE (1944–   )
b. 2/12 Meriden, MS. Country singer, hit "Hank Williams, You Wrote My Life" 1976, *Greatest Hits, Just Good Ol' Boys*.

BANGLES, THE
CDs & albums *All Over the Place, Everything, Greatest Hits*, video *Greatest Hits*. "Walk Like an Egyptian," "Manic Monday."

BARBER, SAMUEL (1910–1981)
b. West Chester, PA. Composed Symphony No. 1 introduced on NBC Symphony under Arturo Toscanini 1938. Composition *Vanessa* won 1958 Pulitzer Prize & Piano Concerto No. 1 the 1963 Prize. Opera *Antony and Cleopatra* at Metropolitan Opera in NY City 1966. Died 1/23.

BARBIERI, LEANDRO "GATO" (1933–   )
b. Rosario, Argentina. Tenor saxist, joined **Don Cherry* Quintet** 1966, at Avery Fisher Hall in NY City in 1980, *Caliente, Para Los Amigos, Tropico*, etc.

BARBOUR, DAVID M. "DAVE" (1912–1965)
b. Flushing, NY. Guitarist/songwriter, married singer Peggy Lee*, they wrote "Mañana."

BARDENS, PETE
CDs & albums *Speed of Light, Water Colors, See One Earth*.

BARNES, CHARLIE (1913–1991)

b. Charles Daly, 10/26 New York, NY. Saxist/singer/bandleader, formed first band in 1933, led Disneyland Band in California 1972. "Clap Hands," "Here Comes Charlie Barnes," on *Giants of the Big Band Era.* Died 9/4/91.

BARNES, GEORGE (1921–1977)

b. Chicago, IL. Guitarist, with ABC radio 1946/51, had own duos & quartets 1960s/70s. Died 9/5 Concord, CA.

BARNES, MAX D.

Songwriter, won country music award for "Chiseled in Stone," with Vince Gill co-wrote "Look at Us" 1992. His son Max T. Barnes co-wrote "Love-Me" with Skip Ewing.

BARRETT, SYD

CDs & albums *Barrett, The Madcap Laughs, Opel Outtakes.*

BARRETTO, RAY

Won Latin Album Grammy *Soy Dichoso,* January 1992.

BARRIO BOYZZ, THE

Quintet of Freddy Correa, Lorrie Morrero, Robert Vargas, Angel Ramirez, Jr., & David Daville, hip/hop/rap/R&B singers from a NY ghetto, "Stay In School, Education is Cool" anti-drug tour of U.S. from their debut album *Crazy Coolin'* 1993.

BARRON, KENNY (1943–   )

b. Philadelphia, PA. Pianist/composer, recorded with Stan Getz* in Copenhagen, Denmark 1991. With bassist Ray Drummond & drummer Ben Riley album *Lemuria-Seascape* 1992. With Stan Getz* "Soul Eyes" on *People Time,* Grammy 1993.

BARTO, TIZMON

Classical pianist, posed shirtless at the piano on his album cover *Pure Romance* 1992.

BARTZ, GARY LEE (1940–   )

b. Baltimore, MD. Alto/soprano saxist, with tenor saxist Willie

Williams, pianist Benny Green, bassist Christian McBride, & drummer Victor Lewis on *Shadows* 1993.

BASEHEAD
Washington, D.C. folk/blues/funk/hip hop group with singer/ guitarist Michael Ivey, drummer Brian Hendrix, guitarist Keith Lofton, & bassist Bill Conway, *Toys, Play with Toys* 1992.

BASIE, COUNT (1904–1984)
b. William James, Jr., 8/21 Red Bank, NJ, pianist/organist/ bandleader. With O. L. Gaines wrote "One O'clock Jump," honored by President Reagan in The White House in December 1981. Died 4/26 Hollywood, CA. His band continued touring, albums *April in Paris, Basic Basie, Live-at El Morocco* 1992, etc.

BASSETT, LESLIE (1923–)
b. Hanford, CA. Composer, Variations for Orchestra won 1966 Pulitzer prize.

BASSEY, SHIRLEY (1937–)
b. 1/8 Cardiff, Wales. Sang the title song in the James Bond film *Goldfinger* 1964, *Best of Shirley Bassey, Sassy Bassey*.

BATES, KATHERINE LEE (1859–1929)
b. Falmouth, MA. Lyricist, with composer Samuel A. Ward* wrote "America the Beautiful" 1895. Died at Wellesley, MA.

BATTLE, KATHLEEN (1948–)
b. 8/13 Portsmouth, Ohio. Lyric coloratura soprano with Jessye Norman* on *Deutsche Grammophon* 1991, at Carnegie Hall Christmas Concert 1991. With violinist Itzhak Perlman* on D.G 1992. With trumpeter Wynton Marsalis* on *Baroque Duet* 1992. Sang at Lincoln Memorial in Washington, D.C. January 1993, won Grammy 1993.

BATTLEFIELD BAND
CDs & albums *Music in Trust, New Spring, On the Rise*.

BAUZA, MARIO (1911–1993)
Leader of the Afro-Cuban Jazz Orchestra The Legendary Mambo, *King Tanga.*

BAY CITY ROLLERS
Edinburgh, Scotland group founded 1970, hit singles "I Only Wanna be with You," 1976, "You Make Me Believe in Magic" 1977.

BAYES, NORA (c.1880–1928)
b. Dora Goldberg, singer/songwriter, with husband composer Jack Norworth* wrote "Shine On, Harvest Moon" 1908.

BEACH BOYS, THE
California rock group with Alan Jardine, Bruce Johnson, Mike Love, Brian Wilson*, Carl Wilson*, Dennis Wilson*. Dennis had a hit album *Pacific Ocean Blue* but died 12/28/83. Group hits include "Surfin' USA" 1963, "Help Me Rhonda" 1965 music videos *The Beach Boys: An American Bandstand* 1985, *Surfin' Girl & Surfin' USA,* toured US summer of 1992.

BEAL, JEFF
CDs & albums *Liberation, Objects in the Mirror, Perpetual Motion.*

BEASTIE BOYS
Rap group King Ad-Rock (Adam Horowitz), Mike D. (Diamond) & MCA (Adam Yauch), formed about 1987. Album *License to Ill* sold over 4 million copies, "Party", "Basehead" 1992. Launched Ad-Rock out of a cannon, *Check Your Head* 1992, single & video *Pass the Mic* 1992.

BEAT FARMERS
CDs & albums *Glad N Greasy, Loud & Plowed, And Live, Poor & Famous, Tales of the New West, The Pursuit of Happiness.*

THE BEATLES
British group with George Harrison*, John Lennon*, Paul Mc-Cartney*, & Pete Best. Ringo Starr replaced Peter Best as

drummer in 1962. The Liverpool group toured the US and were a sensation. "I Want to Hold Your Hand" sold over 12 million copies. 1967 Grammy for album *Sgt. Pepper's Lonely Hearts Club Band,* 1970 Oscar for the film *Let it Be,* videos *A Hard Day's Night, Help, Magical Mystery Tour,* etc.

BEAUSOLEIL
Singer/fiddler Michael Doucet* of the **Cajun Band.** CDs & albums *Bayou Boogie, Cajun Conja, Live from the Left Coast, Spirit of Cajun Music, La Danse de la Vie,* etc.

BEAUTIFUL SOUTH, THE
British group with singers Paul Heaton (songwriter), Dave Hemingway, Sean Welch, David Stead, Dave Rotheray. Album *The Beautiful South* 1992.

BECHET, SIDNEY (1891–1959)
b. New Orleans, LA. Noted clarinetist/soprano saxist/composer, left New Orleans in 1914 & toured with various bands, led own **New Orleans Creole Band** in NY & Paris 1920s/50s. Involved in a shooting match with guitarist Mike McKendrick & jailed in Paris for 11 months. Died in Paris.

BECK, JEFF (1944–   )
b. 6/24 Surrey, England, guitarist/singer, *Beck-ola, Blow by Blow, Flash, Wired.* With Jed Leiber "Hound Dog" on soundtrack *Honeymoon in Las Vegas* 1992. *Frankie's House* 1993.

BECK, JOE
CDs & albums *Back to Beck, Beck and Sandborn, Friends, The Journey, Relaxin.*

BEE GEES
Barry, Robin, & Maurice Gibb, all born on the Isle of Man, England. Album *Saturday Night Fever* 1977 sold over 15 million copies, first triple platinum album, won 1978 Grammy hit song "Stayin' Alive." Maurice Gibb suffered from alcohol & drug problems but recovered. Singles over the years have been on the top of charts for 27 weeks, *Chicken of the World,*

ESP High Civilization, Spirits Having Flown. On NBC-TV
Entertainment Tonight August 1993.

BEE, MOLLY (1939–   )
b. Holly Beachboard 8/18 Oklahoma City, OK. Country singer in
1950s/60s, hit "I saw Mommy Kissing Santa Claus."

BEERS, ETHELINDA E. (1827–1879)
b. Goshen, NY, lyricist, with composer J. H. Hewitt* wrote the
famous Civil War song "All Quiet on the Potomac Tonight"
1861.

BEIDERBECKE, LEON "BIX" (1903–1931)
b. Davenport, IA. Cornetist/pianist/composer, played in various
bands in 1920s. Suffered a nervous breakdown and died 8/6 in
Queens, NY City.

BELAFONTE, HARRY (1927–   )
b. Harold George, Jr. 3/1 New York, NY. Singer, his LP *Calypso,*
was a top seller. 1953 Tony for *John Murray Anderson's
Almanac. Belafonte '89, Returns to Carnegie Hall,* etc.

BELEW, ADRIAN
Guitarist, *Desire Caught by the Tail, Mr. Music Head, Young
Lions,* etc., at Ultimate Guitar Concert in San Francisco in
September 1992.

BELLAMY BROTHERS, THE
David Bellamy and Howard Bellamy, pop/country singers from
Florida, gold record for *Let Your Love Flow* 1976, *Reality
Check, Rebels without a Clue,* etc.

BELLE, REGINA
Singer with Peabo Bryson* hit single "A Whole New World"
1992 (*Aladdin* theme) Grammy 1994.

BELLSON, LOUIS (1924–   )
b. Louis Balassoni, Rock Falls, IL. Drummer/leader/composer, at
jazz festivals 1960s/80s, *Airmail Special, Dynamite, East Side
Suite,* video *Louis Bellson & His Big Band.*

BELLY
Hit single "Star" on WFIT Playlist in March 1993.

BEMISHI
Bemishi Shearer, singer, daughter of vibraphonist Oliver Shearer, *Womanchild* 1992.

BENATAR, PAT (1952–)
b. Patricia A. Geraldo, 1/10 Brooklyn, NY, singer, platinum albums *In the Heat of the Night* and *Precious Time*, hits "Love is a Battlefield," "Hit Me with Your Best Shot," album *Pat Benatar Hit Videos* 1984, *Live from Earth, Tropico.*

BENEKE, TEX (1914–)
b. 2/12 Fort Worth, TX. Singer/leader, led **Glenn Miller* Orchestra** after Miller's death in 1944, hit songs "The Boogie Woogie Piggy," "One Dozen Roses."

BENNETT, ROBERT R. (1894–1981)
b. 6/15 Kansas City, MO. Composer, his score for *Oklahoma* (film adaptation) won 1955 Oscar. Orchestrated *South Pacific* and some 300 Broadway musicals. Died 8/18 in New York City.

BENNETT, SANFORD F. (1836–1898)
Lyricist, with composer Joseph P. Webster* wrote "In the Sweet Bye and Bye" 1867. Johnny Cash* sang their song on the *Reader's Digest 50 Beloved Songs of Faith* 1992.

BENNETT, TONY (1926–)
b. Anthony D. Benedetto 8/3 New York, NY. Singer, recorded "Cold, Cold Heart" 1951, "I Left My Heart in San Francisco" & won 1962 Grammy. With pianist Ralph Sharon, bassist Pual Langosch, & drummer Joe La Barbera on album *Perfectly Frank* won 1993 Grammy. Sang at a Clinton inaugural ball, Janaury 1993. "Steppin' Out" Traditional Pop Grammy 1994.

BENOIT, DAVID
CDs & albums *Can You Imagine, Digits, Every Step of the Way, Urban Daydreams,* etc.

BENSON, GEORGE (1943–)

b. 3/2 Pittsburgh, PA. Singer/guitarist, won 1976 Grammy for "This Masquerade," at Radio City Music Hall, NY City 1980. *20/20, Bad Benson, Guitar Genius,* CD *Breezin* 1992.

BERBERIAN, CATHY (1928–1983)

b. 7/4 Attleboro, MA. Sang John Cage's* *Fontana Mix,* Luciano Berio's *Circles.* Married Berio. Album *Magnificathy.* Died 3/6 Rome, Italy.

BERG, BOB

CDs & albums *In the Shadows, New Birth, Back Roads* 1992.

BERGEN, POLLY (1930–)

b. Nellie Paulina Burgin 7/14 Knoxville, TN. Singer/actress, dad got her started singing in night clubs. Emmy for film *The Helen Morgan Story* 1957, has starred in numerous films.

BERGMAN, ALAN (1925–)

b. 9/11 Brooklyn, NY lyricist, with wife Marilyn Keith Bergman (b. 11/10/29 Brooklyn) won Oscar for "The Way We Were" 1974, she won 1983 Oscar for songs in *Yentl.*

BERIGAN, R.B. "BUNNY" (1908–1942)

b. Calumet, WI, jazz trumpeter/singer with Benny Goodman* in 1930s. Led own band 1937/42, contracted pneumonia, had a severe hemorrhage, and died 6/2 in a NY City hospital.

BERLIN, IRVING (1888–1989)

b. Israel Baline 5/11 Temun, Russia. Songwriter, wrote "Alexander's Ragtime Band" 1911. "This is the Army Mr. Jones" and "O How I hate to get up in the morning" while a sergeant at Camp Upton during World War I. "Easter Parade" 1933, "God Bless America" 1938, "White Christmas" 1942 & many more. Died 9/22 in NY City.

BERNHARD, SANDRA (1955–)

b. Flint, MI, comedienne/actress/singer CDs & albums *Without You I'm Nothing.*

BERNHARDT, WARREN
CDs & albums *Aint' Life Grand, Hands On, Heat of the Moment.*

BERNIE, BEN (1891–1943)
b. Benjamin Anselwitz in NY City, bandleader, known as the "Ol' Maestro," led bands in 1920s/30s.

BERNSTEIN, LEONARD (1918–1990)
b. 6/25 Lawrence, MA. Conductor/composer, *On the Town, Wonderful Town, Candide, West Side Story* won Grammy 1961. His *Mass* was commissioned by Jacqueline Onassis & performed at the John F. Kennedy Center in Washington, D.C. Died 10/14 NY City.

BERRY, CHUCK (1926–)
b. Charles E. Anderson 10/18 St. Louis, MO. Singer/songwriter wrote "Roll over Beethoven" also recorded by the **Beatles*** in 1964, "Johnny be Good," & "Surfin' USA" made famous by the **Beach Boys***, video with Fats Domino *Rock, Rock, Rock.*

B-52'S
Group from Athens, GA formed 1976 with Kate Pierson, Fred Schneider, Keith Strickland, Cindy Wilson, Ricky Wilson. Party music singers, *Wild Planet* 1980, platinum album *Cosmic Thing* 1989, platinum music video *1979-1989* in 1990, *The B-52's, Whammy, Bouncing off Satellites.* Toured US 1993.

BIBB, LEON (1935–)
b. Louisville, KY, guitarist/gospel singer, album *Leon Bibb in Concert* 1962, toured Russian 1964, on *Someone New* NBC-TV program 1972.

BIG AUDIO DYNAMITE
CDs & albums *No. 10 Upping Street, This Is, Tighten Up Vol. 88, Big Audio Dynamite II, The Globe.*

BIG BOPPER, THE
J. P. Richardson (1935–1959) hit "Chantilly Lace," *Hellooo*

Baby, Best of Big Bopper. Along with Buddy Holly* & Richie Valens*, killed in a plane crash.

BIG BROTHER & THE HOLDING COMPANY
Peter Albin, Sam Andrew, David Getz, James Gurley, lead vocalist Janis Joplin*, had hit single "Piece of My Heart" on album *Cheap Thrills* 1968. Janis Joplin died of a drug overdose 1970. Guitarist Sam Andrew (born 1942) was writing songs in 1992.

BIG DADDY
Los Angeles retro-rockers, albums *Cutting Their Own Groove* 1991, *Sgt. Pepper's* 1992.

BIG DADDY KANE
With Ice-T* & others won 1990 Rap Vocal Grammy for "Back on the Block." Albums *It's a Big Daddy Thing, Long Live the Kane, Taste of Chocolate.*

BIGARD, BARNEY (1906–1980)
b. 3/3 New Orleans, LA, jazz clarinetist/tenor saxist, performed with King Oliver* 1924/27, Duke Ellington* 1927/42, then Louis Armstrong's* **All Stars.** Wrote "Mood Indigo." Died 6/27 Culver City, CA.

BIKEL, THEODORE, M. (1924–)
b. 5/2 Vienna, Austria, guitarist/singer/actor, came to US 1955, *Folk Songs of Israel, Yiddish Theatre & Folk Songs.*

BISHOP, ELVIN (1942–)
b. 10/21 Tulsa, OK. musician. Eighth solo album *Struttin' My Stuff* had a hit single "Fooled Around and Fell in Love." *Don't Let Bossman Get You.* Toured on the Alligator Records 20th Anniversary Tour 1992.

BISHOP, STEPHEN (1940–)
b. Los Angeles, CA. Pianist, soloist with Boston Symphony at Carnegie Hall in 1972.

BISHOP, STEPHEN (1951–)
b. 11/14 San Diego, CA. Singer/songwriter, hits include "Save it

for a Rainy Day" 1976 & "It Might Be You" from the film *Tootsie* 1983.

BITGOOD, ROBERTA (1908–)
b. 1/15 New London, CT. Organist/composer, director of music at Bloomfield College, NJ 1936/47. Married Bert Wiersma. Church organist, first woman president of American Guild of Organists 1982.

BLACK, CLINT (1962–)
b. 2/7 Country singer/guitarist, hit "A Better Man," album *Killin' Time* 1989. Hit single "We Tell Ourselves," *The Hard Way* 1992, video *Put Yourself in My Shoes*. Married actress Lisa Hartman 1991. Clint & Lisa on USO tour to Somalia and on tour with Wynonna Judd* 1993.

BLACK CROWES
Atlanta, GA mainstream rock group with lead singer Chris Robinson*, keyboardist Ed Hawrysch, guitarists Rich Robinson & Marc Ford, drummer Steve Gorman, bassist Johnny Colt. Multi-platinum album *Shake Your Moneymaker* 1990, *The Southern Harmony & Musical Companion* 1992. Toured US 1993.

BLACK HAPPY
Seattle grunge rock group with singer/guitarist Paul Hemenway founded 1992.

BLACK, JAMES M. (1856–1938)
Composer, wrote "When the Roll is Called up Yonder." With lyricist Katherine E. Purvis* "When the Saints Are Marching In" 1896, later changed by others to "When the Saints Go Marching In."

BLACK OAK ARKANSAS
Heavy metal/Dixie boogie group with bass guitarist Pat Daugherty, Wayne Evans, Jimmy Henderson, Stan "Goober" Knight, "Jim Dandy" Mangrum, lead singer Ricky Reynolds. Hit "Jim Dandy to the Rescue" 1973, albums *Best of Black Oak Arkansas, Raunch 'N' Roll.*"

BLACK SABBATH
Pioneer metal British group once fronted by Ozzy Osbourne*, hit "Paranoid." Current singer Ronnie James Dio. *Black Sabbath, Heaven and Hell, Never Say Die, Dehumanizer* 1992.

BLACK SORROWS
Australian rock band with Joe Camilleri (born on Malta) who led **Jo Jo Zep & the Falcons** until 1982. With guitarist Wayne Burt, albums *Harley and Rose* 1982, *Hold on to Me*.

BLACK UHURU
With singer Junior Reed*. CDs & albums *Anthem, Brutal, Iron Storm, Now,* etc.

BLACKMAN, CINDY (1960–)
b. Ohio, jazz drummer/leader, with bassist Clarence Seay, saxist Antoine Roney, & pianist Jacky Terrasson. Pianist Kenny Barron on her third album *Code Red* 1992.

BLADES, REUBEN (1948–)
b. 7/16 Panama City, Panama. He won 1988 Tropical Latin Grammy "Antecedents," albums *Y Son Del Solar Live,* Grammy for *Amor Y Control,* Jan. 1993.

BLAKE, JAMES "EUBIE" (1883–1983)
b. 2/7 Baltimore, MD. Noted black ragtime pianist/composer, wrote "Charleston Rag" 1899. With Noble Sissle* "I'm Just Wild About Harry" in *Shuffle Along* 1921/24. At Carnegie Hall, NY City on 1/20/81 Blake played his "Charleston Rag" & "Memories to You." Died 2/12/83 in Brooklyn, NY.

BLAKE, JAMES W. (1852–1935)
Lyricist, with composer Charles Lawler* wrote "The Sidewalks of New York" 1894 which became the theme song of Alfred E. Smith's presidential campaign in 1928.

BLAKE, NORMAN & NANCY
Won Folk Album Grammy *Just Gimme Somethin' I'm Used To* January 1993.

BLAKEY, ART (1919–1990)

b. 10/11 Pittsburgh, PA. Drummer, formed **Jazz Messengers*** 1953. Toured Europe, played for President & Mrs. Reagan on The White House lawn, September 1981. *Jazz Messenger, Moanin', Feelin' Good, Straight Ahead,* etc. Died 10/16 New York, NY.

BLANCHARD, TERENCE (1962–   )

b. New Orleans, LA. Jazz trumpeter/composer, wrote scores for films *Mo' Better Blues, Jungle Fever, Malcolm X.* Album *Simply Stated* 1992.

BLAND, BOBBY (1930–   )

b. 1/27 Rosemark, TN. R&B singer, hit single "Ain't Nothing You Can Do" 1964, *Best of Bobby Bland, The Soul of Man, Two Steps from the Blues,* etc.

BLAND, JAMES A. (1854–1911)

b. Queens, NY City. Noted black composer wrote "Carry Me Back to Old Virginny" 1878 (adopted as state song of Virginia in 1940). "Oh Dem Golden Slippers" 1879, "In the Evening by the Moonlight" 1879. Buried in Merion, PA.

BLASTERS, THE

Brothers guitarist/singer Phil Alvin, guitarist Dave Alvin, pianist Gene Taylor, bassist Steve Berlin, saxist Lee Allen, *Blaster Collection.*

BLEY, CLARA (1936–   )

b. Oakland, CA. Pianist/composer/leader of a band of nine men. Named Composer of the Year 1980 by *down beat* critics poll. *Social Studies* 1982, *Fleur Carnivore, Sextet,* etc. Married Paul Bley* then Michael Manter.

BLEY, PAUL (1932–   )

b. Montreal, Quebec. Pianist/composer, with jazz bands, then **Paul Bley Quartet.** *Axis/Solo Piano, Open to Love, Syndrome,* etc.

BLIGE, MARY J. (1971–)
Hip-hop singer, *What's the 411?* 1992, singles "Real Love," "You Remind Me" 1992, "Reminisce" 1993. Soul Train Music award as best new R&B Artist, 1992.

BLIND FAITH
English group with Eric Clapton*, Peter "Ginger" Baker on drums & percussion, Rick Grech, Steve Winwood*, hits "Can't Find My Way Home" & "Presence of the Lord" in album *Blind Faith* 1969.

BLOCH, RAYMOND "RAY" (1902–1982)
b. 8/3 Alsace, Germany. Pianist/composer/leader, TV conductor on Jackie Gleason & Ed Sullivan shows 1950/60. Died 3/29 in Miami, FL.

BLOCK, RORY
Singer, album *Ain't I a Woman.*

BLONDIE
Original punk rock group formed 1976 with Clem Burke, Jimmy Destri, Nigel Harrison, Frank Infante, Chris Stein. Lead singer Deborah Harry* b. 7/1/45 Miami, FL. Hits "Call Me" 1980, "Rapture" 1981, "Heart of Glass," albums *Blondie Live* 1983, *Eat to the Beat, Plastic Letter,* video *Blondie Live.*

BLOOD, SWEAT & TEARS
Rock group formed 1968 with blues singer David Clayton-Thomas, Bobby Colomby, Jim Fielder, Dick Halligan, Jerry Hyman, Steve Katz, Fred Lipsuis, Chuck Winfield, Louis Soloff. Album *Blood, Sweat & Tears* won 1969 Grammy, hits "Spinning Wheel," "And When I Die." Later joined by Dave Bargeron, Jerry Fisher, Al Kooper*, Tom Malone, Lou Marini, Jr., George Wadenius, Larry Willis, toured USA 1992.

BLOODS & THE CRIPS, THE
Rival Los Angeles, CA street gang rappers together on album *Bangin' on Wax* 1993.

BLOOMFIELD, MIKE (1943–1981)
b. Chicago, IL. Guitarist/singer/songwriter, *Junko Partner, Super Session.*

BLOSSOM, HENRY (1866–1919)
b. St. Louis, MO. Lyricist, with composer Victor Herbert* wrote "Kiss Me Again" 1905.

BLUE OYSTER CULT
Long Island, NY heavy metal group with Eric Bloom, Albert Bouchard, Joe Bouchard, Rick Downey, Allen Lanier, Donald "Buck Dharma" Roeser. Hit singles "Don't Fear the Reaper" 1976 by Roeser, "Burnin' for You," MTV taped show with Garland Jeffries in Los Angeles 1982. *Agents of Fortune, Career of Evil, Club Ninja,* etc. Toured USA 1992.

BLUEGRASS REUNION
Group with David Grisman, Herb Pedersen, Red Allen, Jim Bachanan, James Kervin, & Jerry Garcia*. Grammy January 1933 for *Bluegrass Reunion.*

BLUES BROTHERS
Singers Jake Blues (John Belushi) & Elwood Blues (Dan Aykroyd), musicians Paul Shaffer, Steve Cropper, Matt Murphy, Donald Dunn, Steve Jordan, Lou Marini, Tom Scott, Tom Malone, & Lan Rubin. *Blues Brothers, Brief Case Full of Blues, The Best of the Blues Brothers.*

BLUES IMPERIALS
On the Alligator Records 20th anniversary tour 1992.

BLUES MACHINE
Led by Koko Taylor* in Chicago 1980, at Avery Fisher Hall in New York City in July 1980.

BOBS, THE
Albums *My I'm Large, New Wave Accapella, Songs for Tomorrow Morning.*

BOCK, JERRY (1928–)

b. New Haven, CT. Composer, hits "Mr. Wonderful" 1956, "Fiorello." With Sheldon Harnick* "Fiddler on the Roof" 1964, "The Apple Tree" 1966.

BODY COUNT

Heavy metal band led by Ice-T*, albums *Body Count* 1992, *Born Dead* 1993.

BOFILL, ANGELA (1955–)

b. New York, NY. Rock singer/songwriter, album *Something About You* in top five on jazz charts. *The Best of Angela Bofill, Intuition, Too Tough,* hit "Under the Moon and Over the Sky."

BOGGUSS, SUZY (1957–)

Country singer/songwriter. With husband Doug Crider co-wrote hit "Letting Go" on gold record *Aces* 1991 (won Country Music Horizon award). Top ten single "Someday Soon," *Voices in the Wind* 1992, "Drive South" 1993, toured with Dwight Yoakum* 1993.

BOILED IN LEAD

Albums *From the Ladle to the Grave, Old Lead, ORB.*

BOLCOM, WILLIAM

Pianist/composer, won 1988 Pulitzer Prize for *12 New Etudes for Piano,* albums *Piano Music by Gershwin, Three Ghost Rags for Piano. Clarinet Concerto* premiered at NY Philharmonic and opera *McTeague* at Lyric Opera in Chicago 1992.

BOLDEN, CHARLES "BUDDY" (1878–1931)

b. New Orleans, LA. Cornetist, led first known jazz band 1900/07, then joined Allen's Brass Band. Ran amok during a parade and was committed to the State Hospital at Angola, LA from 1907/16. Died in Jackson, LA.

BOLLIN, ZUZU (Died 1990)

Dallas blues guitarist during 1950s/80s, albums *Zuzu Bollin* 1984, *Texas Bluesman* 1989.

BOLLING, CLAUDE (1930–)
b. Cannes, France. Albums *Big Band, Jazz a la Francaise, Jazz Brunch, Picnic Suite,* etc.

BOLTON, GUY REGINALD (1884–1979)
b. in England of American parents, came to US. Librettist for Jerome Kern* for *Sally* 1920 which included "Look for a Silver Lining" sung by Marilyn Miller. Also wrote other shows.

BOLTON, MICHAEL
Singer, albums *Michael Bolton, The Hunger, Soul Provider, Timeless,* videos *Soul and Passion, Soul Provider.* Won 1992 Best Male Pop Star Grammy for his new rendition of the 1966 song "When a Man Loves a Woman"; hit single "Steel Bars" 1992, sang "A Change is Gonna Come" at Lincoln Memorial in Jan. 1993, American Music Award for Pop/rock Male Vocalist 1993.

BON JOVI
Heavy metal band with guitarist/singer/songwriter John Bongiovi, guitarists Rob Rock & Richie Samboro, bassist Alex John Such, keyboardist David Bryan, & drummer Tico Torres. Albums *Bon Jovi* 1984, *7800 degrees Fahrenheit* 1985, *Slippery When Wet* 1986 (sold 14 million copies), *New Jersey* 1988 (sold 10 million copies), platinum single "Blaze of Glory" 1990, *Keep the Faith* 1992, videos *Access to All Areas,* "Bed of Roses" on network TV in January 1993.

BOND, CARRIE JACOBS (1862–1948)
b. Janesville, WI. Composer of "I Love You Truly," "When It Comes to the End of a Perfect Day" and other songs.

BOND, CYRUS W. "JOHNNY" (1915–1978)
b. Enville, OK. Guitarist/singer/songwriter, with Gene Autry* 1950/54. Wrote "Cimarron" and other songs. Died 6/13 at Burbank, CA.

BOND, VICTORIA (1945–)
b. 5/6 Los Angeles, CA. Conductor, assisted Andre Previn* in

leading the Pittsburgh Orchestra 1978/80, first woman to co-conduct a major US symphony orchestra.

BONDS, GARY "U.S." (1939–)
b. Gary Anderson 6/6 Jacksonville, FL. Singer/songwriter, hit single "Quarter to Three" 1961; *Best of Gary U.S. Bonds*. With Bruce Springsteen on *Dedication* 1981.

BONELLI, RICHARD (1894–1980)
b. Richard Bunn 2/6 Port Bryan, NY. Baritone in light and grand opera, with Metropolitan Opera, NY 1932–45. Died 6/7 at Los Angeles, CA.

BONO, SALVATORE "SONNY" (1935–)
b. 2/16 Detroit, MI. Singer with wife singer Cherylyn La Pierre Sarkasian formed team of Sonny and Cher*, they were divorced in 1975 and Cher had a successful solo career. Bono married May Whitaker and had two children. His song "I Got You Babe" sold over four million discs. Sang on the soundtrack *Honeymoon in Las Vegas* 1992. Served as mayor of Palm Springs, CA. Elected to U.S. House of Representatives, 1995.

BOOKER, CHUCKII
Keyboardist/singer/songwriter, hit R&B single "Games," album *Nice N' Wild* 1992.

BOOKER T and the MG'S
Rock group with lead guitarist Steve Cropper, drummer Al Jackson*, (d. 1975), bassist Donald "Duck" Dunn, organist Booker T. Jones. Albums *Best of Booker T. and the MG's, Greatest Hits, Melting Pot, Soul Limbo;* hit single "Green Onions" 1962, group disbanded in 1972. Group provided soulful backup numbers for concert in honor of Bob Dylan* at Madison Square Garden in NY City October 1992.

BOONE, CHARLES EUGENE "PAT" (1934–)
b. 6/1 Jacksonville, FL. Actor/singer, married Shirley Foley, daughter of Red Foley. On the Arthur Godfrey Show, NY 1955, had his own TV show, starred in *April Love* 1957. Albums *Greatest Hits, White Christmas*.

BOONE, DEBBY (1956–   )
b. 9/22 Hackensack, NJ. Singer daughter of Pat Boone*. Married Gabriel Ferrer. Hit song "You Light Up My Life" 1977, same hit in 1992.

BORGE, VICTOR (1909–   )
b. 1/3 born Borge Rosenbaum in Copenhagen, Denmark, pianist who combines humor with music. Came to US in 1940. Album *Great Moments of Comedy*. On *Vibrations* public TV 1972, performed with NJ Symphony Orchestra in July 1992, video cassette *The Best of Victor Borge* 1992, toured US in 1990s.

BOSTIC, EARL (1913–1965)
b. Tulsa, OK. Rock & roll alto saxist/composer, hit "Flamingo."

BOSTON
Music group with Brad Delp, Barry Goudreau, Sib Hashian, Tom Scholtz, Fran Sheehan. Album *Boston* 1976 sold 6.5 million copies, *Don't Look Back, Third Stage*.

BOSWELL SISTERS
Singing trio with Connie Boswell (b. 12/3/12 New Orleans, LA died 10/11/76 New York, NY); Martha Boswell (1905–1958), Helvetia "Vet" Boswell (b. 1911 New Orleans). Sisters in films *Big Broadcast* 1932 & *Moulin Rouge* 1934, popular during World War II.

BOURELLY, JEAN PAUL (1961–   )
b. Chicago, IL. Guitarist/singer, has played jazz with Miles Davis, McCoy Tyner, & Elvin Jones; funk with Bell Biv DeVoe, D-Nice, Jazzy Jeff and the Fresh Prince. Album *Trippin* 1992, with Fourplay* on album *Fourplay* 1992.

BOW, WOW, WOW
With lead singer Annabella Irwin (b. 10/31/65 Rangoon, Burma), guitarist Matthew Ashman, drummer Dave Barbarossa. At Hotel Diplomat in NY City on New Year's Day 1982.

BOWIE, DAVID (1947–)
b. David Robert Jones 1/8 London, UK. Pop/rock/singer/
songwriter starred in film *The Man Who Fell to Earth* 1976.
With Brian Eno* on album *Low* 1977. Hit "Let's Dance,"
album *Serious Moonlight* 1984, *Aladdin Sane, Changes, Diamond Dogs, Hunky Dory, Pin Ups, Space Oddity, Black Tie
White Noise* 1993. See Philip Glass*.

BOWLING, ROGER (1944–1982)
Songwriter, "Lucille," "Coward of the Country." Died 12/25 in
Clayton, GA.

BOX TOPS, THE
Soul group with lead singer Alex Chilton (b. 12//28/50 Memphis,
TN), bass guitar/keyboardist Billy Cunningham, organist/
guitarist John Evans, drummer Danny Smythe, lead guitarist
Gary Talley. Hit single "The Letter" 1967. Later drummer
Tom Boggs, bassist/organist Rick Allen, Harold Cloud, and
Swain Scharfer, albums *Boxtops, Dimensions, Non-Stop.*

BOY GEORGE (1961–)
b. George O'Dowd 6/14 Bexley Heath, UK known for make-up
and avant-garde dress. Lead singer for the **Culture Club** rock
band. Hit "Do You Really Want to Hurt Me" 1982, albums
Solid, The Martyr Mantras, on soundtrack for *The Crying
Game* 1993.

BOYD, WILLIAM "BILL" (1910–1977)
b. 9/29 Fannin County, TX. Guitarist/singer/songwriter, disk
jockey in Dallas 1932/67; bandleader for **The Cowboy Ramblers;** wrote "Boyd's Blues," "David's Blues," "Under the
Double Eagle," "Ridin' on a Humpback Mule." Died 12/7 in
Dallas.

BOYS, THE
Pop group, hits "Dial My Heart" 1989, #1 smash "Crazy,"
Pleasure and the Pain, The Saga Continues 1992, video
Messages from The Boys.

BOYZ II MEN
Hip/hop vocal group with Nathan Morris, Wanya Morris, Stockman and Michael McCary. 1991 Grammy for *Cooleyhighharmony*. After gunfire broke out following a concert in Chicago in May 1992 their security guard was killed; Pop single Grammy 1993 for "End of the Road," won 3 Billboard Music Awards, American Music Award 1993, sang at inaugural festivities for President Clinton in Janaury 1993. Hit "In the Still of the Night" 1993.

BRACKEEN, JOANNE
Albums *Breath of Brazil, Fifi Goes to Heaven, Havin' Fun, Where Legends Dwell,* etc.

BRADBURY, WILLIAM B. (1816–1868)
b. York, ME. Composer. With lyricist Anna B. Warner* wrote "Jesus Loves Me" 1859. With lyricist W. W. Walford "Sweet Hour of Prayer" 1860, with lyricist J. H. Gilmore, "He Leadeth Me" 1864. Died in Montclair, NJ.

BRADFORD, CARMEN
Singer. After she left the **Count Basie* Band** in 1992 went solo with her album *Finally Yours.*

BRADLEY, WILL (1912–)
b. Wilbur Schwichtenberg 7/12 Newton, NJ. Trombonist/composer/bandleader, album *Best of the Big Bands.*

BRADY, PAUL
Irish singer/songwriter, *Hard Station, True for You, Back to the Centre, Primitive Dance.* His songs have been recorded by Dave Edmunds, Bonnie Raitt* and Tina Turner*.

BRAFF, REUBEN "RUBY" (1927–)
b. 3/16 Boston, MA. Jazz cornetist/trumpeter, played at 1954 Newport Jazz Festival & subsequent festivals, at Carnegie Hall 1980. Albums *America the Beautiful, Me, Myself and I, This is My Lucky Day,* etc.

BRAGG, BILLY (1957–)
b. 12/20 Essex, UK. Guitarist/singer/songwriter, albums *Back to Basics, Don't Try This at Home, Talking with the Taxman, The Internationale,* 1992, etc.

BRAHMS SEXTETS
Violinists Sharon Robinson, Yo Yo Ma*, Jaime Laredo, Cho-Liang Lin, Isaac Stern*, & Michael Tree, album *Brahms: String Sextets* 1992.

BRANCA, BOBBY
Cornetist, leader of the **Bobby Hackett* Memorial Jazz Band,** first came to US in 1966. Album *Bobby Branca Vol. 1 (1971/76).* With pianist Dave McKenna, clarinetist Dick Johnson, bassist Tony De Fazio 1992.

BRANIGAN, LAURA (1957–)
b. 7/3 Brewster, NY. Singer, hit singles "Gloria" 1982, "Solitaire" 1983, "Self Control" 1984, video *Laura Branigan.*

BRAXTON, ANTHONY (1945–)
b. Chicago, jazz clarinetist/saxist/composer/leader, soloist at Carnegie Hall in NY City 1992. CDs *Anthony Braxton Live, Compositions 88, 151, Four Compositions for QUAR, Seven Compositions,* etc.

BRAXTON, TONI (1967–)
Singer, b. 10/7 no. 1 R&B hit "Love Shoulda Brought U Home" 1992. Won American Music Soul/R&B New Artist award 1994. Grammy 1994 for "Another Sad Song" and for New Vocal Artist and R&B Vocal Performance 1994.

BRAZILIAN RAINFOREST
Albums *Down Chorus, Jungle Journey, Rainforest.*

BREAD
Singer/songwriter David Gates (b. 12/11/40 Tulsa, OK), Mike Botts, James Gordon, (later with Souther-Hillman-Furay Band), James Griffin, Larry Knechtel, Robb Royer. Hit songs

"Make it with You" 1970, "If" 1971, "Diary" 1972, albums *Anthology, Manna, The Best of Bread,* etc.

BREATHE
1988 Top 10 Pop single "Hands to Heaven," album *All That Jazz.*

BRECKER BROTHERS
Saxist Michael & trumpeter Randy Brecker split in 1982; Michael won 1988 Jazz Instrumental award for "Don't Try This at Home." Reunited 1992, hit "Above and Below" track from *Return of the Brecker Brothers* won Grammy 1993.

BRENNAN, J. KEIRN (1873–1948)
b. San Francisco, CA. Singer/lyricist, with music by Ernest Ball* wrote "A Little Bit of Heaven, Sure They Call It Ireland" 1914.

BREWER and SHIPLEY
Folk/rock duo formed 1968, Michael Brewer & Thomas Shipley, hit "One Toke over the Line" 1971, album *Greatest Hits.*

BREWER, SPENCER
Albums *Dorian's Legacy, Emerald/Rumble and Tingstad, The Piper's Rhythm, Portraits.*

BREWER, TERESA (1931–   )
b. 5/7 Toledo, Ohio. Singer/actress, toured on the Major Bowes Amateur Hour from ages 5 to 12, later on the Perry Como* Show and the Ed Sullivan Show. Hit "Till I Waltz Again with You," *Golden Hits, I Dig Big Band Swingers, The Cotton Connection, What a Wonderful World.*

BRICE, FANNY (1891–1951)
Singer/entertainer, star of the Ziegfeld Follies 1910s/20s.

BRICKTOP (1894–1984)
b. Ada Beatrice Queen Victoria Louise Virginia Smith 8/14 Iderson, WV. Singer, sang in night clubs in Paris during World War I and World War II. Died 1/31 in New York, NY.

BRIDGEWATER, DEE DEE (1950–)
b. 5/27 Memphis, TN. Jazz singer/actress, sang with **Thad Jones-*Mel Lewis Orchestra.** Settled in France. *Live in Paris, In Montreux* at the 1990 Jazz Festival (released in 1992).

BRIGATTI BROTHERS
Singers Eddie & David Brigatti with others on album *Live at the Beacon* 1992.

BRIGGS, ARTHUR (1901–1991)
b. St. Georges, Canada, raised in Charleston, SC. Trumpeter/leader, toured Europe in 1920s/30s. Arrested by Nazis in World War II & interned at the St. Denis concentration camp. Led own bands in Paris after 1945. Died 7/16 in Paris.

BROCKMAN, JAMES (1886–1967)
Composer/lyricist with James Kendis*, T. W. Killette, & Nat Vincent wrote "I'm Forever Blowing Bubbles" 1918.

BROMBERG, DAVID
Albums *Best of David Bromberg, How Late'll Ya Play, Out of the Blue, Sideman Serenade.*

BRONX STYLE BOB
b. Bobby Khaleel in NY City, wah-wah/pop singer, album *Grandma's Ghost* 1992.

BROOKS and DUNN
Guitarist Kix Brooks (b. 1955) & singer Ronnie Dunn (b. 1953) won 1992 Country Music Duo award for *Brand New Man,* sang at the show "Boot-Scootin Boogie" (top ten country single 1992). Album *Hard Workin' Man,* won Horizon duo award 1992 for video *Pardners: The Brand New Man.* Country Music Vocal Duo award 1993. Country Duo Grammy 1994 for "Hard Workin' Man."

BROOKS BLUES BAND, LONNIE
Toured on Alligator Records 20th Anniversary tour 1992.

BROOKS, GARTH (1962–)
b. 2/7 Tulsa, OK. Country singer/guitarist, graduated Oklahoma State, married Sandy Mahl 1986. *No Fences* sold 10 million albums 1990, hit album *Ropin' the Wind* 1991 sold 9 million copies. Entertainer of Year 1991 & 92, *The Chase,* 5 million to Dec. 1992. *Beyond the Season* 1992, *The Dance* won 7 awards at Billboard Music awards Dec. 1992. American Music Award Country Vocalist, January 1993 & February 1994.

BROOKS, KAREN
Country singer/songwriter/guitarist. With singer/songwriter/ guitarist Randy Sharp* hit single "A Simple I Love You," album *That's Another Story* 1992.

BROOKS, LONNIE
With The Uppity Blues Woman* album *Christmas on the Bayou* 1992.

BROOKS, PHILLIPS (1835–1893)
b. Boston, MA. Hymnist. With composer L. H. Redner* wrote "O Little Town of Bethlehem" 1868.

BROOKS, SHELTON (1886–1975)
b. Amesbury, Ontario, Canada, raised in Detroit, MI. Composer of "The Darktown Strutters' Ball" 1917, "Some of These Days" sung by Sophie Tucker* 1920, "Honey Gal" sung by Al Jolson* in the Winter Garden, etc. Died 9/6 in Los Angeles, Calif.

BROONZY, BIG BILL (1893–1958)
b. William Lee Conley in Scott, MS. Guitarist/singer/songwriter, wrote "Big Bill Blues," "Mama Let's Cuddle Some More." Died in Chicago of lung cancer.

BROTHERS FOUR
Bob Flick, Michael Kirkland, John Paine, & Richard Foley, albums *Greatest Hits, Greenfield and Other Gold,* "Green-fields" on *Troubadours of the Folk Era Vol. 3* issued 1992.

BROWN, BOBBY (1969–)

b. 2/5, platinum single "On Our Own," top album *Don't Be Cruel* sold 9 million copies. Top single "My Prerogative" 1989, music video *His Prerogative* 1990. "Humpin' Around" R&B single, hit single "Don't Be Cruel," songs peppered with machine-gun raps 1992, Soul/R&B vocalist American Music Award 1993, toured US 1992/93. He married singer Whitney Houston.

BROWN, CHARLES

Album *Boogie Woogie Santa Claus* 1992, won Grammy for blues album *Someone to Love* 1993.

BROWN, CLARENCE "GATEMOUTH"

Albums *One More Mile, Pressure Cooker, Texas Swing, No Looking Back* won Grammy 1993.

BROWN, DENNIS

Albums *Brown Sugar, Hold Tight, Overproof, Slow Down, Visions,* etc.

BROWN, JAMES (1934–)

b. 5/3 Augusta, GA. Rock vocalist/songwriter, sings, shouts, raves, & screams. Called "Mr. Dynamite" and "Soul Brother Number One." Entertained troops in Vietnam 1966. Grammy 1965, 38 gold records in 20 years. *I'm Real, In the Jungle Groove, Love Overdue, Soul Sessions,* etc. Hit "Papa's Got a Brand New Bag" on album *America's Music: Soul I* 1983, *Universal James* 1992. Grammy Lifetime award 1992.

BROWN, LESTER R. "LES" (1912–)

b. 5/12 Reinerton, PA. Leader of **Les Brown and His Band of Renown.** Led bands 1930s/80s, wrote "Sentimental Journey," albums *Anything Goes, Best of the Big Bands,* etc.

BROWN, LEW (1893–1958)

b. Odessa, Ukraine, came to US in 1898. Lyricist, wrote words for the "Beer Barrel Polka" and with Charles Tobias* & Sammy Stept* "Don't sit under the apple tree with anyone else but me" 1942. Died in NY City.

BROWN, MARTY
Country singer/songwriter, *High and Dry* rated 8/9 *CD Review,* February 1992, *Wild Kentucky Skies* 1993.

BROWN, NACIO HERB (1898–1964)
b. Deming, NM. Composer, wrote "The Pagan Love Song" 1929, "Love is Where You Find It," "You were Meant for Me," "All I Do is Dream of You," "Singing in the Rain."

BROWN, OSCAR, JR. (1926–)
b. 10/10 Chicago, IL. Singer/songwriter, wrote "Brown Baby" recorded by Mahalia Jackson* 1960. Master of ceremonies on *Jazz Scene USA* TV show 1962. Album *Sin and Soul.*

BROWN, RAYMOND "RAY" (1926–)
b. Pittsburgh, PA. Bassist with Dizzy Gillespie* & others in 1940s, married singer Ella Fitzgerald* 1948/52. *down beat* polls winner 1953/59. With lyricist Steve Allen composed "Gravy Waltz," albums *Bam, Bam, Bam, Don't Forget the Blues,* etc.

BROWN, RUTH (1928–)
b. 1/12. Singer, known as the R&B Queen in 1950s, hit "(Mama) He Treats Your Daughter Mean" 1953, won Grammy for "Blues on Broadway," albums *Brown, Black & Beautiful, Fine & Mello, Help Good Girl So Bad.* Inducted into the Rock & Roll Hall of Fame in Los Angeles, CA in January 1993.

BROWN, SAWYER
Country singer, albums *Buick, Dirt Road,* hit singles "Cafe on the Corner" 1992, "All These Years" 1993, video *Shakin.*

BROWN, SEYMOUR (1885–1947)
b. Philadelphia, PA. Lyricist. With composer Nat D. Ayer* wrote "Oh, You Beautiful Doll" 1911.

BROWN, T. GRAHAM
Albums *Bumper to Bumper, Come as You Were, You Can't Take It With You,* etc.

BROWNE, JACKSON (1948–   )
b. 10/9 Heidelberg, Germany, came to US. Pianist/singer/
songwriter, hit "Doctor My Eyes" 1971, gold album *The
Pretender* 1976, *For Everyman, Hold Out, Jackson Browne,
Lawyers in Love,* etc., sang on Coca Cola video during the 1992
Olympics in Seville, Spain.

BROWNS, THE
Singers, hit songs "The Three Bells," "Whispering Hope."

BRUBECK, DAVID W. "DAVE" (1920–   )
b. 12/6 Concord, CA. Pianist/composer/leader, formed **Dave
Brubeck Quartet** 1951, new band 1979. Played for President
& Mrs. Reagan on The White House Lawn 1981. *All the Things
We Are, Concord on a Summer Night, Essence of Dave
Brubeck, Jazz Goes to College, Jazz Impressions of New York,*
etc. at Monterey Jazz Festival in California, September 1992.

BRUCE, CAROL (1917–   )
b. 11/15 Great Neck, NY. Actress/singer, on stage in *Do I Hear a
Waltz, Show Boat, Pal Joey.*

BRUCE, JACK
b. 5/14 Glasgow, Scotland. Former member of **Cream***, went
solo, album *Somethin' Else,* launched US tour in March 1993.

BRUFORD, BILL
CDs *Dig, Earthworks, One of a Kind, The Buford Tapes,* etc.

BRUNIS, GEORGE (1902–1974)
b. 2/6 New Orleans, LA. Trombonist/vocalist/leader, with **New
Orleans Rhythm Kings** 1920/24, later with Bobby Hackett,*
Muggsy Spanier,* Art Hodges, Ted Lewis,* Eddie Condon,* &
others. Called "King of the Tailgate Trombone." Died 11/19
Chicago. IL.

BRYAN, ALFRED (1871–1958)
b. Brantford, Ontario, Canada. Lyricist, with composer Fred

Fisher* wrote "Peg O' My Heart" 1913. Died in Gladstone, NJ.

BRYAN, VINCENT (1883–1937)
Lyricist, with composer Gus Edwards* wrote "My Merry Oldsmobile" 1905.

BRYANT, ANITA (1940–   )
b. 3/25 Barnsdall, OK. Noted gospel singer, albums *Abiding Love, How Great Thou Art, Kisses Sweeter Than Wine, Whispering Hope*, etc. Due to her views on homosexuality lost her TV contract promoting orange juice. Appeared on Lawrence Welk shows.

BRYANT, DAN (1833–1875)
b. Daniel W. O'Brien in Troy, NY. Minstrel showman/songwriter, adapting the tune "Zip Coon" (1834) he wrote the words for "Turkey in the Straw" 1861.

BRYANT, RAPHAEL "RAY" (1931–   )
b. Philadelphia, PA. Jazz pianist, albums *Alone with the Blues, Montreaux '77, The Best of Ray Bryant*, etc.

BRYSON, JEANIE (1958–   )
Jazz singer, claims to be the daughter of Dizzy Gillespie.* Debut album with saxist Don Braden, bassist Ray Drummond, trumpeter Wallace Rooney, and pianist Kenny Barron,* June 1993.

BRYSON, PEABO (1957–   )
b. Robert Peabo 4/13 Greenville, SC. Rhythm & blues singer, with Roberta Flack had hit singles "Lookin' Like Love" 1984, & "Born to Love." With Celine Dion "Beauty and the Beast" 1992 (won Grammy 1993), with Regina Belle* "A Whole New World" 1992/93 (won Grammy 1994).

BUCHANAN, ROY
Guitarist, albums *Dancing on the Edge, Livestock, When a Guitar Plays the Blues, You're Not Alone*, etc.

BUCKINGHAM, LINDSEY (1947–   )

b. 10/3 Palo Alto, CA. Guitarist with **Fleetwood Mac,*** then went solo. Five solo records, albums *Out of the Cradle* 1992, on *VH-1 to One* (TV) in January 1993.

BUCKLEY, TIM (1947–1975)

b. 2/17 Washington, D.C. Guitarist/singer/songwriter, albums *Goodbye and Hello* 1967, *Greetings from L.A., Starsailor,* etc. Died 6/29 Santa Monica, CA.

BUCKWHEAT ZYDECO

Accordian group from S.W. Louisiana with accordian player Stanley Dural, Jr. Toured US 1992, albums *One Night Like This, On Track, Taking It Home, Where There's Smoke, Menagerie: The Essential Zydeco Collection.*

BUELLGRASS

Jazz/bluegrass/fusion group led by Buell Neidlinger at first annual Ojai Jazz Festival in California, August 1981.

BUFFALO SPRINGFIELD

Singer/songwriter Jim Messina (b. 12/5/47 Maywood, CA.) musician/singer/songwriter Kenny Loggins,* hit "For What it's Worth," albums *Buffalo Springfield, Retrospective,* etc.

BUFFETT, JIMMY (1946–   )

b. 12/25 Pascagoula, MS. Singer/songwriter, hit singles "Margaritaville" 1977, "Come Monday," albums *Coconut Telegraph, Havana Day Dreamin, Off to See the Lizard, Son of a Sailor,* etc., video *Jimmy Buffett Live.* Lives in Sag Harbor, NY. On top ten grossing tour list 1992, sang at an Inaugural Ball for President Clinton 1993.

BULLARD, FREDERIC FIELD (1864–1904)

b. Boston, MA., teacher/composer, with lyricist Richard Hovey* wrote "For It's Always Fair Weather When Good Fellows Get Together" 1898.

BURKE, BILLIE (1885–1970)
b. Washington, D.C. Actress/singer, married Florenz Ziegfeld.

BURKE, JOE (1884–1950)
b. Philadelphia, PA. Pianist/composer, with lyricist Benny Davis wrote "Carolina Moon" 1928. With lyricist Edgar Leslie,* "Moon Over Miami" 1936. With lyricist Joseph McCarthy,* "Ramblin' Rose" 1948.

BURKE, JOHNNY (1908–1964)
b. Antioch, CA. Lyricist, wrote words for "Pennies from Heaven," "Swinging on a Star" (Academy Award 1944), "What's New?," "Imagination," & other songs. Died in New York City.

BURKE, KEVIN
British/American group, album *Open House.*

BURNETT, CHESTER A. "HOWLIN' WOLF" (1910–1976)
b. 6/10 West Point, MS. Blues singer, formed band in 1940s, hits "Little Red Rooster," "Back Door Man." Sensation at the 1966 Folk Festival, Newport, RI. Died 1/10 Chicago.

BURNETT, ERNIE (1884–1959)
b. Cincinnati, Ohio. Composer, with lyricist George A. Norton* wrote "My Melancholy Baby" 1911.

BURNETT, T. BONE (1948–   )
b. Missouri, singer, "Humans on Earth" on soundtrack *Until the End of the World* 1992. Album *The Criminal Under My Own Hat* won Folk Album Grammy 1993.

BURNING SPEAR
Reggae stars, albums *Jah Kingdom, Man in the Hills, Marcus Garvey, Mek We Dweet.* With Jimmy Cliff* on World Beat '92 tour of the USA.

BURRELL, KENNY (1931–)
b. Detroit, MI. Guitarist/leader, albums *All Day Long, All Night Long, Generation, Guiding Spirit, The Cats,* etc.

BURROWS, ABRAM S. "ABE" (1910–1985)
b. Brooklyn, NY. Librettist, wrote *Guys and Dolls* 1950, *How to Succeed in Business Without Really Trying* 1961. Died 5/17 New York City.

BURTON, GARY (1943–)
b. Anderson, IN. Vibraharpist, albums *Burton and Berklee All Stars, Cool Nights, Reunion with Pat Metheny,* etc. Musician, with Eddie Daniels* *Benny Rides Again* 1992.

BURTON, JAMES (1939–)
b. 8/21 Shreveport, LA. Guitarist, *The Guitar Sounds of James Burton* 1971, *Corn Pickin' & Slick Sliding* 1984.

BUSH, KATE (1958–)
b. 7/30 London, UK. Singer/songwriter, albums *The Dreaming, Hounds of Love, The Kick Inside,* etc., videos *Live at Hammersmith, The Sensual World* 1989.

BUSHWICK, BILL
Rapper, lost an eye due to a gunshot wound. Album *Little Big Man* 1992.

BUTLER, JERRY (1940–)
b. Philadelphia, PA. Soul singer/songwriter, conducted Jerry Butler Workshop in Chicago 1970s. Albums *Best of Jerry Butler, The Ice Man,* appeared on TV program *Street Gold: Street Canal* in Decenber 1992.

BUTLER, JONATHAN
Gospel singer, albums *Deliverance, Gospel Days, More Than Friends,* etc., video *Heal Our Land.*

BUTTERFIELD, CHARLES W. "BILLY" (1917–1988)
b. 1/14 Middletown, Ohio. Trumpeter/fluegelhorn player, with

Artie Shaw,* Benny Goodman,* and others. Died 3/18 North Palm Beach, FL.

BUTTERFIELD, DANIEL (1831–1901)
b. Utica, NY. While in command of a brigade of the Union Army in July 1862, hummed a tune which became ''Taps'' to his bugler Oliver Willcox Norton.

BUTTERFIELD, JAMES A. (1837–1891)
b. Hertfordshire, UK. Composer, came to US in 1856 and settled in Chicago. From a poem by George W. Johnson* wrote the music for ''When You and I were Young, Maggie'' 1866.

BUTTERFIELD, PAUL (1942–1987)
b. 12/17 Chicago, IL. Leader of **Paul Butterfield's Blues Band** from 1965, albums *Better Days, It All Comes Back, Put It in Your Ear, Paul Butterfield Blues Band,* etc.

BUZZIN' COUSINS, THE
Singers John Mellencamp,* Dwight Yoakum,* John Prine,* Joe Ely,* and James McMurty.

BYAS, CARLOS ''DON'' (1912–1972)
b. Muskogee, OK. Tenor saxist, led own bands in 1930s, accompanied Ethel Waters* 1937, then with Count Basie* 1941/43. Went to Europe in 1946 with Don Redman* and lived there, toured Japan 1971. CD *On Blue Star.* Died of cancer in Amsterdam, The Netherlands.

BYRD, CHARLIE (1925–)
b. 9/16 Chuckatuck, VA. Guitarist, with Stan Getz* recorded ''Jazz Samba'' 1962. Influential in the bossa nova craze in the US, gave a recital for Lady Bird Johnson in The White House 1965. Albums *Brazilville, Byrd at the Gate, It's a Wonderful World, The Bossa Nova Years,* etc.

BYRD, DON (1932–)
b. 12/9 Detroit, MI. Trumpeter/fluegelhorn player with **Art Blakey's Jazz Messengers,*** Pepper Adams,* Lionel Hampton,* & others. Albums *Ethiopian Nights* 1972, *Black Byrd*

1975, *Chant* 1980, *125th Street New York City* 1980, *A New Perspective,* Free Form, *First Flight, Harlem Blues,* etc.

BYRD, HARRY (1918–1980)
b. 12/19 Bogalusa, LA. Rock-n-roll pianist in New Orleans. Wrote "Go to the Mardi Gras," "Big Chief." Died 1/30.

BYRDS, THE
Folk/rock band with guitarist/singer/songwriter David Crosby (b.8/14/41 Los Angeles, CA), singer Graham Parsons, Cecil Connor (1946–1973), Skip Battin, Michael & Gene Clark, Chris Hillman (on mandolin solo "Slippin' Away"), Kevin Kelly & Roger McGuinn, hits "Mr. Tambourine Man," "Turn, Turn, Turn" 1965.

BYRNE, DAVID (1952–   )
b. 5/14 Scotland. Leader of the **Talking Heads*** composed music for the Broadway show *The Catherine Wheel* 1981. Byrne left the group, solos *Rei Momo* 1989, *Uh-oh* 1992, toured US 1992.

BYTCHES WITH PROBLEMS
Female rap singers, hits "Two Minute Brother," "We Want the Money," song "Pro-me" attacked Tipper Gore for her stand against explicit music lyrics 1992.

C

CACERES, EMILIO (1897–1980)
b. Rockport, TX. Jazz violinist with big bands of Benny Goodman,* Tommy Dorsey,* & Harry James.* Died 2/9 San Antonio, TX.

CAESAR, IRVING (1895–   )
b. 7/4 New York, NY, wrote lyrics for "Crazy Rhythm." With composer George Gershwin* "Swanee" and with Otto Harbach* and composer Vincent M. Youmans* wrote "Tea for Two" which appeared in *No, No Nanette*.

CAESAR, SHIRLEY (1930–   )
Gospel singer on album *Jubilation Great Gospel Performances Vols. 1 & 2* issued 1992, *He's Working it out for You* (Grammy winner January 1993) on The Stellar Awards TV show "Stand Still" Soul/Gospel Grammy 1994.

CAGE, JOHN MILTON (1912–1992)
b. Los Angeles, CA. Composer of *Sonatas and Interludes* 1940/46, composed *Water Music and Williams Mix* 1952 while throwing Chinese dice for the mix. *Variations* 1958/65 where he used nails and screws between the strings for unusual sound effects. Died of cancer 8/12 in New York City.

CAGES, THE
Pop singers Clayton Cages and Richard Aven, album *Hometown* 1992.

CAHN, SAMMY (1913–1993)
b. New York, NY. Lyricist, wrote English words for "Bei Mir Bist du Schoen" made famous by the Andrews Sisters* 1938. With composer Jule Styne* won Oscar for "Three Coins in a Fountain" 1954. With composer James van Heusen* wrote "All the Way" 1957, "Love and Marriage," & "It's Magic."

CALDWELL, SARAH (1924–   )
b. 3/6 Maryville, MO. Conductor/director, founded Opera Company of Boston 1957, first solo woman conductor.

CALE, J. J. (1938–   )
b. 12/5 Oklahoma City, OK. Guitarist/singer/songwriter, wrote "After Midnight" hit single for Eric Clapton;* albums *Grasshopper, Naturally, Really, Special Edition,* etc.

CALIFORNIA RAISINS
Multi-platinum music video *Meet the Raisins* 1989, album *Sweet Delicious.*

CALL, THE
Albums *Into the Woods, Let the Day Begin, Red Moon, Scene Beyond, Dreams.*

CALLAHAN, J. WILL (1874–1946)
b. Columbus, IN. Lyricist, with composer Lee S. Roberts* wrote "There are smiles that make you happy" 1917.

CALLAS, MARIA (1923–1977)
b. Maria Kalogeropoulou 12/3 New York, NY, Soprano, sang *Norma* at Metropolitan Opera in NY City 1956. Married Giovanni Battista Meneghini, later divorced; linked romantically with Aristotle Onassis in 1960s. Taught at Juilliard 1972. Died 9/16 Paris, France.

CALLOWAY, BLANCHE (1902–1978)
b. Baltimore, MD. Singer/songwriter/bandleader, older sister of Cab Calloway* sang in his bands in 1930s then led own band in Philadelphia. Became first woman disk jockey in the south at station WMBM in Miami Beach, FL in 1950s. Died 12/16.

CALLOWAY, CABELL "CAB" (1907–1994)
b. 12/25 Rochester, NY. Singer/bandleader, led bands in 1920s/40s, noted as a "scat" singer, hit song "Minnie the Moocher." *Best of Big Bands, Jumpin' Five, The Hi de Ho Man.*

CAMEO
Nathan Leftenat, Larry Blackman, & Toni Jenkins, albums *She's Strange, Single Life, Real Men Wear Black* 1992, video *Word Up.*

CAMILO, MICHAEL
Albums *Michael Camilo, On Five, On the Other Hand, Why Not?*.

CAMPBELL, GLEN (1936–)
b. 4/22 Billstown, AK. Country singer/guitarist, hits "Turn Around, Look at Me" 1961, "Rhinestone Cowboy" 1975, "Southern Nights" 1977, won 1968 Grammy for album *By the Time I Get to Phoenix*, has garnered 12 gold and seven platinum albums. Current *Best of the Early Years, Live in London, Unconditional Love*, etc., *Somebody Like That* 1993.

CAMPBELL, LUTHER "LUKE" (1962–)
Rapper with **2 Live Crew*** whose *As Nasty as They Wanna Be* was banned in many US cities because of liberal use of four-letter words. Solo album *Got Something on My Mind* 1992.

CAMPBELL, STACY DEAN (1968–)
Country singer, album *Lonesome Wins Again* 1992.

CAMPBELL, TEVIN
Singer on Top Ten R & B single "Alone With You" October 1992, album *T. E. V. I. N.*

CANCER
Heavy metal band featured in Metalfest VI in Milwaukee: soundtrack *Hell Comes to Your House* 1992.

CANDYMAN
Platinum single "Knockin' Boots" 1990, album *Ain't No Shame in My Game*.

CANDYSKINS, THE
Hit single "Fun?" on WFIT Playlist in March 1993.

CANNED HEAT
Los Angeles blues/rock group with singer Bob "The Bear" Hite, bass guitarist Larry Taylor, guitarists Henry Vestine & Alan Wilson, sang hit "Going Up Country" at Woodstock Festival* in New York in 1969, album *Best of Canned Heat*.

CANNIBAL CORPSE
Albums *Butchered at Birth, Eaten Back to Life.*

CANOVA, JUDY (1916–1983)
b. 11/20 Starke, FL. Comedienne/singer, on Paul Whiteman's radio show, later had *Judy Canova Show* on NBC for 12 years.

CANTOR, EDDIE (1892–1964)
b. Edward Iskowitz in New York, NY, singer/comedian, in Ziegfeld Follies 1910s, starred in *Banjo Eyes* 1941. Died in Beverly Hills, CA.

CAPTAIN & TENNILLE, THE
Daryl Dragon (b. 8/27/42 Studio City, CA) & Toni Tennille*,/ "Love Will Keep Us Together" won 1975 Grammy, album *Greatest Hits.*

CAPTAIN BEEFHEART (1941–)
California blues group originally Don van Vliet, Alex Snoffer, Doug Moon, Gerald Handley, John French. CDs *Lick My Decals Off Baby, Shiney Beast, Spotlight Kid/Clear Spot.*

CARA, IRENE (1959–)
b. 3/18 Bronx, NY City. Actress/singer, sang Oscar winning song theme from *Flashdance.*

CAREY, MARIAH (1970–)
b. 3/27 Huntington, NY. Singer won 1990 New Artist & Pop Vocal Grammys for "Vision of Love," *Mariah Carey* sold 6 million albums 1990, pop single "I'll Be There" with Trey Lorenz* 1992, album *MTV Unplugged,* 1992. Video *The First Vision.* American Music award Pop/rock Vocalist 1993 & Grammy 1993.

CARLIN, GEORGE (1937–)
b. 5/12 New York, NY. Albums *A Place for My Stuff, Class Clown, Indecent Exposure, Parental Advisory,* etc. Video *Carlin at Carnegie Hall.*

CARLISLE, BELINDA (1958–)
Formerly lead singer for the **Go-Go's***, on 1988 Top Ten singles for "Heaven is a Place on Earth," albums *Belinda, Live Your Life Be Free, Runaway Horses,* video *Runaway.*

CARLOS, ROBERTO
Singer, won 1988 Latin Pop Grammy for "Roberto Carlos."

CARLTON, LARRY (1948–)
b. 3/2 Torrance, CA. Guitarist/singer/songwriter, albums *Alone/ But Never Alone, Collection, Discovery, Last Night, Solid Ground, Sleepwalk,* video *Live.*

CARMAN
Gospel singers, platinum music video *Revival in the Land* 1990, albums *Carman, Sunday's on the Way, Addicted to Jesus* 1992.

CARMEN, ERIC (1949–)
b. 8/11 Cleveland, Ohio. Guitarist/singer/songwriter, *Best of Eric Carmen.*

CARMICHAEL, HOAGY (1899–1981)
b. 11/22 Bloomington, IN. Pianist/singer/songwriter composed "Stardust" 1927, "In the Cool, Cool, Cool of the Evening" (1951 Oscar), "Georgia on My Mind." Special tribute to Carmichael at Newport Jazz Festival in NY City 1979. Died 12/27 Rancho Mirage, CA.

CARNEGIE HALL JAZZ BAND
With trumpeter Jon Faddis*, debut in October 1992.

CARNES, KIM (1945–)
b. 7/20 Hollywood, CA. With a deep raw voice sang in Christy Minstrels. Hit "Bette Davis Eyes" Grammy winner 1981. *Best of Kim Carnes, Mistaken Identity, Gypsy Honeymoon* 1993.

CARNEY, HARRY H. (1910–1974)
b. 4/1 Boston, MA. Baritone saxist/clarinetist, joined **Duke**

Ellington* Band 1927— with Ellington for 45 years. Died 10/8 New York, NY.

CARPENTER, MARY-CHAPIN (1959–)

Raised near Washington, D.C. Country guitarist/singer/ songwriter, graduated Brown University. Hit "When Halley Came to Jackson" (about Halley's Comet in Mississippi) won 1992 Country Music Female Vocalist award, wrote "Down at the Twist and Shout," Hit "Come On, Come On" 1992, "I Feel Lucky" won 1993 Grammy. On CBS TV special *Women of Country* in January 1993. Country Music Female Vocalist 1993. Sang on *Christmas in Washington* on NBC 1993. Country Vocal Female Grammy 1994.

CARPENTERS, THE

Brother and sister singers, Karen Ann Carpenter (b. 3/2/50 New Haven, Ct. died 2/4/83 Downey, CA.) and Richard L. Carpenter (b. 10/15/46 New Haven). Hits "Close to You" 1970, "We've Only Just Begun" 1971, album *The Carpenters: A Song for You* 1972. Video *Yesterday Once More.* At the time of Karen's death the pair had sold over 80 million records. Richard continued solo.

CARR, VICKI (1940–)

b. Florencia Bisenta de Casillas 7/19 El Paso, TX. Singer, albums *En Espanol, From the Heart.* Won two Grammys. Married third husband, Dr. Pedro De Leon on 6/5/93 in San Antonio, Tx.

CARREÑO, TERESA (1853–1917)

b. Caracas, Venezuela. World renowned pianist, in 1863 at age nine she played "Listen to the Mocking Bird" (by Septimus Winner) in the White House for President & Mrs. Lincoln. Died in NY City.

CARRERAS, JOSE (1947–)

b. 12/5 Barcelona, Spain. Tenor, won 1990 Grammy for *Carreras, Domingo, Pavarotti in Concert* at the Baths of Caracalla in Rome, Italy. Sang with Diana Ross* & Placido Domingo* in Vienna in December 1992. Albums *Ave Maria/Vienna Choir*

Boys, Recital in Seattle, Lieder Recital, etc. Videos *Comeback Recital in Spain, The Final Romance, Silent Night.*

CARRERE, TIA
Rock & roll singer/actress from Hawaii, in *Wayne's World,* MTV music video *Ballroom Blitz 1992.*

CARROLL, BRUCE
Southern gospel singer, album *Sometimes Miracles Hide* Grammy winner 1993.

CARROLL, DIAHANN (1935–   )
b. Carol Diahann Johnson 7/17 New York, NY, singer/actress. Starred in TV series *Julia* 1968/71. Albums *Diahann Carroll, Fun Life, No Strings, Nobody Sees Me Cry,* etc.

CARROLL, HARRY (1892–1962)
b. Atlantic City, NJ. Composer, with lyricist Harold Atteridge* wrote "By the Beautiful Sea" and with lyricist Joseph McCarthy,* "I'm Always Chasing Rainbows" 1918.

CARROLL, JOE "BEBOP" (1919–1981)
b. Philadelphia, PA. Singer for Dizzy Gillespie* 1949/53, later soloist, then with Woody Herman* 1964/65. Died in Brooklyn, NY.

CARS, THE
Pop quintet formed by Ric Ocasek with Elliot Easton, Greg Hawks, Ben Orr, David Robinson, platinum album *The Cars* 1978, hit "Shake it Up," video *Heartbeat City.*

CARTER, BENNY (1907–   )
b. 8/8 New York City. Saxist/trumpeter/composer. Had own bands 1928/80s, albums *All of Me, All Star Sax Ensemble, My Kind of Trouble,* etc., CD *Harlem Renaissance Suite* 1993 Grammy winner.

CARTER, BETTY (1930–   )
b. Lillie Mae Jones 5/16 Flint, MI. Singer with Lionel Hampton* in late 1940s, toured Japan 1963 with Sonny Rollins.* In show

Don't Call Me Man 1975, 1985 Grammy as Jazz Vocalist for "Look What I Got," album *It's Not About the Melody,* at Miller Lite Jazz Festival in Detroit 1992.

CARTER, CARLENE (1957–)

b. Madisonville, TN, daughter of June Carter and stepdaughter of Johnny Cash.* Country singer/guitarist, hit "I Fell in Love" 1991.

CARTER, CLARENCE

R&B singer, hit "Strokin'," CDs *Between Rock and Hard Places, Dr. C. C., Hooked on Love,* etc., toured US 1992.

CARTER, DIXIE (1939–)

b. 5/25 McLemorenville, TN. Singer/actress, on TV series *Designing Women,* sang "A Taste of Tennessee" for vice president Al Gore in January 1993.

CARTER, ELLIOTT COOK, JR. (1908–)

b. New York, NY. Composer, his Second String Quartet won 1960 Pulitzer Prize & his String Quartet No. 3 won 1973 prize.

CARTER FAMILY, THE

Group known as the "Royalty of American Folk Music," formed 1927. Mother Maybelle Carter (1909–1978) sister-in-law of A. P. Carter (1897–1960) of Maces Springs, VA; Sarah Carter (1898–1979) married A. P. Carter 1915, divorced 1932, she married Coy Bayes 1939; June Carter (b. 6/23/29 Maces Springs) married Johnny Cash* 1966, her songs include "He Don't Love Me Anymore"; Anita Carter (b. 1934); Helen Carter; Carlene Carter*; a postage stamp was issued in 1993 honoring A. P., Sarah, & Maybelle Carter.

CARTER, NELL (1948–)

b. 9/13 Birmingham, AL. Actress/singer, she sang "Back in the High Life," a chilling rendition to her late brother, on ABC TV in July 1992.

CARTER, RON (1937–)

b. Ferndale, MI. Bassist/cellist, formed a quartet, played in The

White House for President and Mrs. Carter in June 1978 and on the White House Lawn for President & Mrs. Reagan in September 1981. With pianist Eubie Blake* & flutist Hubert Laws* at Carnegie Hall NY City 1981. Albums *Blues Farm, Peg Leg, Standard Bearers,* etc.

CARTER THE UNSTOPPABLE SEX MACHINE
British duo Jim Bob (Jim Morrison) & Fruitbat (Leslie Carter), album *1992: The Love Album.*

CARUSO, ENRICO (1873–1921)
b. Naples, Italy, famous tenor with the Metropolitan Opera in New York City 1903/20. *Caruso in Arias, Caruso in Song, The Caruso Edition.*

CASALS, PABLO (1876–1973)
b. Spain. World renowned cellist/composer, played in The White House for President & Mrs. Kennedy. At age 94 conducted his *Hymn to Peace* for the United Nations Assembly. Album *Sacred Choral Works/Escola,* Victor Recordings.

CASE, PETER
Garage rock singer/guitarist with the **Plimsouls** in the 1980s, went solo 1986. Albums *Peter Case, Six Packs of Love* 1992.

CASH, JOHNNY (1932–)
b. 2/26 Kingsland, AK. Country/western singer/songwriter, hits "I Walk the Line" 1964, "A Boy Named Sue" 1969. With Willie Nelson* & Emmylou Harris* on album *The Other Side of Nashville* 1984. *San Quentin, Biggest Hits, Classic Cash, The Sun Years,* etc. With wife June Carter Cash joined evangelist Billy Graham's Crusade in Portland, Oregon in September 1992 and told the crowd how God helped him conquer drug addiction. Sang "The Wanderer" on U2's album *Zooropa* 1994.

CASH, ROSANNE (1955–)
b. 5/24 Memphis, TN. Country/rock singer, daughter of Johnny Cash*, Married Rodney Crowell*, divorced 1991. Album *Seven Year Ache* 1981. 1988 Top Ten Country single "If You

Change Your Mind,'' videos *Interiors, Retrospective,* album *The Wheel* 1993.

CATHEDRALS, THE
Southern gospel singers, album *Camp Meeting Live* 1992.

CATLETT, SIDNEY "BIG SID" (1910–1951)
b. Evansville, IN. Drummer/composer, with various bands 1920s/40s & with Louis Armstrong* 1947/49. While talking with Slam Stewart* at a jazz concert in Chicago died of a heart attack.

CAVEDOGS, THE
Boston alternative rock trio with bassist Brian Stevens, albums *Joy Rides for Shut Ins, The Cavedogs, Soul Martini* 1992.

CETERA, PETER (1944–)
b. 9/13 Chicago, IL. Singer formerly with **Chicago.*** Albums *One More Story, Solitude/Solitary,* adult contemporary top single ''Restless Heart'' in August 1992.

CHAD AND JEREMY
British soft rock duo Jeremy Clyde & Chad Stuart, hits ''Yesterday's Gone,'' ''A Summer Song,'' ''Distant Shores,'' albums *Best of Chad & Jeremy, The Soft Sounds of Chad & Jeremy.*

CHAINSAW KITTENS
Oklahoma band with Tyson Meade, albums *Violent Religion* 1990, *Flipped Out in Singspace* 1992.

CHAMBERS BROTHERS
George, Willie Joe, & Lester Chambers, *Greatest Hits, The Time Has Come.*

CHANNING, CAROL (1923–)
b. 1/31 Seattle, WA. Comedienne/singer, she sang in *Gentlemen Prefer Blondes* 1949, *Hello Dolly* 1964, continued acting in 1970s/90s.

CHAPIN, HARRY F. (1942–1981)
b. 12/7 New York, NY. Singer/songwriter, hit ''Taxi'' 1972,

albums *Greatest Stories Live, Heads and Tails, Portrait Gallery,* etc. Died 7/16 Jericho, NY.

CHAPIN, SAUL (1912–)
b. Brooklyn, NY City. Pianist/songwriter with Sammy Cahn* wrote the English words for "Bei Mir bist du Schön" 1937.

CHAPMAN, MARSHALL
Country guitarist/singer/songwriter, hit "Dirty Dozen" 1987, albums *Take It on Home, Inside Job* 1992.

CHAPMAN, STEVEN CURTIS
Gospel singer, gospel album *The Great Adventure* Grammy winner 1993. "The Live Adventure" Contemporary Gospel Album Grammy 1994.

CHAPMAN, TRACY (1964–)
b. Cleveland, Ohio. Singer/guitarist, hit "Fast Car," on 1988 Top Ten Pop CD *Tracy Chapman,* won 1988 New Artist Grammy, platinum album *Crossroads* 1989, albums *In Living Color* 1991, *Matters of the Heart* 1992.

CHAPPELL, JIM
Albums *Nightsongs and Lullabies, Saturday's Rhapsody, Tender Ritual.*

CHARLATANS UK
With singer Tim Burgess, album *Some Friendly.* "Between 10th & 11th" top on WFIT Playlist 1992.

CHARLES & EDDY
Soul singers Charles Pettigrew and Eddie Chacon, album *Duophonic* 1992.

CHARLES, RAY (1918–)
b. Charles R. Offenberg 9/13 Chicago, IL, composer, director of the **Ray Charles Singers,** won Emmys for "The First Nine Months of Harvest" 1971 and "The Funny Side of Marriage" 1972.

CHARLES, RAY (1930–)
b. Ray Charles Robinson 9/23 Albany, GA. Pianist/singer/ songwriter, became blind at age six. Hit "I Got a Woman" 1955. Arrested in Indianapolis 1961 for possession of narcotics, entered a clinic in California for treatment 1965. At Atlantic City, NJ Jazz Festival in July 1980, on music video *We Are the World* 1985. With Chaka Kahn won 1990 R&B duo for "I'll be Good to You." Videos *An Evening with Ray Charles, Live 1991 at Maccallum Theater, Ray Charles and the Muppets.* R&B Male Grammy 1994 for "A Song for You."

CHAYANNE (1969–)
Puerto Rican singer now performing in Miami, Florida, has earned 18 platinum records since his 1984 album *Chayanne Es Mi Nombre,* album *Provocame* 1993.

CHEAP TRICK
Illinois group known for weird antics, founded in 1977 with Bun E. Carlos, Rick Nielson, Tom Peterson, Robin Zander. Albums *Cheap Trick, Dream Police, Heaven Tonight, One on One, The Doctor, Busted* 1990, video *Every Trick in the Book.*

CHECKER, CHUBBY (1941–)
b. Ernest Evans 10/3 Philadelphia, Pa. Singer/dancer, hit "The Twist" 1960, album *Twist with Chubby Checker* became a nationwide hit 1961. *Limbo Rock* 1962. On TV shows in 1990s. Album *Chubby's Dance Party.*

CHEECH [MARIN] & [TOMMY] CHONG
Albums *Cheech & Chong, Let's Make a New Dope Deal, Sleeping Beauty, Up in Smoke,* etc. Videos *Get Out of My Room, Nice Dreams.*

CHEESECAKE
All-female punk band with singer Denice Monahan, guitarist Cartlin Bermingham, & drummer Colleen Nagle.

CHENIER, CLIFTON
Albums *Boogaloosa Boogie, I'm Here, Live at French Dance, Louisiana Blues & Zydeco.*

CHENILLE SISTERS
Albums *1, 2, 3, Mama I Wanna Make Rhythm,* etc.

CHER (1946–)
b. Cherylyn LaPierre Sarkasian 5/20 El Centro, CA. Pop singer/ actress with husband Sonny Bono* (later divorced). Platinum album *Heart of Stone* 1989, *Cher, Greatest Hits, Love Hurts,* album *Extravaganza: Live at the Mirage.* Sang at Madison Square Garden in NY City May 1992. Also in films *Silkwood* 1983, *Mask* 1985, Oscar for her role in *Moonstruck.*

CHERRY, DONALD E. "DON" (1936–)
b. Oklahoma City, OK. Trumpeter, toured with Ornette Coleman* in 1960s. Lived in Sweden for many years. At Town Hall in NY City in 1980, on *Birdland* TV show in August 1992.

CHERRY, NENEH
Female rapper, album *Raw Like Sushi,* single "Move with Me" on soundtrack *Until the End of the World* 1992.

CHESNUTT, MARK (1964–)
Country baritone albums *Too Cold at Home, Short Stories,* hit single "I'll Think of Something" 1992, *Bubba Shot the Juke Box,* toured US 1992.

CHIC
Band with bassist Bernard Edwards & guitarist Nile Rogers, CD *Sunlake,* album *Chic-ism* 1992.

CHICAGO
Founded 1967 as **Chicago Transit Authority** with Peter Cetera,* Donnie Dacus, Laudir DeOliveira, Terry Kath guitarist (1946– 1978 died of accidental gunshot), singer/keyboardist Robert Lamm, trumpeters Lee Loughnane & James Pankow, Walter

Parazaider, Walt Perry, and drummer Daniel Serphine (hit solo "Hard to Say I'm Sorry" 1982), Cetera solo hit "Glory of Love" 1986. Group hits "Saturday in the Park," top ten single "Look Away" 1989, albums *Chicago I through XIV, If You Leave Me Now, And the Band Played On* 1993. Sold over 20 million albums.

CHIEFTANS
Irish folk singers, *Bells of Dublin, Bonaparte's Retreat, Chieftans 5, 7 & 8, Celtic Wedding,* etc. Videos *Bells of Dublin, An Irish Evening.* With Chet Atkins* "Tahitian Skies" on *Another Country.* Sang with Willie Nelson* & Kris Kristofferson* on *Another Country* 1992. *Belfast* with Roger Daltry* and Nanci Griffith* Grammy winner 1993. Traditional Folk Album Grammy 1994 for "The Celtic Harp."

CHILDRE, DOC LEW (1944–   )
Of Boulder Creek, CA. Pianist/keyboardist, 1992 album *Heart Zones* targets stress reduction and therapy.

CHILLS & THE VERLAINES
New Zealand group with pianist Peter Jeffries, albums *Brave Words, Submarine Bells, The Last Great Challenge in a Dull World* 1992.

CHIPMUNKS
Cartoon characters Alvin, Simon, & Theodore, creations of Dave Seville. Albums *Alvin Show with Dave Seville, Christmas with the Chipmunks, Chipmunks in Low Places* 1992.

CHRISTIAN, CHARLIE (1916–1942)
b. Dallas, TX. Guitarist, brother of pianist Edward, trombonist Emile, & trumpeter/clarinetist Frank. Raised in Oklahoma City. Led his own band in the 1930s, with Benny Goodman* 1939/41. Suffering with tuberculosis Charlie was sent to the Seaview Sanitarium on Long Island, NY 1941. Albums *Genius of the Electric Guitar, Solo Flight.*

CHRISTIE, EDWIN P. (1815–1862)
b. Philadelphia, PA. Minstrel showman/composer, wrote "Goodnight Ladies" 1847.

CHRISTY, JUNE (1925–1990)
b. 11/20 Springfield, IL. Singer with Stan Kenton* 1945/49. Toured Europe late 50s, Australia, Japan, and England 1964/65, at Newport Jazz Festival in NY City 1972. Died 6/21 Los Angeles, CA. *Early June, Something Cool.* Married saxist Bob Cooper 1946.

CHUCK WAGON GANG
Won TNN gospel award 1992.

CHURCH, THE
Australian quartet with singer Steve Kilberg, *Gold Afternoon, Fix, Starfish, Priest-Aura* 1992.

CHURCHILL, FRANK E. (1901–1942)
b. Rumford, ME. Composed music for Walt Disney productions, with various lyricists composed "Who's Afraid of the Big Bad Wolf," "Heigh-ho," "Whistle While You Work."

CHURCHILL, SAVANNAH (1919–1974)
b. New Orleans, LA. Singer for Benny Carter* in 1940s. Died 4/19 Brooklyn, NY City.

CINDERELLA
Albums *Heartbreak Station, Long Cold Winter, Night Songs.*

CLANCY BROTHERS
Albums *In Person at Carnegie Hall, Reunion* with Makem, *Luck of the Irish.*

CLANNAD
Albums *Clannad 2, Fusion, In Concert, Macalla,* etc.

CLAPTON, ERIC (1945–)
b. 3/30 Surrey, UK. Rock musician with **Blind Faith*, Cream*,**

Yardbirds*, appeared in film *Tommy* 1975. went solo, hit "Layla," music video *Eric Clapton—Live '85*, won 1990 rock male vocal for "Bad Love," MTV Best Male Video for *Tears in Heaven* written in memory of his son, 1992 won a Grammy, *Crossroads* 1992. Videos *24 Nights, The Cream of Eric Clapton, Unplugged* won Grammy. Won 6 Grammys 1993. American Music Award Male Artist 1994. Lives in NY City. His son died in 1985 after falling from a high-rise apartment.

CLARK, DAVE (1942–   )
b. 12/15 London, England. Leader of the **Dave Clark Five** 1964/73 with Lenny Davidson, Rick Huxley, Denis Payton, & Michael Smith. Hit singles "Everybody Knows I Still Love You," "Glad All Over."

CLARK, GUY (1941–   )
b. 11/6 Singer/songwriter, toured with Nanci Griffith* & Joe Ely* 1993, *Old Friends, Old No. 1.*

CLARK, PETULA (1932–   )
b. 11/15 Ewell, Surrey, UK. Singer, hit single "Downtown" 1965, albums *Greatest Hits, Live at Royal Albert Hall.*

CLARKE, KENNETH S. "KENNY" (1914–1985)
b. Pittsburgh, PA, drummer, with Roy Eldridge* in 1935, toured Sweden & England, with Ella Fitzgerald*, Benny Carter,* **Modern Jazz Quartet*** & others, at Wolf Trap, Vienna, VA in July 1980. Died 1/26 Montreuilsous-Bois, France.

CLARKE, STANLEY (1951–   )
b. 6/30 Philadelphia, PA. Bassist/singer, formerly with **Return to Forever.*** *Clarke Duke Project, Hideaway, Journey to Love, School Days, Friends 1993.*

CLASH, THE
British group with singer/guitarist Joe Strummer, bassist Paul Simonon, guitarist Keith Levine, and drummer Terry Chimes. Albums *Combat Rock, Give 'Em Enough Rope, London Calling, Story of the Clash*, video *This is Video Clash.*

CLAY, OTIS
Memphis, TN soul singer, hit single "Trying to Live My Life Without You" 1972, album *I'll Treat You Right* 1992.

CLAYTON, WILBUR "BUCK" (1911–)
b. 11/12 Parsons, KS. Trumpeter/arranger, led own bands then with Count Basie* 1936/43, toured Europe 50s, Asia & Europe 60s, active 70s/80s, album *A Swinging Dream.*

CLEGG, JOHNNY & SAVUKA
Albums *Cruel Crazy Word, Shadow Man, Third World Child.*

CLEVELAND, REV. JAMES (1931–1991)
Gospel singer/songwriter, wrote over 400 gospel songs. Died 2/9 Los Angeles, CA.

CLIBURN, VAN (1934–)
b. Harvey Lavan, Jr. 7/12 Shreveport, LA. Pianist, won International Tchaikovsky Competition in Moscow gaining worldwide recognition, received first ticker-tape parade in NY City ever given in honor of musician 1958, gave concerts in 60s/90s.

CLIFF, JIMMY (1948–)
b. James Chambers, Jamaica, West Indies. Reggae singer, albums *Cliff Hanger, Power & the Glory, Reggae Greats-Jimmy Cliff,* videos *Bongo Man, The Harder They Come, Breakout* (reggae Grammy winner 1993).

CLIMAX BLUES BAND, THE
British blues with Colin Cooper, John Cuffley, Peter Haycock, Derek Holt, Richard Jones, George Newsome, & Arthur Wood, started 1969, first US hit "Couldn't Get It Right" 1977.

CLINE, PATSY (1932–1963)
b. 9/8 Virginia Patterson Hensley, Winchester, VA. Country singer/pianist, hits "Crazy" & "I Fall to Pieces," video *The Real Patsy Cline.* Died 3/5 in a plane crash near Camden, TN. A postage stamp was issued in her honor in 1993.

CLINTON, GEORGE (1940–)
b. 7/22 Blainfield, Ohio. Singer/songwriter, hit single "One Nation Under Groove" 1978, *Presents Our Gang Funky.*

CLINTON, LARRY (1909–1985)
b. 8/17 Brooklyn, NY City. Composer/band leader, his tune "The Dipsy Doodle" top hit in late 1930s. Died 5/2 Tucson, Arizona.

CLOCKHAMMER
Group with guitarist/lead singer Bryon Bailey, album *Klinefelter* 1992.

CLOONEY, ROSEMARY (1928–)
b. 5/23 Maysville, KY. Singer, joined Tony Pastor's band 1946, soloist 1949, hit single "Come On-a My House" 1951 sold over one million copies. Albums *For the Duration, Showtunes, Sings Cole Porter, With Love, Tribute to Billie Holiday* 1992, *Girl Singer* won 1993 Grammy.

CLOWER, JERRY (1926–)
b. 9/28 Liberty, MS. Albums *Country Ham, More Good Uns, On the Road, Top Gun.*

COASTERS, THE
Rock & roll band with Carl Gardner, Cornelius Gunter, Adolph Jacobs, later with Gardner, Earl Carroll, Ronnie Bright, & Jim Norman. Hit "Yakety Yak," albums *The Coasters, Their Greatest Recordings.* Carl Gardner & Bobby Nunn on *50 Coastin' Classics* 1992.

COBAIN, KURT (1967–1994)
Songwriter with **Nirvana*** wrote "Smells Like Teen Spirit" (Grammy winner 1993) on their 1991 album *Nevermind.* While on tour in Europe March 1994 Cobain fell ill in Rome after a heroin overdose. Upon returning to Seattle on April 8, 1994, shot himself. His widow Courtney Love is lead singer for the rock band **Hole.**

COBB, ARNETT (1918–   )
b. Houston, TX, tenor saxist with Lionel Hampton* in 1940s, injured both legs in an auto accident 1947. At Newport Jazz Festival in NY City 1977, played in 1970s/80s.

COBB, WILL D. (1876–1930)
b. Philadelphia, PA. Songwriter with Gus Edwards* wrote "School Days" 1906.

COBHAM, BILLY (1944–   )
b. 5/16 Panama. Drummer/songwriter with **Mahavishnu Orchestra.*** *Billy's Best Hits, Picture This, Power Play, Warning,* videos with Louis Bellson,* *Cobham Meets Bellson.*

COCHRAN, EDDIE (1938–1960)
b. Oklahoma City, OK. Singer/songwriter, wrote "Summertime Blues" recorded by **The Who,*** *Early Years, Greatest Hits, Legendary Master Series.* Killed in a car accident while touring England with Gene Vincent.*

COCHRANE, TOM
Canadian rocker formerly with **Red Rider,** hit single "Life is a Highway," solo album *Mad Mad World* 1992.

COCKBURN, BRUCE
Albums *Dancing in Dragon's Jaws, Humans, Inner City Front, World of Wonders.*

COCKER, ROBERT JOHN "JOE" (1944–   )
b. 5/20 Sheffield, UK. Singer/musician with Jennifer Warnes* recorded "Up Where We Belong" on *An Officer and a Gentleman* soundtrack 1982. Albums *Civilized Man, Cocker, Night Calls, One Nite of Sin,* videos *Mad Dogs and Englishmen, Shelter Me.* Sang "With a Little Help from My Friends" at the Woodstock* Festival 1969, album *The Best of Joe Cocker* 1993.

COCTEAU TWINS
British group, singer Elizabeth Frazer, guitarist Robin Guthrie,

bassist Will Heggie, albums *Blue Bell Knoll, Head Over Heels, Treasure,* etc.

COE, DAVID ALLAN (1939–)
b. 9/6 Akron, Ohio. Albums *For the Record/1st Ten Years, Just Divorced, Long-haired Redneck,* songs include "Willie, Waylon and Me" 1993.

COHAN, GEORGE M. (1878–1942)
b. Providence, RI. Songwriter, "Give My Regards to Broadway" 1904, "Mary's a Grand Old Name" 1905, "You're a Grand Old Flag" 1906, "Over There" 1917, his career was depicted in *Yankee Doodle Dandy* (1942) with James Cagney.

COHEN, LEONARD (1934–)
b. 9/21 Montreal, Quebec, Canada. Guitarist/singer/songwriter, albums *I'm Your Man, Recent Songs, The Future* 1992, etc.

COHN, ALVIN G. "AL" (1925–1988)
b. 11/24 Brooklyn, NY City. Tenor saxist/composer, at jazz festivals in NY City, albums *Al & Zoot, Be Loose, From A to Z,* etc. Married singer Mary Ann McCall of Woody Herman's* band.

COHN, IRVING *see* CONN

COLCORD, LINCOLN (1883–1947)
b. at sea off Cape Horn, South America. Lyricist, with composer E. A. Fensted* wrote the "Maine Stein Song" 1901 popularized by Rudy Vallee.*

COLE, LLOYD
Albums *Don't Get Weird on Me Babe, Lloyd Cole 1984/89.*

COLE, NAT "KING" (1917–1965)
b. Montgomery, AL. Singer/pianist/leader, recorded hits "Nature Boy," "Unforgettable," gave a command performance for Queen Elizabeth II in 1960. Hit "Too Young," albums *Big Band Cole, Let's Fall in Love, Love is the Thing,* videos *The Uncomparable, Unforgettable.* Died of lung cancer. A postage stamp was issued in his honor in 1994.

COLE, NATALIE (1949–)

b. 2/6 Los Angeles, CA. Singer daughter of Nat "King" Cole,*
debut album *Inseparable* 1976, sang in Las Vegas, NV & other
cities in 1970s/90s. Won a 1992 Grammy for "Unforgettable"
singing it with her dad's voice dubbed in. Albums *Dangerous,
Natalie Cole Collection.* "Take a Look" Jazz Vocal Grammy
winner 1994.

COLE, RICHIE

Albums *Alto Madness, New York Afternoon, Pure Imagination,
Side by Side, Some Things Speak.*

COLE, ROBERT A. "BOB" (1863–1911)

b. Athens, GA. With lyricist A. M. Hirsch*, the team of Bob Cole
& Billy Johnson wrote "Boola Boola" (1897) which became
the football song of Yale University.

COLE, WILLIAM R. "COZY" (1909–1981)

b. 10/17 East Orange, NJ. Drummer, led own bands in 1920s/30s,
then with Cab Calloway,* Jack Teagarden,* & Earl Hines,* top
record "Topsy." Died 1/29 Columbus, Ohio.

COLEGRASS, MICHAEL

Composer, won 1978 Pulitzer prize for *Deja Vu for Percussion
and Orchestra.*

COLEMAN, ORNETTE (1930–)

b. 3/19 Fort Worth, TX. Saxist/composer, recorded "free jazz"
1960, at Berlin Jazz Days in West Germany in 1960s/70s, on
Birdland TV show July 1992. Albums *Art of the Improvisers,
Forms & Sounds, Love Call, Something Else, Tomorrow is the
Question*, etc.

COLEMAN, SY (1929–)

Singer/songwriter, album *Sweet Charity.*

COLEMAN, WM. J. "BILL" (1904–1981)

b. Centerville, KY. Jazz trumpeter, played in Teddy Hill's band in
Harlem's Savoy Ballroom in 1930s, went to Paris, back in NY

City in 1940s, then returned to live in Paris 1948. He died 8/24 Paris.

COLLECTIVE BLACK ARTISTS ENSEMBLE

At Jazz concerts in NY City in 1970s, later under direction of trombonist Slide Hampton, with pianist Hilton Ruiz, alto saxist James Moody, trumpeters Jimmy Owens & Jon Faddis,* trombonists Britt Woodman & Janice Robinson, alto saxist Frank Weiss 1980s.

COLLIE, MARK

Singer/songwriter, *Born and Raised in Black and White, Hardin County Line, Even the Man in the Moon is Crying* 1993.

COLLINS, ALBERT

Guitarist, *Cold Snap, Don't Loose Your Cool, Frozen Alive, Ice Pickin',* with Branford Marsalis* on blues tour 1993.

COLLINS, JUDITH "JUDY" (1939–)

b. 5/1 Seattle, WA. Singer/guitarist, debut at Town Hall in NY City 1964, hits "Both Sides Now" 1968, *The Judy Collins Concert* 1969, "Send in the Clowns" 1975, albums *Bread and Roses, Home Again, In My Life, Wildflowers,* etc. She sang "Amazing Grace" at the Presidential Gala for Bill Clinton in Jan. 1993.

COLLINS, PHIL (1951–)

b. 1/30 London, England. Member of **Genesis.*** As solo singer won 1985 Grammy for platinum album *No Jacket Required,* won 1990 Grammy for "Another Day in Paradise," *Seriously Live* 1990, platinum video *The Singles Collections*, video *No Jacket Required.*

COLOR ME BADD

Oklahoma City hip-hop/doo-wop with singer Bryan Abrams, Kevin Thornton, Sam Watters, & Mark Collins, video *Scrapbook* 1991, album *Color Me Badd* sold four million copies 1992.

COLTRANE, JOHN (1926–1967)

b. Hamlet, NC. Jazz saxist, formed his own quartet in 1960s, albums *Blue Trane, Coltrane Jazz, Crescent, Dakar,* etc. *A John Coltrane Retrospective: The Impulsive Years* 1992.

COLUMBO, RUSS (1908–1934)
Singer/violinist/leader, while cleaning a loaded hunting rifle accidently shot himself to death.

COLVIN, SHAWN
b. South Dakota, singer/songwriter, won 1989 Grammy for *Steady On,* CD *Fat City* 1992, sang ''You Ain't Goin' Nowhere'' at the concert in honor of Bob Dylan* at Madison Square Garden, Oct. 1992.

COMDEN, BETTY (1919–   )
b. 5/3 Brooklyn, NY City, lyricist with composer Adolph Green* wrote ''The Party's Over,'' ''Just in Time,'' ''New York, New York.''

COMMANDER CODY & HIS LOST PLANET AIR-MEN
Bruce Barlow, Robert Black, Lance Dickerson, William Farlow, George Fayne, Ernst Hager, William Kirchen, Andrew Stein, John Tichy. Albums *Hot Licks, Let's Rock, Live Deep in the Heart of Texas, Lost in the Ozone.*

COMMODORES,THE
Singers from Alabama/Mississippi/Florida with William King, Ronald LaPread, Thomas McClary, Walter ''Clyde'' Orange, Lionel Richie, Jr.*, Milan Williams, hits ''Three Times a Lady'' 1978, ''Sail On'' 1979, albums *All the Greatest Hits, Hot on the Tracks, Nightshift, United, The Commodore's Christmas* 1992.

COMO, PERRY (1912–   )
b. Pierino Roland 5/18 Canonsburg, PA. Singer with Ted Weems's band 1936/42. Hit records ''Till the End of Time'' 1945, ''Prisoner of Love'' 1956, albums *Pure Gold, Today,* etc. Video *Best of Perry Como.* He toured 12 US cities in 1992.

CONCRETE BLONDE
With singer Johnette Napolitano, guitarist James Mankey, drummer Harry Rushakoff (with band when known as **Dream 6**), drummer Paul Thompson on gold album *Bloodletting* 1990, Rushakoff back on CD *Walking in London,* group toured US in 1992, video *Midlife Crisis.*

CONDIE, RICHARD P. (1898–1985)
b. 7/5 Springville, Utah. Conductor/director of the Mormon Tabernacle Choir 1957/74. Died 12/22 Salt Lake City, Utah.

CONDON, ALBERT E. "EDDIE" (1905–1973)
b. Goodland, IN. Guitarist/singer, with various bands 1920s/40s. Had own night club in NY City 1945/67, was reopened in 1970s under new management. CDs *Dixieland Jazz, In Japan, Town Hall Concerts.*

CONFEDERATE RAILROAD
Country sextet from Atlanta, GA with lead singer Danny Shirley, album *Confederate Railroad* 1992, hits "Jesus and Mama" 1992, "Queen of Memphis" 1993.

CONLEY, EARL THOMAS
b. Portsmouth, Ohio. Country singer, albums *Greatest Hits, Too Many Times, Yours Truly,* nominated for country duo 1992 with Keith Whitley.*

CONLEY, EUGENE (1908–1981)
b. 3/12 Lynn, MA. Tenor on CBS *Golden Treasury of Song* 1939 & for several years thereafter. Died 12/18 Houston, TX.

CONN, IRVING (1898–1961)
b. London, England. Name often spelled Cohn. Composer/bandleader in NY City, with lyricist Frank Silver* wrote "Yes, We Have No Bananas" 1923.

CONNELLS
Albums *Boylan Heights, Darker Days, Fun and Games, One Simple Word.*

CONNELLY, MARC (1890–1980)
b. McKeesport, PA. Librettist, with George S. Kaufman* wrote *Helen of Troy* 1926 and other musicals. Died 12/21 NY City.

CONNICK, HARRY, JR. (1967–   )
Pianist/singer/leader, won 1990 Jazz Vocalist Grammy for "We Are in Love," albums *20, Blue Light Red Light, Lofty's Roach Souffle, Twenty-Five* 1992. On top ten grossing tour list, arrested December 1992 for carrying a gun at Kennedy Airport.

CONNIFF, RAY (1916–   )
b. 11/6 Attleboro, MA. Trombonist/leader, album *'S Wonderful* 1956 (sold millions), *Always in My Heart, Concert in Rhythm, Hollywood Rhythm, Somewhere My Love,* etc.

CONRAD, CON (1891–1938)
b. Conrad K. Dober, NY City, composer, with lyricist Billy Rose wrote "Barney Google," with lyricist Benny Davis* co-composed "Margie" (1920) with J. R. Robinson.*

CONTEMPORARIES
Drummer Keno Duke & band in NY City 1970s/80s.

CONTEMPORARY CHAMBER ENSEMBLE
Trumpeter Clark Terry,* trumpeter Jim Maxwell, saxist Zoot Sims,* & soprano Joan Heller performed Charles Schwartz's jazz symphony *Mother---, Mother---* in NY City in January 1979.

CONTI, BILL (1942–   )
b. 4/13 Providence, RI. Composer, wrote theme songs for television's *Dynasty, Falcon Crest, Cagney & Lacey.* Won 1983 Oscar for *The Right Stuff* theme.

COODER, RYLAND P. "RY" (1947–   )
b. 3/15 Los Angeles, CA. Guitarist/composer with **Little Village.*** Movie scores include *The Long Riders* 1980, albums *Pop 'Till You Drop, Borderline, Chicken Skin Music, Jazz, Paris, Texas,* etc. At the Ultimate Guitar Concert in San Francisco,

Sept. 1992. *A Meeting by the River* (with A. M. Batt) World Music Grammy winner 1994.

COOK, WILL MARION (1869–1944)
b. Washington, D.C. Noted black composer, ragtime opera *Clorinda* produced on Broadway, NY City in 1898. Married soprano Abbie Mitchell.

COOKE, SAM (1931–1964)
b. 1/22 Chicago, IL. Singer for the **Soul Stirrers.*** His record "You Send Me" sold over two million copies. Albums *At the Copa, Gospel Soul, Live at the Harlem Square,* etc. Was shot to death in a gun fight in a Los Angeles motel.

COOLEY, DARYL
Won Grammy for soul gospel album *When the Music Stops* 1993.

COOLIDGE, RITA (1945–)
b. 5/1 Nashville, TN. Singer, hit song (written by Peter Allen*) "I'd Rather Leave While I'm in Love," platinum album *Any Time, Anywhere* 1977, CDs *Classic Vol. 5, Greatest Hits, Rita Coolidge.* Married Kris Kristofferson,* later divorced.

COOPER, ALICE (1948–)
b. Vincent Damon Furnier 2/4 Detroit, MI. Singer/songwriter, hits "I'm 18" 1970, "No More Mr. Nice Guy" 1973, albums *A Man Called Alice, Billion Dollar Babies, From the Inside, Goes to Hell, Lace and Whiskey,* etc. , videos *Alice Cooper Trashes the World, Prime Cuts,* album *Hey Stupid* 1992. Lives in Scottsdale, AZ.

COOPER, GEORGE (1838–1927)
b. NY City, lyricist, closest friend Stephen Foster* had in NY City, found Foster bleeding from a shaving accident in a hotel in the Bowery in 1864 & took him to the Bellevue Hospital where he died three days later, With music by Foster, Cooper wrote "Bring Back My Brother to Me" 1862, with J. P. Skelly wrote "Twinkle Twinkle Little Star," with Henry Tucker* "Sweet Genevieve" and hundreds of other songs.

COOPER, STONEY (1918–1977)
b. 10/16 Harman, WV. Fiddler/singer married Wilma Lee Leary & they became a team, joined Grand Ole Opry, Nashville in 1957. Died 3/22 in Nashville, TN.

COOTS, J. FRED (1897–1985)
b. 5/2 Brooklyn, NY City. Composer, wrote songs for Sophie Tucker,* with lyricist Haven Gillespie* wrote "Santa Claus is Coming to Town." Died 4/8 in NY City.

COPELAND, RAY M. (1926–1984)
b. Norfolk, VA. Trumpeter/fluegelhorn player, with Pearl Bailey,* Louis Bellson,* & Thelonious Monk* in 1960s, led own orchestras on Long Island, NY on 1970s. Died 5/18 in NY City.

COPELAND, STEWART
Drummer/composer with **The Police,*** went solo, album *The Rhythmatist,* wrote an opera about the crusades *Holy Blood and Crescent Moon* presented by the Cleveland Opera in 1989.

COPENHAGEN BAND
Led by Thad Jones* and included baritone saxist Sahib Shihab, played at the Berlin Jazz Days in West Germany in 1980.

COPLAND, AARON (1900–1990)
b. Aaron Kaplan 11/14 Brooklyn, NY City. Composer *Symphony for Organ & Orchestra* 1924, ballet *Billy the Kid* 1938 which was revived and won a 1945 Pulitzer Prize, *Concerto for Clarinet & String Orchestra* 1948 adapted for the ballet *The Pied Piper* introduced by the NY City Ballet. Died 12/2 N. Tarrytown, NY.

CORBIN/HANNER
Singers Bob Corbin and Dave Hanner, album *Just Another Hill* 1992.

COREA, ARMANDO A. "CHICK" (1941–   )
b. 6/12 Chelsea, MA. Pianist/composer/leader, led own group

Return to Forever,* solo LP *The Mad Hatter* 1978, with Oscar Peterson won 1980 Grammy as best Jazz Instrumentalists. *down beat* Electric Pianist of Year 1980, won 1988 Grammy for R & B instrumental *"Light Years"*, videos *Chick Corea, Inside Out, Live in Tokyo,* with jazz singer Bobby McFerrin* on album *Play* 1992.

CORY, GEORGE (1920–1978)
b. Syracuse, NY. Pianist/composer, with Douglas Cross* wrote "I Left My Heart in San Francisco" (Grammy winner 1963) sung by Calamae accompanied by composer at 50th anniversary of the San Francisco Opera 1972. Died 4/1 in San Francisco.

CORYELL, LARRY (1943–   )
b. 4/2 Galveston, TX. Guitarist/songwriter, albums *American Odyssey, Shining Hour, Spaces,* etc.

COSMIC ORCHESTRA
Led by Neil Norman with keyboardist Les Baxter of Mexico, Texas 1975/80.

COSMOLOGY
Started 1972 with singer Dawn Thompson, guitarist George Wadenius, trumpeter John D'Earth, trombonist Gary Valentine, pianist Steve Gaboury, at Seventh Avenue South, NY City 1978/79.

COSTELLO, ELVIS (1954–   )
b. 8/25 London, England. Hit "Alison," albums *Almost Blue, Armed Forces, Blood & Chocolate, Imperial Bedroom,* etc. Hit "Days" on sound track *Until the End of the World* 1992.

COTTON, JAMES (1925–   )
b. Quincy, MS. Albums *Cut You Loose, High Compression, Mighty Lone Time,* etc.

COUGAR, JOHN *see* JOHN COUGAR MELLENCAMP

COULTER, PHIL
Albums *Classic Tranquility, Sea of Tranquility, Serenity.*

COUNTRY GENTLEMEN, THE
Group originally Charlie Waller, John Duffy, Eddie Adcock, & Jim Cox, albums *Country Songs Old & New, Featuring Ricky Skaggs, Folksongs & Bluegrass, The Award Winning.*

COUNTRY JOE & THE FISH
Anti-Vietnam War group with Bruce Barthol, David Cohen, "Chicken" Hirsch, Joseph McDonald, & guitarist Barry Nelson. Group appeared at Monterey, CA and Woodstock, NY festivals. Albums *Electric Music/Mind and Body, Feel Like I'm Fixin' to Die, Collected 1965/70,* group sang at the Vietnam War Memorial in Washington, D.C. on 11/11/92.

COVER GIRLS, THE
Hit single "Wishing on a Star" 1992.

COVERDALE/PAGE
Guitarist Jimmy Page (b. 1944) of **Led Zeppelin*** & the **Yardbirds*** & vocalist David Coverdale (b. 1950) of **Deep Purple*** and **Whitesnake*** on album *Coverdale/Page* 1993, pair toured US July/August 1993.

COWBOY JUNKIES
Toronto group, lead singer Margo Timmins, songwriter Michael Timmons, singer John Prine, Peter Timmons, Alan Anton, albums *The Caution Horses, The Trinity Seasons, Whites Off Earth Now, Black-eyed Man* 1992. Texas singer Jimmie Dale Gilmore toured with the band in 1992.

COWSILLS, THE
Barbara, Barry, John, Paul, Richard, Robert, Susan, & William Cowsill, hit single theme from *Hair,* CD *Best of the Cowsills.*

COX, IDA (1889–1967)
b. Cedartown, GA. Singer with **Rabbit Foot Minstrels** at age fourteen, known as the "Uncrowned Queen of the Blues," married pianist Jesse Crump.

CRACKER
Folk/pop/country group with lead singer/songwriter David Lowery formerly of **Camper van Beethoven,** hit single "Teen Angst," album *Cracker* 1992.

CRADDOCK, BILLY "CRASH" (1940–)
b. 6/16 Greensboro, NC. Singer, albums *Back on Track, Sings His Greatest Hits.*

CRAMER, FLOYD (1933–)
b. 10/27 Shreveport, LA. Pianist/singer, joined Grand Ole Opry in Nashville in 1950s, hit "Last Date" 1961, albums *Country Classics, Easy Listening Favorites, Magic Touch of Floyd Cramer.*

CRAMPS, THE
Albums *Bad Music for Bad People, Date With Elvis, Psychedelic Jungle, Stay Sick.*

CRAWDADDY COMBOS
Various groups played in NY City in 1979/80s: **Warren Vache Trio** (cornetist) with drummer Chuck Riggs and pianist Tommy Fay. **Major Holly Trio** (bassist/singer) with tenor saxist Harold Ashby & pianist Dill Jones. **Red Rodney Trio** (trumpeter) with bassist Jack Dryden & pianist Gary Dial. **Vic Dickinson Trio** (trombonist) with drummer Ernie Hackett & pianist Chuck Folds. **Red Rodney Quartet** with bassist Paul Burner, pianist Gary Dial, & drummer Tom Whaley.

CRAWFORD, HANK (1934–)
b. Memphis, TN. Albums *After Hours, Mr. Chips, Night Beat, Soul Survivors,* etc.

CRAWFORD, JAMES S. "JIMMY" (1910–1980)
b. 1/4 Memphis, TN. Jazz drummer with Jimmie Lunceford* 1928/43, later with Ben Webster,* Fletcher Henderson,* played for Broadway shows 1960s/70s. Died 1/27 NY City.

CRAWFORD, RANDY (1952–   )
b. Macon, GA. Singer/songwriter, albums *Rich & Poor, Secret Combination,* hit "Through the Eyes of Love" 1992.

CRAY, ROBERT (1953–   )
Blues guitarist/songwriter/leader of **Robert Cray Band** with drummer David Olsen & keyboardist Peter Boe, replaced by Kevin Hayes & Jimmy Pugh respectively, guitarist Tim Karhatsu added. Albums *Strong Persuader* 1986, *Bad Influence, False Accusations, Midnight Stroll,* etc., won 1988 Grammy for "Don't Be Afraid of the Dark." At Lincoln Memorial, Washington, D.C., in January 1993. Blues Album Grammy *I Was Warned* 1993.

CRAZY HORSE
West Coast rock band. Album *Crazy Horse* 1971, disbanded after guitarist/singer Danny Whitten died of a drug overdose; reformed 1975 with guitarist/singer Frank Sampedra, guitarist/singer Nils Lofgren,* singer/keyboardist Jack Nitzsche, bassist Billy Talbot, drummer Ralph Molina.

CREACH, JOHN "PAPA" (1917–1994)
b. 5/17 Beaver Falls, PA. Violinist/singer with **Chocolate Music Bars** in 1930s/40s, with various groups 50s/60s, joined **Jefferson Airplane*** 1970, formed own combo **Midnight Sun.** Died February 22nd in Los Angeles.

CREAM
British super-rock group formed 1966 with drummer Ginger Baker, bassist/singer Jack Bruce, & Eric Clapton,* hits "Sunshine of Your Love," "Strange Brew," albums *Disraeli Gears, Wheels of Fire, Goodbye Cream.* Short lived trio, video *Strange Brew,* inducted into Rock & Roll Hall of Fame, January 1993.

CREED, LINDA (1949–1986)
Singer/songwriter with Tom Bell wrote hits "Could It be I'm Falling in Love" 1973, "You Make Me Feel Brand New" 1974. Died 4/10 Ambler, PA.

CREEDENCE CLEARWATER REVIVAL
Rock band with Douglas Ray Clifford, Stuart Cook, John Fogerty,* Thomas Fogerty, hits "Proud Mary," "Bad Moon Rising," active in San Francisco 1960s/80s, albums *Bayou Country, Chronicles, Green River, Mardi Gras,* etc., inducted into Rock & Roll Hall of Fame in Los Angeles, CA in January 1993.

CRENSHAW, MARSHALL (1954–)
b. Detroit, MI. Guitarist/singer/songwriter *Life's Too Short,* with Iggy Pop on *Rock 'n' Roll Cities, Detroit,* Nov. 1992.

CRIME & THE CITY SOLUTION
CD *Bride Ship,* "The Adversary" on soundtrack *Until the End of the World* 1922.

CRISS, WILLIAM "SONNY" (1927–1977)
b. Memphis, TN. Alto saxist, led own combos in 1950s/60s, went to Paris 1962 & played in night clubs there, returned to US 1965. Died 11/19 Los Angeles, CA.

CRISTIAN
Won 1993 Latin Pop Album Grammy *Agua Nueva.*

CRITTERS
Combo with Don Ciccone, Christopher Darway, Jack Decker, Kenneth Gorka, James Ryan.

CROCE, JIM (1943–1973)
b. 1/10 Philadelphia, PA. Singer/songwriter, hits "Operator" 1972, "Bad, Bad Leroy Brown" 1973, albums *Live/The Final Tour, Photographs & Memories, Time in Bottle/Love Songs.* Son A. J. Croce (b. 1972) is a pianist/songwriter. Died 9/20 in a plane crash in Natchitoches, LA.

CROCKETT, EFFIE J. (1857–1940)
b. Rockland, ME. To the music of an old song, wrote the words "Rock-a-bye baby in the Tree Top" about 1887.

CRO-MAGS
New York hard core/metal group album *The Alpha and the Omega* 1992.

CROSBY, FRANCES J. "FANNY" (1820–1915)
b. South East, Putnam County, NY. Hymnist, lost her eyesight at age six weeks, married blind musician Alexander van Alstyne. With composer Phoebe Knapp* wrote "Blessed Assurance" 1875. Wrote some 2,000 hymns.

CROSBY, HARRY L. "BING" (1904–1977)
b. 5/2 Tacoma, WA. Crooner/actor, member of the **Rhythm Boys Trio** with **Paul Whiteman's* Orchestra** 1931. Won Oscar as singing priest in *Going My Way* 1944. With Fred Ahlert wrote "Where the Blue of the Night Meets the Gold of the Day,"* biggest hit "White Christmas" 1942. Died 10/1 Madrid, Spain while playing golf. A postage stamp was issued in his honor in 1994.

CROSBY, STILLS, NASH & YOUNG
David Crosby (b. 8/14/41 Los Angeles), Stephen Stills, Graham Nash, Neil Young, later drummer Russ Kunkel. Hits "Woodstock,"* "Teach Your Children" 1970, "Suite: Judy Blue Eyes." Albums *Daylight Again, Live It Up, So Far,* etc. Video *Long Time Comin'.* Crosby was jailed in Texas for drugs in 1980s.

CROSS, CHRISTOPHER (1951–   )
b. Christopher Geppert 5/3 San Antonio, TX. Singer/songwriter "Sailing" Grammy winner 1980, "Arthur's Theme" Oscar winner 1982. Albums *Another Page, Back of My Mind,* etc.

CROSS, DOUGLAS
Lyricist, with composer George Cory* wrote "I Left My Heart in San Francisco," Grammy winner 1993.

CROUCH, SANDRA
Gospel singer, Sandra Crouch & Friends on *With All My Heart,* Grammy winner 1993.

CROWELL, RODNEY (1950–)
b. 8/7 Houston, TX. Singer/songwriter, wrote songs recorded by
  Emmylou Harris.* Married, (later divorced) Rosanne Cash*
  (daughter of Johnny Cash) & produced her albums; with
  Rosanne Cash on Top Ten Country single list "It's Such a
  Small World" 1988 & his own "I Couldn't Leave You If I
  Tried," Album *Life Is Messy* 1992, sang on *A Country Music
  Celebration* on CBS 1993.

CRUISE, JULEE
Album *Floating Into the Night,* single "Summer Kisses, Winter
  Tears" on soundtrack *Until the End of the World* 1992.

CRUMB, GEORGE
Composer, won 1968 Pulitzer Prize for *Echoes of Time and the
  River,* albums *A Haunted Landscape, Celestial Mechanics,
  Idyll for the Misbegotten.*

CRUSADERS, THE
California group with guitarist Larry Eugene Carlton, Wilton
  Felder, Wayne Henderson, "Stix" Hooper, Joe Sample.* Hit
  single "Uptight" (Everything's Alright) 1966, albums *Healing
  the Wounds, Southern Comfort, Street Life, The Crusaders
  Live, The Golden Years.* Carlton's solo album *Sleepwalk* 1982.
  See also the **Jazz Crusaders.***

CRUZ, CELIA
Singer won Grammy for album *Tributo a Ismael Rivera* 1993.

CRYSTALS, THE
Hit single "Da Doo Ron Ron."

CUGAT, XAVIER (1900–1990)
b. 1/1 Barcelona, Spain. Violinist/leader, concert at Carnegie Hall,
  NY City 1925, had own bands in Hollywood, then at Waldorf-
  Astoria Hotel in NY City from 1930s, known as the "Rumba
  King," popularized cha-cha & mambo dances in 1940s/50s.

CULT, THE
Albums *Ceremony, Electric, Love, Sonic Temple.*

CURE, THE
With Pori Thompson, Perry Bamonte, Boris Williams, Robert Smith, Simon Gallup, platinum album *Disintegration* 1989, platinum music video *Staring at the Sea-The Images* 1989, platinum video *The Cure in Orange* 1990, *Picture Show,* hit single "Wish" 1992, *A Letter to Elice* 1992.

CURTIS, KING (1935–1971)
b. Curtis Ousley, Fort Worth, TX. Saxist/leader/composer, staccato style on his tenor sax was called "yackity sax." Stabbed to death on the front steps of his home in NY City.

CURVE, THE
British group with singer Toni Halliday & bassist/songwriter Dan Garcia, US debut album *Doppelganger* 1992, at Manhattan Center Ballroom in NY City in January 1992.

CUSHING, CATHERINE C. (1874–1952)
b. Mt. Perry, Ohio. Composer/lyricist with composer Rudolf Frimil* wrote "L'Amour, Toujours L'Amour."

CYPRESS HILL
Rap singer, hit single "The Pluncky Feel One" won Billboard Music award, December 1992.

CYRUS, BILLY RAY (1962–   )
b. Flatwoods, KY. Country singer with band **Sly Dog.*** Album *Some Gave All* 1992 (sold over 3 million copies), hit single "Achy Breaky Heart" won Country Music award as Best Single & Grammy in January 1993, album *Dreams Come True* 1993.

D

DADA
Hit single "Dizz Knee Land" 1992.

DADDY FREDDY
Reggae hard core singer on album *Ragamuffin Soldier* 1992.

DALE, CLAMMA C. (1948–)
b. 7/4 Chester, PA. Dramatic soprano, sang with Houston & New York Opera companies, won awards for *Porgy & Bess* 1976.

DALTON, LACY J. (1946–)
b. 10/13. Country western singer, albums *Hard Times* 1980, *Lacy J. Dalton* 1980, *Takin' it Easy* 1982, *Crazy Love, Greatest Hits, Lacy J.* 1992.

DALTRY, ROGER (1944–)
b. 3/1 Hammersmith, England. Singer with **The Who,*** performed at Woodstock Festival in NY State 1970, appeared in *Tommy* 1974, *The Kids are All Right* 1979, hit "Rocks in the Head" 1992.

DAMERON, TADLEY E. "TAD" (1917–1965)
b. Cleveland, Ohio. Pianist/composer with Blanche Calloway* in late 1930s, wrote *Soulphony* for Dizzy Gillespie's* Carnegie Hall Concert in NY City 1948, led own band 1953/58 & played in Atlantic City, NJ & other places. Arrested for possession of narcotics and sent to prison in Lexington, KY 1958/60.

DAMN YANKEES
Group with former **Styx*** guitarist/singer Tommy Shaw, guitarist Ted Nugent,* former bassist/singer Jack Blades, & drummer Michael Cartellone, albums *Damn Yankees,* CD *Don't Tread,* toured US 1993.

DAMNED, THE
British rock group, *Final Damnation, Light at the End of the Tunnel, Music for Pleasure, Phantasmagoria,* etc.

DAMONE, VIC (1928–)
b. Vito Farinola 6/12 Brooklyn, NY City. Singer/actor won audition on Arthur Godfrey's Talent Scouts 1945, appeared in films & had his own radio show 1947/49. Served in army 1951/53. Starred in *Hell to Eternity* 1960, albums *Best of Vic Damone,* etc.

DANE, DANA
Hit album *Dana Dane with Fame* 1987.

D'ANGELO, BEVERLY (1954–)
b. Columbus, Ohio. Rock singer/actress, appeared in films *Coal Miner's Daughter* 1980, *Paternity* 1981.

DANIELS, CHARLIE (1936–)
b. 10/28 Wilmington, NC. Guitarist, formed **Charlie Daniels Band,** Nashville 1973. Wrote ''Devil Went Down to Georgia'' 1979 Grammy winner, MTV taped concert at Saratoga Springs, NY 1982, *Decade of Hits, Fire on the Mountain, Full Moon Renegade, Saddle Tramp,* etc., videos *Charlie Daniels, Home-folks & Highways, The Saratoga Concert,* with Wynonna Judd* & Billy Ray Cyrus* at Marysville, CA concert in June 1992. *All Time Greatest Hits* 1993.

DANIELS, EDDIE (1941–)
b. Brooklyn, NY. Tenor saxist/clarinetist, albums *Blackwood, Breakthrough, Memos from Paradise,* with Gary Burton* on *Benny Rides Again.*

DANKS, HART PEASE (1834–1903)
b. New Haven, CT. Composer, with lyricist E. E. Rexford* ''Silver Threads Among the Gold'' 1873.

DANNY & THE JUNIORS
Hit single ''At the Hop.''

DANZIG, GLENN
Soul/death metal singer, with guitarist John Christ, *Danzig II: Lucifer* 1990, *Danzig III: How the Gods Kill* 1992.

DAPOGNY, JAMES
James Dapogny's Chicago Jazz Band, CD *Laughing at Life* 1992.

D'ARBY, TERENCE TRENT
Singer, won 1988 R&B Vocalist Grammy for "Introducing the Hardline According to Terence Trent D'Arby," *Neither Fish nor Flesh* 1989, *Symphony or Damn* 1993, video *Hardline*.

DARIN, BOBBY (1936–1973)
b. Walden Robert Cassotto 5/14 New York, NY. Actor/singer, composed & recorded "Splish, Splash," "Mack the Knife" (Grammy 1959) from *The Three Penny Opera. Best of Splish Splash, The Bobby Darin Story,* etc., video with Linda Ronstadt* *The Darin Invasion.* Married actress Sandra Dee,* later separated, suffered from an irregular heartbeat for 20 years. Died 12/20.

DARLING BUDS
Welsh group with singer Andrea Lewis, guitarists Matt Gray & Harley Farr, bassist Chris McDonagh, & drummer Jimmy Hughes, *Crawdaddy, Erotica* 1993.

DAS EFX
Hit R&B single "They Want EFX" 1992, album *Das EFX*.

DAVID, HAL (1921–)
b. New York, NY. Lyricist, brother of composer Mack David, with composer Burt Bacharach* wrote "What's New Pussycat?" 1965, "Close to You" and other songs.

DAVIS, BENNY (1893–1979)
b. New York, NY. Lyricist/actor, with composers Con Conrad* & J. R. Robinson* wrote "Margie."

DAVIS, CLIFTON (1945–)
b. 10/4 Chicago, IL. Actor/singer, composed "Never Can Say Goodbye" a gold record song.

DAVIS, EDDIE "LOCKJAW" (1921–1986)

b. New York, NY. Tenor saxist with Cootie Williams* & Louis Armstrong* in early 1940s, led own combos 1945/52, with Count Basie* 1957/60s. Albums *Jaws, Jaws Blues, The Best of Eddie Davis.* Died 11/3.

DAVIS, GUSSIE L. (1863–1899)

b. Dayton, Ohio. Black composer, wrote "Irene Goodnight" 1892, "In the Baggage Car Ahead" 1896.

DAVIS, HAL

Songwriter, with Berry Gordy, Willie Hutch, & Bob West wrote "I'll Be There" Grammy winner 1993.

DAVIS, JAMES H. "JIMMIE" (1902–)

b. 9/11 Quitman, LA. Guitarist/singer/songwriter served as governor of Louisiana 1944/48 & again 1960/64, co-authored "You are My Sunshine" and "It Makes No Difference Now."

DAVIS, KATHERINE K. (1892–1980)

b. 6/25 St. Joseph, MO. Pianist/composer. Best known as the composer of "The Little Drummer Boy." Died 4/20 Concord, MA.

DAVIS, MAC (1942–)

b. 1/21 Lubbock, TX. Actor/singer/songwriter, hit song "I Believe in Music" 1972, starred in *North Dallas Forty* 1979, he wrote "In the Ghetto" & other songs for Elvis Presley*. Appeared in *The Will Rogers Follies* on Broadway, New York 1992.

DAVIS, MEYER (1895–1976)

b. 1/10 Ellicott City, MD. Conducted bands in ballrooms and for private parties for many years. Died 4/5 New York, NY.

DAVIS, MILES DEWEY (1926–1991)

b. 5/25 Alton, IL. Jazz trumpeter/leader, formed **Miles Davis Capitol Orchestra** 1948, at 1964 World Jazz Festival in Japan Davis played electric jazz blowing his trumpet through an amplifier with a wah-wah pedal, last tour July 1991. Albums *Agharta, At Last, Blue Moods, Cookin', Kind of Blue,* etc., video *Miles in Paris,* album *DooBop* (Grammy winner 1993). Died 9//28 Santa Monica, CA. *Miles and Quincy Live at Montreux* Jazz Ensemble Grammy 1994.

DAVIS, SAMMY JR. (1925–1990)
b. 12/8 New York, NY. Actor/singer/dancer, appeared in vaudeville at age four with his parents, regular performer in Las Vegas, was hospitalized in 1971 with cirrhosis of the liver. Hit "Candy Man" 1972. Died 5/16 Beverly Hills, CA.

DAVIS, SKEETER (1931–)
b. Mary Frances Penick 12/30 Dry Ridge, KY. Country singer, joined with Betty Jack Davis as the **Davis Sisters** 1949/53, hit song "The End of the World" 1963, albums *She Sings, They Play.*

DAVIS, SPENCER
British rock band **The Spencer Davis Group** with Spencer Davis, Muff Winwood, Stevie Winwood,* Pete York, hit "Give Me Some Lovin'," album *The Best of the Spencer Davis Group.*

DAVIS, WALTER, JR. (1932–1990)
b. Richmond, VA. Pianist, during 1950s with Dizzy Gillespie,* Art Blakey,* & others, led own combos 1960s/70s. Died 6/2 New York, NY.

DAVISON, WILLIAM "WILD BILL" (1906–1989)
b. 1/5 Defiance, Ohio. Jazz cornetist/leader, with various groups in 1920s, led own groups in Milwaukee 1933/41, served in US Army in World War II, at Eddie Condon's* in NY City 1945/60, led own bands 1970s. CDs *Just a Gig, Sweet & Lovely.*

DAWKINS, JIMMY
Chicago blues guitarist/singer, albums *All for Business, Kant Sheck Dees Bluze* 1993.

DAY, DENNIS (1917–1988)
b. 5/21 New York, NY. Singer/actor, sang in Claude Thornhill's*

orchestra while in the Pacific in World War II. Album *Shille-laghs and Shamrocks,* with Jack Benny on radio & TV shows for 25 years. Died 6/22 Bel Air, CA.

DAY, DORIS (1924–   )

b. Doris von Kappelhoff 4/3 Cincinnati, Ohio. Actress/singer, sang in Barney Rapp's band 1941, then with Les Brown,* starred in *The Pajama Game* 1957, *Pillow Talk* 1959. Hit songs ''Secret Love'' & ''Sentimental Journey,'' albums *A Day at the Movies, Greatest Hits, Hooray for Hollywood,* etc.

DAYE, IRENE (1918–1971)

She sang in bands of Mal Hallett & Gene Krupa,* married bandleader Charlie Spivak* 1950.

DAYNE, TAYLOR

Female singer, albums *Tell It to My Heart* 1987, *Can't Fight Fate* 1989, *Trust* 1993.

DAZZ BAND

Jazz band for dancing with Bobby Harris, Keith Harrison, Sennie Skip Martin III, Kenny Pettus, Isaac Wiley, Jr., & Michael Wiley. Hit single ''Let it Whip'' won 1982 Grammy, album *Gh's.*

D. C. TALK

''Free at Last'' Rock/Gospel Grammy winner 1994.

DEAN, BILLY

Country singer, hit singles ''Young Man,'' ''Billy the Kid'' 1992, album *Fire in the Dark,* with Dolly Parton* on *Romeo* 1993.

DEAN, JIMMY RAY (1928–   )

b. Seth Ward 8/10 Plainview, TX. Country pianist/singer/ songwriter, wrote & sang ''Big Bad John'' 1961, ''Dear Ivan'' 1961. Albums *American Originals, Greatest Hits.* Has his own sausage company.

DEARIE, BLOSSOM

Jazz pianist/singer/composer, with guitarist Mundell Lowe, Ray Brown, & Ed Thigpen on album *Once Upon a Summertime.*

DE BARGE
Grand Rapids, MI family group lead singer/keyboardist Eldra "El", Bunny, Randy, Mark, & James DeBarge, hit single "Rhythm of the Night" 1985, albums *All This Love, In a Special Way, In the Storm* 1992.

DECODING SOCIETY
Group led by Ronald Shannon Jackson with Ray Barretto, drummer Jackson, reedman Byard Lancaster, guitarist Vernon Reid, & bassist Melvin Gibbs in Ann Arbor, MI & New York City in 1980s.

DEE, SANDRA (1943–   )
b. Alexandra Zuck 4/23 Bayonne, NJ. Singer/actress, starred in *Gidget* 1959, *Tammy Tell Me True* 1961. Married Bobby Darin,* later separated.

DEELE, THE
1988 Top Ten Black Single for "Two Occasions."

DEE-LITE
With Towa, Super D. J. Dmitry, & singer Lady Kier, single "Groove is in the Heart," albums *World Clique* 1990, *Infinity Within* 1992.

DEEP PURPLE
British rock group, lead guitarist Richie Blackmore, singers Rod Evans & Nicholas Simper, organist/singer Jon Lord, drummer Ian Paice, Thomas Bolin, David Cloverdale, Ian Gillan, Roger Glover, & Glenn Hughes, single "Hit Stone Cold" 1968, albums *Come Taste the Band, Deep Purple, Fireball, Machine Head, Nobody's Perfect,* etc., *Video Singles.*

DEF LEPPARD
British heavy metal band formed in 1977 with drummer Rick Allen (lost an arm in a car crash 1984), guitarist Steve Clark (1960–1992), guitarist Phil Collen, bassist Rick Savage, lead singer Joe Elliott, Pete Willis, later Vivian Campbell. Albums *Hysteria* 1987 sold over 10 million copies, *Pyromania* sold

over five million and on 1988 Top Ten CDs list, multi-platinum videos *Hysteria* & *In the Round in Your Face Live* 1989, albums *Let's Get Rocked, Adrenalize* (sold over 3 million), toured USA 1992.

DeFRANCO, BONIFACE "BUDDY" (1923–)
b. Camden, NJ. Clarinetist/leader, with Gene Krupa,* Tommy Dorsey,* & others in 1940s, led own groups 50s, led **Glenn Miller* Band** 1966/74, resided in Panama City, FL.

DEJOHNETTE, JACK
Drummer/Pianist, with **Directional.*** *ECM Works, Parallel Realties, Special Edition, The Piano Album, Zebra.*

DEKKER, DESMOND (1943–)
b. Kingston, Jamaica, West Indies. Reggae singer/songwriter, hit single "The Israelites" 1969, albums *Dekker's Sweet 16 Hits* 1979, *Compass Point* 1981, etc.

DEKOVEN, H. L. REGINALD (1859–1920)
b. Middletown, CT. Composer of operettas, with lyricist Clement Scott* wrote "Oh Promise Me" 1889.

DEL (1973–)
Singer Teren Jones from Oakland, CA. Album with backup singers The Brides of Frankenstein on *Del The Funkee Homosapien* 1992.

DEL AMITRI
Scottish group with singer Justin Currie, third release *Change Everything* included "The First Rule of Love" & "The Ones that You Love Lead You Nowhere" 1992.

DELANEY & BONNIE
Blues husband & wife team, guitarist/singer Delaney Bramlett & singer Bonnie Lynn O'Farrell Sheridan, later divorced. Albums *Down Home* 1969, *Best of Delaney & Bonnie, On Tour with Eric Clapton.*

DE LARROCHA, ALICIA
Singer won 1988 Classical Soloist Grammy CD *Spanish Fireworks.*

DE MARCO SISTERS
Singers Arlene, Gene, Gloria, & Marie De Marco.

DEMENT, IRIS
Singer, album *Infamous Angel.*

DENVER, JOHN (1943–)
b. 12/31 Roswell, NM. Actor/singer/songwriter, hit single "Take Me Home Country Road" 1971, recorded "Perhaps Love" 1981 with tenor Placido Domingo*. Albums *Back Home Again, Different Directions, I Want to Live, It's About Time, One World,* etc. Toured China in fall of 1992. Lives in Aspen. CO.

DEODATO (1942–)
b. Eumir Deodato 6/22, Rio de Janeiro, Brazil. Keyboardist/songwriter *Deodato, Prelude, Whirlwinds.*

DEPECHE MODE
British group formed 1980 with lead singer David Gaban and singer/songwriter Martin Gore, platinum album *Violator* 1990, *A Broken Frame, Black Celebration, Music for the Masses, Speak & Spell, Songs of Faith and Devotion* 1993, platinum video *101* 1990, videos *Live in Concert, Some Great Videos, Strange,* etc. Toured US Sept./Nov. 1993.

DeROSE, PETER (1900–1953)
b. New York, NY. Composer, with lyricist Mitchell Parish* wrote "Deep Purple" 1933, with lyricist Billy Hill wrote "Wagon Wheels" 1934.

DERRINGER, RICK (1947–)
b. Rick Zehringer 8/5 in Union City, IL. Singer/guitarist with **McCoys** in 1960s, wrote hit "Hang On, Sloopy" 1965, had own band in 1970s.

DESMOND, JOHNNY (1919–1985)

b. Giovanni Alfredo DeSimone 11/14 Detroit, MI. Singer/ songwriter with Gene Krupa,* Glenn Miller,* & Bob Crosby. Album *Johnny Desmond.* Died 9/6 Los Angeles, CA.

DESMOND, PAUL B. (1924–1977)

b. 11/25 San Francisco, CA. Alto saxist with Dave Brubeck* in 1950s/60s. Composed "Take Five," played at Newport Jazz Festivals in NY City. Albums *Easy Living, Late Lament, Pure Desmond, The Best of Paul Desmond.* Died 5/30 New York, NY.

DE SYLVA, GEORGE "BUDDY" (1895–1950)

b. New York, NY. Lyricist, wrote "The Best Things in Life are Free" 1927, "Button Up Your Overcoat," "You are My Lucky Star," "Sonny Boy" 1928 (for Al Jolson*) "Keep Your Sunny Side Up" 1929, with composer Joseph Meyer* "California Here I Come" 1922, with composer Louis Silvers* "April Showers." Died in Hollywood, CA.

DEUTSCH, ADOLPH (1897–1980)

b. 10/20 London, England. MGM musical director in Hollywood, CA, wrote scores for *Annie Get Your Gun* 1950, and *Oklahoma!* (1955 Oscar winner). Died 1/1 Palm Desert, CA.

DEVO

Synthesizer rhythm group from Akron, Ohio. Bob & Jerry Casale, Bob & Mark Mothersbaugh, Alan Myers. Hit "Whip It" 1980, albums *Now it Can Be Told, Q: Are We Not Men? Smoother Noodle Maps,* video *Men Who Make Music.*

DEVOE, BELL BIV

Album *Poison* 1990 (sold 3 million copies).

DE VORZON, BARRY (1934–)

b. 7/31 New York, NY. Composer of "Bless the Beasts and the Children" 1971, "Nadia's Theme" (1977 Grammy winner).

DEXTER, AL (1902–1984)

b. Albert Poindexter 5/4 Jacksonville, TX. Guitarist/singer/

songwriter. Hit "Pistol Packin' Mama" 1943 sold over 10 million copies. Died 1/28 Lewisville, Texas.

DIAMOND, NEIL (1941–   )
b. 1/24 Brooklyn, NY City. Singer/songwriter, wrote "I'm a Believer" 1967, "A Little Bit of Me, a Little Bit of You" (both recorded by **The Monkees,***), hit singles "Song Sung Blues" 1972, "Love on the Rocks" 1980, "Hello Again" 1981, "America" 1981, "Heartlight" 1982, & many more, has over 20 gold or platinum records. Videos *Greatest Hits Live, Love at the Greek*, toured the world 1992.

DIAMOND RIO
Won 1992 Country Music Vocal Group Award, hit single "Norma Jean Riley," with singer Marty Roe album *Close to the Edge* 1992, "In a Week or Two" 1993.

DICKENSON, VICTOR "VIC" (1906–1984)
b. Xenia, Ohio. Trombonist/singer with **Zach Whythe's Chocolate Beau Brummels** 1930s, with Blanche Calloway* 1933/36, then with various bands 1930s/80s, played at Newport Jazz Festivals.

DIDDLEY, BO (1928–   )
b. Ellas McDaniels 12/30 McCombs, MS. Guitarist/singer/songwriter, sang at the Apollo in Harlem, NY City, hits "I'm Sorry," "Who Do You Love?" at 1974 Jazz Festival in Monterey, CA. Albums *Rare and Well Done, The Chess Box, The London Session,* etc.

DIETRICH, MARLENE (1901–1992)
b. Maria Magdalene von Losch 12/27 Berlin, Germany. Singer/actress, in films *The Blue Angel* 1930, *Destry Rides Again* 1939, entertained soldiers in World War II, sang in night clubs. Sang Cole Porter's* hit "The Laziest Girl in Town." Died 5/6 in Paris.

DIETZ, HOWARD M. (1896–1983)
b. 9/8 New York, NY. Lyricist, with Arthur Schwartz wrote "Something to Remember You By" 1930, "Dancing in the

Dark'' 1931, ''That's Entertainment.'' Wrote the lyrics for over 500 songs.

DIFFIE, JOE (1965–)
Country singer on the road 300 days in 1991, hits ''Home,'' ''Ships that Don't Come In'' 1992, albums *A Thousand Winding Roads, Regular Joe,* with Mary-Chapin Carpenter,* on ''Not Much to Ask'' 1992.

DIGABLE PLANETS
Pop/jazz trio with ''Doodlebug'' Craig Irving, ''Ladybug'' Mary Vieira, & ''Butterfly'' Ishmael Butler, R&B hit single ''Rebirth of Slick (Cool Like Dat)'' album *Reachin' (A New Refutation of Time and Space)* 1993.

DIGITAL UNDERGROUND
Platinum album *Sex Packets* 1990, *Sons of the P, This is an Ep Release.*

DILLARDS, THE
Guitarist Rodney Dillard (b. 1942), banjoist Beverly Cotton Dillard, & Doug Dillard, albums *Let it Fly, Mountain Rock, There is a Time,* Rodney's album *Let the Rough Side Drag* 1992.

DILLON, WILLIAM A. "WILL" (1877–1966)
b. Cortland, NY. Composer/lyricist, with Harry von Tilzer* wrote ''I Want a Girl Just Like the Girl That Married Dear Old Dad'' 1911.

DI MEOLA, AL (1954–)
b. 7/22 Jersey City, NJ. Guitarist/songwriter, albums *Cielo E Terra, Electric Rendezvous, Elegant Gypsy, Splendido Hotel,* hit jazz album *Kiss My Axe* 1992, at the Ultimate Guitar Concert in San Francisco in September 1992.

DINNING, MAX (1935–1986)
Singer whose hit song ''Teen Angel'' 1959 was banned in Great Britain because it was too sad. Died 3/22 Jefferson City, MO.

DIO
Albums *Dreamevil, Holy Diver, Sacred Heart, The Last in Line.*

DION AND THE BELMONTS
Singer "Doo-Wop" Dion DiMucci (born 7/18/39 Bronx, NY City), Angelo D'Angelo, Carlo Mastangelo, & Fred Milano, hits "A Teenager in Love" 1959, "Runaround Sue," "The Wanderer," album *Reunion Live at Madison Square Garden.*

DION, CELINE (1978–   )
Singer from Montreal, "If You Asked Me To" on Top Ten singles list June 1992, hit "Nothing Broken but My Heart," with Peabo Bryson duet "Beauty and the Beast" (1993 Grammy winner), album *Celine Dion.*

DIRE STRAITS
Scottish rock group formed 1977 with Dave & Mark Knopfler, John Illsley, & "Pick" Withers, hits "Walk of Life" 1985, "Money for Nothing" 1986, albums *Brothers in Arms, Dire Straits, Love over Gold,* etc., videos *Dire Straits Video Singles, Money for Nothing* 1992.

DIRECTIONS
Band led by drummer/pianist Jack DeJohnette,* trumpeter Lester Bowie, guitarist John Abercrombie,* and bassist Eddie Gomez in New York City in 1977/80s.

DIRTY DOZEN BRASS BAND, THE
New Orleans jazz band founded 1978 with saxists Kirk Joseph, Roger Lewis, & Kevin Harris, albums *The New Orleans Album, Voodo, Open Up Wetcha Gonna Do for the Rest of Your Life* 1992. Sang at Jazz Aspen Festival in Colorado 1992.

DISORDER
British punk/rock group on video cassette *U.K./D.K.* 1984.

DISPOSABLE HEROES OF HIP-HOPRISY
With rappers Rono Tse & Michael Franti, "Television: Drug of

the Nation'' 1992, toured 25 cities starting July 1992, album *Hiphoprisy is the Greatest Luxury,* toured with **U-2** 1992/93.

DIVINYLS
Albums *Desperate, Divinyls, Temperamental, What a Life.*

DIXIE DRUGS
Album *Bring 'Em Back Alive* 1992.

DIXON, GEORGE W. (1808–1861)
Minstrel showman/singer/songwriter, wrote ''Turkey in the Straw'' 1834.

DIXON, MORT (1892–1956)
b. New York, NY. Lyricist, with Billy Rose & composer Ray Henderson* wrote ''That Old Gang of Mine'' 1923, with Henderson* ''Bye, Bye Blackbird,'' with composer Harry Woods* ''I'm Looking Over a Four Leaf Clover'' 1927 and Woods* ''River Stay Away from My Door'' 1931, with composer Allie Wrubel* ''Fare Thee Well'' 1935.

DIXON, WILLIE (1915–1992)
b. Vicksburg, MS. Bassist/blues singer/songwriter, recorded with Muddy Waters* & Memphis Slim,* wrote ''Hootchie Coochie Man'' recorded 1954 by Muddy Waters & others, won 1988 Traditional Blues Album Grammy *Hidden Charms, The Big Three Trio, I am the Blues, The Chess Box.* Died 1/29 Burbank, CA.

D. J. JAZZY JEFF & THE FRESH PRINCE
Won 1991 Grammy for *Summertime.*

D. J. MAGIC MIKE
Rapper, albums *Bass: The Final Frontier, This is How it Should be Done* 1993.

D. J. QUICK
Hit single ''Way 2 Fonky'' 1992, album *Quick is the Name.*

DOANE, WILLIAM H. (1832–1915)
b. Preston, CT. Composer, with lyricist Fanny Crosby* wrote

"Near the Cross" 1869, with lyricist Katherine Hankey "Tell Me the Old, Old Story" 1876.

DR DRE*
b. Andre R. Young, singer, co-founder rap act **N. W. A.***, hit album *The Chronic* 1993 (title is slang for potent marijuana) includes song about the Los Angeles riots—"The Day the Niggaz Took Over," hit "Nuthin' but a 'G' Thang" 1993. 1994 American Music Rap/Hip Hop Artist Award, "Let Me Ride" Rap Solo Grammy 1994.

DR HOOK
New Jersey R & B group, guitarist/singer Dennis Loconiere, keyboardist Billy Francis, drummer John Walters, guitarist Rik Elawit, bassist Jance Garfat, guitarist Rod Smart, albums *Greatest Hits, Revisited, Sloppy Seconds.*

DR JOHN (1941–   )
Mac Rebennack of New Orleans, blues pianist/guitarist, albums *Gumbo* 1972, *In the Right Place* 1973, *Diggin', Gris Gris, In a Sentimental Mood, Goin' Back to New Orleans* (Grammy winner 1993.

DODDS, JOHNNY (1892–1940)
b. New Orleans, LA. Clarinetist/saxist with Kid Ory* intermittently between 1911/19, recorded with Louis Armstrong,* King Oliver,* & Jelly Roll Morton,* led own bands in 1930s, *Blue Clarinet Stomp, Southside Chicago Jazz.* Died in Chicago, IL.

DODDS, WARREN "BABY" (1894–1959)
b. New Orleans, LA. Drummer, brother of Johnny Dodds,* paraded with Bunk Johnson,* with Fate Marable* 1918/21 on river boats, with King Oliver* 20s, recorded with Louis Armstrong* & Jelly Roll Morton.* Led own combos, at 1948 Nice Jazz Festival in France, had strokes 1949/50 but recovered. Died 2/14 Chicago.

DOKKER
With **Van Halen*** on 1988 Ten Top grossing concerts list at East Troy, WI, *Breaking the Chains,* etc., video *Unchain the Night.*

DOLBY, THOMAS
Musician, *Aliens Ate My Buick, Golden Age of the Wilderness,* with others on *Astronauts and Heretics* 1992.

DOLLAR, JOHN W. "JOHNNY" (1933–1986)
b. Kilgore, TX. Singer/songwriter, leader of **Texas Sons** in 1950s, wrote "Big Red" & other songs. Died 4/13 Nashville, TN.

DOLPHY, ERIC ALLAN (1928–1964)
b. Los Angeles, CA. Alto saxist/composer, with **Chico Hamilton* Quintet** 1959/60, had own quintet 1960s, recorded with John Coltrane* & Ornette Coleman.* Albums *Berlin Concerts, Far Cry, Iron Man, Outward Bound,* etc. Suffered with diabetes & died of heart attack on 6/29 in Berlin.

DOMINGO, PLACIDO (1941–)
b. 1/21 Madrid, Spain. Noted tenor, debut with NY City Opera 1966, recorded "Perhaps in Love" with John Denver* 1981, won 1990 Grammy for *Carreras, Domingo, Pavarotti in Concert,* sang with Diana Ross* & Jose Carreras* in Austria in December 1992. Videos *An Evening with Placido Domingo, Placido: A Year in the Life of Domingo.*

DOMINO, ANTOINE, JR. "FATS" (1928–)
b. 2/26 New Orleans, LA. Jazz pianist/composer, hit song "Blueberry Hill" 1956, albums *In Concert, They Call Me the Fat Man, When I'm Walking,* etc., played at the New Orleans Jazz Festival in April/May 1993.

DONAHUE, SAM KOONTZ (1918–1979)
b. 3/8 Detroit, MI. Tenor saxist/trumpeter led own band 1957/79, then with Stan Kenton,* led old Tommy Dorsey* band after 1961 (featuring Frank Sinatra,* played at the 1964 Jazz Festival in Japan. Died 3/22 Reno, NV.

DONALDSON, LOU (1926–)
b. Badin, NC. Albums *Alligator Bogaloo, Lush Life, The Natural Soul,* etc.

DONALDSON, WALTER (1893–1947)
b. Brooklyn, NY City. Composer of "How Ya Gonna Keep 'Em Down on the Farm?" 1919, "My Mammy" 1920 (made famous by Al Jolson*), "Carolina in the Morning" 1922, "Yes, Sir That's My Baby" 1925, "My Blue Heaven" 1927. Died at Santa Monica, CA.

DONEGAN, LONNIE (1951–)
b. 4/28 Glasgow, Scotland. Guitarist/bassist/composer, hits "Rock Island Line," "Does Your Chewing Gum Lose It's Flavor?" toured the US.

DONNELLY, DOROTHY (1880–1928)
b. New York, NY. Lyricist, with composer Sigmund Romberg* wrote words for "Song of Love" 1921 and the "Drinking Song" in the *Student Prince* 1924.

DONOVAN (1946–)
b. Donovan Leitch 5/10 Glasgow, Scotland. Came to US, guitarist/singer, albums *Catch the Wind, Hurdy Gurdy Man, Sunshine Superman,* etc.

DOOBIE BROTHERS, THE
Jeff Baxter, "Little John" Hartman, Mike Hossack, Tom Johnston, Keith Knudson, Michael McDonald,* Tiran Porter, Save Shogren, & Pat Simmons who wrote Doobie hit "Black Water" 1974. Album *Minute by Minute* 1978, group won 1979 Grammy for "What a Fool Believes," albums *One Step Closer* 1980, *Brotherhood, Cycles, Stampede,* etc. Members of the group changed over the years. Simmons began his solo career in 1982.

DOORS, THE
Rock group formed 1966 with drummer John Densmore of Los Angeles, guitarist Robbie Krieger, organist/keyboardist Ray Manzereck, singer Jim Morrison (1944/71), hit single "Light My Fire," albums *Waiting for the Sun* 1969, *An American Prayer* 1978, platinum videos *Dance on Fire* 1985, *The Doors Live at the Hollywood Bowl,* 1989, *Facelift* 1992, etc.

DORHAM, KENNY (1924–1972)
b. Fairfield, TX. Trumpeter, albums *Matador/Inta Somethin, Round Midnight, Septet: Blue Spring, West 42nd Street,* etc.

DORSEY, JIMMY (1904–1957)
b. Shenandoah, PA. Clarinetist/saxist/leader, brother of Tommy Dorsey.* The **Dorsey Brothers** were the first jazz group to broadcast on radio, led their own bands in 1930s/50s. Died of cancer in NY City.

DORSEY, THOMAS ANDREW (1900–1993)
b. 7/1 Villa Rica, GA. Preacher/pianist/songwriter, wrote over 1,000 gospel songs, known as the "Father of Gospel," hit "Take My Hand, Precious Lord" 1932 made famous by Mahalia Jackson,* his "It's Tight Like That" sold 7 million copies. Died 1/23 in Chicago.

DORSEY, TOMMY (1905–1956)
b. Shenandoah, PA. Trombonist, led bands with brother Jimmy* 1920s/30s, led own band 1930s/50s, Albums *Music Goes Round & Round, Dorsey/Sinatra Vols. 1 to 3,* etc. Choked to death on a bone while dining in Greenwich, CT.

DOUBLE TROUBLE
Stevie Ray Vaughan* & **Double Trouble** won Blues Album Grammy for *The Sky is Crying* 1993.

DOUCET, MICHAEL
Singer/fiddler with guitarist Sonny Landreth* on *Bonnie Annee* 1992, with **Beausolid.***

DOUGLAS, JERRY
Hit "Ride the Wild Turkey" on track *Slide Rule* 1992.

DOUGLAS, MIKE (1925–)
b. Michael Delaney Dowd, Jr. 8/11 Chicago, IL. Singer/TV host on the *Mike Douglas Show* 1960s/70s, won four Emmys.

DOWNEY MILDEW

Los Angeles band formed 1988 with singer Charlie Baldonado, singer/songwriter Jenny Homer, album *An Oncoming Train* 1992.

DOWNEY, MORTON (1902–1985)

b. 11/14 Wallingford, CT. Pianist/singer/songwriter, toured Europe 1927, opened own night club The Delmonico 1930, sang over radio, made over 1,500 recordings. Died 10/25 Palm Beach.

DRAPER, RAYMOND A. "RAY" (1940–1982)

b. NY City. Tubist/composer, with John Coltrane* & others in 1950s, with Philly Joe Jones* in Los Angeles in 60s, toured Europe 1969/72, back in Los Angeles in 70s. Died 11/1 in NY City.

DREAD, MICKEY

Albums *Best Sellers, Beyond World War III, Happy Family, Pave the Way*.

DREAD ZEPPELIN

Singer/bassist Gary Bibb, guitarist Carl Joh, percussionist Ed Zeppelin (left the band), bassist Job Job Gabor, drummer Spice, album *It's Not Unusual*.

DRESSER, PAUL (1857–1906)

b. Terre Haute, IN. Composer, brother of novelist Theodore Dreiser, Paul wrote "On the Banks of the Wabash" 1897 (the state song of Indiana), also "My Gal Sal" 1905.

DRIFTERS, THE

Lead singer Clyde McPhatter,* Billy Pinkney, Andrew & Gerhart Thrasher, hits "Save the Last Dance for Me" 1960, "Under the Boardwalk" 1964. Members drifted in and out or died, the new group includes Bill Pinkney with singers Ben E. King, Rudy Lewis, & Johnny Moore with hit singles "There Goes My Baby," "This Magic Moment," "Money Honey," toured US 1992.

D'RIVERA, PAQUITO
Albums *Celebration, Havana Cafe,* single with **Sandoval** "Reunion."

DRIVIN' N' CRYN'
Albums *Fly Me Courageous, Mystery Road, Scarred but Smarter.*

DRY BRANCH FIRE SQUAD
Ohio country quintet with soprano Suzanne Thomas, albums *Born to be Lonesome, Antiques & Inventions, Long Journey* 1992.

DUB BAND
Reggae songs by Jean Binta Breeze on "Tracks" and Jah Lewis on "All Gone Astray" 1992.

DUBIN, AL (1891–1945)
b. Zurich, Switzerland. Lyricist, with composer Joe Burke wrote "Tip Toe Through the Tulips," with composer Harry Warren* "Shuffle Off to Buffalo," "Lullaby of Broadway" (1935 Oscar winner), with composer Jimmy McHugh* "South American Way."

DUCHIN, EDDY (1909–1951)
Pianist/leader, led his own bands in 1930s/40s, albums *Best of the Big Bands, I'll See You in My Dreams.* Died of Leukemia.

DUCHIN, PETER (1937–   )
Pianist/leader, son of Eddy Duchin.*

DUFFIELD, GEORGE, JR. (1818–1888)
b. Carlisle, PA. Lyricist, with composer Adam Geibel* wrote "Stand Up, Stand Up for Jesus" 1858.

DUKE, GEORGE (1946–   )
b. San Rafael, CA. Jazz keyboardist/composer, with **Spectrum.*** Album *Snapshot.* With bassist Kenny Clarke,* & violinist Jean Luc Ponty on album *East River Drive* 1993.

DUKE, VERNON (1903–1969)
b. Vladimer Dukelsy in Pskov, North Russia. Composer, came to US in 1921, wrote scores for the *Ziegfeld Follies* 1934/35, *Banjo Eyes* 1941 starring Eddie Cantor,* *April in Paris* and other songs. Died at Santa Monica, CA.

DUKES OF DIXIELAND
Trombonist Fred J. Assunto (1929–1966) & trumpeter Frank J. Assunto* (1932–1974) & sometimes with Al Hirt.* Albums *Best of Dukes, Tiger Rag, Best of Bourbon Street.* Also with pianist Dick Wellstood.*

DUNCAN, GLEN
Bluegrass singer with Lonesome Standard Time, album *Larry Cordie* 1992.

DUNN, HOLLY
Singer/songwriter, albums *Blue Rose of Texas, Heart Full of Love, Getting It Dunn, Milestones* 1992.

DURAN DURAN
British rock group with lead singer Simon Le Bon, keyboardist Nick Rhodes, and John Taylor. Hit "Hungry Like the Wolf," toured US 1984 with **J. Geils Band***. Albums *Big Thing, Liberty, Seven and the Ragged Tiger, Duran Duran* 1993, video *Decade,* hit single "Ordinary World" 1993.

DURANTE, JAMES F. "JIMMY" (1893–1980)
b. 2/10 New York, NY. Comedian/pianist/vocalist, known as "Ol' Schnozzola." Had his own band 1916, appeared in Broadway plays & in films, wrote "Inka Dinka Doo." Died 1/29 Santa Monica, CA.

DURBIN, DEANNA (1921–)
b. 12/4 Winnipeg, Manitoba, Canada. Singer/actress, appeared in numerous films.

DYLAN, BOB (1941–)
b. Robert Zimmerman 5/24 Duluth, MN. Singer/songwriter, hits

"Blowin' in the Wind" 1962, "The Times They are a Changin' " 1964, "Like a Rolling Stone," "Blood on the Tracks" 1974, video *Bob Dylan & Tom Petty: Hard to Handle, Under the Red Sky* 1991, *Blonde on Blonde, Good as I Been to You* 1992. Celebrated 30 years of recording at a concert at Madison Square Garden in NY City in October 1992.

E

E STREET BAND
Back-up band for Bruce Springsteen with keyboardist/singer Roy Bittan, tenor saxist Clarence Clemons, keyboardist/accordian player Daniel Paul Federici, singer Nils "Lefty" Lofgren,* singer Patty Scialfa, bassist Gary Wayne Tallent, drummer Max M. Weinberg.* Tallent with Springsteen since 1971, Clemons had solo album *Rescue* 1983, Patty "Red" Scialfa with Springsteen since 1984 (currently Springsteen's second wife).

EAGLES, THE
Guitarist/singer/songwriter Don Felder, singer Glenn Frey* (solo album *No Fun Aloud* 1982), guitarist/banjoist Bernie Leadon, Don Henley,* bassist Randy Meiser, Tim Schmidt replaced Meiser 1977, singer Joe Walsh. Double platinum album *The Long Run* 1979, *Natural Progression,* group won 1977 Grammy for *Hotel California,* albums *Desperado, On the Border,* etc., group has sold over 40 million albums. Don Felder recorded title song from film *Heavy Metal* 1981, Leadon formed **RUN C & W***.

EAGLIN, SNOOKS
b. New Orleans, LA. Guitarist, third album *Teasin' You* 1992.

EARLE, STEVE
Country guitarist/singer/songwriter, hit albums *Guitar Town, Copperhead Road.* Album *Essential Steve Earle* 1993. Lives in Fairview, TN.

EARTH, WIND, AND FIRE
Black pop group have sold over 20 million albums since 1970s, Philip Bailey, Roland Bautista, Jessica Cleaves, Larry Dunn, Johnny Graham, Ralph Johnson, Al McKay, Fred White, Andrew Woolfolk, Philip Bailey (who sang "Easy Lover" with Phil Collins* 1984). Hit "Shining Star," albums *All in All, I am, Rise, Spirit, The Eternal Dance* 1992.

EASTER, JEFF & SHERI
Southern gospel singers, *Pickin' the Best/Live* 1992.

EASTERN REBELLION
Jazz pianist Cedar Walton, drummer Billy Higgins, bassist David Williams, tenor saxist Ralph Moore on *Mosaic* 1992.

EASTON, SHEENA (1959–)
b. 4/27 Glasgow, Scotland, singer, moved to California, albums *A Private Heaven, The Lover in Me, What Comes Naturally.*

EBB, FRED (1933–)
b. 4/8 New York, NY. Songwriter won Tonys for *Cabaret* 1967, *Woman of the Year* 1980.

EBERLE BROTHERS, THE
Singers Ray Eberle (1919–1979) singer with Glenn Miller's* orchestra, Bob Eberly (Eberle) (1916–1981), with the Dorsey* Brothers in 1940s, hits "Tangerine," "Green Eyes."

ECKSTINE, BILLY "MR. B" (1914–1993)
b. 7/8 Pittsburgh, PA. Trumpeter/trombonist/vocalist, with Earl Hines,* Budd Johnson* in 1940s, hits "Cottage for Sale" 1945, "Prisoner of Love" 1945, "Blue Moon," toured with Duke Ellington* 1966, with daughter Gina at the Grand Finale in NY City 1980. Albums *Compact Jazz, Everything I Have is Yours, Imagination.*

EDDY, DUANE (1938–)
b. 4/28 Corning, NY. Guitarist/composer/actor, hit singles "Cannon Ball" 1958, "Shazami" 1960, albums *Legend of Rock* 1975, *Greatest Hits* 1979, *Terrific Twangies* 1980, *Rebel Rouser Man, $1,000,000 Worth of Twang.* Inducted into Rock & Roll Hall of Fame in 1994.

EDDY, NELSON (1901–1967)
b. Providence, RI. Baritone, with Jeannette MacDonald* in musicals, they sang "Indian Love Call," "Rose Marie," and others, album with Eleanor Steber *New Moon.*

EDMONDS, KENNETH "BABYFACE" (1956–)
Songwriter, 1990 double platinum album *Tender Lover* included

hits "It's No Crime" & "Whip Appeal," *see also* REID & EDMONDS.*

EDWARDS, GUS (1879–1945)
b. Hohensalza, Germany. Composed "In My Merry Oldsmobile" 1905 with lyricist Vincent Bryan*, "School Days" 1907, with lyricist Ed Madden* "By the Light of the Silvery Moon" 1907. Died in Los Angeles, CA.

EDWARDS, JOAN (1919–1981)
b. 2/13 New York, NY. Singer/songwriter, co-starred with Frank Sinatra* on radio show *Your Hit Parade* 1941/46.

EDWARDS, SHERMAN (1919–1981)
Composed "See You in September" & "Wonderful, Wonderful."

EEK-a-MOUSE
Albums *Mouse and the Man, Mousketeer, Skidip, U-Neck, Wa Do Dem.*

EGAN, RAYMOND B. (1890–1952)
b. Windsor, Ontario, Canada. Lyricist, came to US 1892; with J.R. Alden* and Ange Lorenzo* wrote "Sleepy Time Gal," with composer R.A. Whiting* wrote "Till We Meet Again" 1918.

EGAN, WALTER LINDSAY (1948–   )
b. 7/12 Jamaica, NY City. Guitarist/singer/songwriter, had hit album *HI FI* 1979.

808 STATE
Hit single "Gorgeous" 1993.

EL GRAN COMBO
Won Latin Album Grammy for *Gracias* 1993.

ELDRIDGE, ROY D. (1911–1989)
b. Pittsburgh, PA. Jazz trumpeter/singer. With Horace Henderson 1928, in 30s with Elmer Snowden, Teddy Hill, & others, own combos 1935/41, then with Gene Krupa,* Benny Goodman,* &

Ella Fitzgerald* in 50s/60s, at jazz festivals in 70s, albums *Little Jazz, Loose Walk, Uptown.* Suffered a heart attack 1980.

ELECTRIC FLAG
Guitarist Mike Bloomfield (1944–1981), bassist Harry Brooks, drummer/singer Buddy Miles, organist Herbie Rich, pianist John Simon, tenor Terry Clements, trumpeter Marcus Doubleday, saxist Nick Gravenites, saxist/singer Stemsy Hunter, debut at Monterey Pop Festival 1967. Albums *Electric Flag, Long Time Coming.* Bloomfield album *My Labors* 1971. Hoshal Wright replaced Bloomfield.

ELECTRIC LIGHT ORCHESTRA
British group led by Jeff Lynne (b. 1947), hit single "Video" 1984, albums *Afterglow, Discovery, Elo Olé, Face the Music, Part Two, Time,* etc.

ELEVENTH DREAM DAY
Guitar/rock Chicago quartet, album *El Moodio* 1993.

ELIAS, ELAINE
Albums *A Long Story, Cross Currents, Illusions, Fantasia,* single "So Far So Close," video *New Stars on Blue Note.*

ELISCA, EDWARD (1902–)
b. NY City. Lyricist, with composers V.Youmans,* Elisui & Gus Kahn* wrote "Carioca" for the film *Flying Down to Rio* (with Fred Astaire and Dolores Del Rio) 1933.

ELLIMAN, YVONNE (1953–)
b. 12/29 Hawaii. Singer, appeared in *Jesus Christ Superstar* singing "I Don't Know How to Love Him," video *Yvonne Elliman in Concert* 1981. Sang with Eric Clapton* on his "Ocean Boulevard Tour."

ELLINGTON, DUKE (1899–1974)
b. Edward Kennedy 4/29 Washington, D.C. Pianist/songwriter, led the **Washingtonians** in 1920s, toured Europe 30s, USA 40s, toured world in early 70s. Composed music for "Sophisticated Lady," "Satin Doll," "It Don't Mean a Thing," "Soli-

tude.'' Entertained by President Nixon in The White House. Died 5/24 NY City. Dozens of CDs & albums available, videos *Memories of Duke, Sacred Music of Duke Ellington.*

ELLINGTON, MERCER KENNEDY (1919–)
b. 3/11 Washington, D.C. Trumpeter/leader son of Duke Ellington.* Had own band in 1939, took over father's band 1974, led band for **Sophisticated Ladies** 1980/81.

ELLIOT, RICHARD
Albums *On the Town, Power of Suggestion, What's Inside, Take to the Skies.*

ELLIOTT, ALONZO "ZO" (1891–1964)
b. Manchester, NH. Songwriter with Stoddard King* wrote ''There's a Long, Long Trail A-winding'' 1914 (popular in World War I).

ELLIOTT, "RAMBLIN' JACK" (1931–)
b. Elliott Charles Adnopoz 8/1 in Brooklyn, NY City. Singer/ guitarist, toured Europe 1956/59, ''San Francisco Bay Blues'' on *Troubadours of the Folk Era, Vol. I* in 1992.

ELLIS, DONALD J. "DON" (1934–1978)
b. 7/25 Los Angeles, CA. Trumpeter/leader, played in bands of Charlie Barnet, Maynard Ferguson,* Ray McKinley,* formed own quartet 1962, trumpet soloist at NY Philharmonic 1963/64, led all-star orchestra at Berlin Jazz Festival 1968, composed theme for the film *French Connection* (1973 Grammy winner). Died 12/17 North Hollywood, CA.

ELLIS, HERB (1921–)
b. Farmersville, TX. Guitarist/songwriter, albums *Doggin Around, Roll Call, Soft & Mellow, Soft Shoe.*

ELY, JOE (1947–)
b. 2/9 Lubbock, TX. Country/rock singer, albums *Dig All Night, Down on the Day, Lord of the Highway, Musta Notta Gotta Lotta Honky Tonk Masquerade, Joe Ely and Lucinda Williams* 1993.

EMERSON, LAKE & PALMER
British group 1970/79 with Emerson, singer/musician Gregory "Greg" Lake, & Carl Palmer,* his song "From the Beginning," albums *Brain Salad Surgery, In Concert, Tarkus, Works Vol. 1 & 2*, etc. Palmer formed **Asia*** in 1981.

EMF
With Tom Jones* on **Unbelievable.**

EMMET, JOSEPH K. (1841–1891)
b. St. Louis, MO. Vaudeville actor/songwriter, wrote "Sweet Violets" 1892.

EMMETT, DANIEL D. (1815–1904)
b. Mount Vernon, Ohio. Vaudeville actor/songwriter, wrote "I Wish I Was In Dixie" 1843, "Blue Tail Fly, or Jim Crack Corn" 1846. Was a sensation in the southern states when he sang "Dixie" 1859.

EMOTIONS, THE
Albums *Chronicle Greatest Hits, Rejoice, So I Can Love You, Sunshine.*

ENGLISH, THOMAS DUNN (1819–1902)
b. near Philadelphia, PA. Lyricist, with composer Nelson Kneass* wrote "Ben Bolt."

ENO, BRIAN (1948–   )
British musician/singer albums *Apollo, Music for Airports, Thursday Afternoon*, etc., with John Cole "Wrong Way Up." *Void Dweller* 1992.

ENVIRONMENTS
Albums *Psychologically, Disc 1, 2, 3, Ultimate S, Slow Oceans,* etc.

EN VOGUE
California singers Dawn Robinson, Cindy Herron, Terry Ellis, & Maxine Jones. 1990 debut platinum album *Born to Sing,*

platinum single "Hold On" 1990, hit "My Lovin," "You're Never Gonna Get It," album *Funky Divas* won 1993 American Music award, with Roger Clinton (b. 1956, brother of president) at MTV Inaugural Ball. American Music Soul/R&B Group Award 1994.

ENYA (1962–)
Video *Ornoco Flow* 1992, album *Shepherd Moons* (Grammy winner) 1993.

EPMD
(Erick & Parrish Making Dollars). Long Island rappers Erick Sermon (b. 1969) & Parrish Smith (b. 1968), albums *Strictly Business, Unfinished Business, Business as Usual, Business Never Personal* 1992.

EPPEL, JOHN VALENTINE (1871–1931)
b. Iowa City, IA. Composer/leader, with Frederick K. Logan* wrote "The Missouri Waltz" 1914.

ERASURE
British pop-singers Andy Bell & Vince Clark, albums *Chorus, Crackers International*, video *Erasure—live Wild.*

ERICKSON, ERIC
Singer/songwriter 1966 debut *The Psychedelic Sounds of the 13th Floor Elevators, Where the Pyramid Meets the Eye* 1990.

ERWIN, GEORGE "PEE WEE" (1913–1981)
b. 5/30 Falls City, Nebraska. Trumpeter/leader played in bands of Benny Goodman* & Tommy Dorsey* in 1930s, led own bands 1940s/70s, with Tom Artin's band at Eddie Condon's* in NY City in early 80s. Died 6/20 Teaneck, NJ.

ESTEFAN, GLORIA (1958–)
b. 9/1 Havana, Cuba. Gloria Estefan & **Miami Sound Machine*** platinum album *Cut Both Ways* & platinum video 1989, platinum video *Evolution* 1990. Video *Homecoming Concert.* Broke her back in a 1990 bus accident & now has two 8-inch rods fused to her spine. With husband Emilio bought the

Cardoza Hotel in Miami 1992. Appointed by President Clinton as Public Delegate to the United Nations 1993. Latin Pop Album Grammy for *Mi Tierra* 1994.

ETHERIDGE, MELISSA (1961–   )
Folk/jazz/rock/R&B guitarist/pianist/singer, albums *Melissa Etheridge* 1988, *Brave and Crazy* 1989, with bassist Kevin McCormick on album *Never Enough* (1993 Grammy winner).

ETTING, RUTH (1897–1978)
b. 11/23 David City, Nebr. Torch singer, sang "Shakin' the Blues Away" in Ziegfeld Follies 1927, "Shine On, Harvest Moon" in Follies 1930. Died 9/24 Colorado Springs, Colorado.

EUBANKS, KEVIN
Albums *Face to Face, Opening Night, Promise of Tomorrow.* Guitarist on the *Tonight Show.*

EUGENIUS
Glasgow, Scotland group with lead singer Eugene Kelly, guitarist Garden Keen, bassist Raymond Boyle, and drummer Roy Lawrence, album *Oomalama* 1993.

EUROPEAN RHYTHM MACHINE
Jazz band led by saxist Phil Woods* in 1970s, later his quintet included bassist Steve Gilmore, drummer Bill Goodwin, guitarist Larry Leahy, & pianist Mike Mellillo, album *Song for Sisyphus.*

EURYTHMICS, THE
British group with singer Annie Lennox,* guitarist David Stewart, hit singles "Would I Lie to You?" 1985, "Sweet Dreams are Made of This." Albums *Be Yourself Tonight, Revenge, Savage, Touch,* etc., videos *Live, Greatest Hits Home Video, Sweet Dreams, We Two are One Too.* Lennox left for a solo career.

EVANGELINE
Bluegrass/country guitarist/singers with Rhonda Lohmeyer, Beth McKee, Kathleen Stieffel, Sharon Leger, & Nancy Buchan. Album *Evangeline.*

EVANS, BILL (1929–1980)
b. 8/16 Plainfield, NJ. Pianist/composer, with Herbie Fields, Miles Davis,* & others in 1950s, won *down beat* New Star award 1958, won Grammys in 1958 & 1970. Albums *Compact Jazz*, etc.

EVANS, GEORGE (1870–1915)
b. Wales. Minstrel/songwriter, brought to US in 1877. With lyricist Ren Shields* "In the Good Old Summertime" 1902.

EVANS, GIL (1912–1988)
b. Ian Ernest Gilmore Green in Toronto, Ontario. Pianist/composer, led own band in Stockton, CA 1933/38, with Claude Thornhill* in 40s, with Miles Davis* 50s/60s, toured Japan 1972. *down beat* Arranger of the Year 1980. *Gil Evans & The Monday Night Orchestra, Bud and Bird* (1988 Grammy for Big Band Jazz), video *Gil Evans & His Orchestra*. Died 3/20 Cuernavaca, Mexico.

EVANS, RAYMOND B. "RAY" (1915–   )
b. Salamanca, NY. Lyricist, with composer Jay Livingston* their Oscar-winning songs, "Buttons and Bows" 1948, "Mona Lisa" 1950, "Whatever Will Be Will Be" 1956.

EVERLY BROTHERS
Singers Don (b. 1937) & Phil (b. 1939) both born in Brownie, KY. Hits "Bye, Bye Love" 1957, "Wake Up Little Susie," toured with the **Mamas & Papas.*** Albums *Reunion Concert, The Very Best*, etc., videos *Everly Brothers, Reunion Concert*. Continued touring in the 1990s.

EVERYTHING BUT THE GIRL
Albums *Idle Wild, Everything But the Girl, Language of Life, Love not Money*, etc.

EWING, SKIP
Singer/songwriter with Max T. Barnes wrote songs for Reba McEntire,* Hank Williams, Jr.,* & others, albums *Naturally, The Coast of Colorado, The Will to Love*, song "Love Me" was a hit for Collin Raye.*

EX
Dutch folk/stomp group two disc *Joggers and Smoggers* 1992.

EXILE
Country music group with Buzz Cornelison, Steven Goetzman, Mark Gray, Marion Hargis, Sonny Lemaire, J. P. Pennington, Jimmy Stokley, Les Taylor. Hit "Kiss You All Over" 1978. Albums *Best of Exile, Justice, Keeping it Country, Still Standing,* etc.

EXPERIENCE
Jazz group formed 1955 by J.R. Mitchell & Bayard Lancaster, active 1950s/70s. Erroll Parker's *Experience* featured Lancaster & Michael Carvin in New York City 1981.

EXPLOITED
British punk/rock group video *U.K./D.K.* 1984.

EXPLOSION
Jazz group led by Louis Bellson* in San Jose, CA in 1980s.

EXPOSÉ
Miami female trio, album *Exposure* 1992, video *Exposure.*

EXTREME
Funky rock band with singer Gary Cherone, guitarist Nuno Bettencourt, bassist Pat Badger, & drummer Paul Geary. Album *Extreme II: Pornograffitti* 1990, hit song on album *More Than Words* 1991, CD *Extreme III: Sides to Every Story* 1992 sold half million copies, video *Photograffitti,* group toured US 1992/93.

F

FAB 5 FREDDY (1960–)
b. Frederick Brathwaite, composer/director, *Wild Style* 1980s, host on *YO: MTV Raps*.

FABIAN (1943–)
Fabian Forte b. 2/6 Philadelphia, PA. Hit record "Turn Me Loose" 1958, "Tiger" 1959, sang "Hound Dog Man" in the film of same name.

FABULOUS THUNDERBIRDS
Guitarist Jimmy Vaughn,* singer Kim Watson, bassist Preston Hubbard, drummer Fran Christina. Albums *Butt Rockin': The Fabulous Thunderbirds, Hot Number, Powerful Stuff, The Essential, What's the Word,* at New Orleans Jazz Festival, April/May 1993.

FAD, J.J.
Pop/rap trio, album *Not Just a Fool*.

FADDIS, JON
Jazz trumpeter, albums *Hornucopia, Into the Faddisphere, Legacy*.

FAGAN, DONALD (1948–)
b. Passaic, NJ. Singer formerly with **Steely Dan,*** albums *New Frontier, The Nightly* 1982, *Kamakiriad* 1993.

FAGERQUIST, DONALD A. "DON" (1927–1974)
b. Worcester, MA. Jazz trumpeter with Gene Krupa* in late 1940s, had own combo with singer Anita O'Day,* later with Artie Shaw,* Woody Herman,* & others.

FAHEY, JOHN
Guitarist, albums *Christmas Guitar, God, Time & Casualty, I Remember Blind Joe Death, The Yellow Princess,* etc.

FAIN, SAMMY (1902–1989)
b. 6/17 New York, NY. Singer/songwriter, wrote music for "Wed-

ding Bells are Breaking up that Old Gang of Mine," "I'll be
Seeing You" 1938, "Love is a Many Splendored Thing" 1955,
"Dear Hearts and Gentle People" (those were the words written
on a slip of paper by Stephen Foster* when George Cooper*
found him bleeding in 1864). Died 12/6 Los Angeles, CA.

FAIRFIELD FOUR
Gospel singers, album *Standing in the Safety Zone* 1992.

FAIRPORT CONVENTION
British group, albums *Expletive Delighted, Full House, House
Full, Unhalf Bricking, What We Did on our Holiday,* etc.

FAITH NO MORE
Heavy metal band from San Francisco with singer Mike Patton,
guitarists Jim Martin & Billy Gould, keyboardist Roddy
Bottum, hit single "Epic" 1990, albums *Introduce Yourself,
The Real Thing, Angel Dust,* 1992, rock track "Midlife Cri-
ses," video *Live at the Brinton Academy,* toured US 1993.

FAITH, PERCY (1908–1976)
b. 4/7 Toronto, Ontario. Conductor/composer on Canadian radio
in 1930s, conducted *Carnation Contented Hour* in NY City
40s, musical director for *Coca Cola* show after 1947, wrote
"My Heart Cries Out for You," won 1960 Grammy for
"Theme for a Summer Place," albums *All Time Greatest Hits,
Themes for Young Lovers.*

FAITHFULL, MARIANNE
Albums *A Child's Adventure, Blazing Away, Broken English,
Strange Weather,* video *Blazing Away.*

FARGO, DONNA (1949–)
b. 11/10 Mt. Airy, NC. Country singer/songwriter, hits "Happiest
Girl in the USA," "Funny Face."

FARINA, DAVE (1936–)
b. Brooklyn, NY City. Singer/songwriter formed **Ragtime Jug
Stompers,*** his "Cocaine Blues" on *Troubadours of the Folk
Era, Vols. 1–3* 1992.

FARINA, RICHARD (1936–1966)
Singer/songwriter, team of Richard & Mimi Baez Farina (married folk singer Carolyn Hester, later divorced; married Mimi, sister of Joan Baez), wrote "Pack Up Your Sorrows" recorded by Johnny Cash. Farina was killed in a motorcycle accident.

FARM, THE
Hit "Love See No Color" 1992.

FARMER, ARTHUR S. "ART" (1928–)
b. Council Bluffs, IA. Trumpeter, played in bands of Horace Henderson, Benny Carter,* & others in 1940s, with Lionel Hampton,* Gerry Mulligan* in 50s, led own jazz quartet in 60s. Lived in Vienna, Austria but toured. Albums *Blame It On My Youth, Farmer's Market, Maiden Voyage,* etc.

FARRELL, EILEEN (1920–)
b. 2/13 Willimantic, CT. Soprano/opera/pop singer, albums *I Gotta Right to Sing, Sings Rodgers and Hart, Sings Torch Songs, This Time It's Love,* hit "Lush Life" from *It's Over* 1992, *Here* 1993.

FARRELL, PERRY
Singer with **Jane's Addiction,*** organized new band **Porno for Pyros,*** on Lollapalooza tour 1992.

FASTAWAY
Albums *All Fixed Up, Bad Bad Girls, On Target, Waiting for the Roar.*

FASTER PUSSYCAT
Los Angeles hard rock band, albums *Faster Pussycat, Wake Me Up When It's Over, Whipped* 1992.

FAT TUESDAY'S COMBOS
Jazz trio led by bassist Stan Getz* in NY City in early 1980s.

FATHER MC
Rap singer has recorded with Mary J. Blige.* Album *Father's Day.*

FATTBURGER
Albums *Good News, One of a Kind, Time Will Tell.*

FEARIS, JOHN S. (1867–1932)
b. Richland, Iowa. Composer, with lyricist Laura Smith wrote "Little Sir Echo."

FEINSTEIN, MICHAEL
Singer, albums *Isn't it Romantic, Live at the Algonquin, Pure Gershwin, Sings Irving Berlin, Pure Imagination* 1992, *Sings the Jule Styne Songbook* 1992.

FELDMAN, MORTON (1926–1987)
b. New York, NY. Musician/composer, wrote pieces for piano, string instruments, flute, trumpet, violin, cello, etc. Albums *Crippled Symmetry, Tragic Memories, Viola in My Life,* etc.

FELICIANO, JOSE (1945–)
b. 9/10 Larez, Puerto Rico. Blind guitarist/singer/songwriter, hit "Light My Fire," wrote theme for TV show *Chico and the Man,* album *All Time Greatest Hits.*

FENDER, FREDDY (1937–)
b. 6/4 San Benito, TX. Singer/songwriter, "Before the Next Teardrop Falls" (Grammy 1977 winner).

FENSTED, L.A. (1870–1941)
b. Trondheim, Norway. Composer/bandmaster, with lyricist Lincoln Colcord* wrote the "Maine Stein Song" 1901 popularized by Rudy Vallee.*

FERGUSON, MAYNARD (1928–)
b. 5/4 Verdun, Quebec, Canada. Trumpeter plays many instruments, led own band in Canada 1943/47, came to NY City 1948, with Charlie Barnet, Stan Kenton* 1950/53, led own bands & combos from 50s, toured England 1967/72, at Atlantic City, NJ Jazz Festival, July 1981. Albums *Chameleon, Conquistador,* etc., at International Association of Jazz Educators in San Antonio, TX in January 1993.

FERRANTE AND TEICHER
Arthur Ferrante (b. 1921) & Louis Teicher, duo-pianists/ composers, albums *Greatest Love Songs of All, As Time Goes By, 30th Anniversary on Stage.*

FERRELL, RACHELLE (1961–)
Raised near Philadelphia, PA. R&B singer/pianist/composer, jazz albums *First Instrument, Too Late* 1992, sang her compositions "Welcome to My Love," "I'm Special," "I Know You can Love Me" on tour with guitarist Kevin Eubanks* album *Rachelle Ferrell.*

FERRY, BRYAN (1945–)
British singer, albums *Bete Noir* 1988, *Boys and Girls, In Your Mind,* on soundtrack *Honeymoon in Vegas* 1992, *Horoscope, Taxi* 1993.

FIEDLER, ARTHUR (1894–1979)
b. 12/17 Boston, MA. Conductor with **Cecilia Society** 1926/49, **Boston Pops** 1930/79. Albums *Popular Favorites, An American Salute, Boston Pops Overtures, White Christmas/Boston Pops.* Died 7/10 Brookline, MA.

FIELDS, DOROTHY (1905–1974)
b. 7/15 Allenhurst, NJ. Lyricist, daughter of Lew Fields of the team of Weber & Fields. Wrote words for "I Can't Give You Anything but Love, Baby" 1928, "Lovely to Look At" 1935, "The Way You Look Tonight" (Tony winner 1936). Died 3/28 NY.

FIELDS, GRACIE (1898–1979)
b. Grace Stansfield 1/9 Rochdale, England. Singer/comedienne, sang in night clubs in London and New York City, hits "Now is the Hour" 1945, "Come Back to Sorrento." Died 9/27 Capri, Italy.

FIELDS, SHEP (1910–1981)
b. 9/12 Brooklyn, NY City. Saxist, led own bands in New York City, became famous by blowing through a straw into a glass of water thus making bubbling sounds, known for his "Rippling Rhythm." Died 2/23 Los Angeles, CA.

FIFTH DIMENSION
Pop/soul/rock group with singer Billy Davis, Jr. (of St. Louis, MO.) and his wife Marilyn McCoo* (of Jersey City, NJ), Daniel Beard, Florence LaRue Gordon, Lamonte McLemore, Ronald Townson, won 1967 Grammy for "Up, Up and Away," "Aquarius" 1969, "Wedding Bells Blues" 1969, group sang in Las Vegas in 1970s. Albums *The Glory Days, Greatest Hits on Earth.*

FINE ARTS QUARTET
Irving Ilmer, Abram Loft, George Sorkin, & Leonard Sorkin.

FINE YOUNG CANNIBALS
British trio, *The Raw & the Cooked* 1989 sold over 2 million albums, *Fine Young Cannibals,* video *Live at the Paramount.*

FINN, WILLIAM (1952–)
Composer/lyricist, wrote Broadway show *Falsettos* about his friends dying of AIDS, won two Tony awards 1992.

FIORITO, TED (1900–1971)
b. Newark, NJ. Pianist/songwriter, with lyricists Sam Lewis* & Joe Young* wrote "Laugh, Clown, Laugh." Fiorito died of a heart attack.

FIREFALL
Country/pop group formed 1974 with Mark Andes, Jock Bartley, Larry Burnett, Rick Roberts, hit "You are the Woman" 1976, albums *Firefall, Best of Firefall.*

FIREHOSE
Albums *Flyin' the Flannel, Ragin' Full on.*

FIREHOUSE
Group with lead singer C.J. Snare, guitarist Bill Leverty, bassist/guitarist Ray Richardson, & drummer Michael Foster, album *Firehouse,* hit singles "Don't Treat Me Bad," "Love of a Lifetime" 1990, "When I Look Into Your Eyes" 1992, album *Hold Your Fire* 1992.

FIRESIGN THEATRE
Albums *Dear Friends, Don't Crush the Dwarf, How Can You be in Two Places at Once, I Think We're all Bozos on this Bus.*

FISCHER, CLARE
Albums *Crazy Bird, Free Fall, Lembrancas,* etc.

FISCHER, LISA
R&B singer, won 1991 Grammy for "How Can I Ease the Pain?".

FISCHER, WILLIAM G. (1835–1912)
b. Baltimore, MD. Composer, with lyricist Katherine Hankey wrote "I Love to Tell the Story" 1869.

FISHBONE
Rock group with bassist Norwood Fisher, albums *Realty of My Surroundings, Fishbone, Truth & Soul.*

FISHER, EDWIN J. "EDDIE" (1928–   )
b. 8/10 Philadelphia, PA. Singer, had million selling record "Oh, My Papa," Hit Song "Here Comes Santa Claus," albums *Very Best of Eddie Fisher, Christmas with Eddie Fisher,* etc. Married Debbie Reynolds,* Elizabeth Taylor, Connie Stevens.*

FISHER, FRED (1875–1942)
b. Cologne, Germany, came to US. With lyricist Alfred Bryan* "Peg o' My Heart" 1913, "Chicago." Died in New York City.

FITCH, CLYDE (1865–1909)
b. Schenectady, NY. Lyricist, wrote the words for "Love Makes the World Go Round" 1896.

FITZGERALD, ELLA (1918–   )
b. 4/25 Newport News, VA. Singer, joined Chick Webb* 1934, led bands after Webb died in 1939. Has won eight Grammy awards. At Atlantic City, NJ Jazz Festival 1981, sang at the Infiniti Jazz at the Hollywood Bowl, CA in July 1992.

FIVE BLIND BOYS OF ALABAMA, THE
Includes Baritone Clarence Fountain and Booker T. Jones, quintet was founded in the early forties, albums *My Desire/There's a God Somewhere, Soon I'll be Done, Deep River,* etc.

FIVE-EIGHT
Metallic rock guitar/bass/drum group from Athens, GA, album *I Learned Shut Up* 1993.

FIVE SATINS, THE
Hit single "In the Still of the Night."

FIXX, THE
British new wave group with Charlie Barrett, Cy Curnin, Rupert Greenall, Jamie West-Oram, albums *Shattered Room* 1982, *Reach the Beach* 1983, *Calm Animals,* etc., video *Live in the USA.*

FLACK, ROBERTA (1940–   )
b. 2/10 Black Mountain, NC. Singer, performance at 1971 Newport, RI Jazz Festival was a sensation with her hit "Reverend Lee," album *First Take,* won 1972 Grammy for "The First Time I Ever Saw Your Face" & in 1973 for "Killing Me Softly with His Song," at JVC Jazz Festival in Newport, RI in August 1992. Married bassist Steve Novosel,* later divorced.

FLAMINGOS, THE
Albums *The Flamingos, Best of the Flamingos.*

FLANAGAN, TOMMY (1932–   )
Pianist, albums *Alone Too Long, Montreaux '77, Thelonica,* etc., with bassist George Mraz & drummer Kenny Washington on *Jazz Poet* 1992.

FLATT & SCRUGGS
Country singers from TN, guitarist/singer/songwriter Lester R. Flatt (1914–1979) joined Grand Ole Opry, Nashville 1944 teamed with Earl Scruggs, hits "Cabin in the Sky" 1959, "Go

Home'' 1916, ''The Ballad of Jed Clampett'' (1962 theme song for the *Beverly Hillbillies*). Albums *The World of Flatt & Scruggs, Mercury Sessions Vols. 1 & 2, Greatest Hits.*

FLECK, BELA
Singer leader of the **Fleckstones,** hit ''Magic Fingers'' from album *UFO,* albums *Daybreak, Drive, Natural Bridge,* hit ''UFO Tofu'' 1993 Grammy winner.

FLEETWOOD MAC
Rock group with Lindsey Buckingham,* drummer/singer Mick Fleetwood, Christine* & John McVie, Stephanie ''Stevie'' Nicks,* Bob Welch, Robert Weston. Second best selling album *Rumors* 1977. Buckingham left group 1992 & replaced by Rick Vincent. Hit ''Don't Stop'' was theme song of Democratic National Convention in NY City 1992, group played at an inaugural ball for President Clinton in 1993. Nicks had solo album *Bella Donna* 1981.

FLEXIBLE FLYERS
Jazz band led by Roswell Rudd in Boston 1980s.

FLIM AND THE BB'S
Albums *Big Notes, Further Adventures, New Pants.*

FLOCK OF SEA GULLS
British group with Frank Maudsley, Paul Reynolds, Ali and Mike Score, hit single ''I Ran'' won Grammy 1983, albums *A Flock of Sea Gulls, Best of Flock of Sea Gulls, Magic.*

FLOREN, MYRON (1919–)
b. 11/5 Webster, SD. Accordianist on *Lawrence Welk Show,* * gospel singer, hit ''You'll Never Walk Alone,'' albums *22 of the Greatest Hits, Polkas, Three Accordian Polkas,* etc.

FLORES, ROSIE
Los Angeles country/rock singer/songwriter/guitarist, formerly led **Screaming Sirens*** on the West Coast in late 70s, album *After the Farm* 1992.

FLORESCOPE
Nine-member jazz group led by Chuck Flores at New York Club in San Fernando Valley, CA in 1980s.

FLORIDA BOYS
Southern gospel singers, album *Live* 1992.

FLOTSAM AND JETSAM
Albums *No Place for Disgrace, When the Storm Comes Down.*

FLYING BURRITO BROTHERS, THE
Country music group with Chris Eldridge, Chris Hillman, "Sneaky Pete" Kleinow, Graham Parsons, hit album *Gilded Pace of Sin* 1969. Albums *Further Along, The Flying Burrito Brothers.* Mandolin player Hillman had solo "Slippin' Away."

FOGELBERG, DANIEL G. "DAN" (1951–)
b. 8/13 Peoria, IL. Singer/songwriter, hits "Part of the Plan" 1975, "Leader of the Band" 1982, "Missing You," albums *Captured Angel, Exiles, Home Free, Windows & Walls,* etc.

FOGERTY, JOHN
Albums *Centerfield, Eye of the Zombie, The Blue Ridge Rangers.*

FOGHAT
British group formed 1971 with Roger Earl, David Peverey, Rod Price, Anthony Stevens, hit single "Slow Ride" 1976, albums *Energized, Foghat, Night Shift, Rock N Roll Outlaws,* etc.

FOOTE, ARTHUR W. (1853–1937)
b. Salem, MA. Composer, with lyricist Harriet Beecher Stowe "Still, Still with Thee."

FORD, BENJAMIN F. "WHITEY" (1901–1986)
b. DeSota, MO. Country banjoist/mandolin player known as the "Duke of Paducah," entertained soldiers in World War I, was a member of the Grand Ole Opry in Nashville, TN for 16 years.

FORD, ERNEST J. "TENNESSEE ERNIE" (1919–1991)

b. 2/13 Bristol, TN. Country singer, had own show on CBS & ABC radio 1950/55 then NBC-TV 1955/61, top hits "Mule Train" 1949 & "Sixteen Tons" 1955. Albums *All Time Greatest Hymns, Red, White and Blue.* Died 10/1 Washington, D.C.

FORD, LENA GUILBERT (died 1918)

b. Elmira, NY. With composer Ivor Novello wrote "Keep the Home Fires Burning" 1915. Killed in a German Zeppelin raid on London, England.

FORD, LITA

Albums *Dancin' on the Edge, Dangerous Curves, Out for Blood,* video *A Midnight Snack,* hit "Shot of Poison" 1992.

FORD, ROBBEN

Blues album *Robben Ford & the Blue Line* Grammy winner 1993.

FOREIGNER

British/American rock band sold over 30 million albums & had nine top ten hits including "Feels Like the First Time" & "Double Vision" in 1970s/80s. Toured US 1985, lead singer Lou Gramm left and was replaced by Johnny Edwards. Albums *Agent Provocateur, Double Vision, The Very Best & Beyond* 1992, toured US 1992.

FORESTER SISTERS

Albums *A Christmas Card, Talkin' About Men, You Again,* etc.

FORREST, HELEN (1918–)

b. 4/12 Atlantic City, NJ. Singer with big bands of Artie Shaw,* Benny Goodman* 1930s/40s, in 1945 film *You Came Along* singing "Out of Nowhere."

FORRO, BRAZIL

Accordianist, CD *Music for the Maids and Taxi Drivers* 1992.

FOSTER, RODNEY
Country singer/songwriter formerly duo of Foster & Lloyd, album *Del Rio, TX 1959* (reissued 1992).

FOSTER, STEPHEN C. (1826–1864)
b. Lawrenceville, PA. Songwriter, wrote "Oh Susanna" 1848, "Camptown Races" 1850, "Old Folks at Home" 1852, "My Old Kentucky Home" 1853, "Jeannie with the Light Brown Hair" 1854, "Old Black Joe" 1860, "Beautiful Dreamer" 1863. He cut himself with a razor while shaving and died in NY City. *See also* GEORGE COOPER.*

FOUNTAIN, PETER D., JR. "PETE" (1930–)
b. 7/3 New Orleans, La. Clarinetist/saxist with **New Orleans Junior Dixieland Jazz Band** 1948/49, led own band and with Lawrence Welk* 1950s/60s, continued playing 70s/90s. Albums *Mr. New Orleans, The Best of Pete Fountain, The Blues,* etc.

4HIM
Gospel singers nominated for a Gospel Music award 1993.

FOURPLAY
Pianist Bob James,* guitarist Lee Riteman, bassist Nathan East, & drummer Harvey Mason with guitarist Jean Paul Bourelly* on hit album *Fourplay* 1992.

FOUR SEASONS, THE
Pop group started 1956 with Tommy DeVito, Bob Gaudio, Nick Massi (Nicholas Macioci), & singer Frankie Valli,* hits "Sherry," "Big Girls Don't Cry," "Rag Doll," "My Eyes Adored You."

FOUR TOPS
Singer Abdul Fakir, Renaldo Benson, Lawrence Payton, Levi Stubbs, hits "Baby I Need Your Loving" 1964, "Reach Out I'll Be There" 1966, "I Can't Help Myself," albums *Anthology, Best of the Four Tops, Live,* video *Live at the Park West.*

FOX, CHARLES (1940–)
b. 10/30 New York, NY. Composer, wrote film scores for *Foul Play, Nine to Five,* won Emmy for *Love American Style* 1970 & 1973.

FRAMPTON, PETER (1950–)
b. 4/22 Beckenham, England. Rock singer/songwriter with **Humble Pie Band*** 1972/75, his album *Frampton Comes Alive* (1976) sold over 12 million copies, CD *Shine on-a Collection* 1992. *Peter Frampton* 1994.

FRANCIS, CONNIE (1938–)
b. Concetta Maria Fransconero 12/12 Newark, NJ. Singer on Arthur Godfrey's *Talent Scouts* show at age 12, hit "Who's Sorry Now?" on *Ed Sullivan Show* 1958, sang "Where the Boys Are" in the film of same name 1963, by 1970s had eight gold records. Albums *Christmas in My Heart, The Very Best of Connie Francis.*

FRANKLIN, ARETHA (1942–)
b. 3/25 Memphis, TN. Soul singer, won 1971 Grammy for "Don't Play that Song," 1972 Grammy (fifth straight win). Hits "Freeway of Love" & "Respect" 1985, won 1988 Grammy for "One Lord, One Faith, One Baptism," album *What You See is What You Sweat* 1991. "Someday We'll All be Free" (1992), on *Malcolm X* soundtrack, sang the national anthem at Democratic Convention in NY City 1992, video *The Queen of Soul,* sang at Lincoln Memorial in Washington, D.C. 1993. Married Glynn Turman.

FRANKLIN, REV. C.L.
With Aretha Franklin albums *Never Grow Old, Pressing On, The 23rd Psalm, Two Fishes & Five Loaves of Bread, The Prodigal Son.*

FRANKS, MICHAEL
Singer with guitarist Larry Carlton & pianist Joe Sample,* albums *Burchfield Nines, The Camera Never Lies, One Bad Habit, Skin Dive, Tiger in the Rain, Blue Pacific* 1992.

FRAZIER, DALLAS JUNE (1939–)
b. 10/27 Spiro, OK. Singer/songwriter, with *Cliff Stone's Hometown Jamboree* TV show, hit single "Alley Oop" 1957. Wrote "Georgia," "Elvira."

FREEMAN, LAWRENCE "BUD" (1906–)
b. 4/13 Chicago, IL. Tenor saxist with Tommy Dorsey,* Benny Goodman* in 1930s, mostly in NY City in 60s/70s, with **World's Greatest Jazz Band*** 1969/71. CD *Something to Remember You.*

FRENCH QUARTER COMBOS
Jazz quartet with pianist Dorothy Donegan, saxist Charles Davis, bassist Jerome Hunter, & drummer Ray Mosca in New York City in early 1980s.

FREY, GLENN (1948–)
b. 11/6 Detroit, MI. Guitarist/singer, albums *No Fun Aloud, Soul Searching, The Allnighter.*

FREY, MARVIN (1918–1992)
Of Tarrytown, NY. Minister/composer who wrote over 2,000 gospel songs, hit international single "Kum Ba Yah."

FRICKIE, JANIE (1950–)
b. 12/18 Whitney, IN. Singer/musician, hit single "Down to My Last Broken Heart" 1980, Country Music Association Female Vocalist of Year 1982/83, inducted into Country Music Hall of Fame 1992.

FRIED, GERALD (1928–)
b. 2/13 New York, NY. Composer, wrote score for TV series *Roots* (1977 Emmy winner).

FRIEDMAN, LEO (1869–1927)
b. Elgin, IL. Composer, with lyricist Beth Slater Whitson* wrote "Let Me Call You Sweetheart" 1910.

FRIEND, CLIFF (1893–1974)
b. Cincinnati, Ohio. Songwriter, with Dave Franklin wrote "The Merry-go-round Broke Down" (Warner Brothers "Looney Tunes" cartoon theme) 1937, with Charles Tobias* wrote "Don't Sweetheart Me" 1944 and other songs. Died in Las Vegas, NV.

FRIJID PINK
Thomas Beaudry, Thomas Harris, Richard Stevers, Bary Thompson, Jon Wearing, Craig Webb, & Lawrence Zelanka.

FRIML, RUDOLPH (1879–1972)
b. Prague, Czechoslovakia. Composer, came to US in 1906. Wrote scores for *The Firefly* 1912, *Rose Marie* 1924, *The Vagabond King* 1925, wrote "The Donkey Serenade" introduced by Allan Jones,* with lyricist Catherine Cushing* "Indian Love Call," "L'Amour, Toujours, L'Amour," album *Songs of Frimil.* Died in Hollywood, CA.

FRIPP, ROBERT
Composer/guitarist/leader of **King Crimson*** 1969, debut "In the Court of the Crimson King," with musicians David Sylvian & Trey Gunn, toured Japan. Albums *Evening Star, Show of Hands,* performed in a Guitar Masters Series in NY City 1992.

FRISELL, BILL (1952–   )
Guitarist, albums *Before We were Born, Is That You? Lookout for Hope, Where in the World?* etc.

FRIZZELL, DAVID (1941–   )
b. 9/26 Texas, singer, brother of Lefty Frizzell,* album *The Family's Fine, But This One's All Mine* 1981.

FRIZZELL, WILLIAM O. "LEFTY" (1928–1975)
b. 3/21 Corsicana, TX. Guitarist/singer/songwriter, hits "Always Late," "Don't Stay Away," "Travelin' Blues," "Long Black Veil" 1959, "Saginaw, Michigan" 1964, albums *American Originals, Greatest Hits, Best of Lefty Frizzell.*

FROMAN, JANE (1907–1980)
b. 11/10 St. Louis, MO. Actress/singer, while en route to entertain troops in 1943 she suffered crippling injuries in a plane crash. Inspiration for the film *With a Song in My Heart* 1952. Died 4/22 Columbia, MO.

FUGS, THE
Pop/rock group with John Anderson, Lee Crabtree, Pete Kearney, Tuli Kupferberg, Charles Larkey, Vinny Leary, Bob Mason, Ken Pine, Ed Sanders, Peter Stampfield, Ken Weaver, formed 1965. Known for their anti-Vietnam war songs "Kill for Peace," "The Evil Spirits of the Pentagon."

FULLER, JESS "LONE CAT" (1897–1976)
b. Jonesboro, GA. Guitarist/singer/songwriter, wrote "San Francisco Bay Blues." Died 1/28 Oakland, CA.

FUNICELLO, ANNETTE (1942–   )
b. 10/22 Utica, NY. Actress/singer, sang on Walt Disney's Golden Horseshoe Revue on TV, member of his Mouseketeers 1950s, starred in Beach Party films in 1960s with Frankie Avalon.*

FURAY, RICHIE (1944–   )
b. 5/9 Yellow Springs, Ohio. Guitarist/singer with Stephen Stills* formed **Buffalo Springfield*** 1966, with **Poco*** & **The Souther-Hillman-Furay Band.*** He had three hit singles.

FUTURE KULTURE
Angelique & other dancers on Lollapalooza tour 1992.

G

GABRIEL, ANA
Singer/songwriter, hit "Evidencias" on top of the Latin singles chart, sang at the James L. Knight Center in Miami, FL in 1992.

GABRIEL, PETER (1950–   )
b. 2/13 London, England. Singer/songwriter with **Genesis*** 1969/72, solo career hits "Games without Frontiers," "Shock the Monkey," "Biko," & "Sledgehammer" 1986. With Bruce Springsteen* & others on 1988 Ten Top-grossing concerts list. Won Grammy for "Passion" on *The Last Temptation of Christ* soundtrack 1989, hit album *U.S.* (Grammy winner 1993), *Digging in the Dirt,* videos *POV, Compilation Video. Steam* Short Music Video Grammy 1994.

GAILLARD, BULEE "SLIM" (1906–1991)
b. Detroit, MI. Jazz pianist/composer, wrote "Flat Foot Floogie." Died 2/26/91 in London, England.

GALBRAITH, JOSEPH B. (1919–1983)
b. Pittsburgh, PA. Guitarist with Claude Thornhill* in 1940s, died 1/13 Bennington, VT.

GALE, ERIC (1938–   )
b. 9/20 Memphis, TN. Guitarist/singer, *Ginsing Woman, In a Jazz Tradition, The Eric Gale Band* 1992.

GALLOP, SAMMY (1915–1971)
b. Duluth, MN. Lyricist, wrote "Elmer's Tune." Hanged himself.

GALWAY, JAMES (1939–   )
Superstar Irish flutist, albums *Annie's Song,* with Henry Mancini* on *In the Pink. Galway at the Movies,* toured East Coast of US 1993.

GARBAREK, JAN
Albums *All Those Born with Wings, ECM Works, Legend of 7 Dreams, Wayfarer,* etc.

GARCIA, JERRY (1942–   )
Guitarist with the **Grateful Dead,*** solo albums *Compliments, Jerry Garcia Band, Old and In the Way, Run for the Roses,* etc. In 1992/93 he went on a diet of vegetables and lost 60 pounds. Grateful Dead toured March/April 1993.

GARFUNKEL, ART (1941–   )
b. 11/5 New York, NY. Singer/musician/songwriter, teamed with Paul Simon,* albums *Bridge Over Troubled Waters, The Graduate, Sounds of Silence, Angel Clare, Breakaway, Watermark,* etc. Solo: *Garfunkel, Fate for Breakfast, Scissors Cut.* After they broke up Paul Simon also went solo.

GARLAND, JUDY (1922–1969)
b. Frances Ethel Gumm in Grand Rapids, MI. Singer/actress in *The Wizard of Oz* & other films. Married producer Vincente Minnelli, then Sid Luft. Her daughters Liza Minnelli* & Lorna Luft* are singers. Won 1961 Grammy for *Judy at Carnegie Hall,* sang at London Palladium with daughter Liza in November 1964. Had dozens of albums.

GARLAND, WILLIAM M. "RED" (1923–1984)
b. Dallas, TX. Pianist with Miles Davis* in 1950s, after 1965 mostly in Dallas. Albums *All Morning Long, Dig It With Coltrane,* with Ron Carter on *Crossings, Red Alert,* etc.

GARNER, ERROLL L. (1921–1977)
b. 6/15 Pittsburgh, PA. Jazz pianist/songwriter, played in NY City night clubs in 1940s, toured Europe 1957/58, wrote "Misty" 1959, appeared on Bell Telephone Hour. Albums *Solo Time, Body and Soul, Original Misty, Too Marvelous for Words,* etc. Died 1/2 Los Angeles, CA.

GARRETT, KENNY
Saxist, albums *African Exchange Student, Prisoner of Love,* with pianist Kenny Kirkland & saxist Joe Henderson* on album *Black Hope* 1992.

GARRISON, JAMES E. "JIMMY" (1934–1976)
b. Miami, FL. Bassist with Lennie Tristano,* Philly Joe Jones,* & others in NY City in 1950s, John Coltrane* in 60s, with Alice Coltrane & Elvis Jones in 70s. Died of lung cancer.

GARY PUCKETT & THE UNION GAP
Gary Puckett, Dwight Clement, Kerry Chater, Paul Wheatbread, Martha Withem.

GATLIN, LARRY W. (1948–   )
b. 5/2 Odessa, TX. Lead singer for the **Gatlin Brothers** (with Rudy & Steve Gatlin), country/pop trio. Albums *Greatest Hits, Xmas with the Gatlins,* etc., trio sang at seasonal opening of the Neiman Marcus department store in Dallas in Sept. 1992.

GAUNT, PERCY (1852–1896)
b. Philadelphia, PA. Composer, with lyricist Charles H. Hoyt* wrote "Reuben, Reuben," "The Bowery" 1896.

GAYE, MARVIN (1939–1984)
b. Marvin Pentz 4/2 Washington, D.C. Guitarist/singer, sang in a black club in Detroit 1960s, first gold record *Stubborn Kind of Fellow.* Had several gold & platinum records 1962/83, won two Grammys, hits "Ain't that Peculiar" 1965, "Sexual Healing" 1982, "I Heard it through the Grapevine." Many albums available, video *Greatest Hits Live.* Married Anna sister of Motown mogul Berry Gordy. Died on 4/1 after his father Rev. Marvin Gaye, Sr. shot him during an argument.

GAYE, NONA (1974–   )
Singer, daughter of Marvin Gaye,* lives in Redondo Beach, CA. Debut album *Love for the Future* 1992.

GAYLE, CRYSTAL (1951–   )
b. Brenda Gail Webb 1/9 Wabash, IN. Singer, sister of Loretta Lynn.* "Don't It Make My Brown Eyes Blue" Grammy winner 1978, received Indiana Governor's award 1993. Married Vassilios Gatzimos.

GAYNOR, GLORIA (1949–)
b. 9/7 Newark, NJ. Singer, hits include "Never Can Say Good-bye" 1974, "I Will Survive" 1979, called the "Queen of Disco," CD *Greatest Hits*.

GEIBEL, ADAM (1855–1933)
b. near Frankfurt-am-Main, Germany. Blind composer, came to Philadelphia. Set to music the words "Stand Up, Stand Up for Jesus" written by George Duffield,* With lyricist R.H. Buck wrote "Kentucky Babe" 1896.

GEILS BAND, THE J.
Blues/pop group with Jerome Geils, Stephen Jo Bladd, Magic Dick, Seth Justman, Danny Klein, Peter Wolf, had hit album *Freeze-Frame,* single "Centerfold" 1981. With Duran Duran* albums *MTV Video to Go* & *Live Video* 1984, etc.

GENERATION X
Albums *Kiss Me Deadly, Generation X, Perfect Hits 1975–1981, Valley of the Dolls*.

GENESIS
British pop group with lead singer/drummer Phil Collins,* Tony Banks, Bill Bruford, Peter Gabriel* (left for solo career), Steve Hackett, John Mayhew, Anthony Phillips, Michael Rutherford, John Silver, Daryl Steurmer, Chris Stewart, Chester Thompson, albums *Duke, Foxtrot, Genesis, Invisible Touch,* hit "Hold My Heart" 1992, on We Can't Dance Tour of US 1992. Won Grammy 1993.

GENTRY, BOBBIE (1942–)
b. Roberta Streeter 7/27 Chickasaw County, MS. Singer/songwriter, wrote & recorded "Ode to Billy Joe" 1967 (adapted to film, won three Grammy awards 1976), also had hit "Tuesday's Child," album *Greatest Hits*.

GERARD, RICHARD H. (1876–1948)
b. New York, NY. Songwriter, with composer Henry W. Armstrong wrote "Sweet Adeline" 1903.

GERARDO
Latin singer, hits "Rico Souve," "Dos," "Here Kitty Kitty" 1992, album *Mo Ritmo.*

GERRY & THE PACEMAKERS
British group founded 1959 by Gerry Marsden & managed by Brian Epstein. Albums *Definitive Collection, Gerry & the Pacemakers.*

GERSHWIN, GEORGE (1898–1937)
b. Brooklyn, NY. Composed *Rhapsody in Blue* 1924, *Concerto in F* 1925, *Three Preludes for Piano* 1926, *An American in Paris* 1928. Opera *Porgy & Bess* 1935, "Embraceable You," albums *An American in Paris, Girl Crazy, Porgy & Bess,* etc.

GERSHWIN, IRA (1896–1983)
b. 12/6 New York, NY. Brother of George Gershwin,* wrote lyrics for *Porgy & Bess,* "Lady in the Dark," *An American in Paris.* Died 8/17 Beverly Hills, CA.

GETZ, STANLEY "STAN" (1927–1991)
b. 2/2 Philadelphia, PA. Saxist/leader played with Jack Teagarden,* Jimmy Dorsey,* Benny Goodman,* Woody Herman* in 1940s, with Charlie Byrd* album *Jazz Samba* (started the bossa-nova craze). With Astrud Gilberto* 1964 Grammy for "The Girl from Ipanema" and album *Getz/Gilberto,* with Kenny Barron* album *People Time* at Copenhagen 1991, etc.

GIANT SAND
Pop/punk group from Tucson AZ, album *Center of the Universe* 1993.

GIBB, ANDY (1958–1988)
Singer, hit single "I Just Want to be Your Everything" 1977, by 1979 had sold 15 million records. Died of a heart ailment after ingesting drugs.

GIBBS, TERRI (1954–)
b. 6/15 Augusta, GA. Blind country singer/musician, hit single "Somebody's Knockin' " 1981.

GIBBS, TERRY (1924–)
b. Julius Gubenko in Brooklyn, NY City. Played vibes during 1940s/50s (rated top performer), led own bands, named *down beat* Jazz Player of the Year six times, albums *Flying Home, Sundown Sessions/Dreamband, Vol. 4 Main Stem*, etc.

GIBSON, DEBBIE (1970–)
b. 8/31 New York, NY. Singer/songwriter, on 1988 Top Ten Pop Albums list for *Out of the Blue*, 1988 Female Artist of the Year, platinum video *Live in Concert—The Out of the Blue Tour* 1989, album *Electric Youth* sold over 2 million 1989, video *Live in Concert* 1990. Co-wrote songs on her album *Body Mind Soul* 1993.

GIBSON, DON (1928–)
b. 4/3 Shelby, NC. Guitarist/singer/songwriter, hits "Blue, Blue Sky" 1958, "Sea of Heartbreak" 1961, albums *Country My Way* 1981, *A Legend in His Own Time* 1985, *Best of Don Gibson*.

GILBERT, LOUIS WOLFE (1886–1970)
b. Odessa, Ukraine. Lyricist, brought to USA when one year old, with composer Lewis F. Muir* wrote "Waiting for the Robert E. Lee" 1912, with composer Abel Baer* wrote "Lucky Lindy" 1927.

GILBERTO, ASTRUD (1940–)
b. 3/30 Salvador, Brazil. Singer, wife of guitarist Joao Gilberto later divorced, toured with **Stan Getz* Trio,** with Getz 1964 Grammy for "The Girl from Ipanema" & album *Getz/Gilberto*.

GILL, JOHNNY
Singer, platinum album *Johnny Gill* 1990, *My, My, My,* duet with Shabba Ranks* on "Slow and Sexy" on album *X-tra Naked* 1992. *Provocative* 1993.

GILL, VINCE (1957–)
Country tenor/songwriter, raised in suburbs of Oklahoma City, won 1990 Grammy for "When I Call Your Name," won 1992 Country Music award as Male Vocalist, with Max D. Barnes won

songwriters award for "Look at Us" 1992. Hit single "Our Love Start Slippin' Away," with others on a Country Music Celebration 1993, wrote "I Still Believe in You" with John Barlow Jarvis* Grammy winner 1993. Country Music Entertainer of the Year 1993. Married to country singer Janis Gill.

GILLESPIE, "DIZZY" (1917–)
b. John Birks 10/21 Cheraw, SC. Jazz trumpeter, toured Europe with Teddy Hill 1937, later with Cab Calloway,* Benny Carter,* Charlie Barnet, Earl Hines,* & Duke Ellington.* Formed own band 1945, toured Europe 1956, continued playing 1960s/90s. Dozens of albums, video *Night in Tunisia,* at Infiniti Jazz at Hollywood Bowl in July 1992.

GILLESPIE, HAVEN (1888–1975)
b. Covington, Ky. With composer J. Fred Coots* wrote "Santa Claus is Coming to Town." Died 2/14 Las Vegas, NV.

GILLEY, MICKEY LEROY (1936–)
b. 3/9 Natchez, MS, Singer, hit "Stand By Me" 1980, albums *Biggest Hits, Chasing Rainbows,* etc.

GILMAN, SAMUEL (1790–1858)
b. Gloucester, MA. Lyricist, wrote words for "Fair Harvard" 1836.

GILMORE, CALVIN
Country guitarist/singer opened the first country music theater in Myrtle Beach, SC. Owns & operates Carolina Opry, Southern Country Nights, & Dixie Jubilee. TV show "Room at the Top" broadcast from Branson, MO on Americana Network starting March 1993.

GILMORE, PATRICK S. (1829–1892)
b. Ballyar, Galway, Ireland. Songwriter, wrote the famous Civil War song "When Johnny Comes Marching Home" 1863 (based on an Irish tune). Died in St. Louis, MO.

GIPSY KINGS
1992 Reggae/World Music Album Grammy for *Gipsy Kings Live.*

GISMONTI, EGBERTO
Albums *Danca Das Cabecas, Duss Vozes, Infancia, Sanfona, Sol Do Meio Dia.*

GIUFFRE, JAMES P. "JIMMY" (1921–)
b. 4/26 Dallas, TX. Clarinetist/saxist/composer, in late 1940s with Jimmy Dorsey,* Buddy Rich,* Woody Herman,* toured Europe. Composition *Hex* performed by Orchestra USA 1965, albums *Jimmy Giuffre 3, Liquid Dancers.*

GLASS, PHILIP (1937–)
b. 1/31 Baltimore, MD. Composer, used electrically-amplified wind instruments, wrote "Einstein on the Beach," "Hydrogen Jukebox," "Mapa" (recorded by Brazilian ensemble Uakti), score for *Screens* 1992, opera *The Voyage* at the Metropolitan Opera in NY City. Composed *Low Symphony* based on "Low" by David Bowie* & Brian Eno,* premiered Brooklyn Opera in November 1992.

GLENN, EVANS TYREE (1912–1974)
b. Corsicana, TX. Trombonist with Benny Carter,* Cab Calloway,* Don Redman,* & Duke Ellington,* later formed own quartet in NY City.

GOETZ, E. RAY (1886–1954)
b. Buffalo, NY. Lyricist with Sam Lewis,* Edgar Leslie,* and composer George Meyer* wrote "For Me and My Gal" 1917.

GOFFIN, GERRY (1939–)
Lyricist, wrote "Will You Love Me Tomorrow," "Up on the Roof," "One Fine Day," "The Loco-Motion" with (Carole King*).

GO-GO'S
All female group with Belinda Carlisle* (lead singer since 1978), Charlotte Gaffey, Gina Schock, Kathy Valentine, Jane Wiedlin. Hit album *We Got the Beat* 1982, albums *Talk Show, Vacation,* video *Prime Time.*

GOLD, JULIE
Singer, won 1990 Grammy for "From a Distance."

GOLDSBORO, BOBBY (1941–)
b. 1/18 Mariana, FL. Singer/songwriter, Country Music Association star 1968, hits "Honey," "The Straight Life," album *All Time Greatest Hits.*

GOLDSMITH, JERRY (1930–)
b. 2/10 Los Angeles, CA. Composer of *The Omen* score (1976 Oscar winner).

GOLSON, BENNY (1929–)
b. 1/25 Philadelphia, PA. Tenor saxist/composer, with Bull Moose Jackson, Tadd Dameron,* Lionel Hampton,* Dizzy Gillespie* in 1950s, with Art Farmer* formed **Jazzet** 1959/63, spent 60s composing music. Albums *California Message, In Paris, Time Speaks, The Other Side of Benny Golson.*

GONSALVES, PAUL (1920–1974)
b. Boston, MA. Tenor saxist with Count Basie* & Dizzy Gillespie* in 1940s, with Duke Ellington* after 1950, with Roy Eldridge* on album *Mexican Bandit Meets Pitts.*

GOODMAN, BENJAMIN D. "BENNY" (1909–1986)
b. 5/30 Chicago, IL. Clarinetist/leader with Ben Pollock 1925, formed own band 1934, gave sensational performance at Carnegie Hall Jazz Concert in NY City 1938. Led small groups 1940s/80s, entertained King Hussein of Jordan at State Department dinner in Washington, D.C. in December 1981. Died 6/13 New York, NY.

GOODMAN, STEVEN B. "STEVE" (1948–1984)
b. 7/25 Chicago, IL. Songwriter, wrote "City of New Orleans" a 1972 hit for Arlo Guthrie.*

GOODWIN, J. CHEEVER (1856–1912)
b. Boston, MA. Lyricist, with composer Woolson Morse wrote "Love Will Find a Way" 1890.

GORDON, DEXTER (1923–1990)
b. Los Angeles, CA. Tenor saxist/composer, with Lionel Hampton,* Louis Armstrong,* & Billy Eckstine* in 1940s. Played in NY City in 50s, moved to Copenhagen, Denmark 1962, back in NY City in 70s. Has dozens of albums. Died 4/25 Philadelphia.

GORDON, IRVING (1915–   )
Composer, won 1992 Grammy for "Unforgettable" (written 40 years ago) revived by Natalie Cole.*

GORDON, JIM
Singer/songwriter with Eric Clapton* wrote "Layla," (Grammy winner 1993).

GORDON, MACK (1904–1959)
b. Warsaw, Poland. Came to NY, lyricist, with composer Harry Revel* wrote "Did You Ever See a Dream Walking?" with composer Harry Warren* wrote "Chattanooga Choo Choo," "Springtime in the Rockies" 1942. "You'll Never Know" (Oscar winner 1943).

GORME, EYDIE (1932–   )
b. 8/16 New York, NY. Singer, married Steve Lawrence. Steve & Eydie sang in night clubs in Miami, Los Angeles, Las Vegas, New York, *Best of Eydie Gorme,* etc.

GOSDIN, VERN
b. Woodland, AL. Albums *10 Years of Greatest Hits, Alone, Chiseled in Stone, Out of My Heart,* on Top Ten country Singles list for "Set 'Em Up Joe" 1992.

GOSPEL HUMMINGBIRDS
Grammy 1993 for *Steppin' Out.*

GOTTA BAND
Led by bassist John McVie of **Fleetwood Mac*** & singer Lola Thomas on blues album *John McVie's Gotta Band* 1992.

GOULET, ROBERT (1933–)
b. 11/26 Lawrence, MA. Actor/singer, sang in *Camelot* 1960, *The Happy Time* (won a 1968 Tony), albums *I Wish You Love, The Best of Robert Goulet,* etc. Married Carol Lawrence.

GRABLE, BETTY (1916–1973)
b. St. Louis, MO. Actress/singer, sang in Ted Fiorito's* band during 1930s, then appeared in many films.

GRAFF, GEORGE, JR. (1886–1973)
b. New York, NY. Lyricist, with Chauncey Olcott* & composer Ernest R. Ball* wrote "When Irish Eyes are Smiling" 1912.

GRAND FUNK RAILROAD
Heavy metal group formed 1969 with Donald Brewer, Mark Farmer, Craig Frost, Mel Schacher. First group to have ten consecutive platinum albums, sold over 20 million copies, hit song "We're an American Band," albums *Great Grand Funk Railroad, More of the Best.*

GRAND PUBA
Singer with Brand Nubain, later went solo, album *Reel to Reel* 1992.

GRANT, AMY (1960–)
b. 11/25 Augusta, GA. Soul/rock singer, album *Age to Age* 1983 sold one million copies, hit "Find a Way" was in *Unguarded* 1985. Won 1988 Gospel Vocalist Grammy for "Lead Me On," hit single "I Will Remember You" 1992, chosen Gospel Music Artist of Year 1992, video *Heart in Motion* sold 3 million copies. Lives near Nashville, TN with husband/songwriter Gary Chapman.

GRANT, EDDY (1948–)
b. Edmond M. Grant 3/5 Guyana. Guitarist/singer/songwriter, albums *Fire Under Rock, Going for Broke, Killer on the Rampage,* etc.

GRANT LEE BUFFALO
Los Angeles pop/high octane rock trio with Grant Lee Phillips, Joey Peters & Paul Kimble, album *Fuzzy* 1993.

GRANT, RUPERT (1914–1961)
b. Trinidad, West Indies. Calypso singer/songwriter, with lyricist Morey Amsterdam* wrote "Rum and Coca-Cola" 1943 (based on a tune by Lionel Belasco 1906).

GRANT, TOM
Albums *In My Wildest Dreams, Just the Right Moment, Night Charade,* etc.

GRAPPELLI, STEPHANE (1908–)
b. Paris, France. Jazz violinist in clubs in Paris, recorded with visiting Americans Eddie South, Duke Ellington,* & Oscar Peterson,* toured US 1978/80. Albums *Anything Goes with Yo Yo Ma, Grappelli Meets Kessel, Afternoon in Paris, Satin Doll,* etc.

GRASS ROOTS
Group with Creed Bratton, Rick Coonce, Warren Entner, Robert Grill, Reed Kailing, Joel Larson, & Dennis Provisor, hits "Temptation Eyes," "Heaven Knows," 1967/75, albums *Anthology, Greatest Hits Vols. 1 & 2.*

GRATEFUL DEAD, THE
Blues/rock group started in San Francisco 1966 with lead guitarist Jerry Garcia,* bassist Phil Lesh, Ron "Pig Pen" McKernan on congo drums & harp, guitarist Bob Weir,* drummer Bill Kruetzmann, organist Tom Constanten hit single "Touch of Grey" 1987. 1988 Top Grossing concert at Madison Square Garden in NY City, albums *Grateful Dead, Live/Dead,* etc., Videos *Making of Touch of Grey, So Far,* group toured 1992/93 with Garcia, Lesh, Weir & drummer Mickey Hart. Inducted into Rock & Roll Hall of Fame 1994. Weir had solo album *Bombs Away* 1978.

GRAY, DOBIE (1943–)
b. Brookshire, TX. Singer, hit "The In Crowd" 1965, album *Sing for In Crowds.*

GREAT WHITE
Twice Shy 1989 sold over 2 million albums, albums *Great White, Hooked, Once Bitten, Shot in the Dark,* etc.

GREEN, ADOLPH (1915–)
b. 12/2 New York, NY. Lyricist, with Betty Comden* wrote "The Party's Over," "Just in Time," "New York, New York." Sole writer of "It's Always Fair Weather When Good Friends Get Together."

GREEN, AL (1946–)
b. 4/13 Forrest City, AK. Singer/ordained minister, albums *Call Me, Full of Fire, I Get Joy, Let's Stay Together,* gospel/rap album *Love is Reality* (Grammy winner 1993).

GREEN, BUD (1897–1981)
b. Austria. Brought to US as an infant. With composer Sammy Stept* wrote "That's My Weakness Now." Died in Yonkers, NY.

GREEN, FREDERICK WM. "FREDDIE" (1911–1987)
b. Charleston, SC. Guitarist with Count Basie* 1937 & for many years, recorded with Mildred Bailey,* Billie Holiday,* Benny Goodman,* & Lionel Hampton.* CD *Natural Rhythm.* Died 3/1 Las Vegas.

GREEN, JOHN W. "JOHNNY" (1908–1989)
b. 10/10 New York, NY. Composed music for "Body and Soul," "I Cover the Waterfront." Died 5/15 Beverly Hills, CA.

GREENBAUM, NORMAN (1942–)
b. 11/20 Malden, MA. Singer/songwriter, hit "Spirit in the Sky" 1970 sold two million copies.

GREENFIELD, HOWARD (1937–1986)
Songwriter with Neil Sedaka* wrote "Love Will Keep Us Together" 1975. Died 3/4 Los Angeles, CA.

GREENWOOD, LEE (1942–)

b. 10/27 Los Angeles, CA. Country singer/songwriter, recorded "I O U" 1983, hit single "God Bless the USA." Albums *Holdin' a Good Hand, A Perfect 10, Somebody's Gonna Love You, American Patriot* 1992. Married Kimberly Payne, aged 24, Miss Tennessee 1989. His fifth marriage & her first.

GREER, WM. A. "SONNY" (1903–1980)

b. 12/13 Long Branch, NJ. Drummer with Duke Ellington's* band 1919/51, then with others in 60s, led own bands in 70s. Died 3/23 New York, NY.

GREG KIHN BAND, THE

Rock band formed 1975 with Greg Douglass, Greg Kihn, Larry Lynch, Gary Phillips, Steve Wright. Eighth album *Kihnspiracy* had hit single "Jeopardy" 1983.

GREY, AL (1925–)

b. Aldie, VA. Trombonist/leader of **Al Grey & Friends,** albums *New Al Grey Quintet, Christmas Stockin' Stuffer* 1992.

GRIFFIN, JIMMY (1928–)

b. Chicago, IL. Tenor saxist, with **Bread*** then **The Remingtons,*** albums *Take My Hand, The Cat, The Man I Love,* etc., video *The Jazz Life.*

GRIFFITH, NANCI

Singer/songwriter, Bette Midler* popularized her "From a Distance," Bob Dylan* "Boots of Spanish Leather," Tom Patton "Can't Help but Wonder Where I'm Bound," Townes Van Zant "Tecumseh Valley," & Woody Guthrie "Do Re Me." Album *Other Voices Other Rooms* 1992 (Contemporary Folk Album Grammy 1994), at Carnegie Hall in NY City, March 1993.

GRP ALL-STAR BIG BAND

With 20 players, title album was No. 3 on Billboard's Jazz Chart in August 1992, won Grammy 1992.

GRUBER, EDMUND L. (1879–1941)
b. Cincinnati, Ohio. Composer, while serving in the Philippines for the 5th Artillery, wrote "The Caissons Go Rolling Along."

GRUSIN, DAVE (1934–)
b. Denver, CO. Pianist/composer, albums *Cinemagic, Dave Grusin's Collection, Migration, Night Lines,* etc. *Mood Indigo* Instrumental Arrangement Grammy 1994.

GUARALDI, VINCENT A. "VINCE" (1928–1976)
b. San Francisco, CA. Pianist with Woody Herman* & Cal Tjader* in 1950s, led own trio in 60s, wrote "Cast Your Fate to the Wind" (Grammy award 1962), wrote *Charlie Brown's Christmas* TV special 1965. Died 2/2 Menlo Park, CA.

GUARD, DAVE (1934–1991)
b. near San Francisco, CA. Singer, formed the **Kingston Trio*** in 1957.

GUARNIERI, JOHN A. "JOHNNY" (1917–1985)
b. 3/23 New York, NY. Jazz pianist/composer with Benny Goodman* 1939/40, then with Artie Shaw,* Jimmy Dorsey,* & others. Toured Europe 1974 with Slam Stewart. Died 1/7 Livingston, NJ.

GUESS WHO, THE
Pianist/singer Burton Cummings, Chad Allen, Bob Ashley, Randy Bachman, Bruce Becker, David Inglish, Jim Kale, Greg Leskiw, Vance Masters, Don McDougall, Gary Peterson, Domenic Troiano, Bill Wallace, Ralph Watts, Kurt Winter. Hit singles "These Eyes" 1969, "No Time" 1970, albums *American Women, Live at the Paramount, Wheatfield Soul,* etc. In 1992 Burton Cummings toured with Ringo Starr.*

GUION, DAVID W.F. (1892–1981)
b. 12/15 Ballinger, TX. Composer, wrote "My Cowboy Love Song" 1936, *Texas* for orchestra 1952.

GUNS 'N' ROSES
Rock group with lead singer Axl Rose, guitarist Slash (Saul Hudson), bassist Duff McKayan, guitarist Izzy Stradlin* (quit 1989), drummer Steven Adler (ousted for drug problems 1992). Group on Top Ten CDs list 1988 for *Appetite for Destruction* & single "Sweet Child of Mine," on Top Ten albums list for *G'N'R Lies* 1989, "November Rain" 1992, toured US & South America, played in Paris 1992, Billboard top group 1992, "Live and Let Die" Grammy winner 1993.

GUTHRIE, ARLO (1947–   )
b. 7/10 Brooklyn, NY son of Woody Guthrie.* Guitarist/singer/ songwriter, wrote "Alice's Restaurant" (hit at the 1967 Newport Folk Festival). Wrote "Coming to Los Angeles, bringing a couple of keys [kilograms of narcotics], don't touch my bags, if you please, mister Customs man." Founded the Guthrie Center in Barrington, MA, serves AIDS patients, abused children, & the elderly 1992.

GUTHRIE, WOODROW W. "WOODY" (1912–1967)
b. 7/12 Okemah, OK. Guitarist/singer/songwriter, wrote "This Land is My Land," albums *Dust Bowl Ballads, Sings Folk Songs, Struggle, Worried Man Blues,* etc.

GUY AND RALNA
Gospel singers, hit "Just a Closer Walk with Thee," album *22 Great Songs of Faith.*

GUY, BUDDY (1936–   )
b. Lettsworth, LA. Guitarist/singer, albums *A Man & the Blues, Hold That Plane, Stone Crazy, Damn Right I Got the Blues* 1992, *Feels Like Rain* 1993, Video *Guy,* opened Buddy Guy's Legends, a blues club in Chicago, toured US in 1992. *Feels Like Rain* Contemporary Blues Album Grammy 1994.

H

HACKETT, ROBERT L. "BOBBY" (1915–1976)

b. 1/31 Providence, RI. Guitarist/cornetist, led own band in Boston 1936, with Benny Goodman* at Carnegie Hall concert 1938, then with Horace Heidt, Glenn Miller.* Led own combos, at Eddie Condon's* in NY City 1975. CD *Live at the Roosevelt Grill, Bobby Hackett & Teresa Brewer.* Died 6/7 Chatham, MA.

HADEN, CHARLIE (1937–   )

b. Shenandoah, Iowa. Bassist. Albums *Magico, Quartet West, Silence, Ballad of the Fallen.* With **Quartet West** on *Haunted Heart* (Grammy winner 1993).

HAGAR, SAMMY (1947–   )

b. 10/13 Heavy metal guitarist/singer/songwriter, hit singles "Your Love is Driving Me Crazy" 1982, "I Can't Drive 55" 1989, albums *Standing Hampton, Three Lock Box, Voa.*

HAGGARD, MERLE R. (1937–   )

b. 4/6 Bakersfield, CA. Guitarist/singer/songwriter, hit LP *Strangers* 1965, played at the White House for President & Mrs. Nixon 1973, hit album *Serving 190 Proof, All Night Long, Best of Country Blues, Big City, Chili Factor,* sang on album *Country Music for Kids* 1992. Married singer Bonnie Owens. Filed for bankruptcy in Sacramento, CA on 12/14/92.

HAIG, ALLAN W. "AL" (1924–1982)

b. Newark, NJ. Pianist/composer with Charlie Barnet, Dizzy Gillespie,* & Charlie Parker* in late 40s, with Chet Baker* & Stan Getz* 50s/60s, own combos 70s, at jazz festivals in NY City & Chicago in 1980. Died 11/16 NY City.

HALE, SARAH J. BUELL (1788–1879)

b. 10/24 Newport, NH. Poet, wrote "Mary Had a Little Lamb" 1830, later set to music to the tune "Merrily We Roll Along" from "Goodnight Ladies" by E.P. Christie.*

HALEY, BILL (1925–1981)

b. William John Clifford, Jr. 7/6 Highland Park, MI. Leader of **Bill Haley & the Comets,** rock 'n roll originator with "Rock around the Clock" 1954 (used in the film *Blackboard Jungle* 1955). Haley played at the Legend of Rock 'n Roll concert at Hollywood Bowl, CA 1972. A postage stamp was issued in his honor in 1993.

HALL, ALFRED W. "AL" (1915–1988)

b. Jacksonville, FL. Bassist with Teddy Wilson & Ellis Larkins* in early 40s, then with various combos in NY City, with Eubie Blake* at Newport Jazz Festival in NY City 1960, then with Benny Goodman,* toured Europe, with Tiny Grimes 1971.

HALL, JIM (1930–)

b. Buffalo, NY. Guitarist, albums *All Across the City, Alone Together with Ron Carter, Jazz Guitar, Live at Town Hall,* etc.

HALL, TOM T. (1936–)

b. 5/25 Olive Hill, KY. Country singer/songwriter, wrote "Harper Valley PTA" which sold over 4.5 million copies, albums *Greatest Hits, The Essential Tom T. Hall,* quit touring in 1992.

HALL AND OATES

Singer Daryl Hall (b. 1949) & musician/singer John Oates, hit "Rich Girl" on platinum album *Bigger than Both of Us* 1976, "I Can't Go for That" on album *Private Eyes* 1981, hit single "Maneater" 1982, sang "Philadelphia Freedom" on album *Two Rooms* 1992.

HALPERN, STEVEN

Albums *Crystal Suite, Jonah's Journey, Radiance, Shifting Focus,* video *Summer Wind anti Frantic.*

HAMBLEN, CARL STUART (1908–1989)

b. 10/20 Kellyville, TX. Leader/singer/songwriter, wrote "This Old House" 1954. Died 3/8 Santa Monica, CA.

HAMILTON, FORRESTSTRON "CHICO" (1921–)
b. Los Angeles, CA. Drummer/composer, with Lionel Hampton*
& Lena Horne* in 1940s, with Gerry Morgan & own combos in
50s/80s, toured Europe with Monty Alexander & Art Farmer*
1980. Albums *Reunion, The Dealer*, video *The Jazz Life*.

HAMILTON, SCOTT
Tenor saxist, albums *Plays Ballads, Radio City, Second Set, The
Right Time, Race Point* 1992.

HAMLISCH, MARVIN (1944–)
b. 6/2 New York, NY. Musician/composer, wrote scores for films
The Way We Were, The Sting 1974, won three Oscars, *A Chorus
Line* 1975, album *Ice Castles*. Led sixty-four piece orchestra for
Barbra Streisand's New Year's concerts at MGM Grand Gardens in Las Vegas 1993/94. In 1989 married ABC sports
contributor Tene Blair.

HAMMER (1962–)
b. Stanley Kirk Burrell 3/30 Oakland, CA. Rap vocalist, hit single
"U Can't Touch This" won 1990 Grammy Rap solo, *Please
Hammer Don't Hurt 'Em* sold eight million albums 1990,
album *Too Legit to Quit* 1991 sold three million copies, hit
"Ain't 2 Proud 2 Beg" 1992. Videos *Here Comes Hammer,
Please Hammer-Hurt 'Em, Addams Groove* won Grammy
1993, video *Hammerin Home*.

HAMMERSTEIN, OSCAR II (1895–1960)
b. New York, NY. Lyricist, with composer Jerome Kern* wrote
"Ol' Man River" 1927, shows *Oklahoma!, Carousel*, with
composer Rudolf Friml* and lyricist Otto Harbach* wrote
"Indian Love Call" 1924, with composer Sigmund Romberg*
wrote "Lover, Come Back to Me" 1928.

HAMMOND, JOHN (1943–)
b. New York, NY. Guitarist, albums *Best of John Hammond,
Nobody But You*, video *From Bessie Smith to Bruce Springsteen*, blues album *Got Love if You Want it* (Grammy winner
1993).

HAMPSON, THOMAS (1955–)

Baritone raised in Spokane, WA. Recordings include Cole Porter's* "Kiss Me Kate" and Wagner's "Gotterdammerung." Album *American Dreamer: The Songs of Stephen Foster* 1992.

HAMPTON, BRUCE

Album *Col. Bruce Hampton & Aquarium Rescue Unit.*

HAMPTON, LIONEL (1914–)

b. 4/20 Louisville, KY. Vibist/drummer, recorded with Louis Armstrong,* with Benny Goodman* 1936/40, toured Europe & the world with own band 1950s/60s, at jazz festivals 70s/80s, played in The White House for President & Mrs. Carter 1978 & President & Mrs. Reagan 1981. On cassette *Big Bands at Disneyland: Lionel Hampton* 1984, sang with daughter Chris. Suffered a stroke in Paris on 5/20/92 & was taken to NY City where he recovered. Honored at the Kennedy Center in Washington, D.C. in December 1992.

HANBY, BENJAMIN R. (1833–1867)

b. Rushville, Ohio. Composer of "Darling Nellie Gray" 1856.

HANCOCK, HERBERT J. "HERBIE" (1940–)

b. 4/12 Chicago, IL. Pianist/composer, with Miles Davis* from 1963, at Telluride Jazz Festival in Colorado, July 1980. Electronic jazz composition *Rockit* won 1984 Grammy, at JVC Jazz Festival, Newport, RI in August 1992. Albums *A Jazz Collection, Future Shock, Sound System*, etc., video *Herbie & the Rockit Band.* Played in the White House for President & Mrs. Clinton in June 1993.

HANDY, WILLIAM C. (1873–1958)

b. Florence, AL. Noted black composer, composed the "St. Louis Blues" 1914. Died in New York City. A postage stamp was issued in his honor.

HANOI ROCKS

Albums *All Those Wasted Years, Oriental Beat, Self Destruction Blues*, etc., video *Hanoi Rocks.*

HAPPY JAZZ BAND
Led by Jim Cullum in San Antonio, TX included clarinetist Allen Vachenin in late 1970s/80s.

HAPPY MONDAYS
Hits "Pills, Thrills N Bellyaches," "Yes, Please" 1992.

HARAN, MARY CLEERE
Alto, pop/jazz singer, debut album *There's a Small Hotel* 1992.

HARBACH, OTTO (1873–1963)
b. Otto Hauerbach in Salt Lake City, UT. Lyricist, with composer Rudolf Friml* wrote "Indian Love Call," "Rose Marie," with Jerome Kern* "Smoke Gets in Your Eyes" 1933.

HARBURG, E.Y. "YIP" (1898–1981)
b. New York, NY. Lyricist, wrote "April in Paris" 1932, "It's Only a Paper Moon" 1933, "Over the Rainbow" 1939 (Oscar winner) "How are Things in Glocca Morra?".

HARDIN, LILLIAN "LIL" (1898–1971)
b. Memphis, TN. Jazz pianist known as a barrelhouse player, with King Oliver's* band, married to Louis Armstrong* 1924/38. Was playing the "St. Louis Blues" for a memorial to Armstrong in Chicago when she collapsed and died.

HARDIN, TIM (1941–1980)
b. 12/23 Eugene, OR. Singer/songwriter, wrote "If I Were a Carpenter" recorded by Bobby Darin,* Bob Seger,* & others. Died 12/29 Hollywood, CA.

HARDLINE
Band with guitarist Neal Schon, Johnny Gioeli, Joey Gioeli, Todd Jensen & Deen Castronovo on album *Double Eclipse* 1992.

HARMONICATS, THE
Hit song "Peg O' My Heart."

HARMONY
b. Pamela Scott. Female rapper, album *Let There be Harmony.*

HARNICK, SHELDON (1924–)
b. Chicago, IL. Songwriter, with composer Jerry Bock* "Fiddler on the Roof" 1964.

HARP, EVERETTE
Jazz musician, hit album *Everett Harp* 1992.

HARRELL, TOM
Jazz trumpeter. Albums *Form, Sail Away, Stories,* etc.

HARRIS, BENJAMIN "LITTLE BENNY" (1919–)
b. New York, NY. Trumpeter with Earl Hines* & John Kirby in 1940s, various times with Benny Carter,* Charlie Parker,* Coleman Hawkins,* & others. Composed *Ornithology, Crazeology* recorded by Charlie Parker, composed *Lion's Den* recorded by Vick Dickenson*.

HARRIS, CHARLES K. (1867–1930)
b. Poughkeepsie, NY. Composer wrote "After the Ball is Over" 1892.

HARRIS, EMMYLOU (1947–)
b. 4/2 Birmingham, AL. Singer, won Grammys 1976/77, Country Music Association Female Vocalist of Year 1980, with Johnny Cash* & Willie Nelson* on *The Other Side of Nashville* 1984, albums *Angel Band, Blue Kentucky Girl, Luxury Liner,* etc. Won The Nashville Network Humanitarian award 1992, Grand Marshal for 40th annual Christmas Parade in Nashville 1992, on CBS special *Women of Country* in January 1993, *Emmylou Harris & the Nash Ramblers at the Ryman* (Grammy winner).

HARRIS, GENE (1933–)
b. Benton Harbor, MI. Pianist, albums *Black & Blue, Listen Here, Tribute to Count Basie, World Tour 1990,* etc.

HARRIS, LARNELLE
Gospel singer, won 1988 Gospel Vocalist Grammy for "Christmas," won Grammy 1993 for "I Choose Joy."

HARRIS, PHIL (1904–)
b. 6/24 Linton, IN. Drummer/leader, with **Lofner-Harris Band** 1920s/30s, conducted the Jack Benny radio series, album *1933*. Married actress Alice Faye.

HARRISON, GEORGE (1943–)
b. 2/25 Liverpool, England. Singer/songwriter with the **Beatles*** 1960s/70s. On 1988 Top Ten Pop Singles list for "Got My Mind Set on You," albums *All Things Must Pass, Cloud Nine, Concert for Bangladesh,* etc. Won top honor on the 1992 Billboard Music awards television show in December 1992.

HARRY, DEBORAH ANN "DEBBIE" (1945–)
b. 7/1 Miami, FL. Punk singer known as "Blondie,"* hit "Call Me" 1980, appeared on commercials.

HART, LORENZ (1895–1943)
b. New York, NY. Lyricist, wrote "With a Song in My Heart" 1934, "Blue Moon" 1934, "This Can't be Love" 1938. On Opening night of the Rodgers* & Hart musical *A Connecticut Yankee,* Hart disappeared. After a two-day search he was found suffering with pneumonia, died three days later in New York City.

HARTFORD, JOHN C. (1937–)
b. 12/30 New York, NY. Guitarist/singer/songwriter, wrote "Tall, Tall Grass," "Gentle on My Mind" 1967 recorded by Glenn Campbell & some 200 other singers, appeared at folk festivals, hit "Me Oh My, How Time Flies," albums *Catalogue, Mark Twang.*

HARTMAN, DAN
Pop singer/songwriter, hit single "I Can Dream About You" 1984. CD *Instant Replay.*

HARVEY, P.J. (1969–)
British pop/blues/punk guitarist/singer/songwriter Polly Jean
Harvey with bassist Stephen Vaughn & drummer Robert Ellis,
album *Dry* 1992.

HASTINGS, THOMAS (1784–1872)
b. Washington, CT. Composer, with lyricist A.M. Toplady composed "Rock of Ages" 1830.

HATHAWAY, DONNY (1945–1979)
b. 10/1 Chicago, IL. Sang with Roberta Flack,* hits "Where is the
Love?" 1972, "The Closer I Get to You" 1978. Albums
*Collection, Everything is Everything, The Best of Donny
Hathaway.*

HAVENS, RICHIE (1941–)
b. 1/21 Brooklyn, NY City. Singer/electric guitarist, played in
Greenwich Village coffee houses in NY City, sang "Freedom"
at Woodstock Festival 1969, hit "Here Comes the Sun" 1971,
CDs *Collection, Mixed Bag, Now, Richard P. Havens 1983,*
etc., at the concert in honor of Bob Dylan* at Madison Square
Garden in NY City in October 1992.

HAWES, HAMPTON (1928–1977)
b. Los Angeles, CA. Blues/jazz pianist named Arrival of the Year
by Metronome 1956. Album *Great Leaves of Summer.* Died
5/28 Los Angeles, CA.

HAWKINS, COLEMAN "BEAN" (1904–1969)
b. St. Joseph, MO. Tenor saxist with **Mamie Smith's Jazz
Hounds** 1921/23, with Fletcher Henderson* 1924/34, recorded
"Body and Soul" 1939, led own combos 1940s/60s, dozens of
CDs & albums. Died in New York City.

HAWKINS, ERSKINE R. (1914–)
b. Birmingham, AL. Composer/leader at Savoy Ballroom in NY
City 1940s/50s, later quartet in the Catskill Mountains, NY.
Albums *Tuxedo Junction, Original Tuxedo Junction.*

HAWKINS, RONNIE (1935–)
b. 1/10 Huntsville, AL. Singer/harmonica player, leader of **The Hawkins,** disbanded 1976. Album *Best of Ronnie Hawkins.*

HAWKINS, "SCREAMIN' JAY" (1929–)
b. Jalacy Hawkins, Cleveland, Ohio. Vocalist/pianist/saxist, albums *Screamin' Jay Hawkins* 1960, *Screamin' the Blues* 1979.

HAWKINS SINGERS, EDWIN
Gospel singers, "Oh Happy Day" 1969 was first gospel song to make Pop Top 5, albums *Mass Choir, Jubilation: Great Gospel Performers, Vols. 1 & 2,* 1992.

HAWKINS, SOPHIE B. (1966–)
Singer, album *Tongues & Tails,* "Damn I Wish I was Your Lover" on Top Ten singles list June 1992, single "I Want You" 1992, New Artist Grammy winner 1993.

HAWKINS, TRAMAINE
Singer, reigning gospel queen, won 1990 Grammy for *Tramaine Hawkins Live,* her hit "Spirit Fall Down on Me" brought wrath of the church, sang "He Shall Purify" at Stellar Music Awards 1993.

HAWKS, ANNIE S. (1835–1918)
b. Hoosick, NY. Hymnist, with composer Robert Lowry* wrote "I Need Thee Every Hour" 1872.

HAYES, ISAAC (1942–)
b. 8/20 Covington, TN. Organist/soul singer/songwriter, wrote score for *Shaft* (Grammy & Oscar winner 1972). Albums *Hot Buttered Soul, Hotbed, Live at Sahara Tahoe, Love Attack,* etc.

HAYES, PETER LIND (1915–)
b. 6/25 San Francisco, CA. Actor/composer/singer, with wife Mary Healy* on radio & TV in 1950s, hosted TV series "When Television was Live" 1975.

HAYES, ROLAND (1887–1976)

b. 6/3 Curryville, GA. Noted black tenor, gave recital at Symphony Hall (Boston 1917), toured Europe 1920/23, gave performance for King George V in Berlin 1924, taught at Boston University after 1950. CD *Art Songs*. Died 12/31 Boston, MA.

HAYMES, JOE (1908–   )

b. Marshfield, Missouri. Pianist/leader during 1930s led own bands at Roseland Ballroom and other clubs in NY City.

HAYMES, RICHARD "DICK" (1917–1980)

b. 9/13 Buenos Aires, Argentina. Pop singer in early 1940s, hits "It Can't be Wrong," "You'll Never Know," albums *Best of Dick Haymes, Easy to Listen To*. Died 3/28 Los Angeles, CA.

HAYNES, ROY OWEN (1926–   )

b. Roxbury, MA. Drummer with Luis Russell & Lester Young* 1947/49, accompanist for Sarah Vaughan 1953/58, then led own quartets, *down beat* New Star 1962, at Jazz Festivals in NY in 1970s/80s.

HAYNES, WARREN

Guitarist/singer/songwriter with the **Allman Brothers**,* solo album *Tales of Ordinary Madness* 1993.

HAYS, LEE (1914–1981)

b. Little Rock, AK. Singer, with Pete Seeger* sang with the **Almanac Singers,** after World War II with the **Weavers.*** With Seeger wrote "If I Had a Hammer." Died 8/26 North Tarrytown, NY.

HAYS, WILLIAM S. "WILL" (1837–1907)

b. Louisville, KY. Composer, during the Civil War travelled through the Confederate lines as a war correspondent, wrote "The Drummer Boy of Shiloh" 1862. Captured in New Orleans and charged with writing seditious songs: imprisoned by Union commander General Ben Butler. Wrote "We Parted by the River" 1866 & other songs.

HAZA, OFRA
Won Grammy 1993 for reggae world music album *Kirya*.

HAZELWOOD, LEE (1929–)
b. 7/9 Mannford, OK. Sang duets with Nancy Sinatra,* "Jackson" 1967, "Some Velvet Morning" 1968, album *Nancy and Lee*.

HEALY, MARY (1918–)
b. 4/14 New Orleans, LA. Actress/singer, wrote "Only Twenty-five Minutes from Broadway" 1961. Married Peter Lind Hayes.*

HEAP, JAMES A. "JIMMY" (1902–1977)
b. Taylor, TX. Singer/songwriter, leader of the **Melody Masters** 1947/64, then the Jimmy Heap Show, wrote "Ethyl in My Gas Tank" and other songs. Died 12/4 Burnet, TX.

HEART
Heavy metal band with Mark Andes, Denny Carmassi, Mike Derosier, Roger Fisher, Steve Fossen, Howard Leese, Ann & Nancy Wilson,* album *Dreamboat Annie* 1976 sold 2.5 million copies, *Brigade* 1990 sold 2 million albums, albums *Bad Animals, Bebe Le Strange, Heart, Little Queen*, etc. Ann & Nancy Wilson on a four-song CD *Lovemongers* featured "Battle of Evermore" & "Crazy for You" 1992.

HEARTBREAKERS
Formed in 1975 with guitarists ex-**Dolls** Johnny Thunder & Walter Luse, bassist Richard Hill & ex-Dolls drummer Jerry Nolan who soon left the band (which was reformed in 1983). Johnny Thunder & the original **Heartbreakers** performed in London, album *Dead or Alive* 1986.

HEATH, PERCY (1923–)
b. Wilmington, NC. With Miles Davis* & Charlie Parker* in 1940s, Dizzy Gillespie* 1950/52, **Modern Jazz Quartet*** 1952/74. Formed **Heath Brothers Band** with saxist Jimmy Heath, pianist Stanley Cowell, & guitarist Tony Purrone, in New York City 1970s/80s, album *Brothers & Others*.

HEATWAVE
Rock group formed 1975, brothers/singers Johnnie & Keith Wilson, born Dayton, Ohio; guitarist Eric Johns, bassist Mario Mantese, guitarist Jessie Whitten, drummer Ernest Berger. Albums *Greatest Hits, Too Hot to Handle.*

HEAVY D AND THE BOYZ
Platinum album *Big Tyme* 1989, *Peaceful Journey.*

HEDGES, MICHAEL
Albums *Aerial Boundaries, Breakfast in the Field, Taproot, Watching My Life Go By.*

HEIFETZ, JASCHA (1901–1987)
b. 2/2 Vilna, Lithuania, Russia. Concert violinist, family fled Russia & settled in San Francisco. Won Grammys 1961/62 & 1964. Albums *Showpieces, The Heifetz Collection, Toscanini Collection,* etc. Video *Piatigorsky.*

HEIGHTS, THE
Debut single "How Do You Talk to an Angel" went gold 1992.

HEINDORF, RAY (1908–1980)
b. 8/25 Haverstraw, NY. Composer/conductor, won Oscars for scores for *Yankee Doodle Dandy* 1942 and *Music Man* 1962.

HELD, ANNA (1865–1918)
b. Warsaw, Poland. Singer, came to America in 1896 with her lover Florenz Ziegfeld, became famous singing "Won't You Come and Play Wiz Me?" 1896.

HELM, LEVON
Album *Levon Helm & The RCO All-Stars.*

HELMS, BOBBY (1933–   )
b. 8/15 Bloomington, IN. Country singer had hit single "Jingle Bell Rock" in 1950s. The Bobby Helms Theater opened in Myrtle Beach, SC in 1993.

HELMUT
New York punk/metal quartet, album *Meantime* 1992, "In the Meantime" won metal with vocal Grammy award 1993.

HENDERSON, J.FLETCHER "SMACK" (1897–1952)
b. Cuthbert, GA. Pianist/composer/leader, brother of Horace Henderson, accompanied singer Ethel Waters* 1921, led Roseland Band in NY City 1924/29, led own bands 30s/40s. Paralyzed by a stroke on 12/21/50, never recovered. Died in NY City.

HENDERSON, JOE (1937–)
b. Lima, Ohio. Jazz saxist/composer, albums *Blue Note Years, Inner Urge, Mode for Joe, Our Thing, Lush Life* (Grammy winner 1993), won Triple Crown *down beat* poll for Best Artist, Album, & Tenor Saxist. Played at Arkansas Ball with Ben E. King* & President Bill Clinton on saxophone in January 1993. *Miles Ahead Jazz* Instrumental Grammy 1994.

HENDERSON, LYLE C. "SKITCH" (1918–)
b. 1/27 England & raised in Halstead, MN. Had big band at Hotel Pennsylvania, NY City with singer Nancy Read, conducted NBC TV Tonight Show after 1962, founded **N.Y. Pops** 1983, toured US with his Pops Orchestra 1992/93.

HENDERSON, RAY (1896–1970)
b. Buffalo, NY. Composed music for "That Old Gang of Mine" 1923, "Bye, Bye Blackbird," "Five Foot Two, Eyes of Blue," "Sonny Boy" 1928 for Al Jolson,* "Button Up Your Overcoat," "You are My Lucky Star." Died in Greenwich, CT.

HENDRICKS, BARBARA (1948–)
Soprano from Stephens, AK lives in Switzerland, album *Bach: Magnificant* 1992, served as UN Goodwill Ambassador, sang "He's Got the Whole World in His Hands" at the Presidential Gala for Bill Clinton in January 1993.

HENDRICKS, JOHN C. "JON" (1921–)
b. Newark, Ohio. Drummer/singer/songwriter, teamed with Dave

Lambert (1917–1966) and Annie Ross to form Lambert, Hendricks, & Ross* 1956 with Hendricks writing the jazz twisting lines. Won a series of *down beat* and *Playboy* polls as Number One Jazz Vocal group. Yolande Lavan later replaced Ross. Hendricks formed a new group with his wife Judith, daughter Michelle, son Eric backed by pianist Richard Wyands, bassist Lisle Atkinson, & drummer Al Harewood in NY City in 1980s. Album *Freddie Freeloader.* Hendricks was honored by National Endowment for the Arts, American Jazz Masters award in January 1993.

HENDRIX, JAMES M. "JIMI" (1942–1970)
b. 11/27 Seattle, WA. Guitarist/singer, hit single "Are You Experienced?" 1967. Albums *Crash Landing, Cry of Love, Kiss the Sky,* videos *Jimi Hendrix,* etc. Died of an overdose of drugs.

HENLEY, DON (1947–   )
b. 7/22 Gilmer, TX. Singer left **The Eagles*** for a solo career, hit single "Dirty Laundry" 1982, platinum album *The End of Innocence* 1988/89, sang duet "Walkaway Joe" at 1992 Country Music Awards with Trisha Yearwood*.

HERBERT, VICTOR (1859–1924)
b. Dublin, Ireland. Composer/bandmaster of 22nd Regiment NY National Guard 1893. Composed music for "I Love Thee, I Adore Thee" 1897, "Gypsy Love Song" 1898, "Babes in Toyland" 1903, "Ah, Sweet Mystery of Life" in *Naughty Marietta* 1910. Album *Cello Concert/Marriner.* Died of a heart attack in New York City.

HERDMAN, PRISCILLA
Albums *Seasons of Change, Star Dreamer, Voices,* etc.

HERITAGE HALL JAZZ BAND
New Orleans touring band included drummer Freddie Kohlman, clarinetist Manuel Crusto, pianist Ellis Marsalis,* bassist Walter Payton, trombonist Fred Lonzo, trumpeter & featured soloist Teddy Riley in 1980s.

HERMAN, JERRY (1932–   )
b. New York, NY. Composer, wrote scores for *Hello Dolly* 1964 & *Mame*. Album *An Evening with Jerry Herman.*

HERMAN, WOODROW C. "WOODY" (1913–1987)
b. 5/16 Milwaukee, WI. Clarinetist/saxist/singer, during 1930s with Isham Jones's Juniors, led own band at Roseland in Brooklyn, known as "The Band that Played the Blues," his recording of "Woodchoppers' Ball" became famous, band later known as "The Thundering Herd." Died 10/29 Los Angeles, CA.

HERMAN'S HERMITS
English group with Karl Greene, Keith Hopwood, Derek Leckenby, Peter Noone, Barry Whitman, toured US in 1960s. Hit "Mrs. Brown You've Got a Lovely Daughter" 1965.

HERMANN, BERNARD (1911–1975)
b. 6/29 New York, NY. Composer, wrote themes for Hitchcock films including *Psycho* 1960, wrote over 60 radio & film scores. Died 12/24 Los Angeles, CA.

HERSHEY, JUNE (1909–   )
b. Los Angeles, with composer/husband Don Swander* wrote "Deep in the Heart of Texas" 1941.

HERZOG, ARTHUR, JR. (1901–1983)
b. New York, NY. Songwriter, wrote blues song "God Bless This Child" sung by Billie Holiday.* Died 9/1 Detroit, MI.

HEWITT, JAMES (1770–1827)
b. Dartmoor, England. Composer, came to New York City in 1792. With lyricist Ann Julia Siddons* composed the opera *Tammany, or the Indian Chief* 1794. *See also* JAMES RALPH.*

HEWITT, JOHN HILL (1801–1890)
b. New York, NY. Composer/pianist, made weekly visits to the White House where he gave piano lessons to Alice Tyler, daughter of President John Tyler 1842/45. With lyricist Ethel Lynn Beers* "All Quiet Along the Potomac Tonight" 1861.

HEYMAN, EDWARD (1907–)
b. New York, NY. Lyricist, with Robert Sour* & composer Johnny Green* wrote "Body and Soul," "I Cover the Waterfront," and with Billy Rose & Green "I Wanna Be Loved."

HEYWARD, DuBOISE (1885–1940)
Lyricist, wrote "Summertime," "A Woman is a Sometime Thing."

HEYWOOD, EDWARD, JR. "EDDIE" (1915–)
b. 12/4 Atlanta, GA. Pianist/composer, accompanist for Billie Holiday,* organized own band 1943, wrote "Canadian Sunset," played at Carnegie Hall in NY City in June 1980.

HIATT, JOHN
Singer with **Little Village,** albums *Bring the Family, Riding with the King, Slow Turning, Stolen Moments,* etc.

HIBBLER, AL (1915–)
b. 8/16 Little Rock, AK. Blind singer, with Duke Ellington's* band. At Louis Armstrong's* funeral in 1971 Hibbler sang "Nobody Knows the Trouble I've Seen." Album *After the Lights Go Down.*

HICKS, JOHN
Blues/jazz pianist, albums *Two of a Kind, Is That So, Power Trio,* with saxist Joshua Redman, trombonist Al Grey, & trumpeter Clark Terry* on album *Friends Old and New* 1992.

HI-FIVE
Waco, TX hip-hop/R&B singers Mack Sanders, Treston Irby, Tony Thompson, Roderick Clark, & Russell Neal. Album *Keep It Goin On* 1992. Hit single "She's Playing Hard to Get" 1992. Clark broke his neck in a car accident in August 1992.

HIGGINBOTHAM, JACK "J.C." (1906–1973)
b. Social Circle, GA. Trombonist, with pianist Eugene Landrum's Jazz Band in 1920s, then with Fletcher Henderson,* Louis

Armstrong* in 30s, with Henry "Red" Allen 1940/47, led own bands in 50s/70s. Died in New York City.

HIGGINS, ELBERT "BERTIE" (1946–   )
b. Tarpon Springs, FL. Singer/songwriter, hit single "Key Largo" 1982.

HIGH FIVE
Hit R&B single "Quality Time" 1993.

HIGHLEY, BREWSTER M. (1823–1911)
b. Rutland, Ohio. With composer D.E. Kelly,* wrote "Home on the Range" 1873, now the state song of Kansas.

HIGHWAY 101
Hit single "Bing, Bang, Boom," albums *Highway 101, Paint the Town,* etc.

HILL, MILDRED J. (1859–1916)
b. Louisville, KY. Organist, arranged the music "Good Morning to All" 1893 which later became "Happy Birthday to You" with words by her sister Patty Smith Hill. "Happy Birthday to You" is sung more often than any other song in the history of the world.

HINES, EARL K. "FATHA" (1905–1983)
b. 12/28 Duquesne, PA. Pianist/composer/vocalist, during 1920s with Louis Armstrong,* Zutty Singleton,* & others, led own bands 1930s/40s, joined Louis Armstrong's* **All-Stars** 1948, led own bands in 50s/80s. Albums *Blues So Low (for Fats), Harlem Lament, Piano Man, Way Down Yonder in New Orleans.* Died 7/22 Oakland, CA.

HINTON, MILTON J. (1910–   )
b. Vicksburg, MS. Bassist with Cab Calloway* 1936/51, then with others. Honored by National Endowment with the Arts American Jazz Masters award in January 1993.

HIROSHIMA
Albums *Another Place, East, Go, Hiroshima, Ongaku,* etc.

HIRSCH, ALLAN M. (1878–1951)
Graduated from Yale University in 1901, with composers Bob Cole* & Billy Johnson 1898 wrote the Yale song "Boola Boola" 1901.

HIRT, ALOIS M. "AL" (1922–   )
b. 11/7 New Orleans, LA. Trumpeter, played in bands of Tommy Dorsey,* Ray McKinley,* & Horace Heidt in 1940s, during 60s led own Dixieland Jazz Bands, had own TV show 1965, gave concert for Hurricane Andrew victims in Louisiana 1992, albums *Cotton Candy, Al & Pete Fountain on Super Jazz,* etc.

HITCHCOCK, ROBYN
Guitarist, albums *Robyn Hitchcock and the Egyptians on Element of Light, Globe of Frogs, Groovy Decoy,* with singers Andy Metcalf & Morris Windsor on *Perspex Island* 1992.

HITE, ROBERT E., JR. (1943–1981)
b. 1/26 Torrance, CA. Bluegrass singer known as "The Bear," hit song "On the Road Again." Died in Los Angeles, CA.

HO, DON (1930–   )
b. 8/13 Kakaako, Hawaii. Singer known for Hawaiian songs, album *Greatest Hits.*

HODGES, JOHNNY "RABBIT" (1906–1970)
b. Cambridge, MA. Alto saxist with Willie the Lion Smith* in 1920s, with Duke Ellington* 1928/51, and again 1955/70. Albums *Compact Jazz, Triple Play, With Wild Bill Davis, In a Mellow Tone.* Died of a heart attack.

HOFFMAN, AL (1902–1960)
b. Minsk, Russia. Songwriter, came to US 1908 & resided in Seattle, WA. With Clem Watts and Bob Merrill* wrote "If I Knew You Were Comin' I'd've Baked a Cake" 1950.

HOLDEN, OLIVER (1764–1844)
b. Shirley, MA. Composer, with lyricist Edward Perronet composed tune "Coronation" for "All Hail the Power" 1793.

HOLDSWORTH, ALLAN
Albums *Sands, Secrets, Velvet Darkness, With a Heart in My Song.*

HOLE, DAVE
Album *Short Fuse Blues.*

HOLIDAY, BILLIE "LADY DAY" (1915–1959)
b. Baltimore, MD. Singer, daughter of guitarist Clarence Holiday, married trumpeter Joe Guy. Recorded with Benny Goodman,* Count Basie,* & others in 1930s, arrested twice on narcotic charges. Videos *The Many Faces of Lady Day, Sound of Jazz.* A postage stamp was issued in her honor in 1994.

HOLLAND, BRIAN (1941–)
Songwriter, with lyricists Eddie Holland (b. 1939) & Lamont Dozier (b. 1941) wrote "Heat Wave," "Stop in the Name of Love," "Baby, I Need Your Loving," hit "Trying to Hold on to My Woman."

HOLLAND, DAVE
Albums *Jumpin In, The Razor's Edge, Triplicate,* etc.

HOLLAND, RANDY
Singer, with Anita Baker* & Skip Scarborough* won 1988 Grammy for R&B song "Giving You the Best I Got."

HOLLIDAY, JENNIFER (1959–)
b. 10/19. R&B singer in Broadway shows *Dreamgirls & Your Arms Too Short to Box with God,* album *I'm on Your Side.* Sang at the Democratic National Convention in NY City 1992.

HOLLIES, THE
British band 1960s/70s with Bernie Calvert, Allan Clarke, Bobby Elliott, Eric Haydock, Tony Hicks, Graham Nash, Mikael Rikfors, & Terry Sylvester. Hit single "He Ain't Heavy, He's My Brother" 1970, albums *Best of the Hollies, Vols. 1 & 2,* etc.

HOLLY, CHARLES H. "BUDDY" (1936–1959)
b. 9/7 Lubbock, TX. Country/rock singer with **Buddy Holly and**

the Crickets, hit single "That'll be the Day." Many albums. Killed in a plane crash from Mason City, IA to Fargo, ND. A postage stamp was issued in his honor in 1993.

HOLLYDAY, CHRISTOPHER
Albums *Christopher Hollyday, The Natural Moment, On Course.*

HOLLY MODAL ROUNDERS
Hit song "Mr. Scarecrow" on album *Troubadours of the Folk Era, Vol. 1* in 1992.

HOLMES, RUPERT (1947–)
b. 2/24 Cheshire, England. Came to America, wrote & recorded the "Pina Colada Song," hit single "Escape."

HOLT, DAVID
Singer, won 1993 Folk Album Grammy *Grandfather's Greatest Hits.*

HONEYCOMBS, THE
English group formed 1963 with Denis Dalziel, John Lantree, Ann "Honey" Lantree, Martin Murray, Alan Ward. First group to have a female drummer, toured America.

HONEYDRIPPERS
With guitarist Nile Rodgers (b. 9/19/52 New York, NY, produces albums for Madonna* & other musicians & singers), album *Honeydrippers Vol. 1.*

HONEYMOON SUITE
Albums *Big Prize, Honeymoon Suite, Racing After Midnight.*

HOODOO GURUS
Albums *Blow Your Cool, Kinky, Magna Cum Louder, Stone Age Romeos.*

HOOKER, JOHN LEE (1917–)
b. 8/22 Clarksdale, MS. Guitarist/singer albums *40th Anniversary, More Real Folk Blues, Plays and Sings the Blues,* etc.,

at the Ultimate Guitar Concert in San Francisco 1992, album *The Healer* 1993.

HOPKINS, JOHN HENRY, JR. (1820–1891)
b. Pittsburgh, PA. He wrote the words & music for the Christmas Carol "We Three Kings of Orient Are" 1863.

HOPKINS, LINDA (1925–   )
b. New Orleans, LA. Singer on Blues Tour with Branford Marsalis* in 1992.

HOPKINS, SAM "LIGHTNIN" (1912–1982)
b. 3/15 Centerville, TX. Guitarist/blues singer, recorded over 100 LP records. Albums *Lost Texas Vols. 1, 2, & 3, Texas Blues, The Herald Recordings*. Died of cancer 1/30 Houston, TX.

HOPKINSON, FRANCIS (1737–1791)
b. Philadelphia, PA. Harpsichordist/organist/composer, signer of the Declaration of Independence, lived in Bordentown, NJ 1775/91. Wrote the words & music for the opera *The Temple of Minerva* 1781.

HOPKINSON, JOSEPH (1770–1843)
b. Philadelphia, Pa., son of Francis Hopkinson.* Lyricist, with composer Philip Phile* wrote "Hail Columbia" 1798.

HORN, PAUL (1930–   )
b. New York, NY. Pianist/composer, albums *Inside the Great Pyramid, Inside the Taj Mahal, Nomad, Peace Album*, etc.

HORN, SHIRLEY (1934–   )
b. Washington, DC. Pianist/singer, albums *Close Enough for Love, I Thought About You, You Won't Forget Me*, ballad album *Here's to Life* (Grammy winner 1993).

HORNE, LENA C. (1917–   )
b. 6/30 Brooklyn, NY. Singer appeared in *Blackbirds* 1939, on USO tours in World War II, toured Europe 1947/59, hit song "Stormy Weather." Albums *Lena Goes Latin, Merry from Lena, Stormy Weather*. Sang at the First Ladies of Song NY

City gala event in February 1993. Married Lennie Hayton, later divorced.

HORNSBY, BRUCE (1954–)

Pianist/singer/songwriter, album *The Way It Is* 1986. With Branford Marsalis* on "Twenty-Nine-Five" track from *Coca-Cola Vol. 3* (Grammy winner 1993). *Barcelona Mona,* with Marsalis. Pop Instrumental Grammy 1994.

HOROWITZ, VLADIMIR (1904–1989)

b. 10/1 Kiev, Ukraine. Concert pianist. Played 1920/30s but suffered from exhaustion 1935 and retired. Resumed career, later became ill again. Won Grammys 1972 & 1988. Married Wanda Toscanini, daughter of conductor Arturo Toscanini. Died 11/1 New York, NY.

HORSZOWSKI, MIECZYSLAW (1892–)

Pianist, albums *Piano/Mozart/Chopin/Debussy, Piano/Mozart/Chopin/Schumann.* Recorded in Philadelphia in 1991, celebrated 100th birthday in March 1992.

HORTON, BIG WALTER

Album *Big Walter with Carey Bell.*

HORTON, JOHNNY (1929–1960)

b. 4/3 Tyler, TX. Guitarist/singer, albums *American Originals, Marty Robinson/Johnny Horton,* etc. Killed in an auto accident.

HORTON, VAUGHN (1911–)

b. Broad Top, PA. Composed "Mockin' Bird Hill."

HORVITZ, WAYNE

With Jazz/rock & roll band the **President,** albums *This New Generation, Miracle Mile* 1992.

HOSCHNA, KRAL (1877–1911)

b. Bohemia, came to NY City 1896. Composer, with lyricist Otto Harbach* wrote "Cuddle Up a Little Closer" 1906.

HOT TUNA
Satellite group of **Jefferson Airplane*** 1972/78 with Jack Cassidy, Papa John Creach,* Jorma Kaukonen, Sammy Piazza, Will Scarlett, Bob Steeler. Albums *America's Choice, Burgers, Phosphorescent Rat, Yellow Fever.*

HOUGH, WILL M. (1892–1962)
b. Chicago, IL. Lyricist, with Frank R. Adams* & composers Joe E. Howard* and Harold Orlob* wrote "I Wonder Who's Kissing Her Now?" 1909.

HOUND DOG TAYLOR
Albums *Hound Dog Taylor and the Houserockers, Natural Boogie.*

HOUSE OF PAIN
Hit single "Jump Around" (1993 Grammy winner) toured US 1992/93, lead singer Everlast (Erik Schrodi b. 1969) was arrested at J.F. K. Airport, NY for having an unloaded pistol in his suitcase, March 1993, later released.

HOUSTON, DAVID (1936–1993)
Country singer, won 1966 Grammy for "Almost Persuaded."

HOUSTON, EMILY D. "CISSY" (1932–   )
b. Newark, NJ. Gospel/soul singer, mother of Whitney Houston,* first to record "Midnight Train to Georgia."

HOUSTON, WHITNEY (1963–   )
b. 8/9 Newark, NJ. Hit singles "Saving All My Love for You" (Grammy winner 1986), "The Greatest Love," on 1988 Top Ten list for "So Emotional," Single "I Will Always Love You" from *The Bodyguard* soundtrack top on Billboard's Hot 100 chart 1992, videos *The Star Spangled Banner, The #1 Video Hits,* "I Belong to You" won Grammy 1993. Swept the American Music awards 1994, three Grammys 1994 including Album *The Bodyguard* and Song "I Will Always Love You." Married singer Bobby Brown.*

HOVEY, RICHARD (1864–1900)
b. Normal, IL. With composer F.F. Bullard* wrote "For It's Always Fair Weather When Good Fellows Get Together."

HOWARD, GEORGE
Jazz saxist, albums *A Nice Place to Be, Dancing in the Sun, Love Will Follow, Personal Reflections,* "Just the Way I Feel" from album *Do I Ever Cross Your Mind* won 1993 Grammy.

HOWARD, JOSEPH E. (1878–1961)
b. New York, NY. Songwriter, with Ida Emerson wrote "Hello, Ma Baby" 1899 the first popular song about the telephone. With Harold Orlob* composed music for "I Wonder Who's Kissing Her Now?" 1909.

HOWARD, MIKI
Hip/hop singer, albums *Come Share My Love, Miki Howard, Femme Fatale* 1992, hit R&B single "Ain't Nobody Like You" 1992.

HOWE, JULIA WARD (1819–1910)
b. New York, NY. Married Samuel G. Howe. While visiting Washington, D.C. she heard the soldiers singing "John Brown's Body" to which she wrote the new words the "Battle Hymn of the Republic" 1861. Randy Travis sang the "Battle Hymn" at the Republican National Convention in Houston, TX in August 1992.

HOWLIN' WOLF (1910–1976)
b. Chester Arthur Burnett 6/10 Aberdeen, MS. Guitarist/harmonica player/singer/songwriter, albums *London Howlin' Wolf Sessions* 1971, *The Chess Box, Chicago: The Golden Years,* etc.

HOYT, CHARLES H. (1860–1900)
b. Concord, NH. Lyricist/playwright, with composer Percy Gaunt* wrote "The Bowery" 1896 and "Reuben, Reuben I've Been Thinking."

HUBBARD, FREDDIE (1938–   )
b. Indianapolis, IN. Musician/leader, at the Playboy Jazz Festival at the Hollywood Bowl 1982, at Miller Lite Jazz Festival in Detroit, September 1992, album *Live at Fat Tuesdays* 1992, dozens of other albums available.

HUDSON BROTHERS, THE
Singers/musicians, William "Bill" Louis II (b. 1949), Mark Jeffrey Anthony (b. 1951), Brett Stuart Patrick Hudson (b. 1953). Had weekly TV show "The Razzle Dazzle Comedy Hour" 1975, hit singles "Rendezvous" 1975, "Help Wanted" 1976.

HUDSON, HELEN
Country singer/songwriter, album *Helen Hudson.*

HUES CORPORATION, THE
Disco/soul group formed 1969 with Tommy Brown, H. Ann Kelly, St. Clair Lee, Karl Russell, Fleming Williams. Hit single "Rock the Boat" 1974.

HUMBLE PIE
British hard rock band formed 1968 with David "Clem" Clemson, Peter Frampton,* Steve Marriott, Gregory Ridley, Jerry Shirley, hit album *Smokin'* 1972, *As Safe as Yesterday, Rockin' the Fillmore, Best of Humble Pie.* Frampton's solo album *Frampton Comes Alive* sold over 12 million copies 1976.

HUMES, HELEN (1913–1981)
b. 6/23 Louisville, KY. Singer with Count Basie* 1938/42, with Red Norvo* in 50s, at Monterey Jazz Festivals, toured Australia. Albums *Songs I Like to Sing, Swingin' with Humes.* Died 9/13 Santa Monica, CA.

HUMPERDINCK, ENGLEBERT (1936–   )
b. Arnold Gerry Dorsey 5/3 Madras, India. Singer, albums *Release Me* 1967, *A Man Without Love* 1969, *The Greatest Hits of Englebert Humperdinck, Hello Out There* 1992. Married &

has two sons & daughter singer/actress Louise Dorsey. Homes in England & in Beverly Hills, CA.

HUNTER, ALBERTA (1895–1984)

b. 4/1 Memphis, TN. Blues singer, sang in night clubs in Chicago & NY City in 1920s, Europe in 30s, on USO tours during World War II. Retired in 1956 but resumed career in 1977. Sang in The White House for President & Mrs. Carter in December 1978. Albums *Amtrack Blues, London Sessions,* etc. Died 10/1 NY City.

HUNTER, IAN (1946–   )

b. 6/3 Shrewsbury, England. Lead singer with **Mott the Hoople,*** went solo, hits "Just Another Night" 1979, on *MTV* at Hotel Diplomat in NY City on New Year's Day 1982. Albums *All American Alien Boy, Shades of Ian Hunter,* etc.

HUNTER, "IVORY JOE" (1911–1974)

b. Kirbyville, TX. R&B singer/pianist, wrote and recorded "Blues at Sunrise" 1944, had a gold record "Since I Met You Baby" 1956. Died of Cancer 11/8 in Memphis, TN.

HUNTER, ROBERT

Albums *Box of Rain, Tale of Robert Hunter, Tiger Rose,* etc.

HUPPFELD, HERMAN (1894–1951)

b. Montclair, NJ. Singer/composer, wrote "As Time Goes By" 1931.

HURT, "MISSISSIPPI JOHN" (1892–1966)

b. Teoe, MS. Guitarist/singer, albums *1928 Sessions, Immortal Mississippi John, Last Sessions, Today,* etc.

HÜSKER DÜ

Minneapolis pop trio with guitarist/singer Bob Mould. Albums *Candy Apple Gray, New Day Rising, Warehouse: Songs and Stories, Zen Arcade.* Mould left and joined rock group **Sugar.***

HUSKY, FERLIN (1927–   )

b. 12/3 Flat River, MO. Country guitarist/singer, albums *Capitol Collection Series, Greatest Hits.*

HUTCHERSON, BOBBY (1941–)
b. Los Angeles, CA. Vibraphonist, albums *Color Schemes, Dialogue, Happenings,* etc.

HUTTON, INA RAY (1916–1984)
b. Odessa Cowan 3/3 Chicago, IL. Singer/leader, called the "Blond Bombshell of Swing," led all-female band in 1930s, then an all-male band, married trumpeter Randy Brooks, sang in various night clubs in 1950s. Died 2/19 Ventura, CA.

HUTTON, MARION (1920–1987)
Singer with **Glenn Miller* Band,** hits "My Heart Belongs to Daddy," "The Jumpin' Jive," "F.D.R. Jones."

HWA
"Hoes Wit Attitude" female rap group.

HYLAND, BRIAN (1943–)
b. 11/12 Woodhaven, NY. Singer, had hit "Itsy Bitsy Teenie Weenie Yellow Polkadot Bikini" 1960. Album *Greatest Hits.*

HYMAN, DICK (1927–)
b. NY City. Pianist/musical director for Arthur Godfrey's radio show in late 1950s, at Newport Jazz Festival 1972 & later years, his **Perfect Jazz Repertory Quintet*** played in NY City, was at Avery Fisher Hall in NY City in June 1960, at Gibson Jazz Concerts, Denver, 1982. Albums *Blues in the Night, Plays Fats Waller, Superpiano: Toronto Live, All Through the Night,* etc.

HYMAN, PHYLLIS
Albums *Living All Alone, Prime of My Life, Under Her Spell.*

HYNDE, CHRISTINE E. "CRISSIE" (1951–)
b. Akron, Ohio. Lead singer for the rock group **The Pretenders.*** Militant vegetarian.

I

IAN, JANIS (1950–)
b. Janis Fink 5/7 New York, NY. Singer/songwriter, hit "At Seventeen" won 1975 Grammy, album *Between the Lines*. Revealed she was a lesbian on her 1993 album *Breaking the Silence*.

IAN AND SYLVIA
Canadian country duo singers Ian and wife Sylvia Fricker Tyson, hit "You Were on My Mind" 1966, albums *4 Strong Winds, Greatest Hits, Northern Journey*.

ICE CUBE (1969–)
Rapper O'Shea Jackson from Los Angeles, formerly with N.W.A. albums *Amerikkk's Most Wanted, Kill at Will, Death Certificate* 1991, *The Predator* 1992.

ICE-T
Rapper Ice-T (Tracy Marrow) and his **Body Count Band*** won 1990 Rap Vocal Grammy with others for "Back on the Block." On Lollapallooza Tour 1991, album *Body Count* included song "Cop Killer" which raised a storm of protests. With Body Count on album *Born Dead* 1993.

IDOL, BILLY (1955–)
b. William Board 11/30 Surrey, England. Singer, punk rock teenage idol, hits "Eyes Without Face," "Catch My Fall" 1984, platinum album *Charmed Life* 1990, *Rebel Yell, Whiplash Smile*, videos *The Charmed Life Videos, Vital Idol*.

IGGY POP (1947–)
b. James Jewel Osterberg 4/21 Ann Arbor, MI. Singer/songwriter, albums *The Idiot, Lust for Life* 1978, *No Fun* 1980, *Choice Cuts* 1984, etc. With others on *Rock 'n' Roll Cities Detroit* on TV November 1992.

IGLESIAS, JULIO (1943–)
b. Julio Iglesias de la Cueva 9/23 Madrid, Spain. Singer/

songwriter, has sold over 100 million albums, earned $48 million 1991/92 per *Forbes* magazine. Albums *1100 Bell Aire Place, In Concert, Julio, Moments,* videos *In Spain, Starry Nights,* album *Calor* won Latin Pop album Grammy 1993.

IMPRESSIONS, THE
Singers Sam Gooden, Fred Cash, Reggie Toniser, Ralph Johnson, hit singles "Gypsy Woman," "Finally Got Myself Together" 1974, album *Greatest Hits.*

INCREDIBLE SWING BAND, THE
Scottish group with Gerlad Dott, Mike Heron, Malcolm McMaistre, Christina "Licorice" McKechnie, Rose Simpson, & Robin Williamson.

INDIA (1970–)
b. India Cabellero in Puerto Rico, singer raised in the South Bronx, NY City, duo with keyboardist Eddie Palmieri on album *Llegó La India . . . via Eddie Palmieri* 1993.

INDIGO GIRLS
Georgia based folk/rock duo of Amy Ray and Emily Saliers, albums *Indigo Girls, Strange Fire,* video *Live at the Uptown Lounge,* singles "Nomads, Indians, Saints," "Let it Be Me" 1992, album *Rites of Passage* Grammy winner 1993.

INGRAM, JAMES (1952–)
b. 2/16 Akron, Ohio. Singer/songwriter, with Patti Austin* hit single "Baby Come to Me" 1982, soloist on "We are the World" 1985, albums *It's Real, It's Your Night, Power of Great Music, Always You* 1993.

INK SPOTS
Singers Billy Bowen (1909–1982), Orville "Happy" Jones, Ivory "Deek" Watson, Bill Kenny, Bernard Mackey (1909–1980), guitarist Charlie Fuqua, hit "If I Didn't Care" 1939, featured Ella Fitzgerald* in 1940s, hit "To Each His Own." Herb Kenny joined group, sang at Avery Fisher Hall in NY City, June 1980. Albums *The Best of Ink Spots, Greatest Hits.*

INNER CIRCLE
Bad Boys Reggae Album Grammy 1994.

INXS
Australian group with Andrew, Jon, & Tim Farriss, Gary Beers, Michael Hutchence, Kirk Pengilly, Daryl Hall, hit singles "Original Sin" 1984, "Need You Tonight" 1988, Top Ten pop album *Kick* 1988, platinum video *Kick the Video Flick* 1989, platinum album *X* 1990, *Welcome to Wherever You Are* 1992, *Beautiful Girl* 1993, toured US 1992/93.

IRON BUTTERFLY
Group with Erik Braun, Ronald Bushy, Lee Dorman, Doug Ingle, Michael Pinera, Lawrence Reinhardt, albums *In-a-gadda-da-vida, Live, Rave Flight.*

IRON MAIDEN
British blues/rock/heavy metal group, albums *Iron Maiden, Killers, Life After Death, No Prayer for the Dying, Power Slave,* etc., videos *Iron Maiden, Maiden England,* album *Fear of the Dark* 1992.

ISAAK, CHRIS (1958–)
b. Stockton, CA. Singer/songwriter, album *Heart Shaped World* 1989 sold 1.5 million copies. Album *Silvertone,* videos *Chris Isaak, Wicked Game* popularized in the film *Wild at Heart,* album *San Francisco Days* 1993. Resides in San Francisco.

ISHAM, MARK
Castalia named the Best Soundtrack, *Film Music, Mark Isham* (Grammy winner 1990), *Tibet, Vapor Drawings,* etc.

ISIS
Album *Rebel Soul.*

ISLEY BROTHERS
Ronald (b. 1941), Rudolph, Marvin (later killed in a car crash), Ernest, & O'Kelly Isley (died in 1986). Hit single "It's Your Thing," albums *3 plus 3, Between the Sheets, Smooth Sailin, Winner Take All,* etc.

ISRAEL VIBRATION
Albums *Praises, Strength of My Life, Why You so Craven?*

ITURBI, JOSE (1895–1980)
b. 11/28 Valencia, Spain. Pianist/conductor/composer, toured Europe, American debut 1928, became conductor of Rochester (NY) Philharmonic 1936. Died 6/28 Los Angeles, CA.

IVES, BURL (1909–)
b. Icle Ivanhoe 6/14 Hunt, IL. Folk Singer, in concert at Town Hall, NY City 1945, appeared on Broadway & in films, *The Big Country* (won 1959 Oscar), appeared in TV commercials 1980s/90s, albums *Have a Jolly Christmas, Little White Duck,* etc.

J

JACKSON, AL JR. (1936–1975)
b. Memphis, TN. Drummer, member of **Booker T & the M.G.'s.***
Killed by a prowler 10/1 in Memphis, TN.

JACKSON, ALAN (1958–)
b. 10/17. Attended high school in Newman, GA. Country singer,
albums *I'd Love You All Over Again, Love's Got a Hold on You,
Don't Rock the Jukebox* 1991, Country Music video award for
Midnight in Montgomery 1992, "She's Got the Rhythm,"
"Chattahoochee" 1993. American Music Country Album
award for *A Lot About Livin' and a Little 'Bout Love* 1994.

JACKSON FIVE, THE
Brothers & sisters born in Gary, IN, Jackie (b. 1951), Tito (b.
1953), Jermaine LaJuane*, Marlon David (b. 1957), & Michael
Joseph Jackson*, hit single "I Want You Back" 1970 sold over
2 million copies, "I'll Be There" 1970, "ABC" was number
one 1970. Also Randy (b. 1961), Janet* (successful solo career)
& La Toya.* *Hitsville USA, The Motown Singles Collection*
1992.

JACKSON, FREDDIE
Albums *Do Me Again, Don't Let Love Slip Away, Just Like the
First Time, Rock Me Tonight.* Hit R&B single "I Could Use a
Little Love" 1992, album *Time for Love* 1992.

JACKSON, JANET (1966–)
b. 5/16 Gary, IN. Sister of Michael Jackson.* Hit single "Control," album *Rhythm Nation 1814* sold over 2 million 1989,
platinum single "Miss You Much" 1989, video *Rhythm Nation
1814*, with Luther Vandross on June 1990 Top singles list for
"The Best Things in Life are Free." "That's the Way Love
Goes" (Grammy Winner 1994), album *janet* 1993.

JACKSON, JERMAINE (1954–)
b. 12/11 Gary, IN. Brother of Michael Jackson.* Singer, video
Jermaine Jackson: Dynamite Videos 1985, albums *Greatest*

Hits & Rare Classics. Jermaine & wife Margaret produced the ABC mini-series *The Jacksons: An American Dream* in November 1992.

JACKSON, JOE (1956–　)
b. Portsmouth, England. Pianist/singer/composer, came to US 1982. Albums *Blaze of Glory, Body & Soul, I'm the Man, Jumpin' Jive, Laughter & Lust, Look Sharp,* etc.

JACKSON, LA TOYA (1956–　)
b. 1/29 Gary, IN. Sister of Michael Jackson,* singer, married Jack Gordon, her manager. He was arrested 4/21/92 for assaulting her with a chair.

JACKSON, MAHALIA (1911–1972)
b. near New Orleans, LA. Gospel/jazz singer, sang at concerts at Carnegie Hall in NY City 1950/56, sang at the inauguration of President Kennedy 1961, at black march on Washington, D.C. 1963, toured Europe 1971. Albums *America's Favorite Hymns, Greatest Hits,* etc. Died of heart disease.

JACKSON, MICHAEL J. (1958–　)
b. 8/29 Gary, IN. Singer with the **Jackson Five,*** went solo, won 1983 Grammys for "Beat It" and album *Thriller,* (bestselling album of all time to date) on video *We are the World* 1985, on 1988 Top Ten Pop compact discs list for *Bad,* multi-platinum video *Moonwalker* 1989, hit "In the Chart" 1992. Honored as Top-selling artist of the decade on Billboard Music Awards in December 1992.

JACKSON, MILTON "MILT" (1923–　)
b. 1/1 Detroit, MI. Vibraphonist, with Dizzy Gillespie,* Woody Herman,* & others, *Bags & Trane, Bags Meets Wes, Soul Route,* etc.

JACKSON, PRESTON (1904–1983)
b. James Preston McDonald in New Orleans, LA. Trombonist, with Terry Weatherfield in 1920s, Louis Armstrong* & others in 30s, led own bands 40s/50s, with Lil Hardin* 1959, at Preservation Hall in New Orleans in 70s.

JACKSON, QUENTIN L. "BUTTER" (1909–1976)
b. Springfield, Ohio. Trombonist, with Duke Ellington* 1948/59, toured Europe with Quincy Jones. Died 10/2 New York City.

JACKSON, WANDA (1937–)
b. 10/20 Maud, OK. Country singer/songwriter, toured with Elvis Presley* 1955/56, sang in Japan & Europe, albums *Greatest Hits, Rocking in the Country.* Honored at a country music festival in September 1992. Married Wendell Goodman.

JACKYL
Atlanta based quintet with Tom Bettini, Jeff Worley, Jesse James Dupree, Chris Worley, & Jimmy Stiff, toured US 1992. Album *Jackyl* 1992. Guitarist Dupree was arrested in Cincinnati on January 11, 1993 for dropping his pants on stage and exposing himself to the audience.

JACOBS, ALBERT T. "AL" (1903–1985)
b. 1/22 San Francisco, CA. Songwriter, wrote "This is My Country," "There'll Never be Another You," & some 300 songs. Died 2/13 Laurel, MD.

JACQUET, J.B. ILLINOIS (1922–)
b. Broussard, LA & raised in Houston, TX. Tenor saxist/bassoonist, hit with Lionel Hampton* on "Flying Home," with Cab Calloway* & Count Basie* in 1940s, led own bands & combos 1950s/90s. Albums *Jacquet's Got It, The Black Velvet Band, The Blues: That's Me.* Played in The White House for Presidents Carter & Reagan. Had his own band at President Clinton's Gala in January 1993.

JADE
Hit R&B singles "I Wanna Love You" 1992, "Don't Walk Away" 1993.

JAGGER, MICK (1943–)
b. 7/26 Dartford, England. Singer/songwriter with the **Rolling Stones,*** albums *She's the Boss, Wandering Spirit* 1993. First wife Bianca, daughter Jade. Married Jerry Hall, separated 1992.

JAM, THE
British rock group founded 1977, lead singer Paul Weller, bassist
Bruce Foxton, cassette *The Jam* 1985, CDs *All Mad Cops,
Snap, Sound Effects, This is the Modern World.*

JAMAL, AHMAD (1930–   )
b. 7/7 Pittsburgh PA. Pianist/composer, had own trio in 1960s,
wrote *Minor Moods, Extensions and One for Miles.* At the
Mellon Jazz Festival in Pittsburgh 1992. Albums *Crystal,
Digital Works, Live at Montreal 1985, Pittsburgh, Rossiter
Road, Poinciana,* etc.

JAMBALAYA CAJUN BAND
With accordianists & fiddlers, album *Joy to the World* 1992.

JAMES, BOB (1939–   )
b. 12/25 Marshall, IN. Keyboardist/composer, albums *Grand
Piano Canyon, Ivory Coast, Obsession, Touchdown,* video *Bob
James Live,* with Earl Klugh on album *Cool* (Grammy winner
1993).

JAMES, "BONEY"
Jazz musician, hit album *Trust* 1992.

JAMES, ELMER (1910–1954)
Bassist/tubist.

JAMES, ELMORE
Guitarist, with John Brim on *John Brim & Floyd Jones, Whose
Muddy Shoes,* with Gladys Knight on 2 CDs *The Fire/Furry
Records Story* 1993.

JAMES, ETTA (1938–   )
Blues/gospel/rock singer, albums *At Last, Gospel Soul of Etta
James, Second Time Around, Seven Year Itch,* etc. Album *The
Right Time* won 1993 Grammy.

JAMES GANG
Tom Bolin, James Fox, Phil Giallombardo, "Bubba" Keith, Roy

Kenner, Dale Peters, Richard Shack, Tom Troiano, Joseph Fidler Walsh, & Bob Webb. Albums *Bang, James Gang Rides Again, Live in Concert, Miami,* etc.

JAMES, HARRY (1916–1983)
b. 3/15 Albany, GA. Trumpeter/leader, with Ben Pollack 1936, formed the **Music Makers** 1963, toured Europe 1970s. Recorded "All or Nothing at All" with Frank Sinatra*. Albums *Best of the Big Bands, Compact Jazz,* etc. Died 7/5 Las Vegas, NV.

JAMES, RICK (1952–)
b. James Johnson 2/1 Buffalo, NY. Singer, hit "Super Freak" on double platinum album *Street Songs* 1981, *Cold Blooded, Glow, Greatest Hits,* etc.

JAMES SEVEN
British pop/rock group, album *Seven,* toured US in 1992.

JAMES WHITE AND THE BLACKS
Punk/jazz group consisting of **James Chance and the Contortions** with the Lurie brothers of the **Lounge Lizards** in 1980s.

JAN AND DEAN
Surf music duo formed 1958 with Jan Berry (b. 4/3/41 Los Angeles) & Dean Torrance, debut hit "Jennie Lee" sold 10 million copies, wrote hit single "Surf City" 1963, albums *All Time Greatest Hits, Best of Jan and Dean.*

JANE'S ADDICTION
Lead singer Perry Farrell* started Lollapalooza tour of US 1991, albums *Jane's Addiction, Nothing's Shocking, Ritual De Lo Habitual,* video *The Fan's Video-Soul Kiss.*Farrell went solo & with Stephen Perkins, Peter di Stefano, & Martyn Le Noble formed **Porno for Pyros** 1993.

JARREAU, AL (1940–)
b. 3/12 Milwaukee, WI. Singer, won Grammys as best jazz vocalist 1978/79, albums *All Fly Home, Breakin' Away, Glow, High Crime, In London, Heaven and Earth* (Grammy winner 1993).

JARRETT, KEITH (1945–)
b. 5/8 Allentown, PA. Jazz pianist/composer, with Roland Kirk & others in 1960s, had own quartet 70s/90s. Albums *Book of Ways, Changeless, ECM Works, Paris Concert, Bach's Preludes & Fugues Op 87* 1992.

JARVIS, JOHN BARLOW
Singer/songwriter, albums *Pure Contours, So Fa So Good, Whatever Works,* with Vince Gill* wrote "I Still Believe in You" (Grammy winner 1993).

JASMINE
Pop/jazz group with saxist/clarinetist/flutist Roger Rosenberg, pianist Bill O'Connell, bassist Lee Smith, drummer/percussionist Steve Berrios, & singer Carmen Lundy in 1980s.

JASON
Jason Ringenberg cowpunk guitarist/singer with **Jason & the Scorchers** in 1980s, went solo on country albums *Devil's Daughter & Already Burned,* heavy metal albums *Try Me & Letter of Love* 1992.

JAY & THE AMERICANS
Brooklyn based group with lead singer John Jay Traynor 1961/62, lead singer David Jay Black 1962/70, Sandy Deane (Sandy Vaguda), Howie Kane, Marty Sanders, Kenny Vance.* Album *Come a Little Bit Closer* 1963, hits "Cara Mia" 1965, "This Magic Moment" 1969, albums *All Time Greatest Hits, Legendary Master Series.*

JAYHAWKS
Minneapolis country/rock band formed 1985 with lead singer/songwriter Mark Olsen, guitarist Gary Louis, bassist Marc Perlman, keyboardist Benmont Trench, albums *The Jayhawks* 1986, *Blue Earth* 1989, *Hollywood Town Hall* 1992.

JAZZ BUTCHERS, THE
Singers, album *Condition Blue* 1992.

JAZZ CRUSADERS
With tenor saxist Wilton L. Felder, flutist Hubert Laws,* drummer Stix Hooper, pianist Joe Sample,* albums *Their Best, Freedom Sounds, The Golden Years* with hit song "Street Life" issued 1992.

JAZZ MACHINE
With drummer Elvin Jones,* bassist Andy McCloud, tenor saxist Pat LaBarbara, guitarist Roland Prince in NY City 1979, toured with saxist Andrew White in 1980s, in Lewistown, NY, 1992.

JAZZ MASTERS
On video *Vintage Collection Vol. 1.*

JAZZ MEMBERS BIG BAND
Organized in Chicago by trumpeter Steve Jensen and trombonist Jeff Lindberg 1978. In 1981 included 17 other instrumentalists.

JAZZ MESSENGERS
Led by Art Blakey* with bassist Charles Fambrough. Album *The Complete Blue Note Recordings of Art Blakey's 1960 Jazz Messengers* issued in 1992.

JAZZMANIA
Duo with trumpeter Ted Curson & bassist Ray Drummond 1979. Also the **Jazzmania All Stars** led by Mike Morganstern with Joe Carroll at Jazzmania in 1980s.

J.B. HORNS
Funk trio with trombonist Fred Wesley & sax men Pee Wee Ellis & Maceo Parker,* album *Funky Good Time/Live* 1993.

JEFF HEALY BAND
Top Five song "Angel Eyes", album *Hell to Pay, See the Light.*

JEFFERSON AIRPLANE/STARSHIP
With singer/songwriter Marty Balin (Martyn Jerel Buchwald b. 1943 Cincinnati), Jack Cassidy, Joey Covington, Spencer Dryden, Paul Kantner, Jorma Kauoknen, Grace Slick.* Hits

"It's No Secret," "Fantastic Lover," "White Rabbit." Albums *After Bathing at Baxter's, Surrealistic Pillow, Takes Off, Volunteers.* Several members formed **Starship** 1985, video *Jefferson Starship. Jefferson Airplane Loves You,* (1960s songs) released in 1992.

JEFFERSON, "BLIND LEMON" (1897–1930)
b. Wortham, TX. Guitarist/singer blind from birth, sang in streets of Dallas from 1917, made some 81 recordings accompanied by Leadbelly* & John White, album *King of Country Blues.*

JEFFERSON, EDDIE (1918–1979)
b. 8/3 Pittsburgh, PA. Singer with Coleman Hawkins* in 1940, hits "Moody's Mood for Love" in 1950s, LP *Main Man* 1979. After leaving a night club in Detroit was shot to death on 5/9/79. Albums *Body & Soul, Godfather of Vocals, Letter from Home.*

JEFFREYS, GARLAND (1944–)
b. Brooklyn, NY. Rock/jazz/soul singer/songwriter, album *Escape Artist* 1981.

JELLY FISH
Rock group with singer/songwriter Andy Sturmer & Roger Manning, album *Split Milk* 1993.

JENKINS, GORDON (1919–1984)
b. 5/12 Webster Groves, MO. Composer/leader, arranger for Benny Goodman* & Paul Whiteman,* orchestra leader for Judy Garland,* Dick Haymes,* & others, composed *Manhattan Suite* 1945. Hit song "Goodnight Irene," CDs *Sophisticated, Soul of the People.* Died 5/1 Malibu, CA.

JENKINS, LEROY (1932–)
b. Chicago. Jazz violinist, album *Leroy Jenkins: Solo Violin* 1984.

JENNINGS, WAYLON (1937–)
b. 6/15 Littlefield, TX. Singer, played electric bass for Buddy Holly* 1958/59, then led own band. Albums *A Man Called Hoss, The Eagle, The Taker/Tulsa & Honky Tonk Heroes,* etc.

JENNINGS, WILL
Songwriter, with Eric Clapton* wrote "Tears in Heaven" about Clapton's son who died after falling off a balcony in New York City. The song won a 1993 Grammy.

JESUS JONES
British primal rock band with singer Mike Edwards, Jerry De-Borg, Gen, Al Joworski, & Ian Baker, album *Perverse* 1993.

JESUS AND MARY CHAIN, THE
British brothers Jim and William Reid, guitarists/singers, *Videos 1985 to 1989,* albums *Automatic, Barbed Wire Kisses, Draklands, Psychocandy,* CD *Honey's Dead* 1992, on Lollapalooza US tour 1992.

JETHRO TULL
British rock group led by Ian Anderson, Mike Abrahams, Barrimore Barlowe, Martin Barre, Clive Bunker, Glenn Cornick, John Evan, & Jeffrey Hammond-Hammond. Hit album *Aqualung, A Passion Play, Catfish Rising, Heavy Horses, Rock Island, Stand Up, A Little Light Music* 1992, video *The First 20 Years.*

JETT, JOAN (1960–)
b. Joan Larkin 9/22 Philadelphia, PA. Pop/heavy metal group **Joan Jett & the Blackhearts** with Ricky Byrd, Lee Crystal, & Gary Ryan. Hit "I Love Rock 'n' Roll" 1982. Also led the **Runaways.** Albums *Good Music, The Hit List, Notorious, Up Your Alley.*

JIMENEZ, FLACO
Pop/jazz singer with **Tex-Mex and The Texas Tornados,*** albums *Arriba El Norte,* solo album *Partners* 1992.

JOBIM, ANTONIO CARLOS (1927–1994)
b. Rio de Janeiro, Brazil. Pianist/guitarist/composer, resided in Los Angeles after 1965, albums *Echoes of Rio, Passarim, Stone Flower,* video *Rio Revisited with Gal Costa.*

JODECI

With Dahin De Grati, Joel "Jo Jo" Hailey, Cedric Hailey, DeVante "Swing" De Grate, hit R&B single "Come Talk to Me" 1992, album *Forever My Lady* 1992 (won Billboard awards).

JODY GRIND, THE

Atlanta group, bassist Robert Hays aged 24, drummer Rob Clayton aged 22 & collaborator Deacon Lunchbox (Timothy T. Ruttenber) aged 41 were killed in a car crash on April 19, 1992 near Montgomery, AL. Singer Kelly Hogan & guitarist Bill Taft were in another vehicle & not involved in the accident. Albums *One Man's Trash is Another Man's Treasure* 1990, *Lefty's Deceiver* 1992.

JOE PUBLIC

Guitarist J.R. (Joseph Sayles), bassist Kevin Scott, keyboardist Jake (Joe Carter), drummer Dew (Dwight Wyatt), R&B hits "Live & Learn," "I Miss You," album *Joe Public* 1992.

JOEL, BILLY (1949–   )

b. 5/9 Bronx, NY City. Pianist/singer, won 1974 Grammy for "Just the Way You Are" *Piano Man,* 1979 Grammy for album *52nd Street,* hit single "Uptown Girl." Album *Storm Front* sold over 2 million in 1989, videos *A Matter of Trust, Billy Joel, Eye of the Storm,* etc. On *Honeymoon in Vegas* soundtrack 1993. Married supermodel Christie Brinkley March 1985, later divorced.

JOHN, ELTON (1947–   )

b. Reginald Kenneth Dwight 3/25 Pinner, England. Pianist/singer/songwriter, hits "Rocket Man," "Philadelphia Freedom," "Sad Songs," videos *The Nighttime Concert, To Russia with Elton.* Bernie Taupin* has been his lyricist for 25 years. The John/Taupin songs were featured on the album *Two Rooms* 1992 sung by various pop singers. Single "The One" on Top Ten adult contemporary list 1992, Grammy 1993. Inducted into Rock & Roll Hall of Fame 1994.

JOHNS, EVAN (1956–   )
Raised in McLean, VA. Guitarist, leader of the **H-Bombs,** albums *Evan Johns and the H-Bombs* 1986, *Rolling Through the Night* 1987, *Rockit Fuel Only* 1992.

JOHNSON, ALBERT J. "BUD" (1910–   )
b. Dallas, TX. Tenor saxist/vocalist, toured Texas 1920s, with Louis Armstrong* & others 30s, Dizzy Gillespie* & others 40s, own combos 50s, with Count Basie* & Earl Hines* 60s, toured Europe 1970, in NY City 80s.

JOHNSON, BUNK (1879–1949)
b. William Geary Johnson in New Orleans, LA. Trumpeter with Buddy Holden in 1890s, **Allen's Brass Band** & others in 1900s/40s, first recorded in 1945, then in 1947 in NY City, later returned to Iberia, LA where he died.

JOHNSON, ERIC
Guitarist, named best overall guitarist in *Guitar Player's Magazine* annual readers' poll, January 1993. Albums *Ah Via Musician, Tones.*

JOHNSON, GEORGE W. (1839–1917)
b. Binbrook, Canada. Lyricist, came to US. With composer James A. Butterfield* wrote "When You and I Were Young, Maggie."

JOHNSON, JAMES L. "JJ" (1924–   )
b. 1/22 Indianapolis, IN. Trombonist/composer, with Benny Carter* 1942/45, Count Basie* 1945/46, toured Europe in 50s. Wrote *Perceptions* recorded by orchestra led by Gunther Schuller* (1961) & performed at Monterey Jazz Festival in California. Albums *The Trombone Master, J.J. Johnson Vols. 1&2.* Moved to California in 1970.

JOHNSON, JAMES P. (1891–1953)
b. New Brunswick, NJ. Pianist/composer, played in NY City & Atlantic City, NJ 1912/19, accompanist for singers Bessie Smith* & Ethel Waters* in 1920s. Wrote "Charleston" with

Cecil Mack (R.C. McPherson)* 1923 and "Carolina Shout." Suffered strokes in 1946 & 1951 and died in a Queens Hospital in NY City.

JOHNSON, JAMES WELDON (1871–1938)

b. Jacksonville, FL. Lyricist/singer/vaudeville actor, with composer/brother John Rosamond Johnson* wrote the official song of the NAACP "Lift Ev'ry Voice and Sing" 1900.

JOHNSON, JOHN ROSAMOND (1873–1954)

b. Jacksonville, FL. Composer, with vaudeville team of Bob Cole* and the Johnson Brothers, composed music for "Lift Ev'ry Voice and Sing."

JOHNSON, LINTON KWESI

Albums *Dread Beat an' Blood, Reggae Greats, Tings on Time,* etc.

JOHNSON, MARV (1939–1993)

R&B singer/songwriter, hits "Come to Me" 1959, "You Got What It Takes," "I Love the Way You Love."

JOHNSON, ROBERT

Video *The Search for Robert Johnson.*

JOLLY BOYS

Calypso/work songs, albums *Pop 'N Mento, Sunshine 'N Water,* with baritone Allan Swymmer on album *Beer Joint & Tailoring* 1992.

JOLSON, AL (1886–1950)

b. Asa Joelson, Russia. Came to America, sang "Mammy" in the film *The Jazz Singer,* with Buddy de Sylva* & Joseph Meyer* wrote "California Here I Come." Died soon after returning from Korea where he had entertained troops. A postage stamp was issued in his honor 1994.

JONES, ALLAN (1907–1992)

b. Old Forge, PA. Singer/actor in the film *The Firefly* 1937 in which he sang the "Donkey Serenade." Died 6/27 of lung cancer in NY City.

JONES, ELVIN RAY (1927–)
b. Pontiac, MI. Drummer, brother of pianist Hank Jones & trumpeter/cornetist Thad Jones,* played in Detroit 1952/56, had own quintet in NY City in 80s, at Playboy Jazz Festival at Hollywood Bowl 1982, **Elvin Jones Jazz Machine*** at Artpark Jazz Festival in Lewistown, NY September 1992.

JONES, ETTA
Albums *Christmas with Etta, Don't Go to Strangers, I'll be Seeing You, Something Nice.*

JONES, GEORGE (1931–)
b. 9/12 Saratoga, TX. Country singer, named best male vocalist by Country Music Awards 1980, "He Stopped Loving Her" rated by *Country America* as top country song of all time, named to Country Hall of Fame 1992 & sang "Rockin' Chair." Married Tammy Wynette* 1968, divorced 1975, married Nancy Sepulvado (his fourth wife) March 1983.

JONES, GLENN (1961–)
b. Jacksonville, FL. Soul tenor/songwriter, with wife Genobia Jeter-Jones, albums *Here I Go Again* 1992, with tenors Trey Lorenz* & Brian McKnight on *I've Been Searchin'* 1992.

JONES, GRACE (1952–)
b. 5/19 Jamaica, West Indies. Singer/songwriter, *Warm Leatherette* 1980, *Island Life* 1985, etc.

JONES, HOWARD (1955–)
b. 3/23 Southampton, England. Singer, albums *Cross that Line, Dream Into Action, Human's Lib, One to One.*

JONES, ISHAM (1894–1956)
b. Coalton, Ohio. Composer/leader, with lyricists Tell Taylor* & Ole Olson wrote "You're in the Army Now" 1917, with lyricist Gus Kahn* wrote "I'll be Seeing You in My Dreams" 1924.

JONES, JONATHAN "JO" (1911–1985)
b. 10/7 Chicago, IL. Jazz drummer with Ted Adams in 1920s,

with Bennie Moten* & Count Basie* in 30s, served in army in World War II, then played with Basie & others, toured Europe with Jazz at the Philharmonic in 60s, in NY City in 70s. Died 9/3 NY City.

JONES, MICHAEL
Pianist, albums *After the Rain, Magical Child, Pianoscapes, Seascapes, Sunscapes.*

JONES, "PHILLY JOE" (1923–1985)
b. Philadelphia, PA. Drummer with local combos in 1940s, later with Zoot Sims,* Miles Davis,* & others, toured Japan 1965, Europe 1969/72, with Byard Lancaster formed jazz/rock group **Le Gran Prix** 1975, at Carnegie Hall, NY City 1980, albums *Blues for Dracula, Drum Song.*

JONES, QUINCY D., JR. (1933–)
Trumpeter/pianist/composer, with Lionel Hampton* & Dizzy Gillespie* in 1950s, toured Europe with his big band 1960, composed "Evening in Paris," *Soundpiece for Jazz Orchestra,* scores for *In Cold Blood* 1967, *The Wiz* 1978, & other films, Grammy awards for albums *The Dude, Lena Horne, The Lady & Her Music* 1982, 1990 Grammy for *Back on the Block.* Jazz Ensemble Grammy 1994 for album *Miles and Quincy Live at Montreux.* Jones has six children, was married to actress Peggy Lipton. Video *Quincy Jones—A Celebration.*

JONES, RICHARD MYKNEE (1889–1945)
b. Donaldsville, LA. Jazz pianist/composer, known as a barrelhouse player, composed "Trouble in Mind" first recorded by "Chippie" Hill, became one of the most recorded blues of all time.

JONES, RICKIE LEE (1954–)
b. 11/8 Chicago, IL. Blues/jazz/folk singer/songwriter, hit "Chuck E's in Love" 1979, albums *Flying Cowboys, Pop Pop, Rickie Lee Jones* 1991, *The Magazine.*

JONES, SISSIERETTA (1868–1933)
b. Portsmouth, VA & raised in Providence, RI. Known as "Black

Patti'' she sang in The White House for President Benjamin Harrison. She was leader of **Black Patti's Troubadours** 1893/1910.

JONES, "SPIKE" (1911–1965)

Leader of **Spike Jones & His City Slickers,** hit "All I Want for Christmas is My Two Front Teeth" 1940s, albums *Dinner Music for People, Spike Jones Christmas, The Best of Spike Jones.*

JONES, THADDEUS J. "THAD" (1923–1986)

b. 3/28 Pontiac, MI. Jazz trumpeter/composer, with Count Basie* 1954/63, formed band with Mel Lewis* 1965, toured Soviet Union 1972. CDs *Mad Thad, Quintet and Sextet, The Magnificent Thad Jones.* Died 8/20 Copenhagen, Denmark.

JONES, TOM (1940–   )

b. Thomas Jones Woodward 6/7 Pontypridd, Wales. Singer/musician, hits "It's Not Unusual" 1964, "What's New Pussycat?" 1965, "I'll Never Fall in Love Again." Toured US 1992. Albums *All Time Hits, The Golden Hits, Greatest Hits, Unbelievable* 1992.

JOPLIN, JANIS (1943–1970)

b. 1/19 Port Arthur, TX. Became a top rock singer, Kris Kristofferson* wrote her biggest hit "Me and Bobby McGee." Albums *Farewell Song, Greatest Hits, In Concert,* etc. Claimed to have kicked the heroin habit before she died in Los Angeles, CA.

JOPLIN, SCOTT (1868–1912)

b. Texarkana, TX. Noted black pianist/composer, known as the "King of Ragtime," wrote "Maple Leaf Rag" 1899, "Slow Drag" 1903, "Stoptime Rag" 1910, "Treemoniana." Albums *King of Ragtime, Piano Music, The Original Rags,* video *Treemonisha.*

JORDAN, LOUIS (1905–1975)

b. 7/8 Brinkley, AK. Alto saxist/singer with Chick Webb* 1936/38, then formed own group **Tympany Five.*** Hits "Ain't

Nobody Here But Us Chickens,'' ''Open the Door, Richard'' 1947, ''Saturday Night Fish Fry'' 1950, toured England with Chris Barber 1962, known as the ''King of the Jukeboxes.'' Died 2/4 Los Angeles, CA.

JORDAN, RONNY (1966–)
Jazz/hip hop guitarist, album *The Antidote* 1992.

JORDAN, SASS
b. England. Blues/rock singer, raised in Montreal. Album *Racine* 1992.

JORDAN, STANLEY
Jazz guitarist, albums *Cornucopia, Flying Home, Magic Touch, Stolen Moments,* video *Cornucopia.*

JOURNEY
Progressive rock band with Jonathan Cain, Aynsley Dunbar, Gregg Rolie, Neil Schon, Steve Smith, Ross Valory, singer Steve Perry,* called ''America's Most Progressive Rock Band'' 1983, hit ''Send Her My Love'' 1983, ''Foolish Heart'' on album *Street Talk* 1984, *Raised on Radio* 1986, *Time* 1992. Perry left band 1992.

JOY DIVISION
Singer Ian Curtis, guitarist Bernard Albrecht, bassist Peter Hook, drummer Stephen Morris. Albums *Closer, Substance, Unknown Pleasures.* Reformed as the New Order.*

JUDAS PRIEST
British heavy metal rock band. K.K. Downing, lead singer Rob Halford, Ian Hill, Dave Holland, Glenn Tipton. Albums *Screaming for Vengeance* 1982, *British Steel, Defenders of the Faith, Hell Bent for Leather, Painkiller,* etc. Singers Halford & Sebastian Bach on rock band **Skid Row's** *B-Side Ourselves* 1992. Video *Fuel for Life.*

JUDD, NAOMI (1946–)
b. 1/11 Ashwood, KY. Country singer, with daughter Wynonna* won 1988 Grammy for ''Give a Little Love'' track from

Greatest Hits. After Naomi became ill in 1991 with chronic hepatitis & retired Wynonna went solo. The Judds had many successful albums, videos *Great Video Hits, Love Can Build a Bridge.*

JUDD, WYNONNA (1964–)

b. 5/3 Ashland, KY. Country singer/guitarist with her mother Naomi,* went solo 1991, hits ''She Is His Only Need,'' ''I Saw the Light,'' ''No One Else on Earth'' 1992, album *Wynonna* sold over one million copies, won Grammy 1993. On CBS *Women of Country* January 1993. Married Larry Strickland, owns a 22-acre farm near Franklin, TN.

K

KAEMPFERT, BURT
Orchestra leader. Album *Best of Burt Kaempfert.*

KAHAL, IRVING (1903–1942)
b. Houtzdale, PA. Lyricist, with Willie Raskin & composer Sammy Fain* wrote "Wedding Bells are Breaking Up That Old Gang of Mine" "I'll be Seeing You" 1938.

KAHN, GUS (1886–1941)
b. Koblenz, Germany. Lyricist, came to America, wrote "Sunshine and Roses" 1913, "Memories" 1915, "Pretty Baby" 1916, "Carolina in the Morning" 1922, "Ain't We Got Fun," and with composer Vincent Youmans* "Carioca" 1933. Died in Beverly Hills, CA.

KAISER, HENRY
Kaiser & David Lindley traveled to the island of Madagascar to record Malagasy folk music for their album *A World Out of Time* 1992.

KAMEN, MICHAEL
Composer, with Sting* & Eric Clapton* wrote "It's Probably Me" for *Lethal Weapon 3,* Grammy winner 1993.

KAMINSKY, MAX (1908–)
b. 9/7 Brockton, MA. Jazz trumpeter/leader, with Red Nichols,* Joe Venuti,* Tommy Dorsey,* Artie Shaw* in 1930s, later with Art Hodes & Jack Teagarden,* during 60s/80s at Jimmy Ryan's & Condon's in NY City.

KANAWA, KIRI TE
Soprano, CDs *The Kiri Collection* 1992, *Kiri Te Kanawa Sings Michael Legrand* 1992.

KANDER, JOHN (1927–)
Composer of *Cabaret, Chicago, Funny Lady.*

KANE, HELEN (1910–1966)
Singer known as the "Boop-boop-a-doop girl" sang "I Wanna Be Loved by You" 1928.

KANSAS
Albums *Best of Kansas, Left Overture, Mesque, Monolith, Point of No Return, Song for America,* video *Kansas.*

KANUCA, RICHARD "RICHIE" (1930–1977)
b. Philadelphia, PA. Saxist/musician, with Stan Kenton,* Woody Herman,* & others in 1950s, with **Roy Eldridge* Quintet** 1966/71, co-led quintet with Blue Mitchell. Died 7/22 Los Angeles, CA.

KASET, ANGELA
Songwriter, wrote "Something in Red" for Lorrie Morgan* 1993.

KATER, PETER
Albums *Gateway, Rooftops, Spirit, Two Hearts,* etc.

KATT, JEANNETTE
California guitarist/singer/songwriter, hit single "When I Do Wrong I Do It So Right" & album *Pink Mischief* 1992.

KAUFMAN, GEORGE S. (1889–1961)
b. Pittsburgh, PA. Librettist/playwright, with Moss Hart & composer Richard Rodgers* wrote "I'd Rather Be Right" 1937, with Morrie Ryskind and George Gershwin,* *Strike Up the Band* 1930.

KAY, CONNIE (1927–)
b. Conrad Henry Kirnon in Tuckahoe, NY. Drummer with Miles Davis,* Lester Young,* Charlie Parker* & Stan Getz* in 1940s/50s, replaced Kenny Clarke* in the **Modern Jazz Quartet,*** disbanded 1974, at Eddie Condon's in NY City 1979/80s.

KAY, HERSHEY (1919–1981)
b. 11/17 Philadelphia, PA. Composer, wrote scores for ballet,

Broadway shows, & films: *Coco* 1969 & *Evita* 1978. Died 12/2 Danbury, CT.

KAYE, SAMMY (1913–1987)
b. 3/13 Lakewood, Ohio. Clarinetist, formed own band in 1930s with Gene Krupa,* Roy Eldridge,* Teddy Wilson,* lead saxist Marty Oscard. His motto was "Swing and Sway with Sammy Kaye." Albums *Dance to My Golden Favorites, The Best of Sammy Kaye, Best of the Big Bands.* Died 6/2 Ridgewood, NJ.

KAZEE, BUELL H. (1900–1976)
b. 8/29 Burton Fork, KY. Folk singer/guitarist, recorded "Rock Island Line" in 1930s. Died 8/31.

KC & THE SUNSHINE BAND
Formed 1973 with singer/keyboardist Harry Wayne Casey, Oliver Brown, bassist/songwriter Rick Finch, drummer Robert Johnson, Denvil Liptrot, Jerome & Ronnie Smith, James Weaver, & Charles Williams. Hits "That's the Way" 1975, "Shake Your Booty" 1976, album *Best of the KC & Sunshine Band.* Singer/songwriter Gary King* left and formed his own band.

KEE, JOHN P.
Gospel singer with Charlotte, NC-based **New Life Community Choir,** at Gospel Music Worskhop, swept the 1991 awards. Album *We Walk by Faith* won Stellar Award January 1993.

KELLER, GRETA (1901–1977)
b. Vienna, Austria. Singer, came to New York 1920s, in musical show *Broadway* 1928, sang in night clubs, with Rod McKuen* recorded "An Evening in Vienna" & other songs. Died 11/4 Vienna.

KELLY, DANIEL E. (1843–1905)
b. Kingston, RI, later lived in Gaylord, KS. Composer, with lyricist Dr. B.M. Highley* wrote "Home on the Range" 1873, now the state song of Kansas.

KELLY, R.
R. Kelly & Public Announcement, "Slow Dance" R&B top single September 1992.

KELP, JOSEPH
No one knows who wrote "The Yellow Rose of Texas." Only the initials "J.K." are given by the publishers Charles H. Brown of Jackson, Tennessee and Firth Pond & Co. of New York City (1858). Charles H. Brown was born in Virginia and was a book-seller in Jackson according to the 1860 U.S. Census. The only composer/arranger of this period with the initials "J.K." was Joseph Kelp who wrote an arrangement of "Aura Lee" published by George Dunn of Richmond, Virginia in 1864.

KEMP, HAL (1905–1940)
b. Marion, AL. Leader, led own bands with singer Janet Blair (Janet Lafferty) in 1930s. See album *Best of the Big Bands.* Was injured in a head-on car crash December 19th and died two days later.

KEMP, JOHNNY
Singer on 1988 Top Ten Black Singles list for "Just Got Paid," album *Johnny Kemp, Secrets.*

KENDIS, JAMES (1883–1946)
b. St. Paul, MN. Composer/lyricist, with James Brockman,* Nat Vincent, and composer John W. Killette wrote "I'm Forever Blowing Bubbles" 1918.

KENDRICK, EDDIE (1940–1992)
b. 12/17 Union Springs, AL. Lead tenor of the **Temptations*** 1963/71 with hits "Get Ready," "The Way You Do the Things You Do." Group had 13 Top Ten hits with singer David Ruffin. Successful solo career on R&B charts, hit "Keep on Truckin'." Albums *At His Best, People Hold Out.* Had a lung removed in 1991 because of cancer, later became ill again & died on 10/5 in Birmingham, AL.

KENNEDY, NIGEL (1972–   )
British virtuoso violinist, his recording of Vivaldi's "The Four Seasons" sold over one million copies, toured US in 1992.

KENNY G. (1956–   )
b. Kenny Gorelick 6/5. Saxist, graduated from University of Washington summa cum laude in accounting, married actress Lyndie Benson. Had platinum music video *Kenny G in Concert* 1990, albums *Live, Duotones, G Force, Silhouette,* video *Kenny G Live,* pop hit instrumental "Theme from *Dying Young*" 1992, "Breathless" 1992, played at inaugural ball for President Clinton in 1993. Won American Music Adult Contemporary award 1994. 1994 Instrumental Composition Grammy for *Forever in Love.*

KENTON, STANLEY N. "STAN" (1912–1979)
b. 2/19 Wichita, KS. Composer/leader, with saxist/flutist Bud Shank in **Shank's Band** in 1950s/70s. Albums *Artistry & Symphonic Jazz, Jazz Collector, The Very Best of Stan Kenton.* Died 8/25 in Hollywood CA the same day Ray Eberle* died in Atlanta, GA.

KENTUCKY HEADHUNTERS
With guitarist Richard Young won 1990 Grammy Country Group Vocal for "Pickin' on Nashville." Lead singer Ricky Lee Phelps & his brother bassist Doug left group for solo careers 1992. Album *Electric Barnyard.* "Only Daddy That'll Walk the Line" Grammy winner 1993.

KEPPARD, LOUIS (1888–1986)
b. New Orleans, LA, brother of Freddie Keppard (1889–1933). Guitarist/tubist, died 2/17 in New Orleans.

KERN, JEROME D. (1885–1945)
b. New York City. Composer, with librettist Oscar Hammerstein II* wrote *Show Boat* 1927 & other musicals, composed music for "Ol' Man River" 1927, "Smoke Gets in Your Eyes" 1933, "The Last Time I Saw Paris" 1940.

KERSHAW, DOUGLAS J. "DOUG" (1936–)
b. 1/24 Tel Ridge, LA. Cajun fiddler known for the classic "Louisiana Moon." Albums *Best of Doug Kershaw, The Cajun Way, The Louisiana Man.*

KERSHAW, SAMMY (1958–)
From Kaplan, LA. Country singer, top records "Cadillac Style" & "Don't Go Near the Water" 1992, album *Haunted Heart* 1993, single "She Doesn't Know She's Beautiful" 1993.

KESSEL, BARNEY (1923–)
b. Muskogee, OK. Guitarist with Charlie Barnet, Artie Shaw,* & others in 1940s, toured Europe with Jazz at the Philharmonic 1952/53, won *down beat* readers' polls 1956/59, with Herb Ellis* 1970s/80s, albums *Kessel Plays Carmen, Kessel Plays Standards, The Artistry of Barney Kessel.*

KETCHUM, HAL (1953–)
From Greenwich, NY. Singer, hit single "Small Town Saturday Night" 1991, albums *Past the Point of Reasons, Sure Love* 1992, leader of **The Alibis** of Austin, Texas.

KEY, FRANCIS SCOTT (1779–1843)
b. Frederick, MD. Lyricist, while a prisoner on a British ship which was bombing Fort McHenry, Baltimore in 1814, saw the American flag still waving over the fort at daybreak when the bombing stopped and wrote "The Star Spangled Banner."

KHAN, CHAKA (1953–)
b. Yvette Marie Stevens 3/23 Chicago, IL. Singer/songwriter with **Rufus Group** 1972/78, went solo, hits "Through the Fire" 1985, "I Feel for You," with Ray Charles* won 1990 Grammy R&B for "I'll Be Good to You," "Love You All My Lifetime," with Stevie Wonder* on *Handel's Messiah: A Soulful Celebration* 1992. World tour was interrupted 9/27/92 when she underwent surgery for an appendectomy. *The Woman I Am* Grammy winner 1993.

KID CREOLE & THE COCONUTS
Singer August Darnell, percussionist Coati Mundi (Andy Hernandez), singers Afriana Kaegi, Cheryl Poirier, & Taryn Haegy. Albums *I, Too Have Seen the Wood, Private Waters.*

KIEDIS, ANTHONY
Lead singer of the alternative rock band **Red Hot Chili Peppers.***

KILAUEA
Hit jazz album *Tropical Pleasures* 1992.

KING, ALBERT (1921–1992)
Guitarist, albums *Blues at Sunrise, Last Session, Lovejoy, Thursday Night in San Francisco.* Died 12/21 Memphis, TN.

KING, B.B. (1925–   )
b. Riley B. King 9/16 Itta Bena, MS. Guitarist/vocalist, played at Newport Jazz Festivals in NY City 1970s/80s, hit single "The Thrill is Gone," albums *Always One More Time, Great Moments with B.B. King, Guess Who, Live at the Apollo,* etc., video *A Night of Red Hot Blues.* Played at the Republican Convention in Houston, TX 1992. Traditional Blues Grammy 1994 for "Blues Summit."

KING, BEN E. (1938–   )
b. 9/28 Saxist/singer. Albums *Stand by Me, The Ultimate Collection.* Played at the Arkansas Inaugural Ball with President Bill Clinton (also on saxophone) January 1993.

KING, CAROLE (1941–   )
b. Carole Klein 2/9 Brooklyn, NY City. Singer/songwriter. Won four Grammy awards: 1971: Album *Tapestry,* hit Singles "It's Too Late," "You've Got a Friend," & Best Female Vocalist. Wrote and sang "Till Their Eyes Shine" on *Lullaby Album* 1992, wrote "Now and Forever" on *A League of Their Own* soundtrack, Grammy winner 1993. Married & divorced lyricist Gerry Goffin,* married bassist Charles Larkey.

KING CRIMSON
British progressive rock band with founder/guitarist Robert Fripp,* drummer Bill Bruford, & two Americans—bassist Tony Levin & singer/guitarist Adrian Belew, on music video *King Crimson: The Noise-Frejus 1982/85, In the Court of Crimson, Islands, Lizard, Starless,* etc.

KING, EVELYN "CHAMPAGNE" (1960–)
b. 7/1 Bronx, NY City. Singer, disco hit "Shame" 1977, album *The Girl Next Door.*

KING, FRANK "PEE WEE" (1914–)
b. Milwaukee, WI. Composer/leader, with Redd Stewart wrote "The Tennessee Waltz" 1946.

KING, FREDDIE (1934–1976)
b. Gilmer, TX. Blues guitarist, played in Chicago night spots, first recorded 1956, albums *Best of Freddie King, Getting Ready, Just Pickin.'*

KING, GARY
Singer/songwriter, with **KC and the Sunshine Band,*** left & formed own band **Gary and the Dream,** toured US 1992.

KING, GLEN (1947–)
b. 12/14. Guitarist/singer/songwriter, Vietnam War veteran. Played in Nashville 1974/79, composed "Welcome Home, Soldier" with lyricist Tony Savant, performed at Robert Carnegie's Playhouse West in North Hollywood, CA.

KING MISSLE
New York band formed in 1987 with singer/songwriter John Hall, David Rick, Roger Murdock, & Chris Xefos. Hit single "Detachable Penis" on album *Happy Hour* 1992, toured US 1992. **King Missle with the Monks of Doom** toured US in 1993.

KING, NANCY
Singer with bassist Glen Moore, pianist Art Lande, & tenor saxist Benny Wallace on album *Potato Radio* 1992.

KING, ROBERT A. (1862–1932)
b. Robert Keiser in New York City. Songwriter, wrote "Beautiful Ohio" 1918, "I Scream, You Scream, We All Scream for Ice Cream."

KING SINGERS
Six men sang "Yesterday" and "Lovely People" on Public Broadcasting TV with the **Boston Pops** in September 1992.

KING, STODDARD (1889–1933)
b. Jackson, WI. Lyricist, with composer Alonzo Elliott* wrote "There's a Long Long Trail A-Winding" 1914 (popular in World War I).

KING, WAYNE (1901–1985)
b. 2/16 Savannah, IL. Bandleader known as the "Waltz King," played in the Aragon Ballroom, Chicago 1927/35, served as a major in Special Services in World War II. Albums *Golden Favorites, The Best of Wayne King.* Died 5/16 in Phoenix, AZ.

KINGDOM COME
With **Van Halen*** & others on 1988 Top Ten grossing concerts list at East Troy, WI. Albums *Hands of Time, Kingdom Come.*

KINGS OF JAZZ
Toured Europe 1974 with trumpeter Pee Wee Erwin,* saxist Kenny Davern, trombonist Ed Hibble, clarinetist/saxist Johnny Mince.

KING'S X
Hard rock trio from Texas with guitarist Ty Tabor, bassist Doug Pinnick, & drummer Jerry Hashill, albums *Out of the Silent Planet, King's X* 1992.

KINGSMEN, THE
Albums *Best of the Kingsmen, Louie Louie* on CD, *The Sceptor Records Story* 1992.

KINGSTON TRIO
With Bob Shane, Nick Reynolds, & Dave Guard,* (later John

Stuart replaced Guard). Albums *Kingston Trio* 1958, *Best of the Best, Capitol Collectors, Made in the USA, Tune Up,* their song "Tom Dooley" on album *Troubadours of the Folk Era-Vol.3* issued 1992.

KINKS, THE
British hard rock group turned pop with guitarist/singer David Davies, Mick Avory, John Beecham, Laurie Brown, hit single "You Really Got Me" 1964; later with lead guitarist/singer Raymond "Ray" Davies, John Gosling, Alan Holmes, Peter Quaife. Bassist Jim Rodford joined group 1978. Ray Davies wrote, scored, & directed the film *Return to Waterloo* 1984. With Elvis Costello, "Days" on soundtrack *Until the End of the World* 1992, albums *Come Dancing, Kink Kronikles, One for the Road, Phobia* 1993.

KIRK, ROLAND T. "RAHSAAN ROLAND" (1936–1977)
b. Columbus, Ohio. Played three instruments simultaneously: tenor sax, stritch alto sax, & manzello soprano sax, toured Europe 1961/64, *We Free Kings, The Man Who Cried Fire, Kirk's Works.*

KIRKPATRICK, WILLIAM J. (1838–1921)
b. Duncannon, PA. Composer, although claimed by others, he is credited for having composed the music for "Away in a Manger" 1886.

KIRSTEN, DOROTHY (1910–1992)
b. 7/6 Montclair, NJ. Lyric soprano with Metropolitan Opera in NY City for 30 years, first opera star to appear on the cover of *Time* magazine. Also appeared in Broadway shows and sang duets with Gordon MacRae.* Died 11/25 Los Angeles, CA.

KISS
Eric Carr, Gene Simmons, Paul Stanley, guitarist Ace Frehley (solo album 1978), drummer/singer Peter Criss of Brooklyn, NY City wrote hit "Beth" 1976 for his wife. Hit single "Rock 'n Roll All Night," albums *Alive, Animalize, Asylum, Crazy Nights, Destroyer, Revenge* 1992, video *X-Treme Close-Up*

1992. Drummer Eric Singer later replaced Criss and guitarist Bruce Kulick replaced Frehley.

KITARO
Albums *Asia, Astral Voyage, Full Moon Stop, India, Kojiki, Silk Road,* video *Live in America, Dream* (Grammy winner 1993).

KITT, EARTHA MAE (1928–)
b. 1/16 North, SC. Singer, appeared in films & TV shows, sang at Cafe Carlyle in NY City 1992, albums *Best of Eartha Kitt, In Person at the Plaza.*

KITTREDGE, WALTER (1834–1905)
b. Merrimac, ME. Composer, wrote the words & music for the popular Civil War song "Tenting on the Old Camp Ground."

KLEMMER, JOHN
Albums *Barefoot Ballet, Lifestyle, Touch,* etc.

KLEZMER CONSERVATORY BAND
Albums *A Touch of Klez, Jumpin' Night, Klez, Yiddish Renaissance.*

KLF
With Tammy Wynette* on album *Justified and Ancient* 1992.

KLUGH, EARL (1953–)
b. Detroit, MI. Jazz guitarist, albums *Crazy for You, Finger Paintings, Heartstring, Life Stories, Soda Fountain Shuffle, Solo Guitar, Whispers & Promises,* etc.

KNAPP, PHOEBE PALMER (1839–1908)
b. New York, NY. Composer, with lyricist Fanny Crosby* wrote "Blessed Assurance" 1873.

KNIGHT, GLADYS MARIA (1944–)
b. 5/28 Atlanta, GA. Singer, formed **Gladys Knight and the Pips,** vocal group 1966 with Merald Knight, Edward Patten, William Guest, Langston George, Eleanor Guest, Brenda Knight. Won two Grammys for "Midnight Train to Georgia" 1973, won

1988 Grammy for "Love Overboard." Albums *Anthology, Neither One of Us, Touch, Visions,* with Elmore James* on 2 CDs *The Fire/Fury Records Story* 1993.

KNOPFLER, MARK
Musician, with Chet Atkins* won 1990 Country Instrumental Grammy for "So Soft, Your Goodbye," *Cal Soundtrack.*

KOEHLER, TED (1894–1973)
b. Washington, D.C. raised in NY City. Lyricist, with composer Harold Arlen* wrote "I Love a Parade" 1931, "Stormy Weather" 1933.

KOLLER, FRED
Songwriter, wrote "Angel Eyes," album *Night of the Living Fred.*

KONITZ, LEE (1927–   )
b. Chicago, IL. Alto saxist with Claude Thornhill* 1947/48, with Miles Davis,* Stan Kenton,* & others in 50s, won *Metronome* poll 1954 & *down beat* poll 1957/58, toured Europe 1965/66, at Carnegie Hall in NY City in June 1980, albums *Round and Round, Subconscious-lee.*

KOOL AND THE GANG
Jazz group formed 1964, later R&B/pop, with singer Robert "Kool" Bell & tenor saxist Ronald Bell from Youngstown, Ohio; George Brown, guitarist Cladys Smith, & flutist/saxist Dennis Thomas all three from Jersey City, NJ; trombonist Cliff Adams, Robert "Spike" Mickens, Michael Ray, singer J.T. Taylor,* Rickey West, & keyboardist Curtis Williams from Buffalo, NY, group had platinum single "Celebration" 1980, videos *Kool & the Gang* 1985, *Decade,* albums *Emergency, Something Special,* etc.

KOOL MOE DEE
Singer with Ice-T* & others won 1990 Rap Vocal Grammy for "Back on the Block," albums *How Ya Like Me, Knowledge is King.*

KOOPER, AL (1944–   )
b. 2/5 Brooklyn, NY City. Rock guitarist/organist/singer with **Blood, Sweat and Tears.***

KOSTELANETZ, ANDRE (1901–1980)
b. 12/23 St. Petersburg, Russia. Conductor, came to New York in 1922, with Metropolitan Opera, conducted CBS radio after 1931, composed *Music for Tomorrow* for New York World Fair 1939, albums *Most Requested Songs, Opera Without Words, Stars & Stripes Forever,* etc. Married opera singer Lily Pons.*

KOTTKE, LEO
b. Athens, GA. Guitarist, albums *A Shout Toward Noon, Balance, Guitar Music, My Father's Face, Regards from Chuck Pink,*etc.

KRAFT, ROBERT
Songwriter with Arne Glimcher wrote "Beautiful Maria of My Soul" (from film *The Mambo Kings*) Grammy winner 1993.

KRAL, IRENE (1932–1978)
b. Chicago, IL. Singer, sister of pianist/singer Ray Kral, toured US coast-to-coast, also Canada &Bermuda 1950s, singer for Maynard Ferguson* & Shelly Manne,* albums *Where is Love* and *Better than Anything.* Married trumpeter Joe Burnett.

KRAMER, WAYNE
Guitarist formerly with **MC 5,** album *Death Tongue* 1992.

KRAUSS, ALISON (1971–   )
Guitarist/singer/leader with **Union Station,*** Bluegrass Grammy 1990 for *I've Got That Odd Feeling, Too Late to Cry, Every Time You Say Goodbye* won Grammy 1993. Joined Grand Ole Opry in Nashville on July 3, 1993.

KRAVITZ, LENNY
Singer, album *Let Love Rule* 1992, toured US 1993.

KREISLER, FRITZ (1875–1962)
b. Vienna, Austria. Violinist, came to NY City, composed *Ca-*

price Viennois for violin, albums *Legendary Performances, The Kreisler Collection, Transcription/Violin/Piano.*

KRIS KROSS
Kris Kelly (b. 1979) & Kris Smith (b. 1979) from Atlanta, GA. Hit singles ''Warm It Up'' 1992, ''Jump'' Grammy winner 1993, Top Ten album *Totally Krossed Out* June 1992, toured US, *Billboard* New Pop Artist 1992, New Artist American Music Award 1993.

KRISMA
Jazz group led by Dave Garfield played in North Hollywood, CA 1978.

KRISTOFFERSON, KRIS (1937–   )
b. 6/22 Brownsville, TX. Singer/songwriter/actor, wrote ''Help Me Make It Through the Night'' & ''Me and Bobby McGee'' (hit for Janis Joplin*), acted in films. Albums *Jesus Was a Capricorn, My Songs, Silver Tongued Devil, Songs of Kristofferson.*

KRONOS QUARTET
With violinist David Harrington, 2nd violinist John Sherba, violist Hank Dutt, & cellist Joan Jeanreneaud, recorded *White Man Sleeps* by white South African expatriate Kevin Volans 1985, albums *Black Angels, Pieces of Africa* 1992.

KRUPA, GENE (1909–1973)
b. Chicago, IL. Drummer/leader, with Mezz Mezzrow & others in 1920s, with Russ Colombo,* Benny Goodman* 1934/38, after a blow-up with Goodman at the Earle Theater in Philadelphia, formed own band in Atlantic City, NJ in April 1938, rejoined Goodman 1943, had own successful band 1944/51, led combos 50s/60s. Arrested in California on a marijuana possession charge but later released. Albums *Compact Jazz, Drummer Man, Gene Krupa and Buddy Rich, Walkman Jazz.*

KUNZEL, ERICH
Pianist, albums *American Jubilee, Mancini's Greatest Hits, Sound of Music/Rodgers/Cincinnati Pops, Star Tracks Vol. II.*

K.W.S.
Hit single ''Please Don't Go'' 1992.

KYSER, JAMES KERN "KAY" (1906–1985)
b. 6/18 Rocky Mount, NC. Leader, his band played in Chicago in
1930s, famous for his ''College of Musical Knowledge,''
toured 40s/60s. Became a Christian Science healer. Album
Sentimental Favorites. Married singer Georgia Carroll.

L

LA BELLE, PATTI (1944–)
b. Patricia Holt 5/24 Philadelphia, PA. Singer with singers Sarah Dash, Nona Hendryx, & organist Andre Lewis, hit "Moon Shadow" 1972. Went solo, hits "New Attitude" 1985, "On My Own" 1986, R&B single "When You've Been Blessed, Feels Like Heaven" 1992, album *Burnin* won 1991 Grammy, video *Live at the Apollo.* Soul/R&B Female Vocalist winner at American Music Awards 1993. Sang on *Christmas in Washington* special (NEC TV) 1993.

LACY, STEVE (1934–)
b. New York City, albums *Futurities Part 1 & Part 2, Rushes, Sempre Amore, The Door.*

LADYSMITH BLACK MANBAZO
Albums *Classic Tracks, Journey of Dreams,* 1987 Grammy for *Folk Recordings for Shake Zulu, Umthombo Wamanzi,* etc.

L. A. EXPRESS
Rock/jazz originally the **Tom Scott Quartet** 1973 with pianist Joe Sample,* included drummer John Guerin in 1974.

LA FACE
Hit album *Boomerang Soundtrack* 1992.

LA FARGO, SCOTT (1936–1961)
b. Newark, NJ. Bassist with Chet Baker* & Barney Kessel* during 1950s, led own trio in NY City 1960/61. Killed in an auto accident in Geneva, New York.

LA 4, THE
With Almedia, Brown, Manne, & Shank, albums *Just Friends, Watch What Happens, Zaca.*

LAINE, CLEO (1927–)
b. 10/26 Southall, England. Jazz singer, joined John Dankworth 1953 (married him 1958), in concert at Tully Hall in NY City

1972, Carnegie Hall 1973, at Wolf Trap Jazz Concert, Vienna, VA. in July 1980, at JVC Jazz Festival, August 1992. Albums *Cleo Sings Sondheim, Jazz, That Old Feeling, Woman to Woman.*

LAINE, FRANKIE (1913–   )
b. 3/30 Chicago. Singer with Fred Croyole in late 1930s, in Hollywood, CA night clubs in 40s, toured England 1954, had own show on CBS 1955/56, albums *Golden Hits, Greatest Hits.*

LAMB, ARTHUR J. (1870–1928)
b. Somerset, England, lived in Providence, RI. Lyricist, with composer H.W. Petrie* wrote "Asleep in the Deep" 1897, with composer Harry von Tilzer* wrote "A Bird in a Gilded Cage" 1900.

LAMBERT, HENDRICKS, & ROSS
Dave Lambert (1917–1966), Jon Hendricks*, & Annie Ross vocal trio formed 1958, albums *Everybody's Boppin', Sing Along with Basie, Twisted/Best of Lambert, Hendricks, & Ross,* etc.

LAMBERT, LOUIS (1835–1910)
b. Charleroi, PA. Lyricist, with composer Patrick Gilmore* wrote popular Civil War song "When Johnny Comes Marching Home" 1863.

LANDRETH, SONNY
b. Louisiana. Slide guitarist/tenor/songwriter, album *Outward Bound* 1992.

LANE, ABBE (1932–   )
b. 12/14 Brooklyn, NY City. Singer/actress, married Xavier Cugat,* later divorced.

LANE, BURTON (1912–   )
b. New York, NY. Pianist/composer, wrote score for *Finian's Rainbow* 1947, "How are Things in Glocca Mora?" 1947, 'On a Clear Day You Can See Forever" 1966.

LANE, CRISTY (1940–)
b. 1/8 East Peoria, IL. Singer, hit "One Day at a Time."

LANE SISTERS
Maiden names Mullican, singers, Lola (b. Macy, IN 1906–1981), Rosemary (b. Indianola, IA 1914–1974), Priscilla (b. 1917 Indianola, IA).

lang, k.d. (1961–)
b. 11/2 Alberta, Canada. Female country/rock singer, albums *Absolute Torch & Twang,* 1989 Country Vocal Female Grammy, *Angle with a Lariat, Shadowland,* video *Harvest of Seven Years, Ingenue* with co-writer Ben Mink,* toured US 1992. New Artist American Music Award 1993, hit "Constant Craving" won Grammy 1993. Proclaimed her lesbianism in July 1993.

LANGFORD, FRANCES (1913–)
b. Frances Newberh 4/4 Lakeland, FL. Popular singer 1930s/40s, with Bob Hope on USO tours during World War II. Hit singles "I'm in the Mood for Love," "I've Got You Under My Skin." Sang with Dick Powell & Rudy Vallee*, sold over 15 million records. Married actor Jon Hall, divorced & in 1955 married Ralph Evenrude who died in 1985.

LANIN, LESTER (1911–)
b. 8/26 Philadelphia, PA. Society bandleader played at wedding receptions of Prince Charles & Lady Diana, Prince Andrew & Fergie, Billy Joel* & Christie Brinkley, for 60th birthday of Queen Elizabeth, and played for all presidents of US since Eisenhower.

LANSON, SNOOKY (1919–)
b. Roy Landman 3/27 Memphis, TN. Singer.

LANZ, DAVID
Albums *Cristofori's Dream, Heartsounds, Nightfall, Return to the Heart,* with Paul Speer *Desert Vision, Natural States.*

LANZA, MARIO (1921–1959)
b. Alfredo Arnold Cocozza, Philadelphia, PA. Tenor, had lead in *The Great Caruso* 1951. Albums *Voice of the Century, Arias and Songs, Sings Caruso Favorites,* etc.

LARKINS, ELLIS (1923–   )
b. Baltimore, MD. Pianist, debut at age eleven with Baltimore City Colored Orchestra, with Billy Moore, Bill Coleman* & Al Hall* in 1940s, with singer Anita Ellis in 70s, at Carnegie Tavern 1978/80s.

LA ROSA, JULIUS (1930–   )
b. 1/2 New York, NY. Singer popular with teenagers in 1950s, hits "Lipstick and Candy," "Rubber Sole Shoes" 1956.

LARSON, NICOLETTE (1952–   )
b. 7/17 Helena, Montana. Hit single "I Only Want to be With You" 1982.

LASH
British quartet, albums *Gola, Scar, Spooky* 1992. Toured US with **Red Hot Chili Peppers*** 1992.

LAST DRIVE
Surf/punk/blues group from Athens, GA. Album *Blood Nirvana* 1992.

LATEEF, YUSEF (1921–   )
b. William Evans in Chattanooga, TN. Flutist/saxist/composer, with Lucky Millinder, Dizzy Gillespie,* & others in 1940s, led own groups in 50s, toured Europe & Japan with Cannonball Adderley* 1962/64, then led own combos. Albums *Encounters, Gentle Giant, Yusef Lateef's Encounters.*

LATEINER, JACOB (1928–   )
b. 5/31 Havana, Cuba. Musician.

LATHROP, JACK
Singer with **Glenn Miller*** **Band** in early 1940s, hit "Beat Me Daddy Eight to the Bar."

LAUPER, CYNTHIA "CYNDI" (1953–   )
b. 6/20 Queens, NY City. Singer, hit album *She's So Unusual* broke record for most Top Ten singles, won Grammy 1984, hit "Girls Just Want to Have Fun," albums *A Night to Remember, True Colors,* video *Live in Paris.* With electronic magic, sang 1947 vocal "Santa Claus is Coming to Town" with Frank Sinatra* on the Special Olympics benefit album *A Very Special Christmas* 1992.

LAVIN, CHRISTINE
Albums *Attainable Love, Beau Woes & Other Problems, Future Fossils, Good Thing Can't Read Mind.*

LAW AND ORDER
Jazz duo with Billy Bang and Butch Morris in NY City in 1980s, album *Guilty of Innocence.*

LAWLER, CHARLES B. (1852–1925)
b. Dublin, Ireland. Composer, came to New York City. With lyricist J.W. Blake* wrote "The Sidewalks of New York" 1894.

LAWRENCE, ELLIOTT (1925–   )
b. 2/14 Philadelphia, PA. Pianist/composer, had own band in late 1940s, musical director & arranger for Broadway musical shows in 1960s.

LAWRENCE, JOEY (1976–   )
TV actor/singer/songwriter on television shows *Gimme a Break* 1983/88 and *Blossom,* hit "Nothin' My Love Can't Fix" on his *Joey Lawrence* album 1993.

LAWRENCE, TRACY
Country singer, hit single "Runnin' Behind" 1992, albums *Sticks & Stones, Tracy Lawrence.* Named New Male Vocalist at Country awards 1993.

LAWRENCE, VICKI (1949–)
b. 3/29 Inglewood, CA. Singer/actress, a regular on the Carol Burnett shows. Hit "The Night the Lights Went Out in Georgia."

LAWS, HUBERT (1939–)
b. Houston, TX. Flutist/composer with **Jazz Crusaders*** 1954/60, with pianist Eubie Blake* & bassist Ron Carter* at Carnegie Hall in NY City 1981. Albums *Rite of Spring, Romeo & Juliet, San Francisco Concert, Best of Hubert Laws,* etc.

LAWSON, YANK (1911–)
b. John R. Lausen 5/3 Trenton, Missouri. Jazz trumpeter with Ben Pollack, Bob Crosby, & Tommy Dorsey* in 1930s/40s, with Bob Haggart 50s, then led own bands, with bassist Haggart co-led **World's Greatest Jazz Band*** 70s/80s.

LAZARUS, EMMA (1849–1894)
b. New York, NY. Poetess who wrote "The New Colossus" 1883 inscribed below the Statute of Liberty in NY harbor 1903. Her *Songs of a Semite* 1883 included "The Banner of the Jew" which became a popular Zionist anthem.

LEADBELLY, HUDDIE (1885–1949)
b. Ledbetter in Mooringsport, LA. Guitarist/composer/vocalist. Got into brawls and spent 1918/25 in prison in Texas & 1930/34 in prison in Louisiana. While in prison he wrote "Easy Rider," "Rock Island Line," "Good Morning Blues," & "Goodnight Irene." Albums *Alabama Bound, King of 12 String Guitar,* etc.

LE BON, SIMON (1958–)
b. 10/26 Singer, with **Duran Duran.***

LE DOUX, CHRIS
(Le Duc) country singer, albums *He Rides the Wild Horses, Old Cowboy Heroes, Rodeo Songs Old & New,* with Garth Brooks* *Watcha Gonna Do With a Cowboy* album (title track won Grammy 1993).

LED ZEPPELIN
British group started 1968 with drummer John Bonham, John Paul Jones, John Baldwin, Robert Plant, & guitarist Jimmy Page. In 1980 John Bonham choked to death after drinking about forty shots of vodka and the group disbanded. Hit single "Stairway to Heaven," video *Song Remains the Same,* platinum 6 LP box set *Led Zeppelin* 1990. Guitarist Page & crooner Harry Connick Jr.* were at a concert in Miami, FL in April 1992. *See also* Coverdale/Page.*

LEE, BRENDA (1944–)
b. Brenda Mae Tarpley 12/11 Atlanta, GA. Singer, hit single "I'm Sorry," gave a command performance for Queen Elizabeth II in 1964. Albums *Brenda Lee, Greatest Country Hits,* CD *Anthology* rated in 8/9 *CD Review* February 1992. Sang at the Optimist International Convention in Louisville, KY 1993.

LEE, JOHNNY (1947–)
b. Texas City, TX. Country singer, hit "Lookin' for Love" in film *Urban Cowboy* 1980. Album *Best of Johnny Lee.*

LEE, PEGGY (1920–)
b. Norma Delores Egstrom 5/26 in Jamestown, ND. Singer/ actress, hit songs "Fever," "Is That All There Is?" won Grammy 1969, recorded "Elmer's Tune" for Benny Goodman,* married Dave Barbour,* toured Japan 1975, with Tony Bennett* 1982. Albums *Peggy Lee, Mirrors, There'll be Another Spring,* etc. Appeared in a wheelchair at a party for k.d. lang in NY City in 1992.

LE FEVRE, MYLON
Pop/gospel singer won 1993 Grammy for *Faith, Hope and Love.*

LEGENDARY BLUES BAND, THE
With bassist Calvin Jones, drummer Willie Smith, guitarist Willie Flynn, singer/harpist Madison Slim. Albums *Keeping the Blues Alive, Ub Da Judge, Wake Up with the Blues, Prime Time Blues* 1992.

LEGENDS OF JAZZ
Los Angeles band formed by drummer/singer Barry "Kid" Hartyn in 1973, group with trumpeter Andrew Blakeney (aged 82) played in Damrosch Park, Lincoln Center, NY City in 1980.

LEGRAND, MICHAEL (1932–)
b. 2/24 Paris, France. Pianist, albums *After the Rain, Le Jazz Grand, Legrand Piano.*

LE GRAN PRIX
Jazz band co-led by drummer Philly Joe Jones* & saxist William Byard Lancaster in 1970s.

LEHMANN, LOTTIE (1888–1976)
b. 2/27 Perlberg, Germany. Lyric soprano with Metropolitan Opera in NY City 1934/45, then gave concerts until 1951. Albums *Lottie Lehmann Sings with Kiepma & Tucker, Sings Wagner/Strauss.* Died 8/26 Santa Barbara, CA.

LEIBER, JERRY (1933–)
Songwriter, with Mike Stoller* wrote "Hound Dog," "Searchin'," "Yakety Yak," and based on "Sweet Genevieve" by Henry Tucker* wrote "Love Me Tender" introduced by Elvis Presley.*

LEIGH, CAROLYN (1926–1983)
b. 4/21 Bronx, NY City. Songwriter, wrote lyrics for "Hey, Look Me Over," "The Best is Yet to Come," and "Young at Heart."

LEIGH, MITCH (1928–)
b. Irwin Michnick 1/30 Brooklyn, NY City. Composed the score for *Man of La Mancha.*

LEIGH, RICHARD
Songwriter with Laying Martine, Jr. wrote "The Greatest Man I Never Knew" popularized by Reba McEntyre* (Grammy winner 1993).

LEMONHEADS
Boston based combo with guitarist/singer/songwriter Evan Dando with guest bassist Juliana Hatfield & drummer David Ryan on album *It's a Shame About Ray* 1992. Bassist Nic Dalton later replaced Hatfield.

LEMPER, UTE
German singer, album *Ute Lemper Sings Kurt Weill*, toured San Francisco, Chicago, & New York City in January/February 1993.

LENNON, JOHN (1940–1980)
b. 10/9 Liverpool, England. Singer/songwriter with **The Beatles.*** With Paul McCartney* wrote "Love Me Do" 1962, "I Want to Hold Your Hand," "She Loves You," "Hard Day's Night," "Can't Buy Me Love," "And I Love Her." Won 1970 Oscar for his score "Let It Be," had hit "Imagine" 1971, married Yoko Ono,* their album *Double Fantasy* won 1981 Grammy. Videos *Imagine, Live Peace in Toronto, Yoko Ono/John Lennon Live in New York City.* Was shot and killed on 12/8 in New York City.

LENNON, JULIAN (1963–   )
b. 4/8 Liverpool, England. Son of John Lennon.* Singer/musician, album *Valotte* 1983, Paul McCartney* wrote John Lennon's hit song "Hey Jude" about him. Video *Stand By Me: A Portrait of Julian Lennon* 1986.

LENNON SISTERS
Singers Dianne (b. 1939 Los Angeles, CA), Peggy (b. 1940), Kathy (b. 1942), Janet (b. 1946). *Best of the Lennon Sisters, 22 Songs of Faith, How Great Thou Art.*

LENNOX, ANNIE (1954–   )
b. 12/25. British singer formerly with **Eurythmics,*** hit single "Why" won MTV video award 1992, sang at 1992 Montreux Jazz Festival in Switzerland, sang "Love Song for a Vampire" on soundtrack *Bram Stoker's Dracula* 1992. Album *Diva* won Grammy 1993.

LENYA, LOTTE (1900–1981)
b. Karoline Blamauer 10/18 Vienna, Austria. Singer/actress, came to US. Won a Tony for the revival of the musical *Three Penny Opera* 1955. Died 11/27 New York City.

LEONARD, EDDIE (1875–1941)
b. Richmond, VA. Lyricist, with composer Eddie Munson wrote "Ida Sweet as Apple Cider" 1903.

LEONETTI, TOMMY (1929–1979)
b. 9/10 North Bergen, NJ. Singer. Died 9/15 Houston, TX.

LERNER, ALAN JAY (1918–1986)
b. 8/31 New York, NY. Lyricist, with composer Frederick Loewe* wrote *Brigadoon* 1942, *My Fair Lady* 1956, *Camelot* 1960, etc. Died 6/14 New York City.

LESLIE, EDGAR (1885–1976)
b. Stamford, CT. Lyricist, with E. Ray Goetz* & composer George W. Meyer* wrote "For Me and My Gal" 1917, with composer Joe Burke* wrote "Moon Over Miami" 1936. Died 1/22 New York City.

LES PAUL & MARY FORD
Singing team of Les Paul (Lester Polsfuss) & his wife Mary Ford (Irene Collen Summers 1924–1977). Hits "Vaya Con Dios," "How High the Moon" 1951. Albums *Hits of Les and Mary,* four CD set *Les Paul: The Legend and the Legacy* 1992. Paul lives in Mahwah, NJ.

LE TRIO CADIEN
With D.L. Menard, Eddie Le Jeune, & Ken Smith won Traditional Folk Album Grammy 1993 for *Le Trio Cadien.*

LETTERMEN, THE
Rock group with Tony Butala, Gary Pike, Jim Pike, albums *For Christmas This Year, Live in Concert, Why I Love Her.*

LEVEL 42
British rock group formed 1980, albums *Running in the Family, True Colours, World Machine,* video *Live at Wembley,* etc.

LEVELLERS, THE
British group with bassist Jeremy, drummer Charlie, & singer Mark Chadwick, album *Levelling the Land* 1992.

LE VERT
Vocal trio with Sean & Gerald Levert (sons of Eddie Levert of the **O'Jays**) & Marc Gordon. Albums *Big Throwdown, Just Coolin, Rope a Dope Style, For Real Tho'* 1993. Baritone Gerald Levert hit R&B single "School Me" 1992, "Can You Handle It?" On 1988 Top Ten Black Singles list for "May Forever Love."

LEWIS, AL (1905–1992)
b. Houma, LA. Banjoist/guitarist played with King Oliver* and the **Preservation Hall Band** in New Orleans, LA.

LEWIS, EPHRAIM
Singer/songwriter, debut album *Skin* 1992.

LEWIS, GARY (1945–)
Singer/guitarist of **Gary Lewis & the Playboys,** son of comedian Jerry Lewis. Served in the army 1967/68. His group had seven top hits including "This Diamond Ring," "Save Your Heart for Me," toured US 1992.

LEWIS, HENRY JAY (1932–)
b. 10/16 Los Angeles, CA. Music director New Jersey Symphony 1968, first black conductor of Metropolitan Opera in NY City 1972. Married soprano Marilyn Horne.

LEWIS, HUEY (1951–)
b. 7/5 San Francisco, CA. **Huey Lewis and the News** formed 1981 with Mario Cipollina, Johnny Colla, Bill Gibson, Chris Hayes, Sean Hopper. Hits "Heart and Soul" 1983, "If This is It" 1984, "The Power of Love" in the film *Back to the Future*

1985, video *The Heart of Rock & Roll* 1985, with others on *People Get Ready: A Tribute to Curtis Mayfield* 1993.

LEWIS, JERRY LEE (1935–   )
b. 9/29 Ferriday, LA. Pianist/singer/comedian, hits "Another Time, Another Place" 1968, "Roll Over Beethoven," "Whole Lotta Shakin' Going On," with **Rolling Stones** on video *Ready Steady Go Vol.2* 1985, video *Shindig: Presents Jerry Lee Lewis* 1992. In March 1993 Lewis moved to Ireland where a law exempts Irish residents from paying income taxes on income derived from creative art.

LEWIS, JOHN AARON (1920–   )
b. La Grange, IL. Pianist/composer with **Modern Jazz Quartet***
1952/74, played with Dizzy Gillespie,* Miles Davis,* & others. Composed numerous pieces of music, albums *Chess Game, Wonderful World of Jazz.*

LEWIS, MEL (1929–1990)
b. Melvin Sokoloff in Buffalo, NY. Drummer/leader, with Bill Colman in 1950s, with Dizzy Gillespie,* Stan Kenton,* & others in 60s, toured Soviet Union 1972, at Newport Jazz Festivals in NY City in 70s/80s, albums *The Lost Art, Naturally,* etc.

LEWIS, RAMSEY E., JR. (1935–   )
b. 5/27 Chicago, IL. Pianist/composer formed own trio 1956, album *The In Crowd* 1963 (Grammy winner), played at Carnegie Hall in NY City in 1970s, albums *Blues for the Night Owl, Keys to the City, Sun Goddess,* etc. At Miller Lite Jazz Festival in Detroit 1992.

LEWIS, SAMUEL M. (1885–1959)
b. New York, NY. Lyricist, with Joe Young* & composer Walter Donaldson* wrote "How Ya Gonna Keep 'Em Down on the Farm?", with composer Ray Henderson* "Five Foot Two Eyes of Blue." With composer Ted Fiorito* wrote "Laugh, Clown, Laugh."

LEWIS, TED (1891–1971)
b. Theodore Leopold Friedman in Circleville, Ohio. Clarinetist/

leader, had his own band. Wore a top hat and his opening line
was "Is ev'rybody happy?".

LIBERACE (1919–1987)
b. Wladziu Valentine Liberace 5/16 West Allis, WI. Pianist, debut at
Carnegie Hall in NY City 1953, wore elaborate costumes and had
candelabras atop his pianos. Albums *Greatest Hits, Here's
Liberace, Best of Liberace.* Died of AIDS 2/4 Palm Springs, CA.

LIBERATION ARMY
Eleven-piece jazz orchestra in San Francisco formed in 1979 with
pianist Jessica Williams, featuring trumpeter Eddie Henderson
and altoist Vince Wallace.

LIEURANCE, THURLOW (1878–1963)
b. Oskaloosa, Iowa. Composer, with lyricist Rev. J.M. Cavanass
wrote "By the Waters of Minnetonka" 1914.

LIFE, SEX AND DEATH
Los Angeles rockers, album *The Silent Majority* 1992, with
Poison* and **Damn Yankees*** toured US 1993.

LIFERS GROUP
Lifetime inmates at Rahway prison in New Jersey on albums
Lifers Group World Tour: Rahway Prison, That's It 1992,
Living Proof 1993.

LIGHT, ENOCH HENRY (1907–1978)
b. 8/18 Canton, Ohio. Percussionist, albums *Big Band Hits of the
'30s, Provocative Percussion.*

LIGHTFOOT, GORDON M. (1939–   )
b. 11/17 Orilla, Ontario, Canada. Singer/songwriter, wrote "If
You Could Read My Mind" 1970, "Sundown" 1974, albums
*East of Midnight, If You Could Read My Mind, Summertime
Dream, Sundown, Waiting for You* 1993, etc.

LILIUOKALANI (1838–1917)
b. Honolulu. Queen of the Hawaiian Islands, songwriter, wrote
"Aloha Oe" 1884.

LILLIAN AXE
Hard rock outfit, albums *Poetic Justice, Love & War* 1992.

LIMELITERS
Formed by Glenn Yarborough* and Lou Gotlieb in 1959. Albums *A Mighty Day, Harmony, Pot Pourri, Reunion,* etc.

LINCOLN, ABBEY (1930–   )
b. Chicago, IL. Singer, married drummer Max Roach,* later divorced. Her singing in Roach's *Freedom Now Suite* 1960 made that album famous. She was named Aminata by the President of Zaire and given the surname Moseka by the Minister of Education when she visited the Congo in 1975. Albums *Abbey Sings Billie Holiday, Abbey is Blue, Talking to the Sun, The World is Falling Down* 1990, *You Gotta Pay the Band* Grammy winner 1993.

LINCOLN CENTER JAZZ ORCHESTRA
With Wynton Marsalis, toured 28 US cities in 1992.

LIND, JENNY (1820–1887)
b. Stockholm, Sweden. Noted soprano known as the "Swedish Nightingale" toured America 1850/52 on a concert tour arranged by showman P.T. Barnum.

LINDSAY, HOWARD (1899–1968)
b. Waterford, NY. Librettist with composer Cole Porter* for *Anything Goes*1934, with composer Irving Berlin* on *Call Me Madam* 1950 (starring Ethel Merman*), with composer Richard Rodgers* on *Sound of Music* (starring Mary Martin).

LITTLE ANTHONY AND THE IMPERIALS
Clarence Collins, Anthony Gourdine, Sam Strain, Ernest Wright, hit single "Tears on My Pillow."

LITTLE CHARLIE AND NIGHTCATS
Albums *All the Way Crazy, The Big Break, Captured Live, Disturbing the Peace.*

LITTLE ESTHER (1935–1984)
b. Esther Phillips 12/23 Houston, TX. Singer, hits "What a Difference a Day Makes," "Double Crossing Blues," "Release Me."

LITTLE EVA (1945–   )
b. Eva Narcissus Boyd 6/29 Bellhaven, NC. Singer, with words & music by Gerry Goffin* and Carole King* had hit "The Loco-Motion" 1962.

LITTLE FEAT
Formed 1969 with guitarist/singer Lowell George, singer/ keyboardist Bill Payne, bassist Roy Estrada, drummer Richard Hayward, albums *Dixie Chicken, Down on the Farm, Hoy Hoy, Let it Roll, Little Feat, Sailin' Shoes, Time Loves a Hero,* etc.

LITTLE MILTON
Albums *Blues 'N' Soul, If Walls Could Talk, Reality, Waiting for Little Milton,* etc.

LITTLE RICHARD (1935–   )
b. Richard Penniman 12/25 Macon, GA. Pianist/singer hits "Tutti Frutti" 1955, "Long Tall Sally" 1956, "Good Golly Miss Molly" 1957, sang at the 1966 Toronto Rock 'n' Roll Revival, albums *22 Classic Cuts, The Essential Little Richard,* etc., children's hit "Itsy Bitsy Spider" 1991, children's album *Shake it All About* 1992, received Lifetime Grammy award in February 1993.

LITTLE RIVER BAND, THE
Country/pop group from Australia started 1975 with Beeb Birtles, David Briggs, John Farnham, Rick Formosa, Graham Gobble, Steve Mousden, Mal Logan, George McArdle, Roger McLachan, Wayne Nelson, Derek Pellici, & Glen Shorrock. Hit single "Reminiscing" 1978. Albums *Greatest Hits,* with others on *The Stars Come Out for Christmas* 1992.

LITTLE TEXAS
Band with Travis Tritt,* & Trisha Yearwood* on 110-city Budweiser Rock 'N' Country Tour 1993.

LITTLE VILLAGE
Soul/rock singers John Hiatt,* Ry Cooder,* Nick Lowe, & drummer Jim Keltner, album *Little Village*, won Grammy 1993.

LITTLE WALTER (1930–1969)
b. Walter Jacobs. Harpist/harmonica player, albums *Boss Blues Harmonica, Hate to See You Go, The Best of Little Walter.*

LIVING COLOUR
With singer Corey Glover won 1990 Hard Rock Grammy for "Time's Up." Albums *Biscuits, Vivid, Stain* 1993, videos *Primer, Tune Tunnel.* Guitarist Vernon Reid with others on *People Get Ready: A Tribute to Curtis Mayfield* 1993.

LIVINGSTON, JAY HAROLD (1915–)
b. McDonald, PA. Pianist/composer, with lyricist R.B. Evans* wrote "To Each His Own" 1946, "Buttons and Bows" 1948, "Que Sera, Sera, Whatever Will Be Will Be" 1956.

L. L. COOL J (1967–)
b. Queens, NY City. Rapper, debut album *Radio,* platinum album *Walking with a Panther* 1989, *Bigger and Deffer,* won 1991 Grammy for "Mama Said Knock You Out" which he sang with his grandmother at Radio City Music Hall in NY City 1992. Album *14 Shots to the Dome* 1993, "Strictly Business" Grammy winner 1993.

LLOYD, CHARLES (1938–)
b. Memphis, TN. Saxist/flutist, played at the San Francisco Fillmore rock palace with Jim Hendrix* & the **Grateful Dead,*** albums *Forest Flowers* 1966, *Fish Out of Water* 1992.

LLOYD WEBBER, SIR ANDREW (1948–)
b. 3/22 London, England, composer. Wrote hit musicals *Jesus Christ Superstar* 1970, *Evita* 1976, *Cats* 1981, *Phantom of the Opera, Sunset Boulevard* 1993. Albums *Aspects of Webber, Variations, The Premiere Collection Encore,* video *Requiem.*

LOCO MIA
Quartet from the island of Ibiza, Spain, album *Loco Mia* (Crazy One) 1992.

LOESSER, FRANK (1910–1969)
b. New York, NY. Composer, wrote words & music "Praise the Lord and Pass the Ammunition" 1942, "On a Slow Boat to China" 1948, wrote scores for *Where's Charley* 1948, *Guys & Dolls* 1950, *How to Succeed in Business Without Really Trying* 1961. Album *Revisited.* Died in New York City.

LOEWE, FREDERICK (1904–1988)
b. Berlin Germany. Came to New York. Pianist/composer, with lyricist A.J. Lerner wrote *Brigadoon* 1947, *My Fair Lady* 1956, *Camelot* 1960, etc. Died 2/13 Palm Springs, CA.

LOFGREN, NILS "LEFTY" (1953–)
b. Chicago, IL. Guitarist/pianist/singer/songwriter with Bruce Springsteen's **E Street Band,*** left for solo career. Album *Crooked Line* 1992 along with Neil Young's* **Stray Gators** band & Ringo Starr's **All-Star Band.**

LOGAN, FREDERICK K. (1871–1928)
b. Oskaloosa, Iowa. Pianist/composer with John V. Eppel* wrote "The Missouri Waltz" 1914, a favorite of President Truman.

LOGGINS, DAVE
Songwriter, "She is His Only Need" won Grammy 1993.

LOGGINS AND MESSINA
Kenny Loggins (Kenneth Clarke b. 1/7/48 Everett, WA, saxist/singer/songwriter) with Jim Messina (b. 12/5/47 Maywood, CA, singer/songwriter). Also with **Buffalo Springfield*** and **Poco.*** Albums *Full Sail, Sittin' In, Mother Lode,* etc. With others on *The Stars Come Out for Christmas* 1992. Loggins played his sax with President Clinton at the Arkansas Ball in January 1993.

LOMBARDO, GUY A. (1902–1977)
b. 6/19 London, Ontario, Canada. Leader of **The Royal Canadians,** played at New Year's Eve for many years. Known for "Sweetest Music This Side of Heaven." Albums *Best of Guy Lombardo, Golden Medleys, Musical Yesteryears, New Year's Eve with Guy Lombardo.* Died 11/5 Houston, Texas.

LONDON, JULIE (1926–   )
b. Julie Peck 9/26 Santa Rosa, CA. Singer/actress sang on radio at age three. Hit "Cry Me a River" 1956. Albums *Best of Julie London, Sings Choicest—Cole Porter.* Married actor Jack Webb of *Dragnet* fame 1947, later divorced.

LONESOME DEBONAIRES
Pop/rock/metal/country NY City band with guitarist/singer Jonathan Gregg, album *Blue on Blond* 1992.

LONNIE BROOKS BLUES BAND
Toured on Alligator Records 20th Anniversary tour 1992.

LOOSE DIAMONDS
Ohio transplant country/rock group with Tracy & Mike Campbell, Corey Mauser, Jud Newcomb, & David Robinson on album *Blue Days, Black Nights* 1993.

LOPES, LISA "LEFT EYE"
Songwriter, with Dallas Austin wrote "Ain't 2 Proud 2 Beg" Grammy winner 1993.

LOPEZ, VINCENT (1895–1975)
b. 12/30 New York, NY. Bandleader popular 1920/30s. Betty Hutton sang in his band. Died 9/20 Miami Beach, FL.

LORBER, JEFF
R&B jazz, keyboardist. His group **Fusion** disbanded in 1986, solo album *Worth Waiting For* 1993.

LORENZO
Hit R&B single "Real Love" 1992.

LORENZO, ANGE (1894–1971)
b. near West Branch, MI. Pianist/composer, with R.A. Whiting*
and J.R. Alden* wrote "Sleepy Time Gal" 1925.

LORENZ, TREY (1969–)
From South Carolina, singer/songwriter, album *Trey Lorenz*
1993.

LOS LOBOS
Albums *By the Light of the Silvery Moon, How Will the Wolf
Survive? Un Nuevo Comienzo, Kiko & the Lavender Moon, The
Neighborhood* won Grammy 1993. Band played on the
Marlboro Music Military Tour of bases 1992, at New Orleans
Jazz Festival April/May 1993.

LOS TIGRES DEL NORTE
Won Mexican/American Grammy 1993 for *Con Sentimiento Y
Sabor.*

LOUIS, LIL
Drummer/musician. **Lil Louis and the World** with singer Joi
Cardwell on album *Journey with the Lonely* 1992.

LOVE
West Coast rock group formed 1965, guitarist/singer/keyboardist
Arthur Lee, guitarist/singer Bryan Maclean, bassist Ken Forest,
guitarist John Echols, drummer Alban "Snoopy" Pfisterer.
Albums *Best of Love, De Capa, Forever Changes, Love,
Revisited.*

LOVE BATTERY
Grunge rockers from Seattle, formed 1989, lead guitarist Kevin
Whitworth, singer/guitarist "Ron Nine" Rudzits, drummer
Jason Finn, & bassist Bruce Fairweather. EP *Between the Eyes*
and *Dayglo* 1992.

LOVE, COURTNEY (1966–)
Front woman for Los Angeles band **Hole,** wife of **Nirvana**'s Kurt
Cobain.* A picture of her pregnant and in a transparent

negligee appeared on the cover of *Vanity Fair* September 1992: it was retouched to airbrush out the cigarette she was holding.

LOVE, DARLENE
Singer with Bette Midler* & Alan Jackson* on film *Home Alone 2: Lost in New York* soundtrack, she sang "He's a Rebel" on *All Alone for Christmas* 1992.

LOVE, MARIE
British female rapper, single "Marie in the Middle," album *Down to Earth.*

LOVELESS, PATTY (1957–   )
Country singer, albums *Honky Tonk Angel, On Down the Line, Patty Loveless, Up Against My Heart.* Suffered a leaking blood vessel on a vocal cord in October 1992. With others on CBS special in January 1993.

LOVEMONGERS, THE
Their songs are included on the soundtrack of the movie *Singles* 1992.

LOVERBOY
Canadian group formed 1978 with Paul Dean, Matt Frenette, Doug Johnson, Mike Reno, Scott Smith. Hit "Queen of the Broken Hearts" 1983, albums *Big Ones, Get Lucky, Wild Side.* Videos *Anyway You Look at It, Loverboy.*

LOVETT, LYLE (1957–   )
b. 1/11, raised in Klein, TX. Actor/singer/songwriter, starred in the film *The Player.* Best Male Country Vocal Grammy 1989 for *Lovett and His Large Band, Lyle Lovett, Pontiac, Joshua Judges Ruth* won Grammy 1993, sang "Stand by Your Man" on film soundtrack *The Crying Game* 1993, music video *Church* won Grammy 1993. 6/27/93 Married actress Julia Roberts.

LOVIN' SPOONFUL
Rock group started in NY City 1965 with John Boone, Joe Butler,

John Sebastian, & Zal Yanovsky, split 1970. Hit single "Do You Believe in Magic," album *Anthology*.

LOWRY, ROBERT (1826–1899)
b. Philadelphia, Pa. Composer wrote "Shall We Gather at the River?" 1864, "Where is My Wandering Boy Tonight?" 1877.

L 7
Female band with guitarist Doonita Sparks, Dee Plakas, Jennifer Finch, & Suzi Gardner, album *Bricks are Heavy* 1992 about an abused housewife who kills her husband with a frying pan.

LUFT, LORNA (1952–)
b. 11/21. Singer, daughter of Judy Garland* & Sidney Luft, half-sister of Liza Minnelli.* Lorna married Jake Hooker, separated 1992. She sang in *Guys and Dolls* on the road.

LUNCEFORD, JAMES M. "JIMMY" (1902–1947)
b. Fulton, MO. Saxist, formed band with Willie Smith* 1929, toured USA, Scandinavia 1937, popular in 1940s. While making a personal appearance in a music store signing autographs, collapsed and died in Seaside, CA.

LU PONE, PATTI
British singer/actress, in Andrew Lloyd Webber's* *Evita* 1980 and *Sunset Boulevard* 1993, album *Back to Broadway* 1993.

LYMON, FRANKIE (1943–1968)
b. Detroit, MI. Singer/songwriter, **Frankie Lymon and the Teenagers,** hit single "Why Do Fools Fall in Love?" 1956 sold over one million copies. Album *Best of Frankie Lymon*. Died from an overdose of drugs.

LYNCH, RAY
Albums *Deep Breakfast, Music of Ray, No Blue Thing, Sky of the Mind*.

LYNN, LORETTA (1935–)
b. Loretta Webb 4/14 Butcher Hollow, KY. Country singer, married Oliver Lynn, Jr. ("Moony") Toured US, Canada &

Europe in 1960s, at Grand Ole Opry, Nashville, 1972. The film *Coal Miner's Daughter* (1977) was based on her life. Video *In Concert: Live at Harrah's*. Toured with President George Bush in 1992 & often sings in Branson, MO. (dubbed the "Hillbilly Las Vegas.")

LYNN, TAMIYA
Singer/songwriter from New Orleans, sang with the **Rolling Stones,** * the Neville Brothers,* & Dr. John,* album *Tamiya Lynn* 1992.

LYNN, VERA
British singer, CD *Greatest Hits,* hit singles "Auf Wiedersehn Sweetheart," "We'll Meet Again" (popular during World War II).

LYNYRD SKYNYRD
Rock group with Robert Burns, Allen Collins, Steve Gaines, Ed King, William Powell, Gary Rossington, Ronnie Van Zandt, and Leon Wilkeson. Gaines & Van Zandt were killed in a plane crash on 10/20/77 in Mississippi. Hit single "Freebird," albums *Best of the Rest, Legend, Street Survivors,* etc. Video *Tribute Tour,* band on the Marlboro Music Military Tour of bases 1992. Album *The Last Rebel* 1993.

LYTE, E.O. (1842–1913)
b. Bird-in-Hand, Lancaster County, PA. Songwriter & college professor at Millersville University, Millersville, PA. Wrote a number of ditties, hit "Row, Row, Row Your Boat." Died at Lancaster, PA.

LYTE, MC
Female hard core rapper, album *Ain't No Other.*

M

MABLEY, MOMS (1894–1975)
b. Loretta Mary Aikin 3/19 Brevard, NC. Singer/comedienne. Album *Funniest Woman in the World*. Died 5/23 White Plains, NY.

MAC DERMONT, GALT (1928–   )
b. 12/19 Montreal. Composer, with libretto by Gerome Ragni and James Rado rock opera *Hair* 1968.

MAC DONALD, JEANETTE (1907–1965)
b. Philadelphia, PA. Singer/actress, starred with Nelson Eddy in films *Naughty Marietta* 1935, *Rose Marie* 1936, *Maytime* 1937; Albums *San Francisco & Other Favorites,* with Nelson Eddy on *Legendary Performance*. Married Gene Raymond.

MAC DONOUGH, GLEN (1870–1924)
b. Brooklyn, NY City. Lyricist, with composer Victor Herbert* wrote *Toyland* 1903.

MAC DOWELL, EDWARD (1861–1908)
b. New York, NY. Pianist/composer, composed "To a Wild Rose" 1896, album *Piano Concerto 1–2/Amato*.

MACK, LONNIE
Albums *Live, Attack Killer V, Wham That Memphis Man,* with Stevie Ray Vaughan* on *Stroke Like Lightning*.

MAC RAE, GORDON (1921–1986)
b. 3/12 East Orange, NJ. Sang with Jo Stafford*; Hit "Whispering Hope" 1949. Broadway shows with Dorothy Kirsten *. With Shirley Jones in *Oklahoma* 1943.

MAD COBRA
Reggae/hip hop singer has recorded with rappers **Geto Boys.** Album *Hard to Wet, Easy to Dry* 1992.

MADDEN, EDWARD (1878–1952)
b. New York. Lyricist, with composer Gus Edwards* wrote "By the Light of the Silvery Moon" 1907.

MADDOX, ROSE (1926–   )
b. 12/15 Boaz, Alabama. Country singer/guitarist with the **Maddox Brothers and Rose,** album *Rose of the West Coast Country.* She also sang with Buck Owens. Honored at a country music event in September 1992.

MADNESS
British rock group formed 1978 with Mike Barson, Mark Bedford, Chris Foreman, Graham "Suggs" McPherson, Carl Smyth, Lee Thompson, & "Woody" Woodgate. Hit single "Our House" 1983, album *One Step Beyond.*

MADONNA (1958–   )
b. Madonna Louise Ciccone 8/16 Bay City, MI. Singer, Hits "Like a Virgin," "Material Girl," *Like a Prayer* sold over two million albums 1989. *I'm Breathless* sold two million albums. *Vogue,* platinum video *Justify My Love* 1990, *Erotica* 1992, single "This Used to be My Playground" 1992. Book of erotica *Sex* 1992. X-rated film *Body of Evidence* was released in January 1993. Married Sean Penn, later divorced.

MAGIC SAM (1938–1993)
b. Samuel Maghetti 2/14 in MS. Blues singer/guitarist, went to Chicago in 1950s, albums *Magic Touch* 1966, *Easy Baby, Give Me Time, West Side Guitar 1957/66, West Side Soul.*

MAHAVISHNU ORCHESTRA, THE
With drummer Billy Cobham, Jr.,* electric violinist Jerry Goodman, keyboardist Jan Hammer, percussionist Rick Laird, guitarist John McLaughlin. Albums *Apocalypse, Birds of Fire, Visions of Emerald Beyond,* etc.

MAKEBA, MIRIAM (1932–   )
b. 3/4 Prospect Township, South Africa. Singer, albums *Eyes on Tomorrow, Sangoma, Welela.*

MAKEM, TOMMY
Albums *Rolling Home, Songbag.*

MALMSTEEN, YNGEVIE
Albums *Marching Out, Rising Force, Trial by Fire Live in Leningrad, Trilogy.*

MALOTTE, ALBERT HAY (1895–1964)
b. Philadelphia, PA. Composer, he composed music for "The Lord's Prayer" 1935.

MAMAS AND THE PAPAS, THE
Singing group founded in the Virgin Islands 1965 with Cass Elliott (Ellen Naomi Cohen 1945–1974); John Phillips;* Michelle Gilliam Phillips b. 4/6/44 Long Beach CA, the wife of John; Dennis Doherty & Spanky McFarlane. Hit song "Monday, Monday," albums *16 Greatest Hits, History of Creeque Alley, Deliver, Farewell to 1st Golden Era.* MacKenzie Phillips b. 11/10/59 daughter of John later joined the group. Dennis Doherty, Spanky McFarlane, & Larrie Bee toured US 1992.

MANCHESTER, MELISSA TONI (1951–)
b. 2/15 New York, NY. Singer/songwriter, was a back-up singer for Bette Midler,* hits "Midnight Blue," "Don't Cry Out Loud" written by Peter Allen,* albums *Greatest Hits, Tribute,* video *Music of Melissa Manchester.* She toured US 1992.

MANCINI, HENRY (1924–1994)
b. 4/16 Cleveland, Ohio. Composer, won Grammys for *The Music from Peter Gunn* 1958, "Moon River" 1961, "Days of Wine and Roses" 1963. Composed music for Broadway shows & films. Albums *Academy Award Collection, Charade, Mostly Monsters/Murders, Pure Gold,* video *Henry Mancini and Friends.* Worked on *Tom and Jerry—The Movie* 1992.

MANDEL, JOHNNY
Composer, instrumental accompaniment for *Here's to Life* title track won Grammy 1993.

MANDRELL, BARBARA ANN (1946–)
b/ 12/25 Houston, TX. Country/pop singer/guitarist, hit "Sleeping Single in a Double Bed." Albums *Greatest Country Hits, Key's in the Mailbox, Morning Sun,* etc. On 5/28/92 Barbara & her husband celebrated their 25th wedding anniversary. She often sings in Branson, Missouri, dubbed the "Hillbilly Las Vegas". Married Ken Dudney.

MANGIONE, CHARLES F. "CHUCK" (1940–)
b. Rochester, NY. Composer/leader, his *Kaleidoscope* was performed by Eastman School of Music in Rochester, *Together* with Rochester Philharmonic. Wrote "Feels So Good" 1978. Albums *Love Notes* 1981, *Best of Chuck Mangione, Fun and Games, Land of Make Believe, Save Tonight for Me,* etc.

MANHATTAN RHYTHM KINGS
Jazz as vaudeville with bassist Brian Nalepka, banjo/guitarist David Lisker, pianist/clarinetist/bassoonist Michael Reeder in NY City in 1980s.

MANHATTAN TRANSFER
Jazz/rock group with Cheryl Bentyne, Tim Hauser, Alan Paul, Janis Siegel, & Laurel Masse (later dropped out). *Vocalese* won three Grammys 1985, *Brasil* 1988 Grammy winner. Albums *Best of Manhattan Transfer, Coming Out, Mecca for Moderns, Rock, Rhythm and Blues,* etc., videos *Live, Vocalese, The Offbeat of Avenues* 1992. With Tony Bennett* on *The Christmas Album* 1992. Awarded Poland's Gold Medal of Music by President Lech Walesa in Warsaw in October 1992.

MANILOW, BARRY (1946–)
b/ 6/17 Brooklyn, NY City. Singer/songwriter, was an accompanist for Bette Midler.* Hit single "Mandy" 1975, albums *Because It's Christmas, Live on Broadway, Showstoppers, This One's for You,* etc., platinum video *Live on Broadway* 1990, *Making of 2:00 AM Paradise.* Sang in Manila on his world tour in November 1992.

MANLY MOONDOG & THE THREE KOOL KATS
Rock/R&B band led by singer/actor Woody Harrelson on tour 1992.

MANN, BARRY (1939–)
Composer, with Cynthia Well* wrote "You've Lost that Loving Feeling" & "Saturday Night at the Movies."

MANN, HERBIE (1930–)
b. Herbert Jay Solomon 4/16 Brooklyn, NY City. Jazz flutist formed Afro-American sextet 1959, toured Africa, Brazil, & Japan in 1960s, at Atlantic City Jazz Festival in July 1980/81. Albums *Bird in a Silver Cage, Memphis Underground, Push Push*, etc.

MANNE, SHELDON "SHELLY" (1920–1984)
b. 6/11 New York, NY. Jazz drummer, opened Shelly Manne's Hole in Hollywood, CA 1960. Albums *My Fair Lady, Shelly Manne & His Friends*, etc. Died 9/26 in Los Angeles, CA.

MANNHEIM STEAMROLLER
Albums *Christmas, Classical Gas, Fresh-Aire Vols. 1 to 6, Yellowstone.*

MANONE, JOSEPH "WINGY" (1904–1982)
b. 2/13 New Orleans, LA. Trumpeter/vocalist. Lost his right arm in a streetcar accident and so was nicknamed "Wingy," Led his own bands 1920s/70s. Died 7/9 Las Vegas, NV.

MANTOVANI
Albums *Christmas with Mantovani, Golden Hits, Memories, World Hits*, etc.

MARABLE, FATE (1890–1947)
b. Paducah, KY. Jazz pianist/leader, played on Mississippi River boats from 1907, formed own band 1917.

MARIA, TANI
Albums *Bela Vista, Come With Me, Forbidden Colors, Love Explosion, Taurus*, etc.

MARIE, TEENA
Albums *Emerald City, It Must be Magic, Ivory, Robbery, Starchild, Wild and Peaceful.*

MARK, MARKY (1971–)
b. Mark Robert Michael Wahlberg. Rapper, albums *Music for People, You Gotta Believe,* Grammy winner 1993. Served 43 days in jail in 1988 for beating a Vietnamese man (Wahlberg said he was high on liquor & marijuana).

MARKS, JOHN D. "JOHNNY" (1909–1985)
b. Mt. Vernon, NY. Composer, wrote "Rudolph the Red Nosed Reindeer" 1949.

MARLEY, BOB (1945–1981)
b. Robert Nesta 2/5 Kingston, Jamaica. Musician/composer/leader of **Bob Marley and the Wailers.** His reggae music combined with Rastafarian faith sold over 20 million records. Hit "Jamming." Albums *Chances Are, Mighty Bob Marley, Burnin', Exodus, Legend, Natty Dread, Uprising,* videos *Bob Marley Story, Legend, Time Will Tell.* Died 5/11 Miami, Florida. Posthumously inducted into Rock & Roll Hall of Fame January 1994.

MARLEY, ZIGGY
Ziggy Marley (son of the late Bob Marley*) **and the Melody Makers** won 1988 Reggae Grammy for *Conscientious Party* & 1989 Grammy for *One Bright Day.*

MARS, CHRIS
Drummer/singer/songwriter formerly with the **Replacements*** a Minneapolis Group. Solo album *Horseshoes and Hand Grenades* 1992.

MARSALA, MARTY (1909–1975)
b. 4/2 Chicago, IL. Trumpeter/leader, brother of Joe Marsala, in brother's band 1936/41 then led own bands in Chicago and San Francisco 1950s/60s. Died in Chicago.

MARSALIS, BRANFORD (1960–)

b. 8/26 New Orleans, LA. Saxist/leader replaced Doc Severinsen* on NBC's Tonight Show (1992) with replacement band of guitarist Kevin Eubanks*, pianist Kenny Kirkland, bassist Bob Hurst, drummer Jeff Watts, percussionist Vicki Randle, trombonist Matt Finders, & trumpeter Sal Marquez. Albums *Beautiful Are Not Yet Born, Crazy Music People, Royal Garden Blues,* etc. Video *Steep, I Heard You Twice the First Time* Grammy winner 1993.

MARSALIS, DELFEAYO

b. New Orleans, LA. Trombonist, jazz solo on *Pontius Pilate's Decision* 1992.

MARSALIS, ELLIS

Pianist at International Association of Jazz Educators in San Antonio, TX in January 1992, albums *Heart of Gold, PNO in E Solo Piano, Homecoming.*

MARSALIS, WYNTON (1961–)

b. 10/18 New Orleans, LA. Jazz trumpeter/composer, at Montreux Jazz Festival, July 1980. First artist to win Grammys for both classical and jazz albums (1984). Top Ten Classical Album 1988 *Baroque Music for Trumpets,* albums *Black Codes, J. Mood, Live at Blues Alley, The Majesty of the Blues,* etc. *Blue Interlude* Grammy winner 1993. Video *Blues and Swing.* Composed *Jazz* (Six Syncopated Movements) for NY City Ballet (performed at Lincoln Center in January 1993). Album *Citi Movement.* Played at the White House for President & Mrs. Clinton June 1993.

MARSHALL TUCKER BAND

Tommy & Toy Caldwell, Jerry Eubanks, Doug Gray, George M'Corkel & Paul Riddle. Albums *A New Life, Carolina Dreams, Long Hard Road, Marshall Tucker Band, Together Forever,* etc.

MARTHA AND THE VANDELLAS

Pop group with lead singer Martha Reeves (b. 7/18/41 Detroit),

Rosalind Ashford, Betty Kelly, Lois Reeves, Annette Sterling, Sandra Tilley. Hits "Heat Wave," "Dancing in the Streets" 1964, "I'm Ready for Love" 1966.

MARTIN, DEAN (1917–   )

b. Dino Crocetti 6/17 Steubenville, Ohio. Singer/actor, met Jerry Lewis while at the 500 Club in Atlantic City, NJ 1946. They appeared in many films, broke up in 1957. Martin had hit song "Return to Me," albums *All Time Greatest Hits, Happy Hour, Swinging Down Yonder.* NBC TV Show in the early 1970s.

MARTIN, FREDDY (1906–1983)

b. 12/9 Cleveland, Ohio. Bandleader 1932/83. Theme song "Tonight We Love." Album *Hits of Freddy Martin.* Died 9/30 Newport Beach, CA.

MARTIN, HUGH (1914–   )

b. Birmingham, AL. Composer, with lyricist Ralph Blane wrote "Buckle Down, Winsocki" 1941, "The Trolley Song" 1944.

MARTIN, MARY (1914–1990)

b. 12/1 Weatherford, TX. Singer/actress won Tonys for *Peter Pan* 1954 and *The Sound of Music* 1959. Album *Sings Richard Rodgers.* Married Richard Halliday, divorced. Mother of Larry Hagman. Died 11/2 Rancho Mirage, CA.

MARTIN, TONY (1913–   )

b. Alfred Norris, Jr. 12/25 San Francisco, CA. Singer, radio debut on the "Lucky Strike Hour" 1932, appeared in films. Served in World War II. Married dancer Cyd Charisse, appeared with her in night club shows in Las Vegas, NV.

MARTINO, AL (1927–   )

b. 10/7 Singer, hit "Spanish Eyes." Albums *Greatest Hits, The Best of Al Martino.*

MARVELETTES, THE

Singers, hit "Please Mr. Postman," albums *Greatest Hits, Playboy.*

MARX, RICHARD
Singer, 1988 Top Ten Album for *Richard Marx, Repeat Offender* 1989, sold over 3 million copies, platinum single "Right Here Waiting," platinum video *Richard Marx Volume I* 1990, hit singles "Take This Heart" 1992, "Hazard" 1992.

MASON, DAVE (1945–)
b. 5/10 Worcester, England. Guitarist/singer/songwriter, albums *Alone Together, Greatest Hits, Let it Flow, Very Best of Dave Mason.*

MASON, LOWELL (1792–1872)
b. Medfield, MA. Composer, with lyricist Isaac Watts wrote "Joy to the World" 1839. With lyricist Sarah F. Adams wrote "Nearer My God to Thee" 1859. When the oceanliner *Titanic* struck an iceberg in 1912 and began to sink into the ocean, the band played "Nearer My God to Thee."

MATERIAL ISSUE
Chicago pop group, single "What Girls Want" 1990, albums *International Pop Overthrow, Destruction Universe* 1992.

MATHIS, JOHNNY (1935–)
b. 9/30 San Francisco, CA. Singer, hit "Too Much Too Little Too Late." Recorded over 76 albums, *A Special Part of Me, For Christmas, Heavenly, In the Still of the Night, That's What Friends are For,* platinum video *Home for Christmas* 1990. On album *Handel's Messiah: A Soulful Celebration* 1992.

MATLOCK, MATTY (1909–1978)
b. 4/27 Paducah, KY. Clarinetist/saxist/flutist with Ben Pollock & Bob Crosby 1930/40s, led own bands. Toured Orient 1964, Europe 1972. Died 6/15 Van Nuys, CA.

MATRIX
Nine-piece jazz band led by pianist/composer John Harmon formed 1974 in Appleton, WI. With trombonist Kurt Dietrich in NY City in late 1970s/80s.

MATTEA, KATHY
Country singer won 1990 Vocal Female Grammy for "Where've
You Been?" albums *From My Heart, Time Passes By, Untasted,
Honey,* video *A Collection of Hits, Lonesome Standard Time*
1992. On CBS special *Women of Country* in January 1993. *Good
News* Country/Bluegrass/Soul Album Grammy 1994.

MATTHEWS, IAN (1945–   )
b. Ian Matthew MacDonald 6/16 Lincolnshire, England. Guitarist/
singer/songwriter, came to US, hit singles "Woodstock" 1977,
"Shake It" 1978.

MAVERICKS, THE
Miami country/Cuban band with David Lee Holt, Robert Rey-
nolds, Paul Deakin, & singer/songwriter Raul Malo, album
From Hell to Paradise 1992.

MAY, E. WILLIAM "BILLY" (1916–   )
b. 11/10 Pittsburgh, PA. Arranger for Charlie Barnet & Frank
Sinatra,* also bandleader. Albums *I Believe in You, Leading the
Good Life.*

MAYALL, JOHN (1933–   )
b. 11/23 Manchester, England. Composer/musician, albums *A
Sense of Place, Archives to Eighties, Blues Breakers, Raw
Blues, Turning Point,* etc.

MAYFIELD, CURTIS (1942–   )
b. 6/3 Chicago, IL. Guitarist/singer/songwriter, albums *Superfly*
1972, *Of All Time* (Classic Collection). *Curtis Mayfield & the
Impressions 1961–1977* CDs 1992. Was disabled when performing in 1990 when a lighting tower collapsed on him. Later
his house burned down.

MAYNOR, DOROTHY (1910–   )
b. 9/3 Norfolk, VA & raised in Greensboro, NC. Soprano, sang at
Berkshire Music Festival in 1939, toured US & Europe 1940s/
50s. Founded Harlem School of Arts in NY City 1966. Married
Shelby Rooks.

MAZE

Rock group formed 1976 in Philadelphia, later went to San Francisco with singer/songwriter Frankie Beverly, keyboardist Sam Porter, percussionist Roame Lowry, McKinley "Bugs" Williams, guitarist Wayne Thomas, bassist Robin Duke, & drummer Joe Provost. Albums *Maze, Life in New Orleans, Maze with Frankie Beverly, We are One.*

MC BRIDE, CHRISTIAN (1972–)

Jazz bassist. Performs with saxist Joshua Redman.

MC BRIDE AND THE RIDE

Hit country singles "Sacred Ground," "Going Out of My Mind" 1992, album *Burnin Up the Road.*

MC BRIDE, MARTINA

Country singer, album *The Time Has Come* 1992, with Garth Brooks on single "Cheap Whiskey."

MC CABE, CHARLES C. (1836–1906)

b. Athens, Ohio. Singer, in 1862 appointed chaplain of 122nd Ohio Infantry, known as the "singing chaplain." Captured in June 1863 at Winchester, Virginia, imprisoned in Libby Prison in Richmond, then released. At the Christian Meeting in Washington, D.C. in February 1864 attended by President Lincoln McCabe sang "The Battle Hymn of the Republic," and the President asked McCabe to sing it again. At another Christian meeting in January 1865 McCabe sang the song again, and President Lincoln joined in the chorus.

MC CANN, LESLIE C. "LES" (1935–)

b. 9/23 Lexington, KY. Jazz pianist/keyboardist/singer, had own trio, toured Europe 1960s. With Left Bank Jazz Society in Baltimore, MD 1980. At Mellon Jazz Festival, Pittsburgh 1992. Albums *Les is More,* with E. Harris *Swiss Movement.*

MC CARTHY, JOSEPH (1885–1943)

b. Somerville, MA. Lyricist, with composer J.V. Monaco* wrote "Shave and a Haircut" 1914, with Joe Burke* "Rambling

Rose" 1918, with composer Harry Carroll* wrote "I'm Always Chasing Rainbows" 1918.

MC CARTNEY, LINDA (1942–)
b. 9/24. Musician, with husband Paul* and **Wings**.

MC CARTNEY, PAUL (1942–)
b. 6/18 Liverpool, England. With the **Beatles,*** hit "Yesterday," wrote "I Want to Hold Your Hand" with John Lennon, "Hard Day's Night," & other songs. "Ebony and Ivory" with Stevie Wonder 1982. Albums *All the Best, Back to the Egg, London Town, Pipes of Peace, Flowers in the Dirt,* etc. Videos *Get Back, Put It There, Special.* Toured the world 1989, toured US 1990/93, *Paul McCartney Up Close* on MTV in February 1993.

MC CLINTON, DELBERT
Rock singer won 1991 Duet Grammy for "Every Time I Roll the Dice," albums *Best of Delbert McClinton, Live in Austin.* With Bonnie Raitt* on "Good Man, Good Woman" (Grammy winner 1991), with Tanya Tucker* "Tell Me About It" track from *Can't Run from Yourself* (won Grammy 1993).

MC CONNELL, ROB
Rob McConnell and the Boss Brass album *Brassy and Sassy* (won Grammy 1993).

MC COO, MARILYN (1943–)
b. 9/30. Pop/gospel singer with *Fifth Dimension.** Sang "I'm Blessed" at the Stellar Music awards in January 1993.

MC CORKLE, SUSANNAH
Jazz singer, album *I'll Take Romance.*

MC CORMACK, JOHN (1884–1945)
b. Athlone, Ireland. Noted tenor, NY debut with Metropolitan Opera 1910, albums *Irish Minstrel, Treasury of Irish Melodies.*

MC CREE, JUNIE (1865–1918)
b. Toledo, Ohio. Actor/lyricist, with composer Albert von Tilzer*

wrote "Put Your Arms Around Me Honey, Hold Me Tight" 1910.

MC DANIEL, MEL (1942–   )
Country singer, album *Greatest Hits.*

MC DONALD, COUNTRY JOE (1942–   )
b. 1/1 El Monte, CA. Guitarist/singer/songwriter, albums *Superstitious Blues, Vanguard Years 1969–75.*

MC DONALD, MICHAEL
b. St. Louis, MO. Pianist/singer/songwriter with Doobie Brothers*, then solo. With Patti LaBelle* "On My Own" 1986. Albums *If That's What It Takes, No Lookin' Back, Take It to Heart,* with others on *Live at the Beacon* 1992.

MC DOWELL, EDWARD A. (1861–1908)
b. New York, NY. Pianist/composer, wrote *To a Wild Rose, To a Water Lily, & Woodland Sketches.*

MC ELROY, THOMAS
Songwriter, with Denzil Foster wrote "My Lovin' (You're Never Gonna Get It)" (Grammy winner 1993).

MC ENTYRE, REBA (1954–   )
b. 3/28 McAlister, OK. Country singer, studied classical violin & piano at College. Albums *Is There Life Out There? It's Your Call, My Broken Heart* (sold two million copies). Won American Music Country Album Female Artist, & Single ("The Greatest Man I Ever Knew") awards, Videos *Reba, Reba in Concert.* Sang at Bally's in Atlantic City, NJ in July 1992. Seven members of her band were killed in a 1991 crash near San Diego, CA. Husband Narvel Blackstock is her manager. 1993 Grammys: Female Artist Country Music Best Performance (with Linda Davis). 1994 Country Vocal Grammy with Linda Davis for "Does He Love You."

MC FARLAND, GARY (1933–1971)
b. Los Angeles, CA. Composer/vibist. Stan Getz* joined the **Gary McFarland Orchestra** on *Big Band Bossa Nova.*

MC FERRIN, BOBBY (1950–)

b. 3/11 New York, NY. Singer, album *Bobby McFerrin* 1980. 1988 Grammy for *Don't Worry, Be Happy,* at JVC Jazz Festival, Newport, RI in August 1992, Teamed with cellist Yo Yo Ma* at Tanglewood 1988 and at concerts in San Francisco & Boston 1992. Album *Hush and Play,* "Round Midnight" track from *Play* won Grammy 1993.

MC 5

(Motor City Five) with lead singer Rob Tyner* (died 1991), album *Kick Out the James* 1968, reissued 1992.

MC GEE, SAM FLEMING (1894–1975)

b. Franklin, TN. Banjoist/singer with **Sam & Kirk McGee from Sunny Tennessee** 1920s/30s, then **Fruit Jar Drinkers** after 1937.

MC GHEE, HOWARD (1916–1987)

b. Tulsa, OK. Jazz trumpeter/composer, with Lionel Hampton* & others in 1940s/50s, organized own big band 1966, with own quintet at Carnegie Hall in NY City, June 1980. Died 7/17 NY.

MC GOVERN, MAUREEN THERESE (1949–)

b. 7/27 Youngstown, Ohio. Singer, sang "The Morning After" on *The Poseidon Adventure* Soundtrack 1973 & "Can You Read My Mind?" on *Superman* soundtrack 1979. Albums *Another Woman in Love, X-Mas with Maureen McGovern, Baby I'm Yours* 1992.

MC GUIRE SISTERS

Singers, Christine (b. 1928), Dorothy (b. 1930), and Phyllis McGuire (b. 1931), all from Middletown, Ohio. Albums *Best of the McGuire Sisters, Greatest Hits.*

MC HUGH, JIMMY (1894–1969)

b. Boston, MA. Composer, with lyricist Dorothy Fields* wrote "I Can't Give You Anything But Love, Baby" 1928, "I'm In the Mood for Love." Also composed "Comin' in on a Wing and a

Prayer'' 1943 (popular during World War II). Died in Beverly Hills, CA.

MC KENNA, DAVE (1930–   )
Pianist, with Gene Krupa* & others in 1950s/60s, toured Europe, Japan & Australia, now living on Cape Cod, MA. Albums *Dancing in the Dark, My Friend the Piano, No More Ouzo for Puzo, Shadows and Dreams.*

MC KINLEY, RAY (1910–   )
b. 6/18 Fort Worth, TX. Drummer/singer with **Dorsey Brothers*** in 1930s, led Glenn Miller's* band after Glenn's death in 1944, led own bands after 1966.

MC KUEN, ROD (1933–   )
b. 4/23 San Francisco, CA. Singer/songwriter, hit ''Jean'' 1969, sang for Queen Elizabeth II of England & for President & Mrs. Kennedy at White House dinners. Won eleven ASCAP awards. In concert at Carnegie Hall in NY City 1972. Albums *LaMer/ the Sea, Listen to the Warm . . ., McKuen Sings McKuen.*

MC LAUGHLIN, JOHN (1942–   )
b. 1/4. British acoustic guitarist. Albums *Best of McLaughlin, Live at the Royal Festival Hall, My Goals Beyond, Shakti, The Mediterranean,* with percussionist Trilock Gurtu on album *Que Alegria* 1992.

MC LEAN, DON (1945–   )
b. 10/2 New Rochelle, NY. Singer/songwriter, hits ''American Pie'' 1971, ''Vincent'' 1972, albums *Best of Don McLean, Classics.*

MC LEAN, JACKIE (1932–   )
b. New York, NY. Alto saxist, albums *4 5 & 6, Dynasty, Lights Out, New Soil, Rites of Passage, Strange Blues.* With pianist Alan Ray Palmer & trumpeter Ray Hargrove on *Rhythm on Earth* 1992.

MC PARTLAND, JIMMY (1907–1991)
b. James Duigald 3/15 Chicago, IL. Trumpeter/leader, with Ben

Pollack 1926/29, with various bands in 30s. Led own bands & combos 1940s/80s. Served in army in Europe 1942/45, married pianist Marian Page 1945. Died 3/13 Port Washington, NY.

MC PARTLAND, MARIAN PAGE (1918–   )
b. Windsor, England. Pianist/composer, toured Europe with USO & married Jimmy McPartland*. Came to NY City with her husband. Wrote "There'll be Other Times" recorded by Sarah Vaughan*, also sung by George Shearing* at Gracie Mansion in NY City in June 1980. Albums *Personal Choice, Plays Benny Carter, Portrait of Marian McPartland, Willow Creek & Ballads,* etc.

MC PHATTER, CLYDE (1931–1972)
R&B singer, formed **The Drifters**,* hits "Money Honey," "A Lover's Question." A postage stamp was issued in his honor in 1993.

MC PHERSON, RICHARD C. (1883–1944)
b. Norfolk, VA. Songwriter (used the pen-name Cecil Mack) wrote the "Charleston" 1923 with Jimmy Johnson*.

MC RAE, CARMEN (1922–1994)
b. 4/8 New York, NY. Pianist/singer. Won *down beat* critics' poll as New Star of 1954, video *Tribute to Billie Holiday.* At Infiniti Jazz at the Bowl, Los Angeles in July 1992. Married drummer Kenny Clarke*, later divorced.

MC RAE, GORDON (1921–1986)
b. East Orange, NJ. Singer, sang duets with Jo Stafford,* hit "Whispering Hope" (music by Septimus Winner 1868). Also sang with Dorothy Kirsten & in NY City night clubs. Died 1/24 Lincoln, Nebraska.

MC RUN
Hit R&B album *Kizz My Black Azz* 1992.

MC SHANN, JAY "HOOTIE" (1909–   )
b. Muskogee, OK. Jazz pianist/singer, led own bands from 1937, played at Carnegie Hall in NY City & Jazz Festivals in Chicago

& Denver 1982, at Kansas City Blues & Jazz Festival, July 1992. Albums *Going to Kansas City, Paris All Star Blues, Swingmatism.*

MC VIE, CHRISTINE
Singer/songwriter with **Fleetwood Mac***, hits "Got a Hold on Me," "Rumors." Album *Christine McVie in Concert* 1984. Wrote "Don't Stop" which was the theme song for presidential candidate Bill Clinton in 1992.

ME PHI ME (1971–)
b. Flint, MI. Resided in Murfreesboro, TN. Rapper with guitarist John Michael Falasz, harmonica player Rags Murtaugh, & keyboardist/bassist Cee Cee Tec, album *One* 1992, group began 25 city tour in July 1992.

MEACHAM, FRANK W. (1856–1909)
b. Brooklyn, NY City. Composed the march "The American Patrol" 1885.

MEADER, VAUGHN
Won 1962 Grammy for album *The First Family.*

MEADOWS, MARION
Albums *For Lovers Only, Keep It Right There* 1992.

MEAT LOAF (1948–)
b. Marvin Lee Aday 9/27 Dallas, TX. Actor/singer lives in Redding, CT & coaches Little League baseball. Albums *Bat Out of Hell, Dead Ringer,* video *Hits Out of Hell. Bat Out of Hell II: Back into Hell* 1994, toured US, "I'd Do Anything for Love (But I Won't Do That)" won Rock Solo Grammy 1994.

MECCA NORMAL
All-female band with lead singer Jean Smith (b. 1959).

MEDITATIONS, THE
Group from Jamaica, West Indies, album *Return of the Meditations* 1993.

MEGADETH
Heavy metal band with singer Dave Mustaine, Nick Menza, David Ellefson, & Marty Friedman. Toured US 1992. Video *Rusted Pieces,* albums *Killing is My Business, Rust in Peace, So Far So Good So What? Countdown to Extinction* (Grammy winner 1993).

MEISNER, RANDY (1946–   )
b. 3/8 Scotts Bluff, Nebr. Singer/musician with **The Eagles** & **Poco,** left for a solo career 1977.

MELANIE (1948–   )
b. Melanie Safka 2/3 New York, NY. Singer, hits "Candles in the Rain" (performed at Woodstock) then "Brand New Key," "The Nickel Song," albums *Am I Real or What? Best of Melanie, Candles in the Rain.*

MELLE MEL
With Ice-T & others won 1990 Rap Vocal Grammy for "Back on the Block."

MELLENCAMP, JOHN COUGAR (1951–   )
b. 10/7 Seymour, IN. Singer/songwriter, hit "Hurt So Good," platinum album *Big Daddy* 1989, albums *American Fool, Nothing Matters, Uh Huh.* Hit "Get a Leg Up," album *Whenever We Wanted* 1992, performed at 5th (1992) and 6th Farm Aid Concerts in Ames, Iowa. Married model Elaine Irving, 3rd wife.

MELLOW MAN ACE
Latin hip-hop, albums *Mentirosa* 1990, *The Brother with Two Tongues* 1992.

MELODIANS
Jamaica reggae group 1965/75, hit "You Don't Need Me" on *Swing and Dine* issued January 1993.

MEMPHIS SLIM (1915–1988)
b. Peter Chatman in Memphis, TN. Pianist/blues singer/

songwriter with Big Bill Broonzy* in Chicago 1939/42. At Carnegie Hall in NY City 1959, London 1960, and Pace des Arts in Montreal, July 1980. Died in Paris.

MEN AT WORK
Australian group with Greg Ham, Colin Hay, John Rees, Jerry Speiser, & Ron Strykert. Hits "Who Can It Be Now?" "Down Under," albums *Business as Usual* 1982, *Cargo,* video *Live in San Francisco.*

MENDES, SERGIO (1946–)
b. Niteroi, Brazil. Singer/pianist, albums *Brazil 66, Arara, Greatest Hits, Brasileiro* (Grammy winner 1993).

MENKEN, ALAN (1950–)
Composer, wrote score for *Little Shop of Horrors.* With Howard Ashman* won 1990 Grammy for "Under the Sea" from *The Little Mermaid.* Wrote the instrumental music and with Ashman the songs for *Beauty and the Beast,* 1993 Grammy winner. 1994 Grammy with Tim Rice* for "A Whole New World" (*Aladdin* Theme).

MENUHIN, HEPHZIBAH (1920–1981)
b. 5/20 San Francisco, CA. Pianist, in concert with her brother violinist Yehudi Menuhin* at Metropolitan Museum of Art concert 1973. Died 1/1 London, England.

MENUHIN, YEHUDI (1916–)
b. 4/22 New York, NY. Violinist, at age ten played a concerto by Beethoven in Carnegie Hall in NY City, then had a successful concert career. On CBS *60 Minutes* in September 1992.

MERCER, JOHNNY (1909–1976)
b. 11/18 Savannah, GA. Singer/songwriter, wrote for Lew Leslie's Blackbirds 1935/36, sang for Paul Whiteman* 1938/39, then with Benny Goodman.* With composer Harold Arlen* wrote "Over the Rainbow" for *The Wizard of Oz* 1939 & "Blues in the Night" 1941, "That Old Black Magic" 1945, & "Ac-cen-tchu-ate the Positive" 1945. With Jerome Kern* "Dearly Beloved" 1942, and with Harry Warren* "On the

Atchison, Topeka and Santa Fe'' 1946. Albums *Johnny Mercer, Songbook.* Died 6/25 Bel Air, CA.

MERCER, MABEL (1900–1984)
b. 2/3 Burton-on-Trent, England. Sang at Bricktop's* in Paris 1931/38, in NY City night clubs 1941/61. At her belated 80th birthday held at Whitney Museum in NY City January 1981 she sang "S'Wonderful." Videos *A Singer's Singer, Cabaret— forever and Always.* Died 4/21 Pittsfield, MA.

MERCHANT, JIMMY
Songwriter with **Frankie Lymon* & The Teenagers,** with Herman Santiago wrote "Why Do Fools Fall in Love?" 1956 (popularized by Lymon). In November 1992 a NY Federal jury ruled that Merchant & Santiago were entitled to royalties.

MERMAN, ETHEL (1909–1984)
b. Ethel Zimmerman 1/19 Astoria, NY City. Sang in musicals *Girl Crazy* 1930, *George White Scandals 1932, Annie Get Your Gun* 1946, *Call Me Madam* 1950, *Gypsy* 1959. Album *You Are the Top.* Died 2/15 New York, NY. A postage stamp was issued in her honor 1994.

MERRILL, HELEN (1929–)
b. New York, NY. Singer, with Gil Evans* on *Just Friends (Stan Getz), Walkman Compact Jazz.*

MERRILL, ROBERT (1919–)
b. 6/4 New York, NY. Baritone, first American to sing 500 performances at Metropolitan Opera in NY City.

MERRILL, ROBERT "BOB" (1921–)
b. Atlantic City, NJ. Lyricist, with Al Hoffman* & Clem Watts wrote "If I Knew You Were Comin' I'd've Baked a Cake" 1950, "Doggie in the Window", "People", "Love Makes the World Go Round" 1961.

METALLICA
With singer/guitarist James Hatfield, Jason Newsted, Kirk Hammett, & drummer Lars Ulrich. 1988 Top Ten music video for

multi-platinum *Home Vid Cliff 'Em All*. With **Van Halen*** & others on 1988 Top Ten grossing concerts, at East Troy, WI., Platinum *2 of One* 1989. 1990 Metal Grammy for ''Stone Cold Crazy.'' 1991 Grammy for *Metallica*. MTV Hard Rock award for *Enter Sandman* 1992, Metal/hard rock American Music Award 1993. Hatfield burned his left hand & both arms in a flashpot accident in Montreal on 8/8/92.

METCALF, LOUIS (1905–1981)
b. St. Louis, MO. Trumpeter with **Andrew Preer & his Cotton Club Syncopators,** Duke Ellington,* Jelly Roll Morton* in 1920, led own bands in Canada 30s/50s & in NY City 60s/70s. Died 10/27.

METERS, THE
Rock group formed 1968 with keyboardist Art Neville, guitarist Leo Nocentelli, bassist Art Porter, drummer Joseph Modeliste, albums *Good Old Funky Music, Look-ka-Py Py*.

METHENY, PAT
Jazz musician, albums *American Garage, Bright Size Life, Letter from Home* (1989 Jazz Fusion Grammy winner), *Offramp, Rejoicing*. ''The Truth Will Always Be'' from *Secret Story* won Grammy 1993. Contemporary Jazz Instrumental Grammy 1994 for *The Road to You*.

METZ, THEODORE A. (1848–1936)
b. Hanover, Germany, came to US. Composer, with lyricist/singer Joe Hayden wrote the music for ''There'll be a Hot Time in the Old Town Tonight'' 1896. The song was adopted by the Rough Riders and Colonel Theodore Roosevelt as their official song during the Spanish-American War.

MEYER, GEORGE W. (1884–1959)
b. Boston, MA. Composer, with lyricist E. Leslie* & E.R. Goetz* wrote ''For Me and My Gal'' 1917.

MEYER, JOSEPH (1894–1987)
b. 3/12 Modesto, CA. Composed ''California Here I Come''

1924, with lyricist Buddy DeSylva* "If You Knew Susie Like I Knew Susie" 1925 & other songs.

MIAMI SOUND MACHINE
Singers Emilio and Gloria Estefan*, album *Primitive Love.*

MICHAEL, GEORGE (1963–   )
b. 6/26 Watford, England. Singer with **Wham!*** Won 1988 Grammy for album *Faith,* hit single "I Want Your Sex," platinum album *Listen Without Prejudice* 1990, had 3 songs on *Red, Hot and Dance* (album for AIDS funds 1992), videos *Faith, George Michael.* Hit single "Too Funky" 1992. "Don't Let the Sun Go Down" with Elton John* (Grammy winner 1993).

MIDLER, BETTE (1945–   )
b. 12/1 Paterson, NJ & raised in Honolulu, Hawaii. Singer/actress, married Harry Kipper. Carnegie Hall debut 1972 in NY City. Called the "Divine Miss M" won Emmy for special "Ol' Red Hair is Back" 1978, video *Art or Bust* with the Harlettes at Minneapolis concert 1983, Top Ten single "Wind Beneath My Wings" (1989 Grammy winner), platinum album *Some People's Lives* 1990, *Divine Madness, Mud Will Fly Tonight, No Frills, Thighs and Whispers,* sang at Lincoln Memorial in Washington, D.C. 1993.

MIDNIGHT OIL
Australian group with singer Peter Garrett, Peter Gifford, drummer Rob Hurst, guitarist/keyboardist Jim Moginie, guitarist Martin Rotsey, bassist Bones Hillman. US album debut *10, 9, 8, 7, 6, 5, 4, 3, 2, 1–1983, Bird Noises, Head Injuries, Dust* 1987, *Midnight Oil, Blue Sky Mining* 1991, video *Black Rain Falls,* toured US 1992/93.

MIDNIGHTERS, THE
With Hank Ballard (b. 11/18/36) Detroit, MI. Hit "The Twist" before Chubby Checker made it famous.

MIDORI (1972–   )
b. Japan. Classical violinist, played with Boston Symphony under

Leonard Bernstein at Tanglewood in 1986, played at The White House for President & Mrs. Reagan. Lives in NY City.

MIGHTY CLOUDS OF JOY
Gospel quintet, album *Best of the Mighty Clouds Vols. 1 & 2*, won Gospel Music Shop award 1992.

MIGHTY LEMON DROPS, THE
Albums *Laughter, The Mighty Lemon Drops, World Without End, Ricochet* 1992.

MIGUEL, LUIS
Won Latin Pop Album Grammy for *Romance* 1993. *Aires* Grammy winner 1994.

MIKE AND THE MECHANICS
Albums *Mike and the Mechanics, The Living Years, Word of Mouth*, video *A Closer Look*.

MILES, BUDDY (1946–   )
b. 9/5 Omaha, NB. Singer/drummer, played in Jimi Hendrix's band **The Gypsies**. Albums *Them Changes, Live* with Carlos Santana, *Sneak Attack* 1991.

MILESTONE JAZZSTARS
Saxist Sonny Rollins, pianist McCoy Tyner, bassist Ron Carter, & drummer Al Foster played at The White House Jazz Festival for President & Mrs. Carter 1978; *Milestone Jazzstars in Concert*.

MILLER, GLENN (1904–1944)
b. Clarinda, Iowa. Trombonist/big band leader, raised in North Platte, NE. With Ben Pollack 1926/28, then with Dorsey Brothers,* formed own band 1937. Entered army as a captain 1942, then as Major Miller led an AEF Orchestra in England. Jazz rendition of "Little Brown Jug" (by Joseph E. Winner* 1869) was popular. His plane was lost after a flight from Bedford, England and never heard from again. Albums *Best of Glenn Miller, Vols. 1 to 3, Classic Glenn Miller, Jazz Collector Edition*, etc.

MILLER, MITCHELL W. "MITCH" (1911–)
b. 7/4 Rochester, NY. Leader hit single "Yellow Rose of Texas" 1955, host of TV series *Sing Along with Mitch* 1961/66. Albums *34 All Time Great Sing-alongs, Sing Along with Mitch.*

MILLER, MULGREW (1956–)
Pianist with Mercer Ellington* & others, went solo, albums *From Day to Day, The Countdown Wingspan,* led own trio on *Time and Again* 1992.

MILLER, ROGER DEAN (1936–1992)
b. 1/2 Fort Worth, TX. Country/pop singer/songwriter, wrote "King of the Road" 1965 (Grammy winner), "Don't We All Have the Right" 1988, popularized by Ricky Van Shelton,* topped the charts. Albums *Golden Hits, King of the Road.* Died 10/25 of cancer in Los Angeles, CA.

MILLER, STEVE (1943–)
b. 10/5 Dallas, TX. Leader/guitarist/singer/songwriter, hit single "Abracadabra." Albums *Book of Dreams, Born 2 Be Blue, Fly Like an Eagle, Live, The Joker,* etc.

MILLI VANILLI
Group, **Girl You Know It's True** sold over 5 million albums 1989, multi-platinum video **In Motion** 1989.

MILLS, FREDERICK A. "KERRY" (1869–1948)
b. Philadelphia, PA. Composed the music for "Meet Me in St. Louis" 1904 (revived in the 1944 movie with Judy Garland*).

MILLS, STEPHANIE
Singer, albums *Christmas, Home, If I Were Your Woman, In My Life: Greatest Hits,* video *Home is Where the Heart Is,* hit single "All Day, All Night" on album *Something Real* 1992.

MILSAP, RONNIE (1944–)
b. 1/16 Robbinsville, NC. Blind country singer/songwriter, hits "Stand By My Woman, Man," "Lost in the Fifties Tonight,"

albums *Back to the Grindstone, Christmas with Ronnie Milsap, Keyed Up,* etc. video *Ronnie Milsap's Greatest Hits.*

MINGO SALDIVARY SUS TREMENDOS CURATO ESPADAS
Group won Mexican/American Album Grammy 1993 for *I Love My Freedom, I Love My Texas.*

MINGUS, CHARLES (1922–1979)
b. 4/22 Nogales, AZ. Jazz bassist/composer, led his own combos, *Meditations on Integration* performed at Monterey Jazz Festival in California 1964, *Mingus Dances* performed by City Center Joffrey Ballet in NY City 1971. Albums *Blues and Roots, Mingus Dynasty, New Tijuana Moods, Oh Yeah, Town Hall Concert.* Suffered from amyothropic lateral sclerosis ("Lou Gehrig's disease") & died 1/5 in Cuernavaca, Mexico.

MINISTRY
British rock group with frontman Al Jourgensen, bassist Paul Barker of Seattle, WA, guitarist Mike Scaccia, & drummer William Rieflin. Albums *With Sympathy* 1983, *Twich* 1986, *The Land of Rape and Honey* 1989, *The Mind is a Terrible Thing to Taste* 1990, *Psalm 69: The Way to Succeed and the Way to Suck Eggs* 1992, video *In Case You are Showing Up.* Toured US with the Red Hot Chili Peppers 1992. "N.W.O." track from *Psalm 69* Grammy winner 1993.

MINK, BEN
Songwriter, with k.d. lang* wrote "Constant Craving" Grammy winner 1993.

MINNELLI, LIZA (1946–   )
b. 3/12 Los Angeles, CA. Singer/actress, half sister of Lorna Luft* daughter of Judy Garland.* Liza sang "Who's Sorry Now" with Judy Garland at a London Palladium concert 1964, won Oscar for *Cabaret* 1972. Albums *Liza with a Z, The Act, Foursider, At Carnegie Hall, Live from Radio City Music Hall* 1992, video *Visible Results.* Married Mark Gero, divorced in 1992.

MINTZER, BOB
Jazz musician, *One Music* Grammy winner 1993.

MIRACLES, THE
With leader/songwriter Smokey Robinson* on *Hitsville USA: The Motown Singles Collection* 1992.

MIRANDA, CARMEN (1909–1953)
b. Marco Canaverez, Portugal. Singer/dancer, taken to Brazil as a child. Hit song "South American Way" in the film of the same name 1940.

MISFITS, THE
New Jersey hard-core rock group with lead singer/guitarist Bobby Steele, albums *Collection, Earth A.D./Die, Die.* Steele left group 1992 for the **Undead.***

MISSING PERSONS
USA new wave group with singer Dale Dozzio, Terry Dozzio, Warren Cuccurullo, & Patrick O'Hearn. Gold album *Spring Season M* 1983, *Best of Missing Persons,* video *Surrender Your Heart* 1985.

MR. BIG
Rock group with guitarist Paul Gilbert (plays his electric guitar with power drill instead of a pick), tool maker Makita sponsored the band on its US tour 1992. Hit single "To Be With You" on album *Lean into It* 1992.

MR. BUNGLE
Punk/pop/rock band wearing masks with singer Mike Patton, Theo Lingyel, guitarist Trey Spruance, Bar McKinnon, Danny Heifety, & bassist Trevor Boy Dunn. Album *Mr. Bungle* 1992.

MR. MISTER
Rock band with Steve Farris, Steve George, Pat Mastelotto, Richard Page. Albums *I Wear the Face* 1982, *Welcome to the Real World* 1985. *Videos from the Real Life, Videos from the Real World.*

MITCHELL, GUY (1925–   )
b. Detroit, MI. Singer, with composer Percy Faith* gold record "My Heart Cries for You," hit song "Heartaches by the Number."

MITCHELL, JONI (1943–   )
b. Roberta Joan Anderson 11/7 Fort McLeod Alabama, raised in Alberta, Canada. Singer/songwriter, hits "Chelsea Morning" 1962, "Big Yellow Taxi." With jazz/pop fusion band on album *Shadows and Light*. Recording concert at Santa Barbara County Bowl 1979, *Refuge on the Roads* 1984, *Blue, Clouds, Dog Eat Dog, For the Roses, Wild Things Run Fast*, etc. Video *Shadows and Light*.

MITCHELL, RICHARD A. (1930–1979)
b. Miami, FL. "Blue" jazz trumpeter, with **Horace Silver* Quintet** 1958/64, toured Japan 1965, later formed own quintet. Album *Rockland*. Died Los Angeles, CA.

MITCHELL, WILLIAM C. "CHAD" (1936–   )
b. 12/5. Leader of the **Chad Mitchell Trio.**

MITCHELL, WILLIE (1928–   )
R&B trumpeter/composer, album *Best of Willie Mitchell* 1980.

MODERN JAZZ QUARTET
Founded 1952, with drummer Kenny Clarke,* bassist Percy Heath,* vibraphonist Milton Jackson, & pianist John Lewis*, drummer Connie Kay* replaced Clarke in 1955. Disbanded 1974 but re-established at the Monterey Jazz Festival in California in September 1992. Albums *Compact Jazz, Concorde, Fontessa, Modern Jazz Quartet, Third Stream Music*, etc.

MODERNAIRES, THE
Ralph Brewster, Bill Conway, Hal Dickinson, & Chuck Goldstein. Ralph Eberle sang with for Glenn Miller* in early 1940s.

MODUGNO, DOMINICO (1928–1994)
Won 1958 Grammy for record "Nel Blu Dipinto Di Blu (Volare)." Died in Lampedusa, Sicily, Italy.

MOFFO, ANA (1934–   )

b. 6/27 Wayne, PA. Soprano, starred in *Madame Butterfly* 1956 &
other Italian films, with Metropolitan Opera in NY City for 12
years. Albums *A Song for You, La Bellissma.* Married Mario
Lanfranchi, Italian film producer.

MOLLY AND THE HEYMAKERS

Country/rock singer, album *Molly and the Heymakers.*

MOLLY HATCHET

Southern blues/boogie/heavy metal band formed 1975 with drum-
mer Barry Borden, Danny Joe Brown, Bruce Crump, Jimmy
Farrar, Dave Hlubek, Steve Holland, Duane Rolland, Banner
Thomas, Riff West. Album *Beating the Odds* sold over two
million copies. Albums *Flirtin' With Disaster, Molly Hatchet,
Take No Prisoners, The Deed is Done, Greatest Hits,* etc.

MONACO, JAMES V. (1885–1945)

b. Genoa, Italy. Composer, came to Chicago in 1891, then to NY
City. With lyricist Joe McCarthy* wrote "Shave and a Hair-
cut," with lyricist Charles Newman* "Six Lessons from
Madame La Zonga."

MONEY, EDDIE

Albums *Eddie Money, Life for the Taking, Nothing to Loose, No
Control, Playing for Keeps,* video *Pictures of Money.*

MONK, THELONIOUS S. (1920–1982)

b. 10/10 Rocky Mount, NC. Jazz pianist 1940s/70s, at Carnegie
Hall & Philharmonic Hall in NY City in 60s, at Newport Jazz
Festivals in NY City 1972/74. Albums *Brilliant Corners,
Himself, Essence of Thelonious Monk, London Collection,
Monk's Blues, Monk's Dreams,* etc.

MONK, T.S. (1950–   )

Jazz/funk drummer, son of Thelonious Monk,* R&B funk hit
"Bon Von Vie" (Gimme the Good Life) 1980s, returned to
jazz on album *Take 1* issued 1992. Played in the White House
for President & Mrs. Clinton June 1993.

MONKEES, THE
Rock group formed 1966 with Mickey Dolenz (b. 1945 Los Angeles), David "Davy" Jones (b. 1946 Manchester, England), Mike Nesmith,* Peter Tork. Hits "Last Train to Clarksville" 1966, "I'm a Believer," had own TV show 1966/68. Albums *Listen to the Band, Missing Links*, etc. Given a Star on the Hollywood Walk of Fame 1992.

MONROE, BILL (1911–   )
b. 9/13 Rosine, KY. Mandolin player/singer/composer, albums *Best of Bill Monroe, Country Music Hall of Fame, Kentucky Bluegrass, Cryin' Holy Unto the Lord, Live at the Opry*. Played in The White House for Presidents Carter, Reagan, & Bush. Played at the Mall in Washington, D.C. & for President Clinton January 1993.

MONROE, VAUGHN (1911–1973)
Singer, advertised Camel cigarettes, hit song "Let it Snow," album *The Best of Vaughn Monroe*.

MONTANA, PATSY (1914–   )
b. Rubye Blevins 10/30 Hot Springs, AK. Singer/songwriter, lead singer for the **Prairie Ramblers** in 1930s, wrote many western songs, honored at a country music concert in September 1992. Married Paul Rose.

MONTGOMERY, JOHN L. "WES" (1925–1968)
b. Indianapolis, IN. Guitarist/composer, with brothers Buddy & Monk* in the **Montgomery Brothers Quartet** and later the **Wynton Kelly Trio.** Albums *Bumpin, California Dreaming, Far Wes, Plays the Blues, Tequila*. Died suddenly of a heart attack in Indianapolis. *The Complete Riverside Recordings* 1993.

MONTGOMERY, JOHN MICHAEL
Country singer, hit single "Life's a Dance" 1993. American Music Country Award 1994.

MONTGOMERY, MELBA JOYCE (1938–   )
b. 10/14 Iron City, TN. Won Pet Milk contest in Nashville, TN 1958, toured overseas for USO in World War II.

MONTGOMERY, WILLIAM H. "MONK" (1921–1982)
b. Indianapolis, Inc. Bassist/composer, in bands with his brothers, with **Red Norvo* Trio** in Las Vegas 1970/72, led bands touring South Africa 1974. Died following a stroke in Las Vegas, NV.

MONTROSE
Rock group formed 1974 with guitarist Ronnie Montrose, singer Sam Hagar, bassist Bill Church, drummer Denny Carmossi. Albums *Mean, Montrose, Paper Money, Mutatis Mutandis.*

MONTY PYTHON'S FLYING CIRCUS
With singer/comedian Eric Idle, hit "The Lumberjack Song" on album *Monty Python Sings, Monty Python's Flying Circus,* etc.

MOODY BLUES
UK rock group with Graeme Edge, Justin Hayward, Denny Laine, John Lodge, Michael Pinder, Ray Thomas, Clint Warwick. Hits "Nights in White Satin," "Your Wildest Dreams" 1986, "I Know You're Out There Somewhere" 1987, albums *Keys of the Kingdom, Days of Future Passed, Long Distance Voyager, To Our Children's Children's Children* 1992. Toured US 1993, *The Moody Blues in Concert at Red Rocks* on PBS in March 1993.

MOODY, JAMES (1925–   )
b. Savannah, GA. Saxist/flutist, albums *Honey, James Moody and the Hip Organ, Little Suite for Harmonica, Something Special, Sweet and Lovely.*

MOONEY, JOHN
"Telephone King" at New Orleans Heritage Festival in April/May 1993, album *Testimony.*

MOORE, CHANTE
Singer with Keith Washington sang "Candlelight and You" on soundtrack *Strictly Business* 1991, solo album *Precious* 1992, "Candlelight and You" on Black Entertainment Network 1993.

MOORE, GARY
Albums *After the War, Still Got the Blues, Wild Frontier.*

MOORE, GEOFF
Gospel Singer, **Geoff Moore and the Distance** won 1993 Grammy for *A Friend Like You.*

MOORE, MELBA (1945–)
b. 10/29 New York, NY. Singer/actress, sang in Broadway musicals *Hair, Purlie,* album *Soul Exposed.* She sang the "Star Spangled Banner" at the Democratic Convention in NY City, July 1992.

MOORE, RENE
Songwriter, with Michael Jackson,* Bruce Swedien, & Teddy Riley wrote "Jam," Grammy winner 1993.

MORELLO, JOSEPH (1928–)
b. 7/17 Springfield, MA. Jazz drummer, became partially blind, active 1950s/80s.

MORENO, RITA (1931–)
b. Rosa Delores Alverio 12/11 Humacao, Puerto Rico. Singer/actress, won four top awards: Emmy, Grammy, Oscar, & Tony, for film *West Side Story,* stage play *The Ritz,* etc. Sang at Epcot Center at Walt Disney World in 1992.

MORGAN, FRANK
Jazz pianist, albums *A Lonesome Thing, Lament, Mood Indigo,* with pianists Kenny Barron,* Tommy Flanagan, Roland Hanna, Barry Harris, & Hank Jones on album *You Must Believe in Spring* 1992.

MORGAN, GEORGE THOMAS (1924–1975)
b. Waverly, TN. Singer/songwriter, wrote "Candy Kisses" 1948, "I'm in Love Again" 1959. Died 7/7 Nashville, TN.

MORGAN, JANE (1920–   )
b. Boston, MA. Sing, hit song "Fascination," album *Greatest Hits.*

MORGAN, JAYE P. (1932–   )
b. 12/3 New York, NY. Night club singer, arrested in 1972 on a marijuana charge & released. Album *What are You Doing.*

MORGAN, LEE (1938–1972)
b. Philadelphia, PA. Trumpeter, with Dizzy Gillespie* & Art Blakey's **Jazz Messengers*** in 1950s, then formed own combos. Albums *Candy, Cornbread, Take Twelve, The Best of Lee Morgan, The Gigolo, Tom Cat,* etc. Was playing at Slugs, an East Village night club in NY City, when his wife walked in and shot and killed him.

MORGAN, LORRIE LYNN (1959–   )
b. 6/27 Country singer, albums *Leave the Light On, Watch Me* 1992, *Something in Red* (Grammy winner 1993), with others on ABC December 1992 & CBS January 1993, hit "What Part of No" 1993.

MORGAN, MELISSA
With Kashif Morgan on 1988 Top Ten Black Singles list for "Love Changes." Her albums *Do Me Baby, The Lady in Me, Still in Love with You* 1992.

MORRIS, GARY (1948–   )
b. 12/7 Fort Worth, TX. Musician/songwriter, wrote "Wind Beneath My Wings," albums *Full Moon, Empty Heart, These Days, Why Lady Why.* Performed at a concert for Governor Gaston Caperton in Charleston, West Virginia in January 1993.

MORRIS, GEORGE P. (1802–1864)
b. Philadelphia, PA. Lyricist, with composer Henry Russell wrote "Woodman Spare That Tree."

MORRISON, VAN (1945–)

b. George Ivan 8/31 Belfast, North Ireland. Guitarist/singer/ composer. Toured US in 1960, albums *A Sense of Wonder, Astral Weeks, Beautiful Visions, His Band and Street Choir, Moon-dance, Period of Transition,* etc., video *The Concert.* Inducted into the Rock & Roll Hall of Fame, Los Angeles 1992.

MORRISSEY

b. Steven Patrick Morrissey. British pop singer with rock band **The Smiths** (dissolved in 1987), album *Bona Drag* and *Kill Uncle,* toured US 1992. Solo album *Your Arsenal* Grammy winner 1993.

MORRISSEY, BILL (1952–)

b. in Connecticut & now lives in New Hampshire. Country blues/folk singer. Album with singer Suzanne Vega,* violinist Johnny Cunningham of the **Raindogs,** pianist Tom McClung, organist Ron Levy, & drummer Doug Plavin on *Inside* 1992.

MORSE, ANNA JUSTINA (1893–1979)

b. Haverhill, MA. Composer, with lyricist J. E. Rankin wrote the music for "God Be With You 'Till We Meet Again" 1941.

MORSE, STEVE

Guitarist Steve Morse with the **Dixie Dregs,** albums *Free Fall, Night of the Living Dregs.* Formed the **Steve Morse Band,** albums *High Tension Wires, Introduction, Southern Street,* hard rock album *Coast to Coast* 1992.

MORTON, JELLY ROLL (1885–1941)

b. Ferdinand LeMenthe in New Orleans, LA. Pianist/singer/ composer, considered one of the greatest jazz pianists, formed his own band in Chicago before 1915, toured with Fate Marable* & W.C. Handy* in 1920s, recorded with Wingy Manone* in 1934 & for the Library of Congress in Washington, D.C. 1938. Albums *Piano Creole 1926/39, Chicago Days,* etc. Died in Los Angeles, CA.

MOSEKA, AMINATA *see* ABBEY LINCOLN*

MOTELS, THE
Rock band with Martha Evans, Brian Glascock, Michael Goodroe, Marty Jourard & Guy Perry. Albums *The Motels* 1983, *Best of Motels/No Vacancy, All for One.*

MOTEN, BENNIE (1894–1935)
b. Kansas City, MO. Pianist/composer, led own bands in 1920s/30s, Count Basie* was a bandmember. Entered a hospital in Kansas City for a tonsillectomy, died there of complications on 4/2.

MOTHER LOVE BAND
Albums *Apple, Shine,* their songs included on the soundtrack of the film *Singles* 1992.

MOTHERS OF INVENTION
Rock/jazz group with Jimmy Carl Black, Ray Collins, Roy Estrada, Bunk Gardner, Don Preston, James Sherwood, Ian Underwood, & Frank Zappa.* Later disbanded.

MOTLEY CRÜE
Heavy metal band with Tommy Lee, Mick Mars, Nikki Sixx, & lead singer Vince Neil (left in 1991). Albums *Shout at the Devil* 1993, multi-platinum video *Uncensored* 1989, platinum video *Dr. Feelgood* 1990, *Decade of Decadence, Girls, Girls, Girls, Theatre of Pain, Too Fast for Love.* New lead singer John Corabi (formerly with Scream*).

MOTORHEAD
British rock band album *1918,* with growler Lemmy and guitarist Ozzy Osbourne on album *March or Die* 1992.

MOTT THE HOOPLE
British rock group. Albums *All the Young Dudes, Greatest Hits, Mott.*

MOUNTAIN
Rock group with Leslie West, bassist Felix Pappalardi, guitarist David Perry, & drummer Corkey Laing, albums *The Best of Mountain, Twin Peaks.*

MOUSKOURI, NANA
Singer. Albums *Alone, Ma Verite, Nana, Tiena Viva, Why Worry?, The Magic of Nana Mouskouri.*

MOYET, ALISON
British punk/jazz/rock singer, "It Won't Be Long" Grammy winner 1993.

MUDHONEY
Seattle group with Matt Lukin, Dan Peters, Steve Turner, & singer Mark Arm, hit single "Touch Me I'm Sick" 1988. Albums *Every Good Boy Deserves Fudge, Mudhoney, Superfuzz Big Muff, Piece of Cake* 1992.

MUIR, LEWIS F. (1883–1915)
b. Louis F. Meuer in New York, NY. Pianist/ragtime composer, played in honky-tonks in St. Louis in 1900s, with lyricist L. Wolfe Gilbert* wrote "Waiting for the Robert E. Lee" 1912.

MULDAUR, MARIA (1943–)
Blues/rock/jazz/folk/country/gospel singer, hit "Midnight at the Oasis" 1974, with Geoff Muldaur on album *Pottery Pie, Louisiana Love Call* 1993.

MULLIGAN, GERALD J. "GERRY" (1927–)
b. 4/6 New York/NY. Baritone saxist/composer, led own bands 1960s/80s, wrote "Disc Jockey Jump" recorded by Gene Krupa* 1947, *Music for Baritone Saxophone and Orchestra* performed by Neophonic Orchestra 1966, at Carnegie Hall in NY City 1980, at Monterey Jazz Festival in California in September 1992. Albums *Round Midnight with T. Monk* & the Concert Jazz Band, Lonesome Boulevard, Symphonic Dreams,* etc., video *Jazz in America.*

MURPHEY, MICHAEL MARTIN
Country singer, albums *Cowboy Songs, Best of Michael Martin Murphey, Best of Country, River of Time.*

MURPHY, EDDIE
Comedian/singer. Hit singles "Boomerang," "Mo Money," albums *Eddie Murphy, How Could It Be?*, video *Delirious.*

MURPHY, MARK (1943–)
b. Syracuse, NY. Pianist/singer, albums *Bop for Kerouac, Night Mood, Beauty and the Beast.*

MURPHY, MELVIN "TURK" (1915–1987)
b. 12/16 Palermo, CA. Jazz trombonist/composer, led own groups from 1940s, opened Earthquake McGoon's Club in San Francisco in 1960 and played there through 1980s.

MURPHY, PETER
Rock singer with British band **Bauhaus** for four years in 1980s, went solo, at Roseland in NY City in June 1992, album *Deep, Love Hysteria* hit "Holy Smoke" 1992.

MURPHY, STANLEY (1875–1919)
b. Dublin, Ireland. Lyricist, came to New York, with composer Percy Wenrich* wrote "Put on Your Old Grey Bonnet" 1909.

MURRAY, ANNE (1945–)
b. 6/20 Springhill, Nova Scotia. Singer, called the "Canadian Songbird." Gold record *Snowbird* 1970. Toured US 1970s/80s/90s. Albums *Christmas Wishes, Country Hits, New Kind of Feeling,* Sang Canadian National Anthem at World Series in Toronto 1992.

MURRAY, DAVID (1955–)
b. Berkeley, CA. Jazz flutist/saxist/composer of "Hope Scope" & "Dexter's Dues." Albums *I Want to Talk About You, Ming's Samba, Shakill's Warrior* 1992, with pianist McCoy Tyner* & drummer Elvin Jones* on album *David Murray Special Quarter* 1992.

MUSSELWHITE, CHARLES
CDs *Memphis, Tennessee, Ace of Harps, Signatures.*

MUSSO, VIDO (1913–1982)
b. 1/17 Carrini, Italy. Jazz tenor saxist/clarinetist, played in bands of Benny Goodman* & Stan Kenton* 1940s, then led own groups. Performed in Las Vegas from 1957. Died 1/9.

MYLES, ALANNAH
Singer, won 1988 Rock Vocal Female Grammy for "Black Velvet," albums *Alannah Myles, Rockinghorse* (Grammy winner 1993).

MYSTERE DES VOIX BULGARES, LES
Bulgarian women's choir on album *From Bulgaria With Love* 1992, considered the world's finest Balkan disco album.

MYSTIC MOODS ORCHESTRA
Albums *Another Stormy Night, Emotions, Love Token, Stormy Memories, Summer Moods*.

N

NABORS, JIM (1932–)
b. James Thurston 6/12 Sylacauga, AL. Actor/singer, played Gomer Pyle on *The Andy Griffith Show,* sang on Bob Hope's Christmas show for GI's overseas 1971, toured states 1970s/80s, albums *Jim Nabors 22 Great Hymns & Country Favorites* 1983, *Sincerely/Town 'N' Country, The Lord's Prayer,* etc.

NAJEE
Pop/R&B saxist, won Jazz Album Soul Train Music award for album *Just an Illusion* 1993.

NANCE, WILLIS "RAY" (1913–1976)
b. Chicago, IL. Jazz cornetist/violinist/singer, led own sextet in 1930s, with Duke Ellington* on and off 1940s/71, at Town Hall in NY City in December 1975. Died 1/28 NY City.

NARELL, ANDY
Albums *Little Secrets, Slow Motion, The Hammer.*

NASCIMENTO, MILTON
Albums *A Barca Dos Amantes, Anima, Milton's Taxi,* etc.

NASH, GRAHAM (1942–)
b. 2/2. Musician, albums *Songs for Beginners, Wild Tales.*

NASH, JOHNNY (1940–)
b. 8/19 Houston, TX. Reggae singer, hit "I Can See Clearly Now" 1972, albums *Johnny Nash Album* 1980, *Stir It Up* 1981.

NASHVILLE BLUEGRASS BAND
Albums *Boys are Back in Town, Home of the Blues.* Bluegrass Grammy 1994 for *Waitin' for Hard Times To Go.*

NATIONAL JAZZ ENSEMBLE
Formed by bassist Chuck Israels 1973, played at Jazz Forum in NY City in 1980s.

NATURAL BRIDGE
Jazz group with Mike and Randy Brecker* in Washington, D.C. in 1980s.

NAUGHTY BY NATURE
Hit R&B single "Hip Hip Hooray" 1993.

NAVAIRA, EMILIO
Won Mexican/American Album Grammy 1993 for *Unsung Highways*.

NAVARRO, THEODORE "FATS" (1923–1950)
b. Key West, FL. Trumpeter with Andy Kirk, Illinois Jacquet, & others in 1940s. Fats recorded with Benny Goodman*, Billy Eckstein,* & others. Albums *Royal Roast Sessions, Tad Dameron Band.* Tuberculosis & narcotics caused his death in NY City.

NAZARETH
Scottish rock group with Peter Agnew, Manny Charlton, Dan McCafferty & Darrell Sweet. Albums *Expect No Mercy, Hair of The Dog, Hot Tracks, Razamanaz.*

N'DOUR, YOUSSOU
Senegalese singer now lives in NY City, on 1988 Top Ten Grossing Concerts in Philadelphia. Albums *Nelson Mandela, Set, The Lion, Eyes Open* (Grammy winner 1993).

NEAR, HOLLY
Singer, albums *Hang in There, Singer in Storm, Sky Danes, Speed of Light,* etc.

NELSON (1968–)
Rock duo of twin brothers Gunnar & Matthew Nelson, sons of the late Ricky Nelson.* Video *After the Rain* 1991.

NELSON, BILL
Pianist, albums *Catalogue of Obsessions, Character of Dreams, Chance Encounters, Summer of God's Piano,* etc.

NELSON, HARRIET HILLIARD (1912–1994)
b. 7/18 Des Moines, Iowa. Singer/actress, started as a singer in Ozzie Nelson's* orchestra, then married him. *Ozzie & Harriet on Videos Vol. 1 to 6.* Died October 2, 1994 at Laguna, California.

NELSON, OLIVER (1932–1975)
b. St. Louis, MO. Jazz saxist/flutist/composer with Jeter-Pillars in 1940s, with Wild Bill Davis after 1956, wrote *Soundpiece for Orchestra* conducted by composer at Light Music Week in Stuttgart, Germany 1964. Albums *Black, Brown and Beautiful, Blues and the Absolute Truth.* Died 10/27 in Los Angeles, CA.

NELSON, OSWALD G. "OZZIE" (1906–1975)
b. 3/20 Jersey City, NJ. Bandleader. Led bands in NY City, with wife Harriet* started the *Ozzie and Harriet* show on radio 1943, then on TV 1952/65, *Ozzie's Girls* on NBC 1972. Died 6/3 in Hollywood, CA.

NELSON, "RICKY" (1940–1985)
b. Eric H. 5/8 Teancck, NJ. Singer/actor, son of Harriet & Ozzie Nelson.* Before age 21 he had sold over 35 million records, hit single "Hello Mary Lou." Albums *Greatest Hits, In Concert, The Best of Ricky Nelson.* Died 12/31 in DeKalb, TX in a plane crash.

NELSON, SANDER "SANDY" (1938–   )
b. 12/1 Santa Monica, CA. Drummer, albums *Teenbeat, 20 Rock 'n' Roll Hits* 1983.

NELSON, SKIP
Singer, sang for **Glenn Miller* Band** in early 1940s, hit "I Don't Want to Walk Without You."

NELSON, WILLIE (1933–   )
b. 4/30 Abbott, TX. Singer/musician/actor, won Grammy for "Blue Eyes Crying in the Rain" 1975, "Georgia on My Mind" 1978, on music video *We are the World* 1985. Albums *Always on My Mind, Half Nelson, Shotgun Willie*, etc. Videos *Bar-*

barosa, Greatest Hits Live, Some Enchanted Evening. Hit album *Red Headed Stranger.* Had troubles with the Internal Revenue Service owing $16 million, toured US for a tequila maker 1992, with Sinead O'Connor* on *Across the Borderline* 1993. Inducted into Country Music Hall of Fame 1993.

NERO, PETER (1934–   )
b. Bernard Nierow 5/22 New York, NY. Pianist, with Paul Whiteman* in 1950s, played in night clubs, in concert for George Gershwin's* 75th anniversary at Philharmonic Hall in NY City 1972. Albums *Anything but Lonely, Greatest Hits, Summer of '42,* etc.

NESMITH, MICHAEL (1942–   )
b. 12/30 Houston, TX. Country rock, with the Monkees,* left group 1969, solo album *Newer Stuff.*

NETHERTON, TOM
Gospel Singer, hits "How Great Thou Art," "Whispering Hope."

NEVILLE, AARON (1940–   )
The man with the "Golden Voice," from New Orleans, with the Neville Brothers, Art, Charles, & Cyril. Album *Yellow Moon* 1989. Spent two years in jail for auto theft. Hits "Over You," "Tell It Like It Is," "Voodoo," with singer Linda Ronstadt won 1990 Duo Grammy for "All My Life," & with Linda hit "Don't Know Much" & album *Warm Your Heart* 1991. Album *The Grand Tour* 1993, at New Orleans Jazz Fest in April 1993. Sang on *Christmas in Washington* NBC special 1993.

NEVIN, ETHELBURT W. (1862–1901)
b. Edgeworth, PA. Composer, composed music for poem by Robert C. Rogers* became "The Rosary" 1898, with lyricist Frank L. Stanton* wrote "Mighty Lak'a Rose" 1901.

NEW BOHEMIANS
Lead singer Edie Brickell married songwriter Paul Simon.* They had a son born 12/28/92 in NY City.

NEW DETROIT JAZZ ENSEMBLE
With Marcus Belgrave in Detroit, MI 1979/80s.

NEW EDITION
Albums *Greatest Hits, Heart Break, New Edition,* etc. Video *Past and Present.*

NEW GRASS REVIVAL
Albums *Live, New Grass Anthology, On the Boulevard.*

NEW HAWAIIAN BAND
Albums *Hawaii's Greatest Hits Vols. 1 & 2.*

NEW KIDS ON THE BLOCK
Singers Jonathan Knight (b. 1968) & Jordan Knight (b. 1970) both from Worcester, MA, Joe McIntyre (b. 1972 Needham), Donnie Wahlberg (b. 1969), & Danny Wood (b. 1969) both from Boston, *Merry, Merry Christmas* sold over 2 million albums 1989, platinum single "Hangin' Tough" 1989, *Step by Step* sold 3 million albums 1990, *New Kids on the Block,* videos *Hangin Tough, Hangin Tough Live, Step by Step.*

NEW ORDER
Group formerly **Joy Division***, albums *Low-life, Power, Corruption and Lies, Substance, Technique,* video *Substance.*

NEW ORLEANS BLUES SERENADERS
Group led by trumpeter Jabbo Smith* in NY City in 1980s.

NEW ORLEANS NIGHTHAWKS
Jazz band led by bassist Vince Giodano with trumpeters Jimmy Maxwell & Dave Brown; trombonist Bobby Peing, saxists Artie Baker & Clarence Hutchenrider; banjoist Mike Peters; drummer Eddie Davis & pianist John Varro late 1970s/80s.

NEW ORLEANS RAGTIME AND FUNERAL BAND
Led by clarinetist/comedian Woody Allen at Michael's Pub in NY City in late 1970s & early 80s.

NEW POWER GENERATION *see* PRINCE

NEW RAGTIME BAND
With clarinetist Barney Bigard* toured Switzerland in 1975.

NEW YORK DOLLS
Albums *New York Dolls, Lipstick Killers, Too Much Too Soon.*

NEW YORK JAZZ GREATS
Trumpeters John Faddis* & Tom Harrell*; saxist Lew Tabackin, pianist Mulgrew Miller*, bassist Ray Drummond, & drummer Carl Allen.

NEW YORK JAZZ QUARTET
With tenor saxist Frank Wess, pianist Roland Hanna, bassist Ron Carter*, & drummer Ben Riley 1974/75.

NEW YORK JAZZ REPERTORY ORCHESTRA
Group toured Soviet Union 1975, later led by Dick Hyman* 1979/80s.

NEWHART, BOB (1929–)
b. 9/29 Oak Park, IL. Comedian/TV actor, won 1960 Grammy for album *Button Down Mind, Best of Bob Newhart.*

NEWMAN, CHARLES (1933–1978)
b. Dallas, TX. Lyricist, with composer James V. Monaco* wrote "Six Lessons from Madame La Zonga" and other songs.

NEWMAN, RANDY (1943–)
b. 11/28 Los Angeles, CA. Singer/songwriter, hit song "Short People" in album *Little Criminals,* with Linda Ronstadt* on video *Randy Newman at the Odeon* 1985, *Good Old Boys, Land of Dreams, Sail Away, Trouble in Paradise.*

NEWSBOYS
Gospel singers won Grammy 1993 for "Not Ashamed."

NEWTON, JUICE (1952–)
b. 2/18 Virginia Beach, VA. Singer, hit single "Angel of the Morning" 1981, album *Greatest Country Hits.*

NEWTON, WAYNE (1942–)
b. 4/3 Norfolk, VA. Singer, hit "Danke Schoen" 1963, albums *Moods and Moments, The Best of Wayne Newton.* Nightclub performer in Las Vegas, NV, with an estimated yearly income of $10 million, filed for $20 million bankruptcy in August 1992. He opened his $14 million theater in Branson, MO in May 1993.

NEWTON-JOHN, OLIVIA (1947–)
b. 9/26 Cambridge, England. Singer/actress won 1974 Grammy for "I Honestly Love You" composed by Peter Allen,* with John Travolta in film *Grease* 1978, top song "Physical" 1981. Albums *Come on Over, Greatest Hits, Warm and Tender, Back to Basics* 1992. Videos *At the Universal Amphitheatre, Physical, Soul Kiss.* Postponed her 1992 tour after been diagnosed with breast cancer.

NICHOLS, ERNEST L. "RED" (1905–1965)
b. Ogden, Utah. Cornetist, led the **Syncopating Five** later called the **Royal Palms Orchestra** in Atlantic City, NJ in 1923, then led the **Five Pennies** & other bands & groups 1930s/60s. Died on 6/28 of a heart attack in Las Vegas, NV.

NICKS, STEPHANIE "STEVIE" (1948–)
b. 5/26 Phoenix, AZ. Singer with **Fleetwood Mac,** * went solo, albums *Bella Donna* 1981, *Rock a Little, Timespace, Wild Heart,* videos *I Can't Wait, Live at Red Rocks.*

NIGHT RANGER
Rocker group with Jack Blades, Alan "Fitz" Fitzgerald, Brad Gillis, Kelly Keagy, Jeff Watson. Hit "Sister Christian" on album *Midnight Madness* 1983, *7 Wishes, Dawn Patrol.*

NIGHTHAWKS
With guitarist/singer Otis Rush, Jim Thackeray, Jan Zukowski,

Peter Ragusa, & Mark Wenner in NY City 1979/80s. Guitarist Thackeray joined the **Assassins** then **King Snake.** Toured US 1992.

NILSSON, HARRY (1941–1994)
b. Brooklyn, NY City. Grammy winning Country Singer known for "Without You" & "Everybody's Talkin'" from the film *Midnight Cowboy.* Albums *A Little Touch of Harry Nilsson, Nilson Schmilsson, Son of Schmilsson, The Point.* Suffered a heart attack on 2/14/92 in Los Angeles, CA, died 1/15.

NINE INCH NAILS
Album *Pretty Hate Machine.* On Lollapalooza Tour 1991, hit "Broken" 1992, video *Happiness in Slavery* 1992, song "Wish" from album *Broken* won Grammy 1993.

NIRVANA
Seattle based rock group with guitarist/singer/leader Kurt Cobain*, bassist Chris Novoselis, & drummer David Grohl. On Top Ten charts for album *Nevermind* 1992, *Bleach, Incesticide* 1992. Cobain (b. 1968) married Courtney Love* front woman of the Los Angeles band **Hole** February 1992. Band won MTV award, best new artist for "Smells Like Teen Spirit," sold 3.5 million copies. Cobain's wife posed pregnant for *Vanity Fair* 1992. Cobain committed suicide 4/8/1994.

NITTY GRITTY DIRT BAND, THE
Country band with Ralph Barr, Chris Darrow, Jimmie Fadden, Jeff Hanna, Jim Ibotson, Bruce Kunkel, John McEven, Leslie Thompson. Won 1989 Grammy as Best Country Group, albums *20 Years of Dirt: Best of the Nitty Gritty Dirt Band, Live Two 5,* with Willie Nelson* & others on *Another Country* 1992.

NITZER, EBB
Albums *Belief-1988, Ebbhead, Showtime, That Total Age.*

NIXON, MOJO
Band **Mojo Nixon and the Toadliquors** with raunchy album *Horny Holidays* 1992.

NO SPRING CHICKENS
Folk singer Peggy Seeger, half sister of Pete Seeger* and widow of British folk giant Ewan MacColl, teamed with Irish singer Irene Scott on album *Almost Commercially Viable* 1992.

NOBLE, RAY (1907–1978)
b. Brighton, Sussex, England. Composer, led bands for many years, with Jimmy Campbell, Reg Connelly, and Rudy Vallee*, wrote "Good Night Sweetheart, 'Til We Meet Again." Died 3/3 London, England.

NOONAN, PADDY
Albums *Christmastime in Ireland, Irish Dew, Irish Party.*

NORMAN, JESSYE (1946–   )
Soprano, created a stir when she sang "Liebestod" at Tanglewood 1972, albums *Amazing Grace, Spirituals, Song Recital,* video *Hohenems Festival Live.* With soprano Kathleen Battle* on *Deutsche Gramophon* 1991. Album of pop songs *Lucky to be Me* 1992.

NORTH, ALEX (1910–1991)
b. 12/4 Chester, PA. Composer, wrote scores for over 50 films. Died 9/8 in Los Angeles, CA.

NORTON, GEORGE A. (1880–1923)
b. St. Louis, MO. Lyricist, with composer Ernie Burnett* wrote "My Melancholy Baby" 1911.

NORVO, KENNETH "RED" (1908–   )
b. 3/11 Beardstown, IL. Pianist/vibist, led own bands in late 1920s/30s, with Benny Goodman* 1944, Woody Herman* 1946, led own bands 1950s/80s. Albums *Improvisions, Just a Mood, Legendary Trio, The Forward Look.* Married singer Pearl Bailey.*

NORWORTH, JACK (1879–1959)
b. Philadelphia, PA. Songwriter with words by his wife singer Nora Bayes* wrote the music for "Shine On, Harvest Moon"

1908, with composer Albert von Tilzer* wrote "Take Me Out to the Ball Game" 1908.

NOTTINGHAM, JAMES E., JR. (1925–1978)
b. Brooklyn, NY City. Trumpeter with Willie Smith's **Great Lakes Navy Band** in 1940s, then with Lionel Hampton,* Count Basie,* Artie Shaw,* and Benny Goodman.* Died 11/16 in Brooklyn.

NOVA, ALDO
Albums *Aldo Nova, Blood on the Bricks, Subject, Tricks.*

NOVALS, GUIOMAR (1895–1979)
b. Sao Paulo, Brazil. Pianist, debut in Paris 1907, debut in New York 1915, played in New York City in 1930s/40s. Married composer Octavio Pinto.

NOVOSEL, STEVE (1950–   )
b. Farrell, PA. Bassist with pianist McCoy Tyner,* saxist Andrew White, vibist Milt Jackson,* singers Joe Williams,* Shirley Horn,* Donny Hathaway,* & Novosel's ex-wife Roberta Flack* on album *Live at the Floating Jazz Festival* 1992.

NRBO
Albums *At Yankee Stadium, Peek a Boo/Best of NRBO, Scraps, Wild Weekend,* etc.

NUGENT, MAUDE (1873–1958)
b. Brooklyn, NY City. Singer/composer, wrote "Sweet Rosie O'Grady" 1896.

NUGENT, TED (1949–   )
b. 12/3 Detroit, MI. Hard rocker/guitarist/leader/singer/song-writer, albums *Cat Scratch Fever, Free for All, If You Can't Lick 'Em, Penetrator.* Activist for People for the Ethical Treatment of Animals. Toured US 1992/93 with Tommy Shaw and **Damn Yankees.***

NUNN, TERRI
Lead singer/songwriter with **Berlin,** left group in 1987 & went solo, album *Moment of Truth* 1992.

N.W.A.
Rappers with Dr. Dre* (Andre R. Young), Ice Cube (O'Shea Jackson), Eazy-E (Eric Wright), single "F. . . the Police" 1988, platinum album *Straight Outta Compton* 1989. After some of their entourage weren't allowed in the Sheraton Hotel in New Orleans a riot broke out & the group was arrested May 1992. Group disbanded & Dr. Dre went solo. Eazy-E on album *Temporary Insanity* 1992.

NYLONS, THE
Albums *The Nylons, Four on the Floor, Happy Together, Rockapella.*

NYRO, LAURA (1949–)
Albums *Christmas and Beads of Sweat, Eli and the 13th Confession, New York Tendaberry,* etc.

O

OAK RIDGE BOYS, THE
Country/pop group with tenor Joe Bonsall (b. 1948 Philadelphia, PA), Duane Allen,* Richard Sterban, & baritone William Lee Golden (later replaced by Steve Sanders). Hits "Elvira" 1981, "So Fine" 1982, albums *American Dreams, Best of the Oak Ridge Boys, Greatest Hits Vols. 1 to 3, Together, Unstoppable,* etc. Sang in the White House for President & Mrs. Bush in November 1992.

OCEAN, BILLY (1952–   )
b. 1/21 Trinidad, West Indies. Singer, resides in London, England. Albums *Greatest Hits, Nights, Suddenly,* etc.

OCHS, PHILIP DAVID (1940–1976)
b. El Paso TX. Songwriter, many of his hits like "Draft Dodger Rag" were political protests. Albums *A Toast to Those Gone, Broadside Tapes, Gunfight at Carnegie Hall, The War is Over.*

O'CONNELL, HELEN (1921–1993)
b. 5/23 Lima, Ohio. Popular in 1940s, toured with Jimmy Dorsey* Orchestra, sang at Disney World in September 1992. Died 9/9 in San Diego.

O'CONNELL, MAURA
Singer, Irish transplant, sang at Senator Ted Kennedy's wedding 1992, album *Blue is the Color of Hope* 1992.

O'CONNOR, MARK
Violinist albums *Championship Years, Stone from Which Arch Was, The New Nashville Cats.* Won Horizon Country music award 1992. *Country Music* Musician of the Year 1993.

O'CONNOR, SINEAD (1966–   )
b. 12/8 Dublin, Ireland. Singer won 1990 Alternate Music Grammy for *I Do Not Want What I Haven't Got* (sold 2 million albums). Videos *The Value of Ignorance, Year of the Horse.* While on NBC *Saturday Night Live* show 10/3/92 she said:

"Fight the real enemy" and tore up a photo of Pope John Paul II. Later explained that the Vatican had "used marriage, divorce and birth control and abortion to control us through our children and fear."

O'DAY, ANITA (1919–)
b. Chicago, IL. Scat singer with jazz bands & combos 1940s/80s. Albums *Anita, Anita O'Day Sings Winners, In a Mellow Time, Sings Cole Porter.*

ODETTA (1930–)
b. Odetta Felious Cordon 12/31 Birmingham, AL, raised in Los Angeles & sang in night clubs there. At Town Hall 1959 & Carnegie Hall in NY City 1960. Albums *Christmas Spirituals, The Essential Odetta,* with Dr. John* on *Strike a Deep Chord: Blues Guitars for the Homeless* 1992.

O'HARA, GEOFFREY (1882–1967)
b. Chatham, Ontario, Canada. Songwriter, came to NY City to live, wrote the words and music for the popular World War I song "K-K-K-Katy" 1918.

O'HEARN, PATRICK
Albums *Ancient Dreams, Between Two Worlds, El Dorado, Indigo, Mixup, River's Gonna Rise.*

OINGO BOINGO
Albums *Boingo Live, Dead Man's Party, Good for Your Soul, Nothing to Fear, Skeletons in the Closet,* etc.

O'JAYS, THE
With Walter Williams, Sam Strain, Edward Levert,* hits "Use Ta Be My Girl" 1977, "Girl Don't Let It Get You Down" 1980, albums *Emotionally Yours, Let Me Touch You, Serious, Ship Ahoy.* The O'Jays/Whispers toured US 1992.

OLCOTT, CHAUNCEY (1860–1932)
b. Buffalo, NY. Singer/composer, wrote "My Wild Irish Rose" 1899, with Rita Johnson Young* & composer Ernest R. Ball*

"Mother Machree" 1910, with Ernest Ball* and George Graff* wrote "When Irish Eyes are Smiling" 1912.

OLD AND NEW DREAMS
With bassist Charlie Haden,* trumpeter Don Cherry,* tenor saxist Dewey Redman, & drummer Ed Blackwell awarded best Jazz Album of Year 1979 for *Old and New Dreams,* played at Town Hall 1980.

OLD SKULL
Wisconsin teenage group, album *C.I.A. Drug Fest* 1992.

OLDFIELD, MIKE (1953–)
b. 5/15 Reading, Berkshire, England. Guitarist/composer, albums *Islands, Killing Fields, Oldfield, Tubular Bells,* etc.

OLIVER, JOE "KING" (1885–1938)
b. Abend, LA, Cornetist/composer, with Kid Ory* 1917/19, led the **Creole Jazz Band** & the **Dixie Syncopators** 1920s/30s, wrote "Dr. Jazz," "Canal Street Blues." Died in Savannah, GA.

OLIVER, MELVIN J. "SY" (1910–1988)
b. 12/17 Battle Creek, MI. Jazz trumpeter/vocalist with **Zach White and His Chocolate Beau Brummels** 1927, arranged for Jimmie Lunceford* & Tommy Dorsey,* led own bands 1940s/80s on tour and in NY City.

OLIVOR, JANE
Albums *Chasing Rainbows, First Night, Jane Olivor in Concert, Stay the Night,* etc.

OLMAN, ABE (1888–1984)
b. Cincinnati, Ohio. Pianist/composer, with lyricist Ed Rose composed "Oh Johnny, Oh Johnny, Oh" 1917.

O'NEAL, ALEXANDER
Albums *Alexander O'Neal, All Mixed Up, All True Man, My Gift to You,* video *Live in London.*

O'NEILL BAND, SEAN
Singers/musicians, albums *50 Irish Drinking Songs, 50 Irish Party Songs, 50 Irish Pub Songs.*

100 PROOF (AGED IN SOUL)
Album *Greatest Hits.*

ONO, YOKO (1933–)
b. 2/18 Tokyo, Japan. Musician, married John Lennon* 1969, with Lennon *Double Fantasy* (Grammy winner 1981), wrote "Happy Christmas (War is over)" with Lennon, albums *Onobox, Walking on Thin Ice* includes her chilling vocals & Lennon's stunning guitar.

ORB, THE
Hit "U.F. Orb" 1993.

ORBISON, ROY (1936–1988)
b. 4/23 Wink, TX. Singer/guitarist, hits "Ooby-Dooby" 1956, "Crying" 1961, "Oh Pretty Woman," platinum album *Mystery Girl* 1989, Pop Male Vocal Grammy 1990 for *A Black and White Night, In Dreams, Rare Orbison, The Sun Years,* etc., video *A Black and White Night.* Died 12/6 Nashville, TN.

OREGON
Albums *Crossing, Distant Hills, Ecotopia, Essential Oregon, Moon and Mind, Winter Light,* etc.

ORIGINALS, THE
Albums *Baby I'm for Real, Portrait of the Originals,* etc.

ORLANDO, TONY (1944–)
b. Michael Anthony Orlando Cassavitis 4/3 New York, NY. Singer, with **Dawn** had hit "Tie a Yellow Ribbon 'Round the Old Oak Tree" 1973.

ORLEANS
Guitarist Larry Hoppen, bassist Lance Hoppen, keyboardist Bob

Leinbach, R.A. Martin on horns, drummer Wells Kelly, hit single "Love Takes Time" 1979, album *Still the One.*

ORLOB, HAROLD (1885–1982)
b. Logan, Utah. Composer, with lyricists Will M. Hough* & Frank R. Adams,* and composer Joe E. Howard* "I Wonder Who's Kissing Her Now" 1909. Died on 6/25/82. 1939 Oscar with lyricist E.Y. Harburg for "Over the Rainbow."

ORMANDY, EUGENE (1899–1985)
b. 11/18 Budapest, Hungary. Conductor of Philadelphia Orchestra for 44 years. Final performance at Carnegie Hall in NY City on 5/6/80. Died 3/12 in Philadelphia, Pa.

ORRALL, ROBERT ELLIS
Pop/country singer, hits "Boom, It was Over," "It's My Lucky Day," album *Flying Colors* 1993.

ORY, EDWARD "KID" (1886–1973)
b. La Place, LA. Trombonist/singer, led own band in New Orleans 1911/19, then in California. Recorded first known jazz records by a black musician, "Creole Trombone" & "Society Blues," 1921. Wrote & recorded "Muskrat Ramble" 1926, with Louis Armstrong's* band, toured 1920s/60s, moved to Hawaii 1966, at 1971 New Orleans Jazz Festival. Albums *Favorites, Legendary Kid, New Orleans Jubilee.* Died in Honolulu, Hawaiian Islands.

OSBORNE, JEFFREY (1948–   )
b. 10/9 Providence, RI. Singer, hits "On the Wings of Love" 1982, "Soldier of Love" 1990, performed in *Joseph and the Amazing Technicolor Dreamcoat"* 1992, albums *Don't Stop, Emotional, Jeffrey Osborne, One Love One Dream, Only Human,* etc.

OSBORNE, MARY (1921–1991)
b. Minot, ND. Jazz guitarist on Jack Sterling radio show 1952/63, in Bakersfield, CA after 1967, played "God Bless this Child" on album *A Memorial* 1992.

OSBOURNE, JOHN "OZZY" (1949–)

b. 12/3 Birmingham, England. Former lead singer for **Black Sabbath,*** most of his solo albums have gone gold, albums *Bark at the Moon, Blizzard of Oz, Diary of a Madman, Just Say Ozzy, No More Tears,* 1992. Videos *Don't Blame Me, The Ultimate Ozzy, The Wicked Videos.* Ended his solo career at a concert in Costa Mesa, CA in November 1992. 1994 Metal Grammy for "I Don't Want to Change the World."

OSLIN, K.T. (1942–)

b. Crossit, AK. Country singer, once worked as a Broadway chorus girl, won 1988 Country Vocalist Grammy for "Hold Me" track from *This Woman.* Albums *80's Ladies, Love in a Small Town.* Sang "Tumbling Tumbleweeds" with Roy Rogers* on album *Tribute to Roy Rogers* 1992.

OSMOND, DONALD C. "DONNY" (1958–)

b. 12/9 Ogden, Utah. Singer/actor with **The Osmonds** from age four, co-starred with sister on *Donny and Marie Show* 1976/79, albums *Donny Osmond, Eyes Don't Lie.*

OSMOND, MARIE (1959–)

b. 10/13 Ogden, Utah. Singer, starred with **The Osmonds**—Alan, Donny, Jay, Jimmy, Marie, Merrill, & Wayne from age seven. Albums *Best of Marie Osmond, I Only Wanted You, There's No Stopping Your Heart.*

OSTANEK, WALTER

Musician/bandleader, album *35th Anniversary* won Polka Grammy 1993. Polka Grammy 1994 for *Accordingly Yours.*

OTIS, JOHNNY (1921–)

b. John Veliotes 12/28 Vellejo, CA. Musician/singer/songwriter, hit single "Willie and the Hand Jive," *J. Otis—The Capitol Years.*

OUTFIELD, THE

Albums *Bangin, Deep Voices of Babylon.*

OUTLAWS, THE
Country/rock singers Harvey Dalton Arnold, Rick Cua, David Dix, Billy Jones, Henry Paul, Hughie Thomasson, & Monte Yono. Hit "(Ghost) Riders in the Sky" 1980. Albums *Bring It Back Alive, Greatest Hits, The Outlaws*.

OVERSTREET, PAUL
R&B singer/songwriter. Has written 25 Ten Top hits including "Still Out There Swingin'," "Take Some Action," "Head Over Heels," albums *Heroes, Sowin' Love, Love is Strong* 1992.

OWENS, BUCK (1929–   )
b. Alvis E. Owens, Jr. 8/12 Sherman, TX. Singer/musician, joined Bill Woods' band in Bakersfield, CA 1950, later formed his own band, with Harlan Howard wrote "Foolin' Around" and other songs. Albums *Act Naturally, All Time Greatest Hits, Hot Dog*. Sang on album *Country Music for Kids* 1992.

OZAWA, SEIJI (1935–   )
b. 9/1 Hoten, Japan. Conducted San Francisco Symphony Orchestra, album *20th Century Bach* with Boston Symphony 1992. Video *Ozawa*.

P

PABLO CRUISE
Rock group with Bud Cockrell, David Jenkins, Cory Lerios, & Steve Price, later John Pierce & Angelo Rossi. Albums *A Place in the Sun, Worlds Away.*

PADEREWSKI, IGNACE JAN (1860–1941)
b. Kurilovka, Poland. Famous pianist, toured US 1900s/10s, elected premier of Poland in 1919. Toured US again 20s. Albums *The Art of Paderewski, Chopin, Polish Fantasia, Great Pianists of a Golden Era,* etc. Died in NY City.

PAGE, PATTI (1927–)
b. Clara Ann Fowler 11/8 Clarence, OK. Singer, had own show on a Tulsa radio station, promoted the "Tennessee Waltz," later on many guest shows. Albums *Christmas with Patti Page, Greatest Hits, Golden Hits.*

PALMER, JOHN F.
Composer, with lyricist Charles B. Ward* wrote "The Band Played On" 1895.

PALMER, ROBERT (1949–)
b. 1/19 Batley, Yorkshire, England. Singer won 1988 Rock Vocalist Grammy for "Simply Irresistible." Albums *Clues, Don't Explain, Double Fun, Heavy Nova, Pressure Drop, Sneakin' Sally Through the Alley.* Videos *Riptide, Super Nova, Ridin' High* 1992, hit "Every Kinda People" 1992.

PARADES, CARLOS
Guitarist, CD *Guitarra Portugesa.*

PARIS
Oakland, CA rapper, album *Sleeping with the Enemy* includes "Bush Killa" about an assassin stalking President George Bush (1992).

PARIS, JACKIE (1926–1977)

b. Nutley, NJ. Guitarist/singer, with Lionel Hampton* & others, married singer Anne Marie Moss and they were a vocal team in NY City night clubs. Died 7/10 New York, New York.

PARISH, MITCHELL (1900–   )

b. Shreveport, IL. Lyricist, with composer Hoagy Carmichael* wrote "Star Dust" 1927, with composers Billy Rose & Irving Mills wrote "Deep Purple" 1939, with composer Will Hudson wrote the "Organ Grinder's Song."

PARKER, CHARLIE "BIRD" (1920–1955)

b. Kansas City, MO. Alto saxist/composer, co-founder with Dizzy Gillespie* of the "bop" movement, made the celebrated cross-over swing-to-bop at a Red Norvo* session in June 1945. At a tragic session on July 29, 1946 Parker went berserk & was committed to the Camarillo State Hospital in California for seven months. Albums *At Storyville, Bird at the Roost Vols. 1, 2, 3, Easy Bird, Walkman Jazz,* video *Bird: Triumph Celebrating.* Died in New York City.

PARKER, GRAHAM (1950–   )

British pop/rocker guitarist/singer, albums *Howlin Wind, Mona Lisa's Sister, Pourin' it All Out, Struck by Lightning, Burning Questions* 1992.

PARKER, MACEO

R&B alto saxist, with trombonist Fred Wesley & tenor saxist Pee Wee Ellis on album *Mo Roots, Roots Revisited, Funky Good Time* 1993, with Bernie Worrell on *Blacktronic Science* 1993.

PARKER, RAY, JR. (1954–   )

b. 5/1 Detroit, MI. Singer/songwriter, hit "Ghostbusters" 1984, albums *Greatest Hits, I Love You Like You Are, Sex and the Single Man.*

PARLIAMENT

Albums *Chocolate City, Clones of Dr. Frankenstein, Mothership Connection, Motor Booty Affairs, P-funk Earth Tour,* etc.

PARNELL, LEE ROY
East Texas country singer, hit "What Kind of Fool Do You Think I Am?" 1992, albums *Lee Roy Parnell, Love Without Mercy* 1992.

PARSONS, ALAN PROJECT
Albums *Eye in the Sky, I Robot, Pyramid, Vulture Culture.*

PARTCH, HARRY (1901–1974)
b. Oakland, CA. Composer, wrote "Windsong" 1958 & other pieces. Album *Bewitched.* Died in San Diego, CA.

PARTON, DOLLY (1946–)
b. 1/19 Sevierville, TN. Singer/actress, hit "Here You Come Again" on first gold record 1976, film debut *Nine to Five* 1980. She wrote "I Will Always Love You" 1974 remade for *The Best Little Whorehouse in Texas* 1982, *Honkey Tonk Angels* 1993. "Dollywood" theme park is in Sevierville. Married Carl Dean.

PASS, JOE (1929–1994)
b. New Brunswick, NJ. Guitarist, toured with Tony Pastor, arrested on a narcotics charge & spent 3 years in a US Public Health Hospital in Ft. Worth, TX. Played in Las Vegas and arrested again, entered Synanon Clinic in Santa Monica, CA 1961 which cured him of the habit. Won *down beat* New Star Award 1963 & *down beat* Guitarist of the Year 1980. *Albums Appassionato, Blues for Fred, One for My Baby, Summer Nights,* etc. Died May 23, 1994 at Los Angeles.

PATITUCCI, JOHN
Bassist with Chick Corea* & **Return to Forever***. Albums *On the Corner, Sketchbook.*

PATTI, SANDI (1956–)
Gospel superstar has won five Grammys & sold over 6 million albums. Album *Finest Moments.* Won Gospel Music Top Female Vocalist 1981–1992. After 13 years of marriage filed for divorce against John Helvering 1992.

PAVAROTTI, LUCIANO (1935–)
b. 10/12 Modena, Italy. Tenor, toured US & Australia with Joan Sutherland & her husband conductor Richard Bonynge. Made his debut at Metropolitan Opera in NY City in *La Boheme* 1968, sang with Beverly Sills in Philadelphia 1972, won 1988 Classical Vocal Artist Grammy, won 1990 Grammy for *Carreras, Domingo, Pavarotti in Concert.* Videos *Christmas, Distant Harmony in China, Gala Concert, Pavarotti,* etc. Sang at Tel Aviv Square in Israel in October 1992.

PAVEMENT
Garage rockers from Stockton, CA with singer guitarist S.M., guitarist Spiral Stairs, bassist Mark Ibold, drummers Garry Young & Bobby N. Released *Slay Tracks 1933–69* in 1989, *Perfect Sound Forever* 1991, CD *Slanted and Enchanted* declared Best Album of 1992 by *Spin* magazine.

PAXTON, THOMAS R. "TOM" (1937–)
b. 10/31 Chicago, IL. Singer/songwriter, raised in Bristol, OK, served in army, sang in night clubs in NY City. Albums *1 Million Lawyers, It Ain't Easy, Politics Live, Very Best of Tom Paxton.*

PAYCHECK, JOHNNY (1941–)
b. Donald Lytle 5/31 Greenfield, Ohio. Country singer, hit "Take this Job and Shove It." Albums *Country Spotlight, Greatest Hits Vols. 1 & 2, Paycheck and Bo Diddley on Live at the Lone Star.*

PAYNE, FREDA (1945–)
b. 9/19 Detroit, MI. Singer, hit "Band of Gold" 1970, album *Greatest Hits.*

PAYNE, JOHN
Singer/bassist with **Asia*** on album *Aqua* 1992.

PAYNE, JOHN HOWARD (1791–1852)
b. NY City. Singer/lyricist, with composer H.R. Bishop wrote "Home, Sweet Home" 1823.

PEARL JAM
Seattle group with singer Eddie Vedder,* Mike McCready, Stone
Gossard, Dave Albruzzese, & Jeff Ament. Hit album *Ten*
reached platinum, free tickets for a concert in Seattle caused a
traffic jam lasting four hours in September 1992. Rock album
Jeremy won Grammy 1993. Group won New Artist Metal/Hard
Rock award, American Music Awards, January 1993.

PEARL, LESLIE
b. Bucks County, PA. Singer/songwriter, hit "If the Love Fits,
Wear It" 1982.

PEARL, MINNIE (1912–   )
b. Sarah Ophelia Colley 10/25 Centreville, TN. Country singer
known as the "Queen of Country Comedy from Grinder's
Switch" which was three miles from her home. She made her
debut at the Grand Ole Opry in Nashville in 1940. Nashville
Network program honored her in October 1992.

PEBBLES, ANN
Memphis blues singer/songwriter, hit "I Can't Stand the Rain"
1973, on 1988 Top Ten Black Singles Chart for "Girlfriend."
Married pianist Donald Bryant who co-wrote her songs. Albums *Always, Pebbles, Giving You the Benefit* 1992, with
guitarist Thomas Bingham on *Full Time Love* 1992.

PEERCE, JAN (1904–1984)
b. 6/3 New York, NY. Leading tenor with Metropolitan Opera in
NY City 1941/66, sang with his brother-in-law tenor Richard
Tucker. Peerce composed "Bluebird of Happiness" 1976. Album *Art of the Cantor*, video *If I Were a Rich Man*. Died 12/15.

PEIFFER, BERNARD (1922–1976)
b. Epinal, France. Pianist, came to Philadelphia 1954, at Montreal
Jazz Festival in Canada 1962, led the **Bernard Peiffer Jazz
Trio.** Died 9/7 Philadelphia, PA.

PELISSIER, VICTOR (1760–1820)
b. France. French horn virtuoso/composer, played first horn in Old

American Company, New York City in 1793. With book by John Hodgkinson, composed the music for *The Launch, or Huzzah for the (Frigate) Constitution* 1797.

PELL MELL
Seattle rock group led by Steve Fisk, album *Flow* 1992.

PENDERGRASS, THEODORE D. "TEDDY BEAR" (1950–)
b. 3/26 Soul singer, *Life is a Song Worth Singing* double platinum album, his concert at the Greek Theatre in Hollywood was recorded in 1979, on Top Ten Black Singles list for "Joy" 1988. Albums *Love Language, Truly Blessed, Working It Back.* Paralyzed in an auto accident.

PENGUIN CAFE ORCHESTRA
Albums *Broadcasting from Home, Penguin Cafe Orchestra, When in Rome.*

PENISTON, CECE
Hit R&B single "Keep on Walkin'" 1992, album *Finally.*

PENN, MICHAEL (1960–)
Singer/guitarist, albums *March* 1989, *Free-for-all* 1992.

PENSYL, KIM
Albums *3 Day Weekend, Pensyl Sketches #1, 2 & 3.*

PEPPER, ARTHUR E. "ART" (1925–1982)
b. 9/1 Gardena, CA. Alto/tenor saxist with Stan Kenton* 1943/52. Led own combo in Los Angeles but suffered with bouts of alcohol and narcotics. Won *down beat* critics' award as Alto Saxist of Year 1980. Albums *Gettin' Together, Intensity, Meets the Rhythm Section, Modern Jazz Classics, Smack Up,* etc.

PERFECT CIRCLE, THE
Hard rock/jazz group formed by guitarist Gabor Szabo 1975 in Los Angeles, CA.

PERFECT JAZZ REPERTORY QUINTET
With pianist Dick Hyman,* trumpeter Pee Wee Erwin,* bassist Milt Hinton,* drummer Bobby Rosengarden, alto saxist/ clarinetist Johnny Mince replaced Bob Wilbur. Played at Michael's Pub in NY City 1978/81.

PERKINS, CARL (1933–)
b. 4/9 Jackson, TN. Singer/songwriter, albums *Jive after Five, Best of Carl Perkins, Up Through the Years.* Wrote "Blue Suede Shoes."

PERLMAN, ITZHAK (1945–)
b. 8/31 Tel Aviv, Palestine (now Israel). Violinist, played *Brahm's Violin Concerto* with London Symphony in Daytona Beach, FL 1991 & with Florida Symphony in January 1993. Albums *Encores, Traditional Jewish Melodies,* etc. Video *Beethoven Violin Concerto* with Kathleen Battle* on *The Bach Album.*

PERRY, STEVE (1949–)
b. 1/22. Singer with rock band **Journey.*** Went solo 1992 with album *Street Talk.*

PERSON, HOUSTON
Albums *Basics, The Party, Why Not?*

PERSPECTIVE
Hit album *Mo Money Soundtrack* 1992.

PERSUASIONS, THE
Albums *A Capella, Comin' at Ya, Good News, No Frills.*

PET SHOP BOYS
Albums *Actually, Behavior, Disco, Introspective Please.*

PETER, PAUL AND MARY
With Peter Yarrow,* Noel Paul Stookey,* and Mary Travers, hit "Blowin' in the Wind" (Grammy winner 1963). Group disbanded 1971, revived in 1980s. Albums *Best of Peter, Paul and*

Mary, Moving, In Concert, Reunion. Video *25th Anniversary.* Trio sang at the American Reunion on the Mall in Washington, D.C. in January 1993.

PETE ROCK & C.L. SMOTH
Rap singers on album *Mecca and the Soul Brother* 1992.

PETERS, BERNADETTE (1948–   )
b. Bernadette Lazzara 2/28 Queens, NY City. Singer/actress, won a Tony for *Song and Dance* 1986, starred in Stephen Sondheim's* musical *Into the Woods* 1987, sang "Water Under the Bridge" at *Sondheim: A Celebration at Carnegie Hall* in June 1992.

PETERS, ROBERTA (1930–   )
b. Roberta Peterman 5/4 New York, NY. Soprano, debut at Metropolitan Opera in NY City 1950, during summers sang at Covent Gardens in London 1950s/60s, soloist at Carnegie Hall in NY City 1972, sang at Christmas Concert at Carnegie Hall to benefit the AIDS Research Program 1992.

PETERSON, OSCAR E. (1925–   )
b. 8/15 Montreal, Quebec. Jazz pianist/singer, toured with Jazz at the Philharmonic 1950/54, Best Instrumentalist Grammy 1980, Jazz Instrumentalist Grammy 1990 for *The Legendary Oscar Peterson Live at the Blue Note,* 4 CDs *Exclusively* 1992.

PETERSON, RAY
Hit "Tell Laura I Love Her" about a love-struck hero killed in an auto accident.

PETRA
Gospel singers won 1993 Grammy for *Unseen Power.*

PETRIE, HENRY W. (1857–1925)
b. Bloomington, IL. Composer, with lyricist A.J. Lamb* wrote "Asleep in the Deep" 1897.

PETRUCCIONI, MICHAEL
Musician, albums *Michael Plays Petruccioni, Music, Note H Notes, Playground, Power of Thee.*

PETTIFORD, OSCAR (1922–1960)
b. Okmulgee, OK. Bassist/composer. His father's band included their eleven children & toured 1936/41. With Duke Ellington* & others in 1940s, led own bands in 50s, wrote "Black-eyed Peas and Collard Greens," "Tricrotism." Album *Monmartre Blues*. Died in Copenhagen, Denmark.

PETTY, TOM (1950–)
b. 10/20 Gainesville, FL. Formed **Tom Petty and the Heartbreakers** 1975 with Ron Blair, Mike Campbell, Stan Lynch, Benmont Tench, album *Damn the Torpedoes* 1979 sold over 2.5 million copies, hit "Refugee," album *Full Moon Fever* 1989 sold over 2 million. Petty toured with Bob Dylan's **Traveling Wilburys.*** Album *Tom Petty: Pack Up the Plantation* 1992.

PHILE, PHILIP (1734–1793)
b. Philip Pfeil in Germany. Violinist/composer/conductor of Theatre Royal in New York, NY 1779. He composed "The President's March" played in the presence of George Washington at the John Street Theatre on November 24, 1789. This tune was used by Joseph Hopkinson* for "Hail Columbia" 1798. Phile died in Philadelphia.

PHILLIPS, ESTHER (1935–1984)
b. Esther Mae Jones 12/23 Galveston, TX. Singer known as "Little Esther" toured with Johnny Otis* 1949/52, sang with the **Beatles*** on BBC-TV in London 1965, at jazz festivals in NY City & Redondo Beach, CA in 1970s/80s. Album *From a Whisper to a Scream* 1972, *Confessin' the Blues*, *Way to Say Goodbye*, etc.

PHILLIPS, "PAPA" JOHN (1935–)
b. 8/30 Parris Island, SC. Singer with the **Mamas and the Papas.*** Had a lung transplant at UCLA Hospital on 7/4/92.

PHILLIPS, L.Z.
The first copyright of the words in 1919 show Phillips as the author, with composer Offenbach, of "The Marines Hymn— From the Halls of Montezuma to the Shores of Tripoli."

PHISH
Album *Junta.*

PIAF, EDITH (1915–1963)
Singer, sang in night clubs, albums *At Carnegie Hall, At the Paris Olympia, Voice of the Sparrow, Her Complete Recording.*

PIAZZOLIA, ASTOR
Composer, won 1993 for "Oblivion" track from *Symphonic Tango.*

PICKENS SISTERS
Singers popular in 1930s, Jane Pickens Langley Hoving died 2/21/92 in Newport, Rhode Island aged 83.

PICKETT, WILSON (1941–   )
b. 3/18 Prattville, AL. Singer/songwriter, hit "The Midnight Hour", albums *Best of Wilson Pickett, Greatest Hits.* Began serving a prison term for drunken driving January 1994.

PIERCE, BILLIE GOODSON (1905–1974)
b. Pensacola, FL. Pianist, younger sister of Sadie Goodson who sang in Buddy Petit's band. Billie was accompanist for blues singer Bessie Smith. Married Dede Pierce* & toured with the **Grateful Dead,*** Jefferson Airplane,* & other rock groups. Billie & Dede led the **Preservation Hall Band*** in New Orleans.

PIERCE, JOSEPH D. "DEDE" (1904–1973)
b. New Orleans, LA. Trumpeter/cornetist, married Billie Goodson.* Dede & Billie accompanied Ida Cox on tours, appeared in *Great Performances* series at Philharmonic Hall in NY City & also led the **Preservation Hall Band*** in New Orleans. Dede became blind.

PIERCE, WEBB (1926–1991)
b. 8/8 West Monroe, LA. Singer/songwriter, led his own band, with M. Freeman wrote the "Last Waltz." Album *Greatest Hits.* Died 2/24 Nashville, TN.

PIERPONT, JAMES S. (1822–1893)
b. Boston, MA. Composer, wrote words & music for "Jingle Bells" 1857. Died in Winter Park, FL.

PINK FLOYD
British rock group with Syd Barrett, Dave Gilmour, Nick Mason, Roger Waters, & Rick Wright. LP *Dark Side of the Moon* on top of charts for almost two years. *A Momentary Lapse of Reason* on 1988 Top Compact Discs. Albums *Animals, Atom Heart Mother, Final Cut, More, Shine On* 1992. In 1988 on Top Ten-grossing concerts at Giants Stadium, East Rutherford, NJ. Videos *Delicate Sound of Thunder, The Wall.*

PINZA, EZIO (1892–1957)
b. Rome, Italy. Noted basso with the Metropolitan Opera in NY City 1926/46, his voice recorded in the musical *South Pacific* 1949. Albums *Ezio Pinza, Opera Arias: Aida.*

PIRATES OF THE MISSISSIPPI
Album about the homeless, *A Street Man Named Desire* 1992.

PIRNER, DAVID
Songwriter, 1994 Rock Song Grammy for "Runaway Train."

PITNEY, GENE (1941–   )
b. 2/17 Rockville, CT. Tenor/songwriter, hit singles "That Girl Belongs to Yesterday," "I Must be Seeing Things." Album *Anthology.*

PITTS, WILLIAM S. (1830–1918)
b. Orleans County, NY. Composer, wrote "Church in the Wildwood; or Little Brown Church in the Dell" 1857. He died in Brooklyn, NY City. The Mike Club Congregation sang the song on the *Reader's Digest 50 Beloved Songs of Faith* issued in 1992.

PLAN B
West Berlin quartet with lead singer/guitarist Johnny Haeusaler, a drummer, & two more guitarists. Album *The Greenhouse Effect* 1992.

PLANT, ROBERT
On 1988 Top Ten CDs list for *Now and Zen*, albums *Marie Nirvanna, Pictures at Eleven, Principle of Moments, Shaken N Stirred.*

PLASMATICS, THE
With John Beauvoir, Wes Beech, Neal Smith, Richie Stotts, Wendy O. Williams, & Stu Deutch. Albums *New Hope for the Wretched, Coup d'Etat* 1982.

PLATER, ROBERT "BOBBY" (1914–1982)
b. Newark, NJ Alto saxist/flutist with **Savoy Dictators** 1937 then with Tiny Bradshaw, led 93rd Division Band in World War II. With Lionel Hampton 1946/64 then with Count Basie.*

PLATTERS, THE
Singing group formed 1953 with David Lynch (1930–1981), Herb Reed, Paul Robi, Zola Taylor, Tony Williams* (died 8/14/92). Hits "Only You" 1955, "Smoke Gets in Your Eyes" 1958, "The Great Pretender." Albums *Golden Hits, Greatest Hits, The Very Best of the Platters.*

P. M. DAWN
New Jersey hip-hop/rap group with lead singer Prince B, album *Of the Heart of the Soul and of the Cross, The Utopian Experience* 1992, *The Bliss Album* 1993, single "I'd Die Without You" 1993.

POCO
With Paul Cotton, Richie Furay,* George Grantham, Jim Messina, Randy Meisner, Tim Schmit, Rusty Young, & later Kim Bullard, Charlie Harrison, Steve Chapman. Hit album *Deliverin', Head Over Heels, Poco, The Forgotten Trail, The Very Best of Poco.*

POINTER SISTERS
Pop/R&B singers, first black women to appear at Grand Ole Opry, Nashville, TN. Anita (b. 1948), Bonnie (b. 1954), Ruth (b. 1946), all born in East Oakland, CA. Hits "Fire" 1979, "He's

So Shy" 1980, "I'm So Excited" 1982. First pop group to appear at San Francisco Opera House. Albums *Black & White, Break Out, Hot Together,* etc. In 1978 Bonnie Pointer left the group for a solo career, hit single "I Can't Help Myself" 1979.

POISON
Rock band with front man Bret Michaels, on Top Ten singles list for "Every Rose Has Its Thorn" 1989, *Flesh and Blood* sold two million albums 1990, *Look What the Cat Dragged In, Open Up and Say Aah, Swallow This Live,* with guitarist Richie Kotzen on gold album *Native Tongue* 1993 and video *Stand* 1993.

POLICE, THE
British rock group with Stewart Copeland,* Andy Summers,* Gordon "Sting" Sumner.* Hit "Every Breath You Take" 1983. Albums *Ghost in the Machine, Outlandos D'Amour, Zenyatta Mondatta,* videos *Brimstone & Treacle, Every Breath You Take, Synchronicity.*

POMUS, JEROME "DOC" (1926–1991)
Composer, wrote "A Teenager in Love" and "Save the Last Dance for Me."

PONS, LILY (1904–1976)
b. 4/12 Cannes, France. Coloratura soprano, American debut at Metropolitan Opera in NY City 1931. In 1956 celebrated her 25th anniversary with the opera company. Albums *Art of the Coloratura, Opera Arias.* Died 2/13 in Dallas, Texas.

PONSELLE, ROSA (1894–1981)
b. Rosa Ponzillo 1/22 Meriden, CT. Soprano, debut at Metropolitan Opera in NY City 1918. Albums *Arias and Songs, I Have Sung My Songs.*

PONTY, JEAN-LUC
Violinist, albums *Cosmic Messenger, Enigmatic Ocean, Fables, Open Mind, Individual Choice, Storytelling,* etc.

POP, IGGY (1947–   )
b. April 21 James N. Osterberg in Ann Arbor, Michigan. Rock

singer/drummer. Albums *Blah, Blah, Blah, Brick by Brick, Instinct, Lust for Life, The Idiot.* **Iggy Pop & the Stooges,** album *Raw Power.*

POP WILL EAT ITSELF
Hit single "The Looks of the Lifestyle" 1993.

PORNO FOR PYROS
Band organized by Perry Farrell* on Lollapalooza Tour 1993.

PORTER, COLE (1892–1964)
b. Peru, IN. Composer, wrote "What is This Thing Called Love?" 1929, "Night and Day" 1932, "Begin the Beguine" 1935, "My Heart Belongs to Daddy" 1938, "Don't Fence Me In" 1944, "I've Got You Under My Skin," "You'd be so Nice to Come Home To." Albums *Fifty Million Frenchmen, Kiss Me Kate/Alfred Drake, Night and Day/Porter Songbook, You're the Top, etc.*

PORTRAIT, PORTRAIT
Four trumpeters from Los Angeles, Tulsa, & Providence, R.I., hit "Here We Go Again."

POSIES, THE
Seattle grunge band with Ken Stringfellow, Jon Auer, David Fox, and Mike Musburger, CDs *Dear 23* 1990, *Frosting on the Beater* 1993.

POSSE, THE
Michael Wolff leader of Arsenio Hall's band The Posse married actress Polly Draper 1992. Wolff played in The White House for President Bill Clinton in January 1993.

POST, MIKE
Composer won 1988 Instrumental Composition Grammy for *The Theme from L.A. Law.*

POULTON, GEORGE R. (c. 1830–1867)
Composer. With lyricist William W. Fosdick* (1825–1862) wrote "Aura Lea" 1861. "Love Me Tender" by Vera Matson &

Elvis Presley* is based on the tune "Aura Lea." Poulton died in Lansingburg, NY.

POWELL, EARL "BUD" (1924–1966)

b. New York, NY. Pianist with Cootie Williams's* band 1943/44, later with Dizzy Gillespie,* Sid Catlett, & others, in France 1959/64. Albums *Amazing Bud Powell Vol. 1 & 2, Jazz Giants,* etc. Suffered with tuberculosis & died in Brooklyn, NY City.

POWELL, EVERARD S., JR. (1907–1976)

b. New York, NY. Clarinetist/saxist with Fats Waller,* Cab Calloway,* & others in 1950s, later with Ray Charles.* Died 10/31 in NY City.

POWELL, JANE (1928–)

b. Suzanne Burce 4/1 Portland, OR. Singer/actress, in many musicals including *Seven Brides for Seven Brothers* 1954.

POWELL, TEDDY (1906–)

b. Alfred Paolella 3/1 Oakland, CA. Guitarist, with Abe Lyman's band 1927/38 then led own bands in New Jersey, NY City, Chicago, Miami, etc.

POWNALL, MRS. MARY ANN (1751–1796)

b. England. Actress/singer, known as Mrs. Wrighten in England. Female lead in *Tammany,* in NY City 1794, the first opera composed by American James Hewitt.* Sang "Washington and Liberty" and an "Address to the Ladies" at the City Theatre in Charleston, South Carolina on February 22, 1796, then died.

PRAIRIE OYSTER

Toronto country/rock band with singer/leader Russell de Carle, guitarist/vocalist Keith Glass, albums *Different Kind of Fire* 1990, *Everybody Knows* 1992.

PRATT, AWADAGIN (1966–)

From Normal, IL. Pianist, first black concert pianist to win the Naumburg Competition at Avery Fisher Hall, Lincoln Center, NY City in May 1992. He then toured the U.S.

PRATT, CHARLES E. (1841–1902)
b. Hartford, CT. Songwriter, wrote "Bring Back My Bonnie to Me, or My Bonnie Lies Over the Ocean" 1882.

PRAY FOR RAIN
Gospel singers won 1993 Grammy for *Pray for Rain.*

PRESERVATION HALL BAND
With cornetist/vocalist/leader DeDe Pierce,* his wife pianist/singer Billie Pierce,* clarinetist Willie Humphrey, & trombonist Jim Robinson* as of 1973. Later with Willie Humphrey & his brother trumpeter Percy Humphrey, pianist/vocalist Sting Miller, banjo/vocalist Marvin Kimball & trombonist Frank Demond played at Avery Fisher Hall in NY City 1979. At this time there were four different Preservation Hall Bands from New Orleans touring the U.S. Albums *Best of the Preservation Hall Jazz Band, New Orleans Vols. 1 to 4.*

PRESLEY, ELVIS ARON (1935–1977)
b. 1/8 Tupelo, MS. Rock 'n Roll idol, guitarist/singer. Raised in Memphis, TN, appeared on *Louisiana Hayride,* Shreveport, LA. 1954, served in US Army in Germany 1958/60, acted/sang in numerous films. Hits "Hound Dog," "Blue Suede Shoes," "Love Me Tender," "Heartbreak Hotel," "All Shook Up," "Jailhouse Rock." Had 110 gold and platinum records which sold over 100 million copies. Died 8/16 in Memphis, TN apparently from an overdose of drugs (unconfirmed). Left his widow Priscilla and a daughter Lisa Marie. A postage stamp was issued in his honor in January 1993.

PRESS, WOLFGANG
Hit rock track *A Girl Like You* 1992.

PRESTON, WILLIAM E. "BILLY" (1946–)
b. 9/9 Houston, TX. Organist/singer/composer, hits "Space Race" 1974, "You are So Beautiful" 1975, "With You I'm Born Again" 1979, album *Best of Billy Preston.*

PRETENDERS, THE
Rock group founded 1978 by Christine Elaine "Crissie" Hynde* singer/songwriter & James "Jimmy" Honeyman-Scott (1956–1982), Martin Chambers, Peter Farndon, Malcolm Foster, Robbie McIntosh, hit album *Learning to Crawl, Get Close, Packed, Pretenders,* video *Singles.* Group with U-2 Top Ten grossing Concerts at Los Angeles Coliseum 1988.

PREVIN, ANDRE (1929–   )
b. 4/6 Berlin, Germany. Pianist/conductor, brought to Los Angeles 1938, wrote compositions for the piano, etc. Conducted Pittsburgh Symphony, albums *Uptown, Old Friends.* In concert with Fredericka von Stade* at Carnegie Hall, NY City in December 1991. Married Dory Langdon,* lived with actress Mia Farrow.

PREVIN, DORY LANGDON (1925–   )
b. 10/22 Rahway, NJ. Singer/songwriter, married Andre Previn.* Wrote "Pepe" with music by her husband.

PRICE, JESS (1910–1974)
b. Memphis, TN. Drummer/vocalist, with Count Basie,* Ida Cox,* Louis Armstrong,* & others in 1930s/40s, then led own bands, at Monterey Jazz Festival in CA 1971. Died of cancer.

PRICE, KENNY (1931–1987)
b. 5/27 Florence, KY. Guitarist/singer, served in Korean War, started with radio station WLW in Cincinnati 1954, hits "Walking on New Grass," "Pretty Girl," "Pretty Clothes, Pretty Sad."

PRICE, LEONTYNE (1927–   )
b. 2/10 Laurel, MS. Soprano, debut in *Four Saints in Three Acts* 1952, sang in *Porgy and Bess,* with San Francisco Opera & Metropolitan in NY City after 1961. Albums *A Christmas Offering, Puccini, Arias (Heroines).*

PRICE, LLOYD (1932–   )
b. New Orleans, LA. Singer, hit single "Stagger Lee," albums *Greatest Hits, Lawdy, Lloyd Price.*

PRICE, RAY (1926–)
b. 1/26 Perryville, TX. Singer/songwriter, hit "Crazy Arms." Albums *Essential Ray Price, Happens to be the Best*, etc.

PRICE, SAMMY (1908–1992)
b. Honey Grove, TX. Pianist, "King of Boogie Woogie," played in NY City & toured, led the **Bluesicians** in Europe 1955/56, toured Europe again 1969. Album **Rib Joint.**

PRICE, STEVE
Musician/singer, hit "Love Will Find a Way" 1978.

PRICE, TONI
Female singer from Philadelphia, PA. Album *Swim Away* 1993.

PRIDE, CHARLEY (1938–)
b. 3/18 Sledge, MS. Guitarist/singer, first black star of country music, hit "Kiss an Angel Good Morning." Won Country Music Male Vocalist of Year & Entertainer of Year 1971, won Grammy 1972. Albums *Best of Charley Pride, Christmas in My Home Town, Greatest Hits.*

PRIEST, MAXI
Reggae singer, albums *Best of Me, Bona Fide*. With Shabba Ranks* on hit "House Call" 1992.

PRIMA, LOUIS (1912–1978)
b. 12/7 New Orleans, LA. Jazz trumpeter/composer, led own bands in New Orleans in 1920s, various bands in 1930s/60s. With wife Keely Smith* (later divorced) had hit "That Old Black Magic." Composed "Sing, Sing, Sing" 1936, "Robin Hood" 1944, "A Sunday Kind of Love" 1948. Albums *Louis Prima, Zooma*, etc.

PRIMROSE QUARTET
Singer William Primrose (1904–1982) b. Glasgow, Scotland, formed his quartet in 1978. Lived in US & died in Provo, Utah.

PRIMUS
California Bay area trash/funk trio with singer/bassist Les Clay-pool, Tim Alexander, & Larry Lalonde, albums *Frizzle Fry, Sailing the Seas of Cheese, Suck on This,* on Lollapalooza '93 Tour.

PRINCE (1958–)
b. Prince Roger Nelson 6/7 Minneapolis, MN. Funk singer/musician/composer, won Oscar for score of film *Purple Rain* 1985, toured US 1987, *Batman* soundtrack sold over 2 million albums 1989, platinum single "Batdance" 1989, platinum video *Sign of the Times* 1989, MTV award to **Prince and the New Power Generation** for *Cream* 1992, album *Symbolism, Prince,* single hits "Money Don't Matter 2 Night" 1992 & "7" 1993. Videos *Get Off, Sexy M.F.,* toured US 1993.

PRINE, JOHN (1947–)
Singer, albums *Bruised Orange, Common Sense, John Prine, Pink Cadillac, Storm Windows, Sweet Revenge, The Missing Years* 1992.

PROCLAIMERS
Singing pop duo of twin brothers Craig and Charlie Reid (b. 1963) from Leith, Scotland. Hit "I'm Gonna Be (500 miles)" on album *Sunshine on Leith* 1989. Hit song on *Benny and Joon* film soundtrack 1993.

PROCOL HARUM
British rock group with Gary Brooker, Matthew Fisher, Robert Harrison, David Knights, Keith Reid, Ray Royer, Robin Trower, & Barry Wilson. Hit "A Whiter Shade of Pale," albums *A Salty-Dog, Broken Barricades, Chrysalis Years, Shine on Brightly,* album dedicated to Barry Wilson* who died in 1989 in Oregon—*The Prodigal Stranger* 1992.

PROCOPE, RUSSELL (1908–1981)
b. NY City. Alto/soprano saxist/clarinetist, with Jelly Roll Morton* & Chick Webb* 1929/31, with Fletcher Henderson* & others in 1930s, served in army, with Duke Ellington* 1945/74,

at Jazz Gala at Montauk, Long Island, NY in November 1980. Died 1/21.

PROFESSOR LONGHAIR
Album *Crawfish Fiesta.*

PRYSOCK, ARTHUR (1929–)
b. Spartanburg, SC. Singer, albums *Today's Love Songs, Walkman Compact Jazz.*

PSYCHEDELIC FURS
Albums *Book of Days, Forever Now, Midnight to Midnight, Mirror Moves, Psychedelic Furs, Talk, Talk, Talk.*

PUBLIC ANNOUNCEMENT
With singer R. Kelly, hit R&B single "Honey Love" 1992, album *Born Into the '90s,* 1992.

PUBLIC ENEMY
Rap group with Flavor Flav, Chuck D. (Carlton Ridenhour), James Bomb, Terminator X, Agent Attitude, Brother Mike, & Brother James. Platinum album *Fear of a Black Planet* 1990, Videos *Fight the Power-live, Tour of a Black Planet, By the Time I Get to Arizona* showed politicians being killed. *Hazy Shade of Criminal* dramatized FBI agents gunning down a black family 1992. Group added Sister Souljah,* single "Buck Whylin'." Album *Enemy Strikes Live* sold 3 million copies, won Grammy 1993 & *Greatest Misses* also won a Grammy. Flav was charged with firing a gun at a Bronx neighbor in 1993.

PUBLIC IMAGE, LTD
With bassist Jan Wobble* who later left the group. Albums *Happy, Public Image, Ltd., Second Edition.*

PUENTE, TITO (1923–)
b. 4/20 New York, NY. Conductor/leader, albums *El Rey, Goza Mi Timbal, Mambo, Diablo, Sensacion, Out of This World, Un Poco Loco.* Performed at the JVC Jazz Festival, Newport, RI in August 1992.

PULLEN, DON
Albums *Evidence of Things, Unseen, New Beginnings, Random Thoughts, The Sixth Sense, Don Pullen* 1992.

PURDIE, BERNARD (1939–)
b. 6/11 Elkton, MD. Drummer, album *Shaft* 1976.

PURE PRAIRIE LEAGUE
With bassist Michael Reilly, guitarist/singer Jeff Wilson, keyboardist Michael Connor, drummer Billy Hinds. Hit single "Let Me Love You Tonight" 1980, albums *Bustin' Out, Live-taking the Stage, Two Lane Highway.*

PURVIS, KATHERINE E.
Lyricist, with composer James M. Black* wrote "When the Saints Are Marching In" 1896, later revised by others to "When the Saints Go Marching In."

PUTNAM, CURLY (1930–)
b. Princeton, AL. Singer/songwriter, wrote "Green, Green Grass of Home." a gold record 1967.

Q

QUARTERFLASH
Rock group with Jack Charles, Rick DiGiallonardo, Rich Gooch, Mary Ross, Rindy Ross, Brian David Willis. Hit single "Harden My Heart" 1981, albums *Quarterflash, Quarterflash/Take Another.*

QUARTET, THE
Jazz quartet with Kenny Burrell,* Jimmy Smith,* Grady Tate, & Stanley Turrentine* at the Monterey Jazz Festival in California in September 1992.

QUATRO, SUZI (1950–)
b. 6/3 Detroit, MI. Singer, albums *Suzi Quatro, Greatest Hits 1980, Main Attraction* 1992.

QUEEN
British rock group with singer/musician Freddie Mercury (Frederick Bulsara 1946–1991 b. Zanzibar), John Deacon, Brian May, Roger Taylor. Hit single "Another One Bites the Dust" on the album *We are the Champions* & hit "Bohemian Rhapsody," video *The Works* 1984. Albums *A Kind of Magic, Hot Space, Innuendo Jazz, Live Killers,* etc. On Top Ten albums for *Classic Queen* in June 1992, video *Queen: Live in Budapest.* Mercury died of AIDS in November 1991 & left an estate of $15 million.

QUEEN LATIFAH (1970–)
Rapper, hits "Fly Girl" 1991, *Ladies First,* on Fox TV show *Rock the Vote* in September 1992. Albums *All Hail the Queen,* "Latifah's Had It Up 2 Here" Grammy winner 1993.

QUEENSRYCHE
Seattle, WA lyrical metal band with lead singer Geoff Tate, platinum video *Mindcrime* 1989, album *Empire* sold over 2 million copies. *Operation, Live Crime, Queensryche, Rage for Order, The Warning,* video *Building Empires* 1992.

QUESTIONAIRES, THE
Mainstream rock band with lead singer/songwriter Tom Littlefield, album *Anything Can Happen.*

QUICKSILVER MESSENGER SERVICE
Rock group with John Cipollina, Gary Duncan, Gregory Elmore, David Freiberg, Nick Hopkins, Dino Valenti. Albums *Quicksilver* 1971, *Solid Silver* 1975, *Maiden of the Cancer Moon* 1983.

QUIET RIOT
Heavy metal band with Frankie Banal, Carlos Cavazo, Kevin DuBrow, Rudy Sarzo. Debut album *Mental Health* 1983 sold over four million copies, *Condition Critical, QR, Quiet Riot III.*

R

RABBITT, EDWARD T. "EDDIE" (1941–   )
b. 11/27 Brooklyn, NY City. Singer/songwriter, hits "Kentucky Rain," "I Love a Rainy Night." Albums *Best Years of My Life, Jersey Boy, Ten Years of Greatest Hits,* etc.

RADIATORS, THE
With bassist Reggie Scanlan & his "fish–head" music on albums *Law of the Fish, Total Evaporator, Zigzagging Thru Ghostland.* At the New Orleans Jazz Heritage Festival in April/May 1993.

RAFFERTY, GERRY (1947–   )
b. 4/16 Paisley, Scotland. Guitarist/singer/composer, albums *Can I Have My Money Back?* 1971, *Stealers Wheel* 1973, *Right On Down the Line.*

RAFFI (1949–   )
Multi–platinum video *Raffi in Concert with Rise and Shine Band* 1989, *Everything Grows, Singable Songs, Very Young, Evergreen Everblue* 1992. Sang at the *Salute to Children* program at Kennedy Center in Washington, D.C. in January 1993.

RAGTIME JUG STOMPERS
Led by Dave van Ronk,* Dave Farina,* and Sam Charters.

RAINBOW
Albums *Bent Out of Shape, Blackmore's Rainbow, Difficult to Cure, Finyl Vinyl, Rainbow Rising,* etc.

RAINDOGS
With Violinist Johnny Cunningham, albums *Border Drive in Theater, Lost Souls,* with singers Bill Morrissey,* Suzanne Vega,* & others on *Inside* 1992.

RAINEY, MA (1886–1939)
b. Gertrude Melissa Nix Pridgett, Columbus, GA. Singer, married William "Pa" Rainey 1904 & toured with **Rabbit Foot**

Minstrels. Led her own **Georgia Jazz Band** in 1930s, also toured with pianist Lovie Austin.* Known as the "Mother of the Blues." Album *Ma Rainey's Black Bottom.*

RAINGER, RALPH (1901–1942)

b. New York, NY. Pianist/composer, with lyricist Leo Robin* wrote "June in January," "Thanks for the Memory" 1938. Killed in an airplane crash.

RAITT, BONNIE (1949–)

b. 11/8 Los Angeles, CA. Singer/songwriter, won 1989 Grammy for album *Nick of Time,* won 1992 Grammy for "Something to Talk About," also for *Luck of the Draw,* & three awards for "Good Man, Good Woman" with Delbert McClinton.* Sang duets with her father John Raitt at a Boston Pops Concert in May 1992.

RALPH, JAMES (1698–1762)

b. Philadelphia, PA. Librettist for the comic opera *The Fashionable Lady* produced in London 1730 and in New York City 1750, the first opera written by a native born American. Friend of Benjamin Franklin. *See also* James Hewitt.*

RAMEY, SAMUEL (1942–)

b. 3/28 Colby, KS. Basso, sang on album remake of the Broadway show *Kismet* 1992.

RAMONES, THE

With Dee Dee, Joey, Johnny, and Marky Ramone, albums *Brain Drain, Halfway to Sanity, Ramones Mania, Too Tough to Die.* Joey Ramone wrote "Censorship" 1991. Album *Mondo Bizarro* 1992, videos *Lifestyles of the Ramones, Rock & Roll High School.*

RANDALL, JAMES RYDER (1839–1908)

b. Baltimore, MD. Lyricist, wrote "Maryland, My Maryland" (became the state song of Maryland) based on the music of the German Christmas carol "Tannenbaum, O Tannenbaum" (Christmas tree). Died in Augusta, GA.

RANDOLPH, BOOTS
Country saxist/singer, albums *Country Boots, Sentimental Journey, Yakety Sax,* etc.

RANGELL, NELSON
Albums *In Every Moment, Nelson Rangell, Playing for Keeps.*

RANKIN, KENNY
Albums *After the Roses, Because of You, Inside, Silver Morning,* etc.

RANKS, NARDO
b. Gary Aloysious Henderson, singer with **Yellow Bird,*** album *Rough Nardo Ranking* 1992.

RANKS, SHABBA (1960–   )
b. Rexton Fernando Gordon in St. Ann's Parish, Jamaica. Reggae/dancehall rapper, R&B hits "Wicked in Bed" 1989, "Mr. Loverman," and with Maxi Priest* duet "Houst Call," won 1992 Grammy for album *Raw as Ever* & 1993 Reggae Album Grammy for *X-rated Naked.*

RAPHAEL
Singer won Latin pop album Grammy 1993 for *Ave Fenix.*

RAPP, DANNY (1941–1983)
b. Philadelphia, PA. Singer with **Danny and the Juniors,** hit single "At the Hop" 1957. Died 4/4 in Quartsize, PA.

RARE EARTH
Rock group with Gil Bridges, Edward Cuzman, Peter Hoorelbecke, Kenny James, Ray Monette, Mark Olson, John Persh, Rob Richards, & Michael Urso. Hit "Get Ready" 1970. Albums *Ecology, Greatest Hits Rare Classic, In Concert.*

RASBACH, OSCAR (1888–1975)
b. Dayton, KY. Pianist/composer, wrote operettas *Dawn Boy* and *Open House,* composed music for Joyce Kilmer's poem "Trees."

RASCALS, THE

Soul/rock group with singer Eddie Brigati (b. 1946 NY City), keyboardist/singer Felix C. Cavaliere (b. 1944 Pelham, NY), guitarist Gene Cornish (b. 1946 Ottawa, Canada), drummer Dino Danelli (b. 1945 NY City). Started 1965 in Garfield, NJ as Young Rascals, hits "How Can I Be Sure," "Groovin' " 1967, "Good Lovin'." Brigati & Cavaliere composed most of their songs.

RASKIN, DAVID

Composer, wrote the theme song for the film *Laura*.

RASKIN, MILTON W. (1916–1977)

b. Boston, MA. Jazz pianist with Wingy Manone* & Gene Krupa* in 1930s, with Tommy Dorsey,* Teddy Powell, & Alvino Rey in 1940s.

RASPBERRIES, THE

Pop group formed 1973 with singer/songwriter Eric Carmen,* drummer Jim A. Bonfanti, guitarist Wally C. Bryson, Michael McBride, Scott McCord, David Smalley. Hits "Never Gonna Fall in Love Again" 1975, "All By Myself" 1975, on *Capitol Collectors Series*.

RATT

Had platinum video *Ratt: The Video* 1989, *Detonator Video-action* 1991, albums *Dancing Undercover, Invasion of Privacy, Out of the Cellar, Ratt and Roll, Reach for the Sky*.

RAVEN, EDDY

Singer on 1988 Top Ten Country singles list with "I'm Gonna Get You" and "Joe Knows How to Live," album *Temporary Sanity*.

RAWLS, LOUIS A. "LOU" (1936–   )

b. 12/1 Chicago, IL. R&B singer, debut with Dick Clark at Hollywood Bowl, albums *At Last, It's Supposed to be Fun, Legendary-Best Blue Note, Stormy Monday*, video with

Duke Ellington *The Lou Rawls Show*. Sang "When you say Budweiser" at a Little League baseball game in Williamsport, PA which caused some controversy in 1992.

RAY, JOHN A. "JOHNNY" (1927–1990)
b. 1/10 Dallas, OR. Singer, hits "Cry," "The Little Cloud that Cried" 1951, "Just Walkin' in the Rain." Albums *Remember, The Best of Johnny Ray*. Charged with soliciting a man in a bar in Detroit in 1959 but was acquitted. Died 2/24.

RAYE, COLIN
b. De Queen, AK & raised in Texarkana. Country singer, album *All I Can Be* 1991, "In This Life" no. 1 in September 1992, "Love Me" written by Skip Ewing* hit in 1992, "I Want You Bad" 1993 hit, with Dolly Parton* on *Romeo* 1993. Married Connie Parker 1980, divorced 1987.

RAYLETTES
Female back-up trio for Ray Charles.*

RAZAF, ANDY (1895–1973)
b. Andreamenentania Paul Razafinkeriefo in Washington, D.C., nephew of Queen Ranavalona II of Madagascar. With Harry Brooks & composer Fats Waller* wrote "Ain't Misbehavin'," "Honeysuckle Rose," "S'posin." Died in Los Angeles, CA.

RED DEVILS
Blues singers/musicians, album *King King* 1992.

RED HOT CHILI PEPPERS
Los Angeles alternative band formed 1983 with singer Anthony Kiedis,* bassist Flea (Michael Balzary), drummer Chad Slovak, & guitarist Hillel Slovak who died in 1988 of a heroin overdose & was replaced by John Frusciante (replaced by Arik Marshall). Albums *Mother's Milk* 1989, *Blood Sugar Sex Magik* sold almost 3 million copies, *Freaky Styley, Red Hot Chili Peppers*, videos *Live, Positive Mental, Octopus*. Hits "Suck My Kiss" 1992, "Under the Bridge" Grammy 1993 & "Give It Away" Grammy 1992.

REDBONE, LEON
Jazz/blues guitarist/singer, albums *Champagne Charlie, No Regrets, From Branch to Branch, Super,* with cornetist Scott Black & bassist/saxist Vince Giordano on *Up a Lazy River* 1992.

REDDING, OTIS (1941–1967)
b. 9/9 Dawson, GA. Singer, hit "The Dock of the Bay." Albums *Dictionary of Soul, Otis Blue/Sings Soul,* etc. Videos *Pain in My Heart, The Immortal.* Killed at Lake Monona, WI when his private plane crashed. A postage stamp was issued in his honor in 1993.

REDDY, HELEN (1942–   )
b. 10/25 Melbourne, Australia. Singer/songwriter, came to US. Hit "I Am Woman" became feminist theme song, albums *Helen Reddy's Greatest Hits, Lust for Life.* Toured US in 1990.

REDMAN, DON (1900–1964)
b. Piedmont, WV. Jazz saxist/singer, with **McKinney's Cotton Pickers** & others in 1920s, recorded with Louis Armstrong* 1931, led own bands 30s/40s, album *1936–1949.*

REDMAN, JOSHUA (1969–   )
Jazz saxist with Christian McBride,* album *Wish* on top of the charts November 1993.

REDNER, LEWIS H. (1831–1908)
b. Philadelphia, PA. Organist, with lyricist Rev. Phillips Brooks* composed "O Little Town of Bethlehem" 1868.

REED, DEAN (1939–1986)
b. Denver, CO. Singer, sang "Tutti Frutti" & "Blue Suede Shoes" in Moscow and became known as the "Frank Sinatra of Russia."

REED, JERRY (1937–   )
b. Jerry Hubbard 3/20 Atlanta, GA. Singer/songwriter, hit "When You're Hot, You're Hot," albums *East Bound and Down, The Bird.*

REED, JIMMY (1925–1976)
b. Mathis James Reed 9/16 Leland, MS. Guitarist/singer/ songwriter, albums *Big Boss Blues, The Best of Jimmy Reed.*

REED, LOU (1942–   )
b. 3/2 Long Island, NY. Guitarist/singer/songwriter, with **Velvet Underground,*** hits "Walk on the Wild Side," "What's Good." Albums *Berlin 1973, Legendary Hearts, Mistrial, Transformer,* videos *A Night with Lou Reed, The New York Album Video,* on soundtrack *Until the End of the World* 1992, album *Magic and Loss* 1993.

REESE, DELLA (1932–   )
b. Delaresse Taliaferra 7/6 Detroit, MI. Singer, joined Mahalia Jackson's* troupe at age 13, toured world. Album *Mel Torme* & Della Reese in Concert* at Jubilee Auditorium, Edmonton, Canada.

REEVES, DIANNE
Albums *Dianne Reeves, I Remember, Never Too Far.*

REEVES, JIM (1923–1964)
b. 8/20 Panola County, TX. Singer, has sold over 60 million records, hits "Four Walls," "I Can't Stop Loving You," "He'll Have to Go." Albums *Twelve Songs of Christmas, Welcome to My World* issued in 1993. Killed in a plane crash.

REEVES, MARTHA (1941–   )
Singer, Martha Reeves and the Vandellas, albums *Greatest Hits, Heat Wave, Watch Out,* etc.

REG
Chicago Christian/rock band, with Wendi & Glenn Kaiser (lead singer/guitarist), founded in 1970s as the **Resurrection Band,** albums *Awaiting Your Reply & Wave,* toured US in 1990s.

REGINA, ELIS
Albums *Elis and Tom, Essa Muther, The Art of Elis Regina.*

REID, JUNIOR (1965–)
Reggae singer from Jamaica, West Indies, with **Black Uhuru*** in the 1980s, album *Long Road* 1992.

REID, MIKE
Country singer/songwriter, album *Turning for Home,* sang his own songs on album *Twilight Time* 1992.

REID AND EDMONDS
Songwriters Antonio "L.A." Reid (b. 1958) & Kenneth "Baby-face" Edmonds with Daryl Simmons, "End of the Road" Grammy winner 1993. Reid and Edmonds opened their second recording studio in Atlanta, GA called La Face Records in 1993.

REIVERS, THE
Albums *End of the Day, Pop Beloved, Translate Slowly.*

R. E. M.
With singer Michael Stipe, Mike Mills, Peter Buck, & Bill Berry. Albums *Dead Letter Office, Document, Life's Rich Pageant, Out of Time, Reckoning,* etc. Videos *Pop Screen, Succumbs, This Film is on R. E. M., Tourfilm, Drive* 1992. Won 1991 Grammy for "Losing My Religion," hit album *Out of Time* 1991. On soundtrack *Until the End of the World* & album *Automatic for the People* 1992.

REMINGTONS, THE
James Griffin (formerly with **Bread***), Richard Mainegra, & Rick Yancey, album *Blue Frontier* 1992.

REMLER, EMILY
Albums *East to West, Retrospective Vols. 1 & 2, Take Two, Transitions.*

RENAISSANCE
British group, albums *Tales of 1001 Nights Vols. 1 & 2.*

REO SPEEDWAGON
Rock group with Kevin Cronin, Neal Doughty, Alan Gratzer,

Bruce Hall, Greg Philbin, Gary Richrath, album *High Fidelity* sold over 6 million copies, hit single "Can't Fight This Feeling" 1985. Albums *Decade of Rock & Roll, Good Trouble, Nine Lives, Wheels are Turnin'*, etc. Toured US 1992/93.

REPLACEMENTS
Leader Paul Westerberg* of Minneapolis, drummer Chris Mars.* Albums *All Shook Down, Don't Tell a Soul, Let it Be, Pleased to Meet You*. Westerberg left the group, sang "Dyslexic Heart" on soundtrack *Singles* 1992.

RESTLESS HEART
With lead singer Larry Stewart, on Top Ten country singles list 1988 for "Bluest Eyes in Texas." Albums *Restless Heart, Wheels* videos *Big Dreams in a Small Town, Fast Movin' Train Video*. Stewart left the band. Album *Big Iron Horses* 1992, "When She Cries" won Grammy 1993.

RETURN TO FOREVER
Jazz group led by pianist Chick Corea* with singer Flora Purim, (later replaced by Gail Moran) & bassist Stanley Clarke* who went solo. Albums *Return to Forever, Music Magic, Romantic Warrior*, etc.

REVEL, HARRY (1905–1958)
b. London, England. Pianist/composer, came to US 1929, with lyricist Mack Gordon* wrote "Did You Ever See a Dream Walking?" 1933, "Paris in the Springtime" 1935. Died in NY City.

REVELATION ENSEMBLE
Led by James Blood Ulmer played at Moers International Jazz Festival in West Germany summer of 1980.

REVERE, PAUL (1937–)
b. 1/7, formed **Paul Revere and the Raiders** with Charlie Coe, Joe Correrro, Mark Lindsay, Freddy Weller. Albums *Here They Come, Legend of Paul Revere, Midnight Ride*.

REXFORD, EBEN E. (1841–1916)

b. Johnsburg, NY. Lyricist, with composer H.P. Danks* wrote "Silver Threads Among the Gold" 1873.

REY, ALVINO (1911–   )

b. 7/1 Oakland, CA. Electric guitarist/leader, featured on King Family TV series in 1960s.

REYES, CLAUDIO (1945–1992)

Latin singer died of a heart attack while undergoing penis enlargement. Plastic surgeon Dr. Richard Samities of Miami, FL was charged with manslaughter (*USA Today*, 3/26/93).

REYNOLDS, DEBBIE (1932–   )

b. 4/1 El Paso, TX. Singer/actress, starred in *The Unsinkable Molly Brown* 1964, *Singin' in the Rain* 1952. Album *Best of Debbie Reynolds*.

REYNOLDS, MALVINA (1900–1978)

b. San Francisco, CA. Singer/songwriter, wrote "What Have They Done to the Rain?" (popularized by Joan Baez* and Bob Dylan*) also other songs. Died 3/18 Oakland, CA.

REYNOLDS, ROGER (1934–   )

Composer, won 1989 Pulitzer prize for *Whispers Out of Time.*

RHODE, RON

Albums *Cottage, Corn Silk, Unforgettable.*

RICE, THOMAS D. "DADDY" (1808–1860)

b. NY City. Early minstrel showman/songwriter, friend of Stephen Foster.* Wrote the words to "Jim Crow," which became his lifetime hit.

RICE, TIM

Songwriter. 1994 Grammy for "A Whole New World" (*Aladdin* theme) with Alan Menken.

RICE, TONY
Albums *Backwaters, Church Street Blues, Cold on the Shoulder, Native American, Tony Rice.*

RICH, BERNARD "BUDDY" (1917–1987)
b. New York, NY. Jazz drummer/leader, with Artie Shaw* & others in 1930s, with Tommy Dorsey* 40s, Harry James & Dorsey 50s/60s, led own bands 1966/74, at Atlantic City Jazz Festival in 1980. Albums *Rags to Riches, Rich Versus Roach, Walkman Jazz, Time Being,* etc. Died 4/28 Los Angeles, CA.

RICH, CHARLES A. "CHARLIE" (1932–)
b. 12/14 Forrest City AK. Pop/country pianist/songwriter, hits "Behind Closed Doors" 1973, "The Most Beautiful Girl," albums *Greatest Hits, Pictures and Paintings* 1992.

RICHARD, ZACHARY
Albums *Mardi Gras Mambo, Woman in the Room, Zach's Bonton, Snake Bite Love.*

RICHARDS, KEITH
Guitarist with **Rolling Stones,*** solo album *Talk is Cheap* 1988, **Keith Richards & His X-Pensive Wives*** with Waddy Wachtel, Ivan Neville, Bernard Fowler, & Steven Jordan on *Main Offender* 1992.

RICHIE, LIONEL (1949–)
b. 6/20 Tuskegee, AL. Lead singer of the **Commodores,*** then went solo. Hits "All Night Long," "Hello," "Say You, Say Me," had nine number one songs in nine years, won 1984 Grammy for album *Can't Slow Down,* on video *We Are the World* 1985. R&B single "Do It to Me" 1992. Videos *All Night Long Concert, The Making of Dancing.* Had three throat operations for the removal of polyps from his vocal chords in June 1992. After 18 years of marriage divorced Brenda in 1991.

RIDDLE, NELSON (1921–1985)
b. 6/1 Oradell, NJ. Pop/jazz leader/composer/musician, with Frank Sinatra* in 1950s, won 1974 Oscar for score for *The*

Great Gatsby. Formed own bands, albums *Riddle Touch,* video *Linda Ronstadt with Nelson Riddle.*

RIDERS IN THE SKY
Albums *Best of the West, Horse Opera, Riders Radio Theater, Saddle Pals, Merry Christmas from Harmony Ranch* 1992, etc.

RIGHT SAID FRED
British trio, single "I'm Too Sexy" 1992, video release showing weight lifters sold 2.5 million copies, toured US to promote album *Up* 1992.

RIGHTEOUS BROTHERS
Duo formed in 1962 with Bobby Hatfield and Bill Medley, hits "You've Lost that Lovin' Feelin'," "Soul and Inspiration," "Unchained Melody" 1965, albums *Best of Righteous Brothers, Anthology 1962–1974,* video *Shindig Presents Righteous Brothers.*

RILEY, JEANNIE C. (1945–)
b. Jeannie C. Stephenson 10/19 Anson, TX. Pop/country singer, hit "Harper Valley PTA," album *Diamond Rio* 1992.

RIPPERTON, MINNIE (1948–1979)
b. 11/8 Chicago, Il. Singer, hits "Lovin' You" 1974. Had a five-octave voice range. Died 7/12 Los Angeles, CA.

RIPPINGTONS, THE
Albums *Curves Ahead, Kilimanjaro, Moonlighting, Tourist in Paradise, Weekend in Monaco.*

RISING SONS
Blues/country/rock singers with 1964 recordings featuring Taj Mahal* & Ry Cooder on *Rising Sun* released in 1992.

RITCHIE FAMILY, THE
Cheryl Mason Jacks, Gwendolyn Oliver, Cassandra Ann Wooten.

RITCHIE, JEAN (1922–)
b. 12/8 Viper, KY. Country singer/songwriter, youngest of four-

teen children, all singers, wrote "Let the Sun Shine on Me" and other songs. Album with Doc Watson *Live at Folk City*.

RITENOUR, LEE
Jazz guitarist, albums *Captain Fingers, Color Rit, Earth Run*, etc., *Wes Bound* (tribute to Wes Montgomery) 1993.

RITTER, W. MAURICE "TEX" (1907–1974)
b. 1/12 Murval, TX. Singer/actor. Singing cowboy in over 60 films, *High Noon* won an Oscar 1957. Album *Greatest Hits*.

RIVERS, JOHNNY (1942–)
b. 11/7 New York, NY. Singer, hit "Poor Side of Town," albums *Anthology, Best of Johnny Rivers, Good Rockin'*.

ROACH, MAXWELL "MAX" (1925–)
b. Brooklyn, NY City. Jazz drummer, with Charlie Parker* at Paris Jazz Festival 1949, led own groups 1950s/60s, composed *Freedom Now Suite* performed by his ex-wife Abbey Lincoln* 1980. Elected to *down beat* Hall of Fame 1980. Albums *Jazz in 3/4 Time, Scott Free, The Long March, 1 & 2, To the Max*.

ROACH, STEVE
Albums *Dreamtime Return, Structures from Silence, World's Edge*.

ROB BASE
Album *It Takes Two* (1988) sold over 1.7 million copies, *The Incredible Base* (1989) sold over 600,000 copies.

ROBBINS, MARTY (1925–1982)
b. Martin David Robinson 9/26 Glendale, AZ. Country/western singer, won Grammy for "El Paso" 1959. Albums *A Lifetime of Song, American Originals 1976–82, Essential, Biggest Hits*.

ROBERTS, DANIEL C. (1841–1907)
b. Bridgehampton, NY. Hymnist, with composer G.W. Warren* wrote "God of Our Fathers" 1876.

ROBERTS, LEE S. (1884–1949)
b. Oakland, CA. Composer, with lyricist J. Will Callahan* wrote "There are Smiles That Make Us Happy" 1917.

ROBERTS, MARCUS (1963–)
Pianist/composer, albums *Deep in the Shed* 1990, *Alone with Three Giants* 1991, *The Truth is Spoken Here*. Wrote 9 of 17 compositions for his album *As Serenity Approaches* 1992, played in honor of Vice President Al Gore in January 1993.

ROBESON, PAUL (1898–1976)
b. 4/9 Princeton, NJ. Bass singer/actor, sang "Ol' Man River" in *Show Boat* various times between 1928/36. Albums *American Balladeer, Essential Paul Robeson, Ballad for America*, etc.

ROBIN, LEO (1895–1984)
b. 4/6 Pittsburgh, PA. Lyricist, with composer Ralph Rainger* wrote "Thanks for the Memories" Bob Hope's* theme song, won an Oscar 1938. Also wrote "Diamonds are a Girl's Best Friend."

ROBINSON, CHRIS
Blues/raunch vocalist for the **Black Crowes,*** country/folk/rock album *Lost Together* 1992.

ROBINSON, EARL H. (1910–1991)
b. 7/2 Seattle, WA. Singer/composer, composed the music for the ballet *Bouquet for Molly* and also wrote songs.

ROBINSON, J. RUSSELL (1892–1963)
b. Indianapolis, IN. Pianist/composer, with Con Conrad* composed "Margie" 1920 with lyricist Benny Davis.*

ROBINSON, JAMES N. "BIG JIM" (1890–1976)
b. Deeringe, LA. Trombonist, with Papa Celestin & others in 1920s, own band 30s, Bunk Johnson* 40s, Octave Crosby & others in 50s, toured with Billie & Dede Pierce* in 60s, with **Preservation Hall Band*** in New Orleans in 70s.

ROBINSON, WILLIAM "SMOKEY" (1940–)
b. 2/19 Detroit. **Smokey Robinson & the Miracles** founded 1957, with Pete Moore, Claudette Rogers Robinson, Bobby Rogers, & Ronnie White. Hits "I Second that Emotion" 1965, "The Tears of a Clown" 1970, "My Girl," "Ooh Baby Baby." Albums *Love, Smokey, Quiet Storm, Double Good Everything* 1992.

ROBOTS, THE
New York City singers with Ben Nitze & Joe Mendelson plus a shifting roster of ten, disco/rap/soulful/pop album *Rise Robots Rise* 1992.

ROCHES, THE
Albums *No Trespassing, Nurds, The Roches, Speak, We Three Kings.*

ROCKETS, THE
With Donnie Backus, John "Bee" Badanjek, David Gilbert, Bobby Neil Haralson, Jim McCarty, & Dennis Robbins.

ROCKPILE
British pub/rock group 1976–81 with Billy Bremer, Dave Edmunds, Nick Lowe, & Terry Williamson. Album *Seconds of Pleasure* 1980. Lowe had single hit "Cruel to be Kind" 1978.

ROCKWELL (1964–)
b. Kennedy Gordy 3/15 Detroit, MI, son of Berry Gordy, Jr. Singer, in the chorus for Michael Jackson* hit "Somebody's Watching Me" 1984.

RODGERS, JIMMIE (1933–)
b. 9/8 Meridian, MS. Guitarist/singer/songwriter, hit "Honeycomb." Albums *Best of Jimmie Rodgers, Country Legacy, First Sessions.* A postage stamp was issued in his honor in 1978.

RODGERS, JIMMIE (1897–1933)
b. James Rodgers Snow 9/18 Camus, WA., son of Hank Snow.*

344 / Rodgers, Richard

Yodeler. Albums *Chicago Bound, Early Years, Ludella, America's Blue Yodeler, Down the Old Road, The Gambler,* etc.

RODGERS, RICHARD (1902–1979)
b. 7/28 Long Island, NY. Composer, with lyricist Lorenz Hart* wrote musicals Babes in Arms 1937 & other shows; with Oscar Hammerstein II* wrote *Oklahoma* 1943, *South Pacific* 1949, *The Sound of Music* 1959 & other shows. Albums *Richard Rodgers Songbook, Victory at Sea.*

RODRIGUEZ, JOSE LUIS
Singer won Latin Pop album Grammy 1993 for *El Puma En Ritmo.*

ROGER
On 1988 Top Ten Black Singles chart for "I Want You Man."

ROGERS, KENNETH R. "KENNY" (1938–   )
b. 8/21 Houston, TX. Country singer, hits "The Gambler," "She Believed in Me." Albums *Back Home Again, 25 Greatest Hits,* etc. *Great Video Hits.* Sang at Lincoln Memorial in January 1993.

ROGERS, MILTON M. "SHORTY" (1924–1994)
b. 4/14 Great Barrington, MA. Jazz trumpeter with Red Norvo* 1942/43, in US Army 1943/45, then with Woody Herman* & led own combos, wrote music for the London show *That Certain Girl* 1966, albums *Short Stops, Swings, Wherever the Five Winds Blow.*

ROGERS, ROBERT C. (1862–1912)
b. Buffalo, NY. Poet, with composer Ethelburt Nevin* wrote "The Rosary" 1898.

ROGERS, ROY (1912–   )
b. Leonard Slye 11/5 Cincinnati, Ohio. Singer/actor, with the **Sons of the Pioneers*** 1932/38, TV series *The Roy Rogers Show* 1951/64. Called "King of the Cowboys." With Clint Black* nominated as Country Duo for 1992. Married Dale Evans.

ROLAND, GENE (1921–1982)
b. Dallas, TX. Jazz musician, played in 8th Air Force Band with Jimmy Giuffre* in World War II, with Stan Kenton,* Woody Herman* & others 1950s/60s, led own bands in 1970s.

ROLLING STONES, THE
British rock group formed 1962 with Mick Jagger,* guitarists Keith Richards*, bassist Bill Wyman, Brian Jones (1943–1969, died from an overdose of drugs), drummer Charlie Watts. Mick Taylor (guitarist) and Ron Wood (guitarist) were later additions to the band. Jagger & Richards wrote "Satisfaction" 1965, hits "Honky Tonk Woman," "Hang Fire." Platinum album *Steel Wheels* 1989, videos *The Continuing Adventures* 1990, *25 X 5, Rewind,* etc. Taylor left the band after a short stint in the 1970's. Wyman left the group in 1993.

ROLLINS, HENRY
Hard-core rocker/front man for **Rollins Band** on Lollapalooza Tour 1991, albums *The End of Silence* 1992, *Boxed Life,* video *Talking from the Box* 1993 from his May 1992 performance in Los Angeles.

ROLLINS, THEODORE W. "SONNY" (1930–   )
b. 9/7 New York, NY. Jazz tenor saxist, won *down beat* critics' poll as New Star of Year 1957, recorded with Don Cherry* & others in 1960s, had own quartet in 70s, played in The White House for President & Mrs. Carter 1978 with **Milestone Jazzstars,** won *down beat* critics' award as Tenor Saxist of Year 1980. Video *Saxophone Colossus,* many albums, *Alternatives* 1992.

ROLLINS, WALTER E. "JACK" (1907–1973)
Lyricist, wrote the words for "Frosty the Snowman."

ROMANTICS, THE
With George "Coz" Canler, Rich Cole, Jimmy Marinos, Wally Palmer, & Mike Skill. Top Ten single "Talking in Your Sleep," gold album *In Heat* 1983, *What I Like About You, Hits.*

ROMBERG, SIGMUND (1887–1951)
b. Szegedin, Hungary. Composer of "Auf Wiederschen" 1915, "Lover Come Back to Me" 1928, "When I Grow Too Old to Dream." Wrote scores for *Maytime, The Student Prince, Desert Song, Blossom Time.* Albums *Music/Dragon, Hollywood Bowl, Student Prince.*

ROME, HAROLD JACOB (1908–   )
b. 5/27 Hartford, CT. Composed music for "Sunday in the Park," "Franklin D. Roosevelt Jones," & scores for Broadway shows.

RONETTES, THE
Veronica "Ronnie" Bennett, sister Estelle Bennett, & cousin Nedra Talley. Hit single "Be My Baby" 1963. Veronica married producer Phil Spector, divorced in 1974.

RONEY, WALLACE
Trumpeter with his brother saxist Antoine Roney & pianist Jacky Terrasson on album *Seth Air* 1992.

RONSTADT, LINDA (1946–   )
b. 7/15 Tucson, AZ. Singer, starred in *The Pirates of Penzance* 1981, hit single "You're No Good," won 1988 Mexican American Album Grammy for *Canciones de Mi Padre,* platinum albums *Cry Like a Rainstorm, Like the Wind* 1989, with Aaron Neville* won 1990 Duo Grammy for *All My Life,* videos *What's New?, With Nelson Riddle.* On *The Mambo Kings* soundtrack 1992, album *Mas Canciones* won Grammy 1993, *Frenesi* Grammy 1993.

ROOT, GEORGE F. (1820–1895)
b. Sheffield, MA. Composer known for his Civil War songs, with lyricist H.S. Washburn* wrote "The Vacant Chair" 1862, also wrote "The Battle Cry of Freedom, or Rally 'Round the Flag Boys" 1863 & "Tramp, Tramp the Boys are Marching" 1864.

ROREM, NED (1923–   )
b. Richmond, IN. Composer, won 1976 Pulitzer prize for *Air*

Music. Albums *Poems of Love and the Rain, Quaker Reader/ Crozier, Violin Concerto/Bernstein,* etc.

ROSE, VINCENT (1880–1944)
b. Palermo, Italy. Pianist/violinist/composer, came to US 1897, with John Schonberger wrote "Whispering," also composed music for "Avalon," "Blueberry Hill."

ROSENFELD, MONROE H. (1861–1918)
b. Richmond, VA. Composer, using the pen-name F. Belasco wrote "Johnny Get Your Gun" & "With All Her Faults I Love Her Still" 1888.

ROSNES, RENEE
Jazz pianist, with **Rosnes Trio** on *Without Words* 1993.

ROSS, DIANA (1944–   )
b. 3/26 Detroit, MI. Singer with the **Supremes,*** starred in *Lady Sings the Blues,* won Tony 1977. Albums *Ain't No Mountain, Diana, Force Behind the Power, Swept Away,* video *The Visions of Diana Ross.* Sang with Jose Carreras* & Placido Domingo* in Vienna on TV in December 1992, sang at the Lincoln Memorial in Washington, D.C., January 1993. Married Arne Naess.

ROSS, JEROLD "JERRY" (1926–1955)
b. New York, NY. Lyricist, with composer Richard Adler* wrote songs for *The Pajama Game* 1953 (which included "Hernando's Hideaway") and songs for *Damn Yankees* 1954.

ROSS, LANNY (1906–1988)
b. 1/19 Seattle, WA. Singer/composer.

ROSTROPOVICH, MSTISLAW (1927–   )
b. Soviet Union. Famed cellist, married opera star Galina Vishnevskaya, conductor of National Symphony Orchestra, Washington, D.C. from 1977. Album *Return to Russia.* Was conducting in Greece when informed he was honored by the J.F. Kennedy Center for the Performing Arts in 1992.

ROTH, DAVID LEE (1955–)
b. 10/10 Bloomington, IN. Lead singer with **Van Halen,*** had best selling album *Crazy from the Heat,* albums *A Little Ain't Enough, Eat 'Em and Smile, Skyscraper,* platinum video *David Lee Roth* 1990. Arrested on 4/16/93 for soliciting drugs in Greenwich Village Park, NY City, charges were later dropped.

ROTH, LILLIAN (1910–1980)
b. 12/13 Boston, MA. Singer. Died 5/12 New York, NY.

ROUSE, CHARLIE
Albums *Takin' Care of Business, Unsung Hero,* etc.

ROWAN, PETER
Albums *All on a Rainy Day, Dust Bowl Children, Peter Rowan.*

ROXETTE
Singing duo on the international Join the Joyride 1991/92 tour, album *Live-ism* 1992.

ROXY BLUE
Singers, album *Want Some?* 1992.

ROXY MUSIC
British rock group with singer/songwriter Bryan Ferry (b. 1945), Brian Eno, John Gustafson, Eddie Johnson, Andrew MacKay, Phil Manzanera, & Paul Thompson. Albums *Avalon, Country Life, Flesh & Blood, Manifesto, Siren,* etc. Video *Total Recall.* Ferry had a solo album *Let's Stick Together* 1976.

ROYAL, BILLY JOE (1942–)
Singer, hit single "Down in the Boondocks" 1965, albums *Looking Ahead, Out of the Shadows, Tell It Like It Is, The Royal Treatment, Billy Joe Royal* 1992, video *Out of the Shadows.*

ROZALLA
Singer, album *Everybody's Free* 1992.

RUBIN, VANESSA
Jazz singer, album *Pastiche* 1993.

RUBINSTEIN, ARTHUR (1887–1982)
b. 1/28 Lodz, Poland. Pianist/conductor, lived in Paris but fled to US when the German armies overran France, settled in Hollywood, CA. Albums *Piano Sonata/Van Passen, Tchaikovsky Piano Trio, Works by Schumann, The Rubinstein Collection,* etc.

RUBY, HARRY (1894–1974)
b. New York, NY. Songwriter, wrote the music for "Daddy Long Legs," "I Wanna Be Loved by You" sung by Helen Kane,* "Who's Sorry Now?", "Three Little Words," etc.

RUDE BOYS, THE
Cleveland funk/gospel quartet with Joe Little, Edward Banks, Larry Marcus, & Melvin Sephus. Albums *Rude Awakening* 1990, *Rude House* 1992.

RUFFIN, JIMMY (1939–   )
5/7 Meridian, MS. Singer, hits "What Becomes of the Broken Hearted?" 1966, "Hold on to My Love" 1980. Jimmy & David Ruffin on *Motown Superstars Vol. B.*

RUIZ, MILTON
Albums *A Moment's Notice, Doin' It Right, El Camino, Something Grand.*

RUN C&W
Rhythm & bluegrass group with Bernie Leadon formerly of the **Eagles,*** album *Into the Twang-First Century* 1993.

RUN D.M.C.
Hard core rap group with Run (Joseph Simmons), DMC (Daryl McDaniels), & Jam Master Jay (Jason Mizell), hit "Raisin' Hell." Albums *Run D.M.C.* 1984, *King of Rock* 1985, *Raisin' Hell* 1986 sold over three million copies, *Tougher than Leather* sold over 1.3 million, *Down with the King* 1993.

RUNDGREN, TODD (1948–   )
b. 6/22 Upper Darby, PA. Singer/musician, albums *A Wizard, A True Star, Anthology 1968–85, Healing, A Capella* 1992, etc.

RUSH
Canadian rock group with singer Geddy Lee, guitarist Alex Liefson, percussionist Neil Peart, John Rutsey. Albums *Power Windows* 1985, *A Farewell to Kings, Caress of Steel, Fly by Night, Presto, Rush* 1992, etc. Videos *A Show of Hands, Chronicles, Through the Camera's Eye.*

RUSH, TOM (1941–   )
b. 2/8 Portsmouth, NH. Singer/songwriter, albums *Take a Little Walk with Me, Blues, Songs, Ballads, Circle Game, The Best of Tom Rush.*

RUSHEN, PATRICE LOUISE (1954–   )
b. 9/30 Los Angeles, CA. Flutist/pianist/singer/composer, toured with Melba Liston, Abbey Lincoln,* The Sylvers,* Gerald Wilson, & others. Album *Straight from the Heart.*

RUSHING, JAMES A. "JIMMY" (1903–1972)
b. Oklahoma City, OK. Pianist/singer in Los Angeles clubs in 1920s, with Bennie Moten* 1929/35, with Count Basie* 1935/46, recorded "Boogie Woogie" 1937, had own bands in 50s/70s. Albums *The Essential, You and Me That Used to Be.*

RUSSELL, BRENDA
b. Brooklyn, NY City. Pianist/singer/songwriter, hit "Piano in the Dark" 1988, albums *Get Here, Kiss Me with the Wind* 1992, *Soul Talkin'* 1993, album *Greatest Hits* 1992 included Grammy winners "Piano in the Dark" & "So Good, So Right."

RUSSELL, CHARLES E. "PEE WEE" (1906–1969)
b. Maple Wood, MO, raised in Muskogee, OK. Clarinetist/saxist with Bix Beiderbecke,* Red Nichols,* & others in 1920s/30s, with Muggsy Spanier* & others in 40s, led own bands in 50s/60s, played at President Nixon's inaugural ball in Wash-

ington, D.C. 1969. Albums *Portrait of Pee Wee, We're in the Money.*

RUSSELL, GEORGE (1923–   )
b. Cincinnati, Ohio. Pianist/composer/leader, wrote "Concept" 1953, led own sextet 60s/70s, at Carnegie Hall in NY City 1972, conducted Italian Radio Jazz Orchestra & Swedish Radio Jazz Orchestra in Europe in 1980s. Albums *African Game, So What, Status Seekers, The Outer View.*

RUSSELL, LEON (1941–   )
b. 4/2 Lawton, OK. Singer with British group **Mad Dogs** in 1970, went solo, albums *Best of Leon Russell, Carney, Willow the Wisp,* with keyboardist Bruce Hornsby* on *Anything Can Happen* 1992, his first disc since 1981.

RYDELL, BOBBY (1942–   )
b. Robert Ridarelli 4/26 Philadelphia, PA. Singer with Paul Whiteman's* band at age nine, joined **Rocco and the Saints** 1959. Sang at the Legend of Rock 'n Roll show at the Hollywood Bowl in 1972.

RYDER, MITCH (1945–   )
b. William S. Levise, Jr. 2/26 Detroit, MI. Lead singer with **Mitch Ryder and the Detroit Wheels,** soul band, later went solo, hit "Jenny Take a Ride" 1965, album *Best of Ryder and Detroit* toured US in 1990s.

RYPDAL, TERJE
Albums *Blue with the Chasers, Singles Collections, Waves, Undisonus.*

S

SADE
Pop group with Helen Folasade Adu b. 1/16/60 Nigeria, Africa. Debut album *Diamond Life* 1984 sold over six million copies, album *Promise* was platinum 1988, *Stranger than Pride, Love Delux* 1992, *Diamond Life Video,* with bassist Paul Denman & trumpeter Rick Braun toured US 1992/93.

SADLER, BARRY (1941–)
b. Leadville, Ohio. Singer/songwriter, wrote ''The Ballad of the Green Berets'' 1966.

SAFFIRE
Blues group with pianist Ann Rabson, guitarist Gaye Todd Adegbalola, & bassist Earlene Lewis formed 1988, LP *Saffire* 1990, *Uppity Blues Woman, I Wasn't Born Yesterday, Parent Christmas* 1992, *Hot Flash* 1992.

SAGER, CAROL BAYER (1947–)
b. 3/8 New York, NY. Lyricist, married songwriter Burt Bacharach.* With composer Marvin Hamlisch* she wrote the words ''They're Playing Our Song'' 1979.

SAIGON KICK
Florida metal band with singer Matt Kramer, guitarist Jason Bieler, bass guitarist Tom De File, & drummer Phil Varone formed 1988, hit ''Love is on the Way'' 1992, second album *The Lizard.*

SAINTE-MARIE, BEVERLY ''BUFFY'' (1941–)
b. 2/20 Craven, Saskatchewan, Canada. Singer/composer. An American Indian, she has written over 300 songs, won Oscar for best song from the film *An Officer and a Gentleman* 1982, album *Coincidence* 1992.

SALERNO-SONNENBERG, NADJA
Violinist, album *Mendelssohn Concerto in E Major.*

SALT N' PEPA
Female rap group with rappers Salt (Cheryl James), Pepa (Sandy Denton), hit "Express Yourself" 1990, single "Start Me Up" in film *Stay Tuned* 1992, *Black Magic,* at Roseland, NY June 1992.

SAM AND DAVE
Pop/soul duo with Sam Moore (b. 1935 Miami, FL) & Dave Prater (b. 1937 Ocilla, GA). Hit singles "Soul Man" & "Soul Sister Brown Sugar." Albums *Best of Sam and Dave, Hold on I'm Comin.*

SAM THE SHAM AND THE PHARAOHS
Rock group with Butch Gibson, David Martin, Jerry Patterson, Domingo Samudio, & Ray Stinnet. Album *Best of Sam the Sham and the Pharaohs.*

SAMPLE, JOE
Keyboardist/pianist with **The Crusaders.*** Albums *Ashes to Ashes, Rainbow Seeker, Poles, Spellbound, Voices in the Rain.*

SANBORN, DAVID (1948–   )
b. St. Louis, MO. Funk/jazz alto saxist, won 1988 Grammy for Pop Instrumental "Close Up," hits "Bang Bang," "Upfront" Grammy winner 1993. Video *Love and Happiness,* toured West Coast US 1992.

SANCHEZ, PONCHO
Albums *Cambias, Chilli Con Soul, Fuente, La Familia, Papa Gato.*

SANDERS, PHAROAH
Albums *Karma, Moonchild, Shukuru,* etc.

SANDOVAL, ARTURO
Cuban trumpeter/composer, "I Remember Clifford" Grammy winner 1993, *Dream Come True,* wrote "Mambo Caliente" track on *The Mambo Kings* soundtrack, won Grammy 1993.

SANDS, TOMMY (1937–)
b. 8/27 Chicago, IL. Singer. Hits "Teenage Crush," "Cutie Wootie." Married Nancy Sinatra,* daughter of Frank Sinatra,* later divorced.

SANSONE, MAGGIE
Plays Dulcimer, guitar, & hammer. Albums *Mist and Stone, Sounds of the Seasons 1 & 2.*

SANTANA, CARLOS (1947–)
b. 7/20 Autlan, Mexico. Leader of rock group **Santana.** Hit "Black Magic Woman," 1988 Rock Instrumental Grammy for *Blues for Salvador,* albums *Abraxas, Amigos, Borboletta, Festival, Lotus,* video *Viva Santana,* with **Hardline** on album *Double Eclipse* 1992, "Gypsy/Grajonca" track from *Milago* won Grammy 1993.

SATRIANI, JOE
Guitarist, albums *Dreamer #11, Flying in a Blue Dream, Not of This Earth, Surfing with the Alien* 1987, *The Extremist* Grammy winner 1993.

SAUTER, EDWARD E. "EDDIE" (1914–1981)
b. 12/2 Brooklyn, NY City. Trumpeter/composer, worked with Charlie Barnet & Red Nichols* 1935/39, with Benny Goodman* 1939/44, arranger for Tommy Dorsey,* Artie Shaw* & others, with Bill Finegan formed band 1952/57, wrote music for "All the Cats Join In" from *Make Mine Music.* In Germany 1960s/70s. Died in Nyack, NY.

SAVATAGE
Albums *Gutter Ballet, Hall of the Mountain.*

SAVOY BROWN
Albums *Hellbound Train, Kings of Boogie, Live and Kicking, Shake Down,* etc.

SAWYER BROWN
Albums *Greatest Hits, Shakin, Somewhere in the Night,* etc.

SAWYER, CHARLES C. (1833–1891)
b. Mystic, CT. Lyricist, with composer Henry Tucker* wrote the Civil War song "Weeping Sad and Lonely."

SAYERS, HENRY J. (1854–1932)
b. Toronto, Ontario, Canada. Composer, wrote the words & music for "Ta-ra-ra-boom-der-e" introduced by Lottie Collins in London and in New York 1892 where it became a sensation. Died in NY City.

SCAGGS, WILLIAM R. "BOZ" (1944–   )
b. 6/8 Dallas, TX. Singer, hit "Lowdown" won 1976 Grammy, albums *Middle Man, Moments, My Time, Silk Degrees,* with others on album *Live at the Beacon* 1992.

SCALA, FRANCIS (1819–1903)
b. Italy. Composer/leader, came to USA, leader of the U.S. Marine Band 1855/71, composed "Mrs. Lincoln's Polka" which the band played in The White House for President and Mrs. Lincoln in February 1862.

SCARBOROUGH, SKIP
Singer, with Anita Baker* & Randy Holland* won 1988 Grammy for R&B song "Giving You the Best I Got."

SCARBURY, JOEY (1955–   )
b. 6/7 Ontario, CA. Hit "Believe It or Not" 1981 was theme for TV show *Greatest American Hero.*

SCARTAGLEN
Kansas group singing Irish sons, CD *Last Night's Fun.*

SCHIFF, ANDROS (1953–   )
b. Hungary. Pianist, lives in NY City, performs with his wife violinist Yuriko Shiokawa, albums *Gimpel the Fool, Mozart Piano Works,* & piano concerts on *Bach, Brahms, Mozart,* 1992.

SCHLITZ, DON
Songwriter with Mary-Chapin Carpenter* wrote "I Fell Lucky," Grammy winner 1993.

SCHULLER, GUNTHER (1925–)
b. 11/22 New York, NY. First horn with Cincinnati Symphony 1943/45, later with Metropolitan Opera in NY, president of New England Conservatory of Music from 1967, formed New England Conservatory Jazz Repertory Orchestra, album *Jumpin in the Future.*

SCHUMAN, WILLIAM HOWARD (1910–1992)
b. New York, NY. Violinist/composer, his *Symphony No. 3* was introduced by the Boston Symphony under Koussevitsky 1941, won Pulitzer Prize 1943 for his *Secular Cantata No. 2, American Festival Overture,* ballet *Undertow* 1945, *Symphony No. 6* performed by Dallas Symphony 1949. Died 2/15 New York City.

SCHUUR, DIANE
Blind jazz singer, sang at the Jazz Aspen Festival in Colorado in June 1992, at Playboy Jazz Festival, Los Angeles. Albums *Pure Schuur, Schuur Thing, Timeless, In Tribute* 1992, video *Schuur and the Basie Orchestra.*

SCHWARTZ, ARTHUR (1900–1984)
b. 11/15 Brooklyn, NY City. Composer, with Howard Dietz* wrote over 500 songs including "Dancing in the Dark" 1931, "That's Entertainment." Died 9/3 in Kintnersville, PA.

SCHWARTZ, DAVID
Composed "*Northern Exposure* Theme" (TV show), won Grammy 1993.

SCHWARTZ, GERARD (1947–)
b. 8/19 Weehawken, NJ. Trumpeter/composer/conductor, album *Sound of Trumpet.*

SCOFIELD, JOHN (1952–)
Electric guitarist with **Spectrum**,* band included guitarist Bill Frisell*, bassist Charlie Haden,* & drummer Joey Baron. Albums *Blue Matter, Flat Out, Electric Outlet, Meant to Be, Time on My Hands, Grace Under Pressure* 1992.

SCORPIONS, THE
Rock group formed 1971 with Francis Buchholz, Matthias Jabs, Klaus Meine, Herman Rarebell, Rudolph Schenker. Toured US 1979/80, with **Van Halen*** & others on 1988 Top Ten Grossing Concerts list, East Troy, WI. Albums *Animal Magnetism, Blackout, Crazy World, In France, Virgin Killa,* videos *First Song, To Russia with Love.*

SCOTT, HAZEL D. (1920–1981)
b. 6/11 Port of Spain, Trinidad, West Indies. Pianist/singer in New York night clubs from 1940s, had her own trio at St. Regis & Sheraton Hotels. Married Adam Clayton Powell, Jr. in 1945. Died 10/2 in New York of cancer of the pancreas.

SCOTT, LITTLE JIMMY
Tenor, with his trio on *All the Way* Grammy winner 1993.

SCOTT, TOM (1948–)
b. Los Angeles, CA. Saxist, formerly with pop/rock group **Express,** albums *Blow it Out, Desire, Streamlines, Them Changes.* In 1992 formed jazz group with trumpeter Randy Brecker,* tenor saxist Pete Christlieb, trombonist George Bohanon, pianist Kenny Kirkland, drummer Will Kennedy, & percussionist Mike Fisher on album *Born Again* 1992.

SCOTTO, RENATA (1935–)
b. 2/24 Savona, Italy. Opera singer, video *Prima Donna-Tokyo.*

SCREAM
Lead singer John Corabi left the group to join **Motley Crüe.***

SCREAMING SIRENS
West Coast all-female cowpunk outfit led by Rosie Flores* in 1970s, she went solo in 90s.

SCREAMING TREES
Seattle group, albums *Invisible Lantern, Uncle Anesthesia,* hits "Sweet Oblivion" & "Nearly Lost You" 1992, their songs on film soundtrack *Singles* 1992, with **Soul Asylum*** & **Spin Doctors*** toured US in 1993.

SCRUGGS, EARL (1924–)
b. 1/6 Flint Hill, NC. Guitarist/singer/songwriter, with **Flatt & Scruggs***, hits "Cabin in the Sky," "Petticoat Junction," won Grammy 1969 for "Foggy Mountain Breakdown," with the **Bluegrass Boys,** Joan Baez,* Bob Dylan,* & others on album *Scruggs: A Festival of Music* 1972.

SCULL, GUY H. (1876–1920)
b. Boston, MA. Composer. Before graduating from Harvard College in 1898, composed music for Kipling's poem "Gentlemen Rankers" with music Tod B. Galloway adapted, and Meade Minnigerade & George S. Pomeroy wrote Yale's "The Whiffenpoof Song" in 1909.

SEALS, DAN
R&B singer, albums *Greatest Hits, On Arrival, The Best of Dan Seals, Walking on Wire* 1992.

SEALS, SON
Blues singer, albums *Living in the Danger Zone, Midnight Sob, Lonesome Christmas* 1992.

SEALS and CROFTS
Dash Crofts (b. 1940 Cisco, TX), singer/songwriter & Jim Seals (b. 1942 Sidney, TX), hit singles "Hummingbird" & "I'll Play for You," video *Seals and Crofts Live* 1981.

SEARS, EDMUND H. (1810–1878)
b. Berkshire County, MA. Hymnist, with composer R.S. Willis*
wrote "It Came Upon a Midnight Clear" 1857.

SEBASTIAN, JOHN (1944–   )
b. 3/17 Singer, album *The Best of John Sebastian.*

SECADA, JON (1963–   )
b. Cuba, resides in Miami, FL. Singer, on top singles "Just
Another Day," album *Jon Secada* sold 1.1 million copies,
Latin Pop Album Grammy for *Otro Dia Mas Sin Verte,* sang at
Lincoln Memorial in Washington, D.C. January 1993.

2ND 11 NONE
Album *2nd 11 None* 1991 sold over 400,000 copies.

SECUNDA, SHOLOM (1894–1974)
b. Alexandria, Russia. Composer, came to US, with lyricists
Sammy Cahn* & Saul Chaplin* wrote "Bei Mir bist Du
schon" 1933, popularized by the Andrews Sisters.*

SEDAKA, NEIL (1939–   )
b. 3/13 Brooklyn, NY City. Singer/songwriter, wrote "Breaking
Up is Hard to Do" 1960, with Howard Greenfield*, "Love will
Keep Us Together" 1975, albums *My Friend, Rave Sedaka,*
video *In Concert.*

SEEGER, PETER "PETE" (1919–   )
b. 5/3 New York, NY. Banjoist/singer/songwriter, founded **Alma-
nac Singers** 1940, served in World War II, organized **The
Weavers*** 1949, wrote "Kisses Sweeter than Wine," "Where
Have All the Flowers Gone?". With Lee Hays* wrote "If I Had
a Hammer." Albums *Carnegie Hall Concert, Essential Pete
Seeger,* etc., sang "This Land is Your Land" on album *Ben and
Jerry's Newport Folk Festival 1989/90* issued 1992. Received
Lifetime Grammy Award in February 1993.

SEELY, JEANNIE (1940–   )
b. 7/16 & raised in Titusville, PA. Country singer celebrated her

25th anniversary on radio & television with Grand Ole Opry in Nashville in September 1992.

SEGER, BOB (1945–   )

b. 5/6 Ann Arbor, MI. Singer/musician with **The Silver Bullet Band,** had triple platinum albums *Stranger in Town* 1978, *Against the Wind* 1980. Albums *Beautiful Laser, Like A Rock, The Fire Inside,* etc. His "Old Time Rock n Roll" hit the top of the 40 Jukebox Singles of All Time (updated in 1992). Won Male Vocalist Grammy 1993.

SELDOM SCENE, THE

Scene 20-20th Anniversary Concert Grammy winner 1993.

SEMBELLO, MICHAEL (1956–   )

b. Philadelphia, PA. Singer/guitarist. Guitarist for Stevie Wonder* 1973/79, had hit single "Maniac" from film *Flashdance* 1983.

SEVERINSEN, CARL H. "DOC" (1927–   )

b. 7/7 Arlington, OR. Band leader, led *Tonight Show* orchestra 1967/92, Albums *Doc Severinsen, Facets, Once More . . . With Feeling,* & *Unforgettably Doc* 1992. Toured with his band 1992/93.

SEX PISTOLS

British rock group formed 1978 with Paul Cook, Steve Jones, Johnny Rotten, Sid Vicious,* albums *Live at Chelmsford, Never Mind the Bollocks,* videos *U.K./D.K.* 1985, *The Great Rock and Roll Swindle.*

SEXTANTS, THE

San Francisco pop/rock quartet from Las Cruces, NM with singer/guitarist Brennan Hester, singer/bassist Lori Hester Arthur, singer/guitarist Max Butler, & drummer Matt Boudreaux. Debut album *Lucky You.*

SHA NA NA

Rock group with Lenny Baker, John "Bowser" Bauman, Johnny Contrado, "Dennis" Frederick Greene, "Jocko" John, Dan

McBride, "Chico" Dave Ryan, Tony Santini, "Screamin'" Scott Simon & Donald York, performed at Woodstock Festival in NY State 1969, hit single "Shannon" 1976, albums *Rock 'n' Roll Revival, Remember Then.*

SHADOWFAX
Group won 1988 New Age Grammy "Folksongs for a Nuclear Village," albums *Dreams of Children, Shadowfax, Too Far the Whisper, Watercourse Way.* Album *Esperanto* won Grammy 1993.

SHAI
A cappella singers from Howard University in Washington, D.C., Darnell van Rensalier, Carl "Groove" Martin, Garfield Bright, & Marc Gay, hit "If I Ever Fall in Love" & album of same name 1992, R&B single "Comforter" March 1993.

SHAKESPEARE'S SISTER
Singers, Englishwoman Siobhan Fahey & American Marcella Detroit, album *Hormonally Yours* 1992.

SHAKUR, TUPAC
Rapper/Actor. Starred in film *Poetic Justice.* Charged with shooting two off-duty police officers in Atlanta and sodomizing a woman in New York.

SHALAMAR
Rock group formed 1978 with singer Jody Watley, guitarist/singer Jeffrey Daniels & bassist/singer Howard Hewitt, hit "A Night to Remember 1982," album *Greatest Hits '76–'87.*

SHAMS, THE
Amy McMahon-Rigby, Sue Garner, & Amanda Richards, album *Quilt* 1992.

SHANICE (1974–   )
Singer, hit R&B single "Silent Prayer" 1992, album *Inner Child* 1992, "I Love Your Smile" Grammy winner 1993, "Saving Forever for You" 1993.

SHANKAR, RAVI (1920–)
b. 4/7 Benares, India. Violinist/composer, teacher for George Harrison* of the **Beatles** 1965, albums *Inside the Kremlin, Tana Mana, The Sounds of India, Spirit of India,* etc.

SHANNON, DEL (1939–)
b. Charles Westover 12/30 Grand Rapids, MI. Singer, hits "Runaway," "Two Kinds of Teardrops," albums *Little Town Flint, Rock On, Greatest Hits, The Liberty Years.*

SHANNON, JAMES ROYCE (1881–1946)
b. Adrian, MI. Composer/lyricist, wrote the words & music for "Too-ra-loo-ra-loo-ra, That's an Irish Lullaby" 1913 & wrote the words for "The Missouri Waltz" 1916, a favorite of President Harry Truman.

SHANTE, ROXANNE
Female rapper, album *Bad Sister.*

SHARP, RANDY
Singer/songwriter with singer/songwriter Karen Brooks* on album *That's Another Story* 1992.

SHAW, ARTIE (1910–)
b. Arthur Jacob Arshowsky 5/23 New York, NY. Clarinetist/leader, at age 15 played the sax in bands in Florida, etc., formed own band 1936, served in Navy 1942/44 then led own bands. Albums *Begin the Beguine, Best of the Big Bands, Jazz Collector Edition, Rare & Unreleased* 1992. Married actress Evelyn Keyes.

SHAW, ROBERT (1916–)
b. Red Bluff, CA. Founded Robert Shaw Chorale 1948, conducted Atlanta Symphony in GA from 1966, won 1988 Classical Album Grammy for *Verdi,* albums *Battle Cry of Freedom, Festival of Carols, Many Moods of Christmas.*

SHAW, WOODY (1944–1989)
b. Laurinburg, NC. Trumpeter with Kenny Clarke* & others in

Europe 1964, *down beat* readers' poll Trumpeter of Year 1979, at Atlantic City Jazz Festival in NJ, July 1980. Albums *Cassandranite, Imagination.*

SHAZZY
Female rap group with Sherry Raquel Marsh (b. 1971), debut album *Attitude, a Hip Hop Rapsody,* albums *Believe It's So* 1991, *Heartbreaker.*

SHEA, GEORGE BEVERLY (1909–)
b. 2/1 Winchester, Ontario, Canada. Gospel singer on the evangelist Billy Graham's Crusades.

SHEAR, JULES
Singer, resides in the Catskill Mountains, NY. Albums *The Eternal Return* 1985, *The Third Party* 1989, *The Great Puzzle* 1992.

SHEARING, GEORGE (1919–)
b. London, England. Pianist/composer, born blind, came to US in 1947, composed "Lullaby of Birdland" 1952, at Monterey Jazz Festival in CA 1974, Kool Jazz Festival in Orlando, FL 1982. Albums *Alone Together, Compact Jazz, Grand Piano (solo),* etc.

SHEILA E. (1958–)
b. Sheila Escovedo 12/12 San Francisco, CA. Singer/musician, worked with Prince,* hit "The Glamorous Life" 1984, albums *Sex Cymbal, Glamorous Life, Sheila E.,* video *Live Romance 1600.*

SHENANDOAH
Country singers, albums *Extra Mile, The Road Not Taken, Greatest Video Hits,* single "Rock My Baby" 1992.

SHEPP, ARCHIE (1937–)
b. Ft. Lauderdale, FL. Saxist/composer, co-led New York Contemporary Five, at Helsinki Jazz Festival 1964, with quintet in NY Town Hall, July 1980. Album *Goin' Home.*

SHEPPARD, T.G. (1944–)
b. Bill Browser 7/20 Jackson, TN. Country singer/guitarist, sang "Make My Day" with Clint Eastwood 1984. Album *All Time Greatest Hits.*

SHERIDAN, BONNIE (1945–)
Raised in Granite City, IL. Singer/actress in blues/rock duo of guitarist Delaney Bramlett & Bonnie Lynn O'Farrell in 1960s, married Bramlett. Introduced to cocaine, they separated in 1972 & divorced. She married Sammy Sheridan, leader of the Los Angeles rock band the **Bandaloo Doctors.** She acted in sitcoms. Albums *Best of Delaney & Bonnie, Genesis, On Tour with Eric Clapton.*

SHERMAN, BOBBY (1945–)
Pop singer/actor hits "Little Woman," "Easy Come, Easy Go." Lives in Encino, CA with his two sons (divorced in 1981).

SHERMAN, RICHARD M. (1928–)
b. 6/12 New York, NY. Songwriter, won Oscars for song "Chim, Chim, Cheree" and score for film *Mary Poppins* 1964.

SHIELDS, REN (1868–1913)
b. Chicago, IL. Lyricist/actor, with composer George Evans* wrote "In the Good Old Summertime" 1902.

SHIRE, DAVID (1937–)
b. 7/3 Buffalo, NY. Composer, won Grammy for *Saturday Night Fever* 1978, Oscar for *Norma Rae* 1979.

SHIRELLES, THE
Rock 'n roll group with Doris Kenner Jackson, Beverly Lee, Addie "Mick" Harris McFadden, Shirley Alston Owens. Hits "Will You Love Me Tomorrow?" 1961, "Soldier Boy" 1962. They played at the Legend of Rock 'n Roll at Hollywood Bowl 1972, albums *Anthology, 16 Greatest Hits,* "Soldier Boy" on CD *The Scepter Records Story* 1992.

SHOCKED, MICHELLE
Singer, albums *Texas Campfire Tapes* 1986, *Short Sharp Shocked* 1988, *Captain Swing* 1989, *One for the Road* 1992, *Arkansas Traveler* 1993 Grammy winner, video *The Captain Swing Review*.

SHONEN KNIFE
Hit single "Let's Knife" on WFIT Playlist in March 1993.

SHOOTING STAR
Rock group formed 1977, Van McClain, Charles Waltz, Bill Guffrey, Steve Thomas, Ron Verlin, & Gary West. Albums *Touch Me Tonite, Best of Shooting Star*.

SHORE, DINAH "FANNIE" (1917–1994)
b. 3/1 Winchester, TN. Singer/actress, married to actor George Montgomery 1943/62, won ten Emmys for TV shows, albums *Greatest Hits, 16 Most Requested Songs,* famous for the *Dinah Shore Show* on TV 1972/90s. Died 2/24 Beverly Hills, CA.

SHORT, BOBBY (1926–   )
b. Robert Waltrip 9/15 Danville, IL. Pianist/singer, entertained in The White House for President & Mrs. Reagan & Prince Charles of England in May 1981. Video *At the Cafe Carlyle*.

SHORTER, WAYNE
Rocker with **Weather Report.** * Albums *Native Dancer, Phantom Navigator, Speak No Evil, Super Nova,* etc.

SHRIEKBACK
Jazzy/pop album *Big Night Music* 1992.

SHUTTA, ETHEL (1896–1976)
b. New York, NY. Singer, debut at Madison Square Garden at age five doing the cakewalk & singing "Won't You Come Home, Bill Bailey?." Sang & danced in the Ziegfeld Follies. Married bandleader George Olsen, later divorced. Died 2/5 NY City.

SIBERRY, JANE

Albums *Bound by Beauty, No Borders Here, The Speakless Sky, The Walking.*

SICK OF IT ALL

New York rock group with singer Lou Koller, albums *Blood, Sweat and No Tears* 1989, *Just Look Around* 1993, toured US, Japan & Europe.

SIDDONS, ANNE (ca. 1757–d. after 1795)

b. Ann Julia Kemble in England, sister of the great English actress Sarah Kemble Siddons. Her husbands were named Curtis & Hatton, but she called herself Anne Siddons. Came to New York in 1793, with composer James Hewitt* wrote the libretto for the American opera, *Tammany, or the Indian Chief* produced in NY City on March 3, 1794. Mrs. Pownall* had the female lead.

SIEGEL-SCHWALL BAND

Albums *Best of Siegel-Schwall, Where We Walked* 1966–70, *Reunion Concert.*

SILK

Male quintet singers, debut album *Lose Control* 1992, hit R&B single "Freak Me" 1993.

SILLS, BEVERLY (1929–   )

b. Belle Silverman 5/25 Brooklyn, NY City. Coloratura soprano, many years with New York City Opera, won two Emmys & Medal of Freedom 1980. Made her farewell appearance at the opera 10/27/80. Album *The Art of Beverly Sills.*

SILVER BULLET BAND

See BOB SEGER.*

SILVER, FRANK (1896–1960)

b. Boston. Songwriter, with Irving Cohn (Conn)* wrote, "Yes, We Have No Bananas" 1923.

SILVER, HORACE (1928–)

b. 9/28 Norwalk, CT. Jazz pianist/composer, hit compositions "Doodlin'" & "Sister Sadie" in 1950s hard bop. Led a quintet for over 30 years. Albums *Horace Silver & the Jazz Messengers, Songs for My Father, The Best of Horace Silver.*

SILVERS, LOUIS (1889–1954)

b. New York, NY. Pianist/composer, with lyricist Buddy de Sylva* wrote "April Showers."

SIMON, CARLY (1945–)

b. 6/25 New York, NY. Singer/songwriter, hits "Anticipation" 1972, "Nobody Does It Better" 1977 in "James Bond" film, "You're So Vain." Albums *Coming Around Again, My Romance, No Secrets, Torch,* etc. Composed an opera for children *Romulus Hunt* performed at Lincoln Center, NY City, in February 1993.

SIMON, PAUL (1941–)

b. 10/13 Newark, NJ. Singer/songwriter with **Simon & Garfunkel,*** pair split. Simon won 1975 Grammy for album *Still Crazy After All Those Years,* also won Grammy for *Graceland* 1987. Albums *Hearts & Bones, Live Rhythm,* videos, *Concert in Central Park,* etc. Married to Carrie Fisher, divorced, took his third wife Edie Brickell, aged 25, lead singer of New Bohemians,* in June 1992.

SIMON AND GARFUNKEL

Paul Simon* & Arthur "Art" Garfunkel* folk/rock duo, hits "The Sounds of Silence," "Mrs. Robinson" in film *The Graduate* won 1968 Grammy, "Bridge Over Troubled Waters" won 1970 Grammy for song & album. Albums *Bookends, Concert in Central Park, Wednesday Morning 3AM,* etc. Reunited for a benefit for homeless kids in Los Angeles in March 1993.

SIMONE, NINA (1933–)

b. Eunice Wayman 2/21/ Tryon, NC. Pianist/singer/songwriter, played in Atlantic City, NJ night spots in 1954, led own groups in 1970s, played and sang "Let It Be, Let It Be" on Public TV with Boston Pops in September 1992.

SIMPLE MINDS
British rock group formed 1977, albums *In the City of Light, New Gold Dream, Once Upon a Time, Real Life, Sparkle in the Rain.*

SIMPLY RED
British punk rock group started in 1984 with lead singer Mick Hucknall, albums *A New Flame, Men and Women, Picture Book Stars* 1992.

SIMS, ZOOT (1925–1985)
b. John Haley 10/29 Inglewood, CA. Jazz saxist/clarinetist with Woody Herman* & Benny Goodman* late 1940s/50s, toured Europe with Jazz at the Philharmonic 1967, toured Europe & Australia with Goodman 1973, played for President & Mrs. Reagan on The White House lawn in September 1981. Albums *Passion Flower, The Brother with Stan Getz, The Swinger,* etc.

SINATRA, FRANCIS "FRANK" (1915–   )
b. 12/12 Hoboken, NJ. Singer/actor, called "Ol' Blue Eyes" & "Chairman of the Board." Started with Major Bowes, then Harry James,* Tom Dorsey,* & Benny Goodman.* Won Oscar for *From Here to Eternity* 1953 & appeared in other films, won 1959 Grammy for "Come Dance With Me," Grammys 1965 for "September of My Years," 1966 for "Strangers in the Night" & album *A Man and His Music.* Dozens of albums, videos *A Man and His Music* & *Ol' Blue Eyes is Back.* Married Nancy Barbato & had one son & two daughters, then actress Ava Gardner, then actress Mia Farrow, divorced. Presently married to Barbara [Marx] Sinatra.

SINATRA, NANCY (1940–   )
b. 6/8 Jersey City, NJ. Singer, daughter of Frank Sinatra,* recorded "Something Stupid" with her father 1969, "You Only Live Twice" in "James Bond" film, albums *Boots-Greatest Hits, The Hit Years.*

SINCLAIR, JOHN LANG (1880–1947)
b. Boerne, Texas. Lyricist, based on the old tune "I've Been Working On the Railroad" wrote "The Eyes of Texas are Upon You" 1903.

SINGLETON, ARTHUR J. "ZUTTY" (1898–1975)
b. 3/14 Bunkie, LA. Jazz drummer at Rosebud Theater in New Orleans 1915, served in US Navy in World War I, then with Papa Celestin, Fate Marable,* & others. Led own combos in 40s/60s. Married pianist Marge Creath, sister of Charlie Creath. Suffered a stroke and died 7/14 in New York City.

SIOUXSIE AND THE BANSHEES
Rock group formed 1976 with Siouxsie Sioux, Steve Severin, Sid Vicious,* Marco Pirroni. Budgie replaced Vicious on drums. Albums *Hyaena, Peepshow, Superstition, Through the Looking Glass, Tinderbox,* etc. On Lollapalooza Tour 1991.

SIR MIX-a-LOT
Seattle based rock group, hit single "Baby Got Back" won Grammy in January 1993, album *Mack Daddy* 1992, video *Baby Got Back* showing plump posteriors was banned on MTV. Group won American Music Award rap/hip-hop artist January 1993.

SISSLE, NOBLE (1889–1975)
b. 7/10 Indianapolis, IN. Vocalist/leader/songwriter, with Eubie Blake* 1915, drum major in 369th Regimental Infantry Band in France during World War I, formed duo with Blake 1919. With Blake wrote "I'm Just Wild About Harry" 1921. Toured for USO during World War II. Died 12/17 Tampa, Florida.

SISTER PSYCHIC
Seattle trio with guitarist/singer Andy Davenhall on album *Fuel* 1992.

SISTER SLEDGE
Philadelphia rock group with Debbie, Joni, Kathy, & Kim Sledge, their hit "We Are Family" 1979 became the theme song for the Pittsburgh Pirates, world champions, 1979. Album *Heart* 1992.

SIX SHOOTER
Teenage band, 13 to 17 year olds, video *Daddy Don't Sign the Papers* 1992.

SKAGGS, RICKY (1954–)
b. 7/18 Cordell, KY. Singer/musician, won CMA award as best male newcomer vocalist of year 1982. Albums *Country Boy, Don't Cheat in Our Hometown, Family and Friends, Kentucky Thunder,* videos *Ricky Skaggs, Live in London,* "Cotton-Eyed Joe" from soundtrack *Another Country* won Grammy 1993.

SKATENIGS
Hit "Stupid People Shouldn't Breed" 1992.

SKID ROW
Group sold two million albums *Skid Row* 1989, hit single "Quicksand Jesus," album *B-Side Ourselves* 1992 with Rob Halford & Sebastian Bach singing Judas Priest's "Delivering the Goods," video *Say Can You Scream?*

SKINNY PUPPY
Albums *Mind: Perpetual Intercourse, Rabies, Too Dark Park, Vivi Sect Vi,* etc.

SLAUGHTER
Platinum album *Stick It to Ya* 1990, *Stick It Live,* video *From the Beginning,* album *The Wild Life* 1992.

SLEDGE, PERCY
Singer, albums *The Best of Percy Sledge, The Ultimate Collection,* single "When a Man Loves a Woman" on film soundtrack *The Crying Game* 1993.

SLICK, GRACE (1943–)
b. Grace Barnett Wing 10/30 Chicago, IL. Singer, joined **Jefferson Airplane*** (later Jefferson Starship) 1966, married Jerry "Skip" Johnson. Had a daughter by Paul Kantner of the **Jefferson Airplane,*** then divorced Skip. Album *Collectors Item/San Francisco.*

SLOAN
Hot Single "Smeared" on WFIT Playlist in March 1993.

SLY AND THE FAMILY STONE
Sly, Fred, & Rose Stone with Gregg Errico, Lawrence Graham, Jr., Jerry Martini, Cynthia Robinson. Graham left group 1972. Hit "Everyday People," albums *Anthology*, etc. Group inducted into Rock and Roll Hall of Fame, Los Angeles in January 1993.

SMALL FACES
British rock group formed 1965, albums *Small Faces, The Best of British Rock, There are But 4 Small Faces.*

SMALLWOOD, RICHARD
The Richard Smallwood Singers, gospel/rap/rock group with pianist/director Richard Smallwood on album *On Testimony* Grammy winnter 1993.

SMASHING PUMPKINS
Albums *Gish, Lull,* their songs are included on the film soundtrack *Singles* 1992.

SMITH, BESSIE (1895–1937)
b. Chattanooga, TN. Singer, called the "Empress of the Blues," toured with the **Rabbit Foot Minstrels, Florida Cotton Pickers,** then with her own **Liberty Belles** in 1910s. With Charlie Taylor's band in Atlantic City, NJ, toured with own band in 20s. With Benny Carter & others in 30s. While touring with the *Broadway Rastus Show* her car was struck by a truck. Taken to the Afro-American Hospital in Clarksdale, MS, she died the next day, on September 26th. Albums *1923–33, Any Woman's Blues, Complete Recordings, Nobody's Blues But Mine,* etc. A postage stamp was issued in her honor in 1994.

SMITH, CLADYS "JABBO" (1908–1991)
b. Clexton, GA. Jazz trumpeter, with Claude Hopkins, then led his own combos. With Wild Bill Davidson* in Highlights of Jazz Concert at New York University in April 1980.

SMITH, CLARENCE "PINETOP" (1904–1929)
b. Troy, AL. Pianist/singer, accompanist for Ma & Pa Rainey* in 1920s, became famous for his composition "Pine Top's Boogie Woogie." Struck by a stray bullet in the Masonic Hall on New Orleans Street in Chicago during a fracas & died on March 14th.

SMITH, CONNIE (1941–)
b. 8/14 Elkhart, IN. Country singer started in 1963, album *Best of Connie Smith*. Honored at a country music event in September 1992.

SMITH, HARRY B. (1860–1936)
b. Buffalo, NY. Lyricist, with composer Victor Herbert* wrote "I Love Thee, I Adore Thee" 1897 & "Gypsy Love Song" 1898. With composer Ted Snyder* "The Sheik of Araby 1921." Died in Atlantic City, NJ.

SMITH, JIMMIE (1926–)
b. 12/8 Norristown, PA. Albums *Best of Jimmy Smith, Midnight Special, Off the Top, Plays the Blues, Prayer Meetin'*, etc.

SMITH, KATHRYN E. "KATE" (1909–1986)
b. 5/1 Greenville, VA. Singer, best known for her rendition of Irving Berlin's* "God Bless America" 1938. Recorded over 2,000 songs and had 19 number one hits. Album *The Best of Kate Smith*. Died 6/17 Raleigh, NC.

SMITH, KEELY (1932–)
b. 3/9 Norfolk, VA. Singer in Louis Prima's* band in 1950s, married Prima, later divorced. Went solo 1961.

SMITH, LONNIE LISTON
Albums *Dreams of Tomorrow, Love Goddess, Rejuvenation, Silhouettes*.

SMITH, MAYBELLE (1924–1972)
b. Jackson, TN. Singer known as "Big Maybelle," toured Europe. Elected member of the Blues Hall of Fame. In 1970 she gave up

her 27 year narcotics habit but became recurrently ill after withdrawal.

SMITH, MICHAEL W. (1958–   )

Raised in Kenova, W.Va. Gospel singer, after a bout with narcotics he was "re-born" & signed on as a songwriter/keyboardist for Amy Grant.* Albums *Big Picture, Love Stories,* hit "Place in This World" 1991.

SMITH, PATTI (1946–   )

b. 12/31 Chicago, IL. Singer/songwriter, with Bruce Springsteen* wrote & recorded "Because the Night" 1978, albums *Easter, Horses, Radio Ethiopia, Wave,* with others on *Until the End of the World* 1992.

SMITH, REX (1956–   )

b. Jacksonville, FL. Singer/actor, starred in film *Pirates of Penzance* 1980, hit single "You Take My Breath Away" 1981.

SMITH, SAMUEL F. (1808–1895)

b. Boston, MA. To the tune "God Save the King" he wrote the words for "America" 1832.

SMITH, WILLIE "THE LION" (1897–1973)

b. Goshen, NY. Jazz pianist/bassist/composer, played in clubs in Atlantic City, NJ & New York City in 1910s, in Tim Brymm's army band in World War I, wrote piano pieces "Echoes of Spring," "Sneak Away," "Cuttin' Out," "Here Comes the Band." Albums *Pork and Beans,* with Harry James on *Snooty Fruity.*

SMITH, WILLIE MAE FORD (1904–1994)

Gospel singer, known as "Martha Smith" in her early days. Starred in 1982 documentary on gospel music *Say Amen. Somebody.* Album *I'm Bound for Canaanland,* 1994. Died 2/23 in St. Louis, MO.

SMITHEREENS

Albums *Blow Up, Green Thoughts, Smithereens II.*

SMITHS, THE
British rock group formed 1982, albums *Louder than Bombs, Meat is Murder, Rank, The Smiths, Strangeways, We Have Come, The Queen is Dead,* video *The Complete Picture* 1992.

SMITHSONIAN JAZZ MASTERWORK ORCHESTRA
17-piece band plays in Washington, D.C.

SMOKEY MOUNTAIN BOYS *see* ROY ACUFF

SMYTH, PATTY
Singer, album *Never Enough,* with Don Henley* "Sometimes Love Just Isn't Enough" Grammy winner 1993.

SNAP
Platinum single "The Power" 1990, album *World Power,* single "Rhythm is a Dancer" 1993.

SNOOP DOGGY DOG
Gangsta rapper Calvin Broadus (b. 1971) album *Doggystyle* 1993. Faces murder charges for his bodyguard's alleged shooting of a California man in 1993. Performed at the American Music Awards in Los Angeles in February 1994 while on bail.

SNOW (1969–   )
b. Darren O'Brien in Canada. Rapper, hit single "Informer" 1993.

SNOW, HANK (1914–   )
b. 5/9 Liverpool, Nova Scotia. Called the "Singing Ranger," albums *All Time Greatest Hits, Collector's Series.*

SNOW, PHOEBE (1952–   )
b. Phoebe Laub 7/17 New York, NY. Singer/guitarist, with Zoot Sims* & Teddy Wilson* recorded "Harpo's Blues" 1973, sang in New York City night clubs. Albums *Best of Phoebe Snow, It Looks Like Snow, Never Letting Go, Second Childhood, Something Real,* with others on album *Live at the Beacon* 1992.

SNYDER, TED (1881–1965)
b. Freeport, IL. Composer, with lyricists H.B. Smith* & Francis Wheeler composed "The Sheik of Araby" 1921, with lyricists Bert Kalmer & Harry Ruby* wrote "Who's Sorry Now?" 1923.

SOCIAL DISTORTION
Los Angeles rock & roll foursome with guitarist Mike Ness, albums *Prison Bound, Social Distortion, Somewhere Between Heaven & Hell* 1992.

SOCIETY JAZZ BAND
Band led by English born drummer Andrew Hall in New Orleans, LA in 1980s.

SODOM
German trio, album *Tapping the Vein* 1993.

SOFT CELL
British rock group formed 1979 with Marc Almond & Dave Ball, hit single "Tainted Love" on charts for 43 weeks in 1982, album *Memorabilia.*

SON SEALS
Albums *Bad Axe, Midnight Sun.*

SONDHEIM, STEPHEN J. (1930–   )
b. 3/22 New York, NY. Songwriter, wrote lyrics for *West Side Story* 1957, *Gypsy* 1959, wrote score for *Company* a Tony winner 1971, won 1988 Grammy for show album *Into the Woods,* at Carnegie Hall in NY City, Liza Minnelli,* Glenn Close, & Patti Lu Pone sang Sondheim songs, in June 1992. Composed the music for NY show *Putting It Together* with Julie Andrews, 1993.

SONIC YOUTH
NY rock group with Lee Ranaldo, Kim Gordon, Thurston Moore, & Steve Shelley, formed 1981, albums *Confusion is Sex, Daydream Nation* 1988, *Evol. Sonic Death,* video *Geo* 1990, hit rock track *100%* 1992, "Dirty" 1992.

SONNIER, JO-EL
Country singer, albums *Cajun Life, Come on Joe, Have a Little Faith, Hello Happiness Again* 1992.

SONNY AND CHER
Salvatore "Sonny" Bono*. Actor/singer/songwriter, wrote "I Got You Babe" & "The Beat Goes On." Recorded with wife Cher,* had own TV show in early 1970s, later broke up & Cher had a successful solo career. Albums *Best of Sonny & Cher, In Case You're in Love.*

SONS OF THE PIONEERS
Country singers with Dale Evans & Roy Rogers* (b. 1912), singer/songwriter Rob Nolan (1908–1980), Pat Brady, Roy Lanham, Lloyd Perryman, Rusty Richards, & Tim Spencer. Albums *Cool Water, Empty Saddles, Songs of the Trails, Sunset on the Range, Tumbling Tumble Weeds.*

SOTTO, TITTI (1944–1992)
b. Manzanillo,Cuba. Composer, moved to NY City in 1963 & to Miami 1990. Hits "La Esquina Habanera" (a Havana Harbor), "Latino" & "La Habana Espera" (Havana Waits). Died 8/7 Miami.

SOUEZ, INA (1903–1992)
Opera soprano. After World War II joined Spike Jones'* band & warbled wearing a hat adorned with pigeons. Died in Santa Monica, CA.

SOUL ASYLUM
Minneapolis quartet with bassist Karl Meuller, punk singer Dave Pirner, Dan Murphy, & drummer Grant Young on *Grave Dancers Union* 1992, with **Screaming Trees*** & **Spin Doctors*** toured US 1993, video *Runaway Train* includes photos of actual missing children.

SOUL SHAKERS
With gospel singer/songwriter Keith E. Barrow of Chicago, IL (1954–1983).

SOUL STIRRERS
Gospel singers, *A Tribute to Sam Cooke, Resting Easy, The Original Soul Stirrers,* on *Jubilation: Great Gospel Performers Vols. 1 & 2* 1992.

SOUL II SOUL
British group, platinum album *Keep on Movin* 1989, platinum singles "Back to Life" & "Keep on Movin," Caron Wheeler on album *Just Right Volume III* 1992, *Mood* tracks won Grammy 1993.

SOULJAH, SISTER
b. Lisa Williamson, singer, debut album *360 Degrees of Power* 1992, from her song "The Hate that Hate Produced": "Souljah was not born to make white people comfortable . . . if my survival means your total destruction, then so be it." Joined **Public Enemy*** in 1992.

SOUNDGARDEN
Seattle based rock group with guitarist Kim Thayil, singer Chris Cornell, Matt Cameron, & Ben Shepherd. Hit single "Jesus Christ Pose," albums *Louder than Love, Screaming Life and Fopp, Ultramega, Badmotorfinger* 1991, video *Louder than Live,* appeared in film *Singles* 1992, toured US with **Red Hot Chili Peppers,*** "Into the Void" track from *Badmotorfinger* won Grammy 1993.

SOUNDS OF BLACKNESS
Forty-voice pop/gospel troupe choir, albums *The Evolution of Gospel, The Night Before Christmas: A Music Fantasy* 1992, on *Handel's Messiah: A Soulful Celebration,* toured US 1992, Grammy winners, sang at *The Stellar Awards Show* 1993.

SOUP DRAGONS, THE
Scottish group with guitarist Jim McCulloch, hit "Hotwired" 1992, albums *Love God, This is Our Art,* toured US in 1992.

SOUR, ROBERT B. (1905–1985)
b. 10/31 New York, NY. Lyricist, with composer John W. Green*

& lyricist Edward Heyman* co-wrote "Body and Soul" 1930. Died 3/6 New York, NY.

SOUSA, JOHN PHILIP (1854–1932)

b. Washington, D.C. Noted bandleader/composer, led U.S. Marine Corps Band 1880/92, then organized own band. His marches include "Semper Fidelis" 1888, "The Washington Post March" 1889, "El Capitan" 1896, "The Stars and Stripes Forever" 1897. Albums *Hands Across the Sea, Marches and Dances,* etc.

SOUTH, JOE (1942–   )

b. 2/28 Atlanta, GA. Singer/songwriter/musician, hit "Games People Play" won two Grammys 1969, album *Best of Joe South.*

SOUTHER-HILLMAN-FURAY BAND

Rock group with John David Souther, Chris Hillman, Richie Furay,* James Gordon,* Paul Harris, & Al Perkins.

SOUTHERN CROSS

Jacksonville, FL based blues/rock & roll group with singers/guitarists "Whitey" Bryan, bassist Jeremy Lin, Craig Hallmark, & drummer Kevin "Snake" Berry.

SOUTHERN PACIFIC

Albums *County Line, Greatest Hits, Killbilly Hill, Southern Pacific, Zumma.*

SOUTHSIDE JOHNNY (1948–   )

b. John Lyon (12/4 Neptune, NJ), singer/harmonica player of **Southside Johnny and Asbury Jukes,** rhythm & blues band with bassist/vocalist Al Berger, trumpeter Ricky Gazda, singer Kevin Kavanaugh, baritone saxist Eddie Manion, tenor saxist Carlo Novi, trumpeter Tony Palligrosi, Richie Rosenberg, guitarist Billy Rush, & drummer Kenny Pantifallo. Hit single "This Time." Their albums featured songs of Bruce Springsteen,* *Hearts of Stone, I Don't Want to Go Home, Live/Reach Up and Touch, This Time It's for Real,* etc.

SOVINE, WOODROW W. "RED" (1918–1980)
b. 7/17 Charleston, W.V. Singer/songwriter, wrote several songs, formed the **Echo Valley Boys.**

SPACE STATION
Led by Ray Mantilla featuring drummer Joe Chambers at Jazzmania* in NY City in 1980s.

SPANDAU BALLET
Formed 1979 with Tony Hadley, Gary Kemp, Martin Kemp, Steve Norman, & John Keeble, albums *Diamond, Journeys to Glory, True,* & *Parade* video *Over Britain.*

SPANIER, FRANCIS J. "MUGGSY" (1906–1967)
b. Chicago, IL. Cornetist in Chicago in 1920s, with Ted Lewis* & Ben Pollack in 30s, with Miff Mole 1944/48, with Earl Hines* in 50s, led own combos in 60s. Died in Sausalito, CA.

SPANN, OTIS (1931–1970)
b. Jackson, MS. Pianist, half-brother of Muddy Waters.* Albums *Cryin' Time, Walking Blues.*

SPARKS
California rock group formed 1974 with Russell Moel, Ron Moel, Trevor White, Ian Hampton, & Dinky Diamond. Albums *Best of Sparks, Sparks in Outer Space, Ultimate Collection,* etc.

SPEAKEASY JAZZ BABIES
Led by John Bucher & included Woody Allen's **New Orleans Ragtime & Funeral Band*** in NY City in late 1970s/80s with singer Betty Comora.

SPEAKS, OLEY (1874–1948)
b. Canal Winchester, Ohio. Baritone/composer, with words by Rudyard Kipling composed "On the Road to Mandalay" 1907, also wrote that popular World War I song "When the Boys Come Home."

SPECIAL EDITION
Jazz quartet formed by drummer Jack DeJohnette* with alto saxist Arthur Blythe, bassist Peter Warren, & saxist/flutist David Murray, albums *Special Edition* 1980, *Youngest in Charge* 1989.

SPECIAL EFX
Pop/jazz fusion with guitarist Chieli Minucci, percussionist George Jinda, & vocalist Mark Ledford, albums *Confidential, Double Feature, Global Village, Just Like Magic, Modern Manners, Special EFX, Play* 1993.

SPECTOR, PHIL
Pop singers Darlene Love and Ronnie Spector sang on the *Phil Spector Christmas Album* 1962, *Rocking Around the Christmas Tree* 1992 & Phil Spector ablum *Back to Mono* 1992.

SPECTRUM
Jazz group formed by drummer Billy Cobham* 1975 with keyboardist George Duke,* bassist Doug Rauch, & guitarist John Scofield.* Albums *It's Too Hot for Words, Opening Roll.*

SPEERS, THE
Gospel singers won 1993 Grammy for *70th Anniversary Celebration.*

SPENCER, TIM (1908–1974)
b. Webb City. MO. Singer/songwriter, with Roy Rogers* & Bob Nolan formed the **Sons of the Pioneers** 1930, later appeared in films, wrote ''Room Full of Roses.''

SPENT POETS, THE
Rock group from Northern California, album *The Spent Poets* 1992 includes songs ''The Rocks in Virginia's Dress,'' ''He's Living with His Mother Now.'' & ''Special.''

SPICE I
Gangsta rapper/deep funk vocalist describes the war between cops and ''niggas'' on album *In My Neighborhood* & violent drug dealers on ''East Bay Gangster'' on album *Spice I* 1992.

SPIN DOCTORS
Lead singer Chris Barron advocated legalization of marijuana in *High Times* April 1993, with **Screaming Trees*** & **Soul Asylum*** toured US 1993, hit album *Pocket Full of Kryptonite* 1993.

SPINAL TAP
Rock/heavy metal band with original stars Nigel Tufnel (Christopher Guest), David St. Hubbins (Michael McKean), & Derek Smalls (Harry Shearer) in fictional rockumentary *This is Spinal Tap* 1984. Now with guitarists Jeff Beck, Slash, Joe Satriani, & bassist Derek Smalls on album *Break Like the Wind* 1992.

SPINNERS, THE
Albums *Best of the Spinners, One Kind Love Affair.*

SPIRIT
Rock group formed 1967 with Randy California, Ed Cassidy, Mark Andes, Jay Ferguson, John Locke, later Larry Knight replaced Andes. Albums *12 Dreams of Dr. Sardonicus, The Best of Spirit, Time Circle.*

SPIVAK, CHARLIE (1906–1982)
b. 2/17 New Haven, CT. Trumpeter/leader with Paul Specht 1924/30, with Dorsey* Brothers & others in 1930s, then formed own band. Died of cancer 3/1 Greenville, SC.

SPIVEY, VICTORIA (1908–1976)
b. Houston, TX. Pianist/blues singer, at age 12 played piano in local theaters, directed Lloyd Hunter's Serenaders in 1930s. Played in NY City night clubs in 1960s, with Turk Murphy's* band in San Francisco in 70s. Married trumpeter Reuben Floyd, later divorced, married dancer Billy Adams. Died 10/3 NY City.

SPRINGER, MARK ALAN
Songwriter, wrote "Two Sparrows in a Hurricane" for singer Tanya Tucker* 1993.

SPRINGFIELD, DUSTY (1939–)
b. Mary Isobel Catherine O'Brien 4/16 Hampstead, England.

Country/western/soul singer settled in Memphis, TN. First recorded in 1966, hit "You Don't Have to Say You Love Me," album *Golden Hits,* sang "Silver Threads and Golden Needles" on album *Troubadours of the Folk Era, Vol. 3* issued 1992.

SPRINGFIELD, RICK (1949–   )
b. 8/23 Sydney, Australia. Singer, *Rick Springfield: Platinum Video* 1984, albums *Living in Oz, Tao, Working Class Dog.*

SPRINGSTEEN, BRUCE (1949–   )
b. 9/23 Freehold, NJ. Singer/songwriter/leader, album *Born in the USA* 1985 became most popular rock album of all time, on music video *We are the World* 1985, hit "Tunnel of Love" 1987, in 1988 on Ten Top-grossing concerts list with Sting* & others at J.F. Kennedy Stadium in Philadelphia, PA. Multiplatinum video *Anthology 1978–1988,* toured Europe, albums *Lucky Town* 1992, *Souls of the Departed, Human Touch* won Grammy 1993, laser disc includes songs "Glory Days" & "Atlantic City" 1993. Married actress Julianne Phillips, divorced, married singer Patti Scialfa 1991.

SPYRO GYRA
Founded 1978 with saxist/songwriter Jay Beckenstein, vibist Dave Samuels, keyboardist Tom Schuman, & drummer Julio Fernandez. Albums *Access All Dreams, Alternating Currents, Catching the Sun, Three Wishes* 1992, video *Graffiti.*

SQUEEZE
British rock group formed 1974 with John Bentley, Chris Difford, Julian Holland, Harry Kakoulli, Gilson Lavis, Don Snow, Glenn Tilbrook. Paul Carrack (b. 1951), original member of **Ace,** joined Squeeze in 1981. Hit album *East Side Story* 1981. Difford & Tilbrook wrote over 600 songs. Albums *Babylon and On, Cool for Cats, Frank, Play, Sweets from a Stranger,* video *1978–87.*

SQUIER, BILLY (1950–   )
b. 5/12 Wellesley, MA. Singer/guitarist, hits "Everybody Wants You" 1982, "Eye on You" 1984, albums *Creatures of Habit, Don't Say No, Emotions in Motion.*

STAFFORD, JO (1918–)
b. 11/12 Coalinga, CA. Singer, formed **Stafford Sisters Trio** with her two sisters in Hollywood 1935, then joined Tommy Dorsey,* had own radio show 1945/49, with Gordon MacRae* hit song "Whispering Hope," sang on Lawrence Welk* programs 1960s/80s, hit "You Belong to Me." Albums G.I. Joe, *Jo—Jazz'm Music of My Life.* Married Paul Weston.

STANSFIELD, LISA (1966–)
British blue-eyed soul singer, platinum album *Affection* 1989 & platinum single "All Around the World" 1990, hit album *Real Love* 1992, video *Real Life.*

STANTON, FRANK LIBBY (1857–1927)
b. Charleston, SC. Poet, with composer Ethelburt Nevin* wrote "Mighty Lak' a Rose" 1900.

STAPLE SINGERS
Gospel/rock singers originally "Pop" Roebuck Staples, Cleo, Marvis, & Pervis Staples 1960s/80s, albums *Be Attitude: Respect Yours, Chronicle, We'll Get Over.* Group at Meadowlands Theater in New Jersey in June 1992.

STARR, KAY (1924–)
b. Kathryn Stark 7/21 Dougherty, OK. Country/jazz singer, at age eleven had own radio show WRR in Dallas, at age fifteen sang on Grand Ole Opry in Nashville, TN. With Joe Venuti* and Charlie Barnett in 1940s, *Capitol Collectors Series, Greatest Hits.*

STARR, RINGO (1940–)
b. Richard Starkey 7/7 Liverpool, England. Drummer/singer with the **Beatles,** * went solo 1970, starred in **Caveman** 1981, with Paul McCartney on video *Give My Regards to Broad Street* 1984. Formed his **All-Starr Band*** with guitarist Joe Walsh, bassist Timothy B. Schmit, singer/guitarist Nils Lofgren, saxist Tim Cappello, Dave Edmunds, Todd Rundgren, singer/pianist Burton Cummings, drummer Zak Starkey (son of Ringo Starr), on album *Time Takes Time* 1992. Toured US, video *Ringo Starr and His All-Star Band—Live.*

STARSHIP
Members of Jefferson Starship with Don Baldwin, Craig Chaquico, Pete Sears, Grace Slick* & Mickey Thomas. Hit album *Knee Deep in the Hoopla* 1985, *No Protection,* video *Hoopla.*

STATLER BROTHERS, THE
Country quartet wtih brothers Don S. Reid (b. 1945) & Harold W. Reid (b. 1934) plus Philip Balsley & Lew C. DeWitt formed in 1960s, later with Jimmy Fortune. Albums *All American Country, Atlanta Blue, Christmas Card, Live—Sold Out, Maple Street Memories,* etc., won TNN Vocal Group 1992, with Randy Travis* on *The Statler Brothers Show* on TNN-TV November 1992.

STEEL EYES
Hit "Angel Eyes," toured US 1992.

STEEL PULSE
With lead singer David Hinds, albums *Earth Crisis, Handsworth Revolution, Reggae Fever, True Democracy, Victims,* reggae album *Rastafari Centennial/Live in Paris-Elysee Montmartre* 1993 Grammy winner. Eight member band played at Inaugural Parade for President Clinton in January 1993.

STEELEYE SPAN
Albums *All Around My Hat, Back in Line, Below the Salt, Now We are Six,* etc., video *20th Anniversary Celebration.*

STEELY DAN
Rock group with singer/songwriter Donald Fagen,* Jeff Baxter, Walter Becker, Danny Dias, James Hodder, & David Palmer, album *The Nightly* 1982, *Aja, Can't Buy a Thrill, Gaucho, Katy Lied, Royal Scam,* etc. Fagen had solo single "New Frontier" 1983, on NY Rock & Soul Revue album *Live at the Beacon* 1992. Group split up in 1981 but Fagan & Becker reunited for 1993 tour.

STEPPENWOLF
With George Biondo, Robert "Bobby" Cochran, Wayne Cook,

Jerry Edmonton, & John Kay, hit single "Born to be Wild," albums *16 Greatest Hits, Monster,* video *Steppenwolf* 1974.

STEPT, SAM H. "SAMMY" (1897–1964)

b. Odessa, Ukraine. Leader/composer, with lyricist Bud Green* wrote "That's My Weakness Now" 1928, with lyricists Charles Tobias* & Lew Brown* wrote "Don't Sit Under the Apple Tree With Anyone Else But Me" 1942 (popular during World War II).

STERLING, ANDREW B. (1874–1955)

b. New York, NY. Lyricist, with composer C.B. Ward* wrote "Strike Up the Band" 1900 & with composer Harry von Tilzer* wrote "Wait 'Till the Sun Shines Nellie" 1905.

STERN, ISAAC (1920–)

b. 7/21 Kreminiecz, Soviet Union. Violinist, brought to US at age three, debut with San Franciso Symphony at age eleven, toured bases in South Pacific during World War II, with Yo Yo Ma* on Top Ten Classical albums list for *Brahams: Double Concerto* 1992.

STERN, MIKE

Albums *Jigsaw, Odds or Evens, Time in Place.*

STEVENS, CAT (1948–)

b. Stephen Demetri Georgiou 7/21 London, England. Rock singer/songwriter, hit "Moon Shadow" 1971. Became a Muslim in 1981 & changed his name to Yosef Islam. *Tea for the Tillerman,* etc.

STEVENS, CONNIE (1938–)

b. Concetta Ingolia 8/8 Brooklyn, NY City. Singer/actress. With George Burns starred in the TV series *Wendy and Me* 1964/65. Album *Songs of Hank Williams.*

STEVENS, MORTON (1929–)

b. 1/30 Newark, NJ. Conductor/composer of theme songs "You're Dead" 1970 & "Hawaii 5-0" 1974, won Emmys.

STEVENS, RAY (1939–)
b. 1/24 Clarksdale, GA. Silly-song crooner albums *#1 With a Bullet, I Have Returned, Surely You Joust,* etc.

STEWART, JOHN (1939–)
b. 9/5 San Diego, CA. Guitarist/singer/songwriter, hit single "Gold" 1979, albums *Trancas* 1984, *Neon Beach/Line* 1990, etc.

STEWART, LEROY "SLAM" (1914–)
b. 9/21 Englewood, NJ. Jazz bassist/vocalist/leader, with Peanuts Holland in Buffalo, NY 1936/37, recorded "Flat Foot Floogie" with the **Spirits of Rhythm** 1939, with Benny Goodman* & others in 1940s, accompanist for pianist/singer Rose Murphy in late 50s/60s, at jazz concerts in 70s/80s. Album *Shut Yo' Mouth.*

STEWART, LISA
Singer, sang Hank Cochran's "Don't Touch Me" on her album *Lisa Stewart.*

STEWART, RODERICK D. "ROD" (1945–)
b. 1/10 Glasgow, Scotland. Singer/songwriter with **Jeff Beck* Group** 1968/69, **Faces** 69/75, then went solo. Hit single "Maggie Mae," album *Rod Stewart Live at the Los Angeles Forum* 1980, hit "Do You Think I'm Sexy?". Albums *A Night on the Town, Atlantic Crossing, Camouflage, Coast to Coast. Gasoline Alley,* etc. Video *Motown Song,* hit "Once in a Blue Moon" 1992. Inducted into Rock and Roll Hall of Fame 1994. Married model Rachel Hunter 1990 & they live in Beverly Hills, CA.

STEWART, WYNN (1934–1985)
b. 6/7 Morrisville, MO. Country/western singer/leader of **The Tourists** 1960s, hit single, "Something Pretty" 1968.

STILL, WILLIAM GRANT (1895–1978)
b. 5/11 Woodville, MO. Noted black composer, served in U.S. Navy in World War I, composed ballets & operas. In 1945

conductor Leopold Stokowski wrote: "Still is one of our greatest American composers." Still's seventh opera was *Highway No. 1 USA* 1963. Albums *Afro-Symphony, Minatures for Flute, Suite for Violin and Piano,* etc. Died 12/3 Los Angeles, CA.

STILLS, STEPHEN (1945–)
b. 1/3 Dallas, TX. Singer/songwriter/musician, with **Buffalo Springfield,*** then with **Crosby, Stills, Nash & Young.*** Albums *Manassas, Stephen Stills, Stills Alive,* etc. Sang at the Lincoln Memorial in Washington, D.C. in January 1993.

STING (1951–)
British singer Gordon Sumner (b. 10/2 Newcastle, England). "Bring On the Night" won 1987 Best Male Pop Vocal Grammy, hit "If You Love Somebody, Set Them Free," on 1988 Top Ten compact discs list for . . . *Nothing Like the Sun,* won 1991 Grammy for *Soul Cages,* albums *Dream of the Blue Turtle, Nada Como El Sol,* video *Part One.* After living together for ten years married actress Trudie Styler in August 1992. Won 1994 Grammys for "If I Ever Lose My Faith in You" (Male Pop Vocal) and *Ten Summoner's Tales* (Music Video).

STITT, EDWARD "SONNY" (1924–1982)
b. 2/2 Boston, MA. Jazz saxist, son of singer Edward H. Boatner (b. 1898 New Orleans, LA). Stitt won *Esquire* New Star award 1947, led own bands 1949/60s, at Newport Jazz Festivals in NY City in 1970s. Albums *Moonlight in Vermont, Stitt Plays Bird, With the Jazz Messengers.*

STOKES, BRYON (1886–1974)
b. Jackson, MI. Lyricist. With composer F. Dudleigh Vernor,* wrote "The Sweetheart of Sigma Chi" 1912.

STOKOWSKI, LEOPOLD (1882–1977)
b. 4/18 London, England. Conductor of Cincinnati Symphony 1909/12, Philadelphia Symphony 1912/38, later Houston Symphony.

STOLL, GEORGE (1905–1985)
b. 5/7 Minneapolis, MN. Director/composer, wrote film scores *For Me and My Gal* 1942, *Anchors Aweigh* 1945 & won an Oscar.

STOLLER, MIKE (1933–)
Composer, with Jerry Leiber* wrote "Hound Dog," "Searchin'," "Yakety Yak," & "Love Me Tender" introduced by Elvis Presley.*

STOLTZMAN, RICHARD L. (1942–)
b. 7/12 Omaha, Nebraska. Clarinetist, albums *Begin Sweet World, Romance,* etc.

STONE ALLIANCE
Jazz trio formed by tenor saxist Steven Grossman with bassist/pianist Gene Perla & percussionist Don Alias in 1975, played at Newport Jazz Festivals in NY City late 1970s/80s.

STONE, DOUG (1957–)
Baritone country singer, hits "Warning Labels," "Jukebox Without a Country Song," "Come in Out of the Pain" 1992, albums *I Thought It was You, The First Christmas, From the Heart* 1992 (after he had quadruple bypass surgery at age 35), videos *A Video Jukebox, I Thought It was You.*

STONE, SLY (1944–)
b. Sylvester Stewart 3/14 Denton, Texas. Singer, leader of **Sly and the Family Stone.***

STONE TEMPLE PILOTS
Hit single "Sex Type Thing," album *Core* 1993. American Music Pop/Rock New Artist award 1994 for "Sex Type Thing," "Plush" Hard Rock Grammy 1994, also Heavy Metal/Hard Rock award.

STOOKEY, NOEL PAUL (1937–)
b. 11/30 Baltimore, MD. Singer/songwriter with Peter Yarrow* & Mary Ellin Travers,* **Peter, Paul & Mary*** formed 1962.

STORY, LIZ
Albums *Escape of Circus Ponies, Part of Fortune, Solid Colors, Unaccountable Effect.*

STRADLIN, IZZY
Guitarist/songwriter, left **Guns N' Roses*** 1991, solo album *Izzy Stradlin and the Ju Ju Hounds* 1992. Gilby Clarke (who replaced Stradlin) broke his wrist in a motorcycle accident in April 1993, so Stradlin returned to the band for five stadium dates overseas.

STRAIT, GEORGE (1952–)
b. 5/18 Pearsall, TX. Singer, platinum video *George Strait: Live* 1989, albums *Beyond the Blue Moon, Livin' It Up, Right or Wrong, Strait Country, Ten Strait Hits, Holding My Own* 1992, in film *Pure Country* 1993.

STRAY CATS
Rock group formed 1975 with Lee Rocker, Brian Setzer, Slim Jim Phantom (Jim McDonnell), albums *Built for Speed, Rant n' Rave* 1982, *Greatest Hits,* video *Bring It Back Again.*

STRAYHORN, WILLIAM "BILLY" (1915–1967)
b. Dayton, Ohio. Pianist/songwriter, wrote "Something to Live For" 1939 recorded by Duke Ellington,* composed or arranged for Ellington: "Take the A Train," "Johnny Come Lately," "Passion Flowers," "Such Sweet Thunder," "Blood Count."

STREISAND, BARBRA (1942–)
b. 4/24 New York, NY. Singer/actress, album *Barbra Streisand* 1963 Grammy winner, won Oscar 1966 for film *Funny Girl,* albums *Color Me Barbra, Emotion, Guilty, One Voice, People,* etc. Videos *A Happening in Central Park, Color Me Barbra, My name is Barbra, One Voice.* Sang at a Clinton/Gore fund raiser in Los Angeles & at the Presidential Gala in January 1993. Performed at M & M Grand Garden, Las Vegas on New Year's Eve and Day 1994.

STRITCH, BILLY
Pianist/vocalist Billy Stritch leader of a Texas based jazz band with singer Liza Minnelli,* bassist Chip Jackson, & drummer Terry Clark* on album *Billy Stritch* 1992, teamed with Liza Minnelli on "Come Rain or Shine" & "As Long as I Live" 1992.

STROUSE, CHARLES (1928–   )
b. New York, NY. Composer, with lyricist Lee Adams wrote score for *Golden Boy,* with book by Michael Stewart score for *Bye, Bye Birdie,* for films *Bonnie & Clyde, The Night They Raided Minsky's,* score for Broadway show *Annie.*

STRUNZ AND FARAH
Acoustic guitarists Josye Strunz and Ardeshir Farah on albums *Misterious Guitanas, Americas* won Grammy 1993.

STRYPER
Christian hard rock band, had a platinum music video *Live in Japan* 1989, albums *In God We Trust, Soldiers Under Command, Yellow and Black Attack.*

STUART, MARTY
Country singer, with Travis Tritt* toured on their "Return of the No Hats" tour 1992, hit single "This One's Gonna Hurt You." Stuart was inducted into the Country Music Hall of Fame in 1992, with Travis Tritt* won Horizon Country Music award 1992 & 1993 Grammy for "The Whiskey Ain't Workin'".

STUCKY, NATHAN W. "NAT" (1934–1988)
b. 12/17 Cass County, TX. Singer/songwriter, leader of the **Corn Huskers** 1958/59, **Louisiana Hayriders** 1962/66 & **Sweet Thangs** after 1966, sang with Connie Smith. Died 6/24 Nashville, TN.

STULTS, R.M. (1861–1923)
b. Hightstown, NJ. Songwriter, wrote the words & music for "The Sweetest Story Ever Told" 1892.

STYLISTS, THE
Albums *Confessions of a Pop Group, Introducing, Singular Adventures of The Stylists.*

STYNE, JULE (1905–1994)
b. Julius K. Stein 12/31 London, England. Songwriter, came to Chicago in 1913 with his family, with Sammy Cahn* wrote "I've Heard that Song Before" 1941 introduced by Frank Sinatra,* "It's Been a Long Long Time," "Let it Snow, Let it Snow," "Five Minutes More," "Three Coins in a Fountain" 1954 which won an Oscar. Album with singer Michael Feinstein* *Sings the Jule Styne Songbook* 1992. Interviewed on ABC December 1993. Died September 20th in New York City.

STYX
Pop group founded 1963 with John Curulewski, Dennis De Young, Chuck Panozzo, John Panozzo, Tommy Shaw,* & James Young. Hit "Babe" 1979. Dennis DeYoung (b. 2/18/47 Chicago, IL) had solo hit "Desert Moon" 1984. Albums *Best of Styx, Crystal Ball, Kilroy Was Here,* etc., video *Caught in the Act–live.*

SUGAR
Tight rock group with guitarist/singer Bob Mould, bassist David Barbe, & drummer Malcolm Travis. Mould previously was with the Minneapolis pop trio *Hüsker Dü.** Album *Copper Blue* 1992.

SUKMAN, HARRY (1912–1984)
b. 12/2 Chicago, IL. Pianist/composer, hit score of *Song Without End* won an Oscar in 1960. Died on his birthday.

SULLIVAN, MAXINE (1911–1987)
b. Marietta Williams 5/13 Homestead, PA. Jazz singer with **Red Hot Peppers** in Pittsburgh in 1930s, sang with John Kirby 1938/41 & married him, later divorced. With Benny Carter's* band. Sang at Newport Jazz Festivals in NY City in 1980s. Albums *Sings Burton Lane, Songs of Burton Lane, Tribute to Andy Razaf.* Married pianist Cliff Johnson who died in 1970.

SULLIVAN, TOM (1947–)
b. 3/27 Boston, MA. Singer/songwriter, wrote "If You Could See What I Hear" 1976 made into a movie in 1982.

SUMMER, DONNA (1948–)
b. LaDonna Andrea Gaines 12/31 Boston, MA. Singer. Hits "Hot Stuff," "Bad Girls," "Last Dance," "She Works Hard for the Money," albums *Another Place, Another Time, Four Seasons of Love, I Remember Yesterday, Walk Away, etc.* Married Bruce Sudano.

SUMMERS, ANDY
Albums *Charming Snakes, The Golden Wire, Nupterious Barricades, World Gone Strange.*

SUN RA (1914–1993)
b. Herman Blount in Birmingham, AL. Pianist/keyboardist/leader, with Fletcher Henderson* in 1940s, led **Solar Arkestra** & other groups since 1956, with his **Omniverse Jet Set Arkestra** at Blue Note in Denver 1982. Album *Holiday for Soul Dance.*

SUNDAY, THE
R&B hit single "Blind" 1993.

SUPER CAT
Dancehall music group with singer Don Dada, has recorded with rapper Heavy D., album *Don Dada* 1992.

SUPER SAX
Jazz group founded by bassist Buddy Clark & saxist Med Flory in 1972 with pianist Lou Levy. Clark left group 1975, & in 1980s included Jay Migliori, Ray Redd, Lanny Morgan, Jack Nimitz, Frank Delarosa, Conte Candoli, John Dentz, Med Flory, & Lou Levy. Albums *Chasin' the Bird, Joy of Sax, Stone Bird.*

SUPERBAND
Jazz group formed by trumpeter Gerry LaFurn and drummer Charlie Persip in 1979. New 17-piece band played at Jazzmania* in NY City in 1980s.

SUPERCHUNK
Pop/rock quartet from Chapel Hill, NC with singer/guitarist Mac McCaughan, bassist Laura Ballance, guitarist Jim Wilbur, & drummer Jon Wurster founded 1989, album *No Pocky for Kitty* 1992.

SUPERSUCKERS
Garage rock album *The Smoke of Hell* 1992.

SUPERTRAMP
British rock group with Bob Benberg, Richard Davies, John A. Helliwell, Roger Hodgson, & Dougie Thompson. Albums *25th Anniversary Series, Breakfast in America, Crime of the Century, Crises? What Crises? Paris, Supertramp,* etc.

SUPREMES, THE
Detroit pop singers started 1962 with Florence Ballard (1943–1976), Cindy Birdsong, Diana Ross,* Jean Terrell, & Mary Wilson. Hits "Stop In the Name of Love," "Baby Love," first group to have five consecutive top hits on the best seller lists, albums *Floy Joy, Hits and Rare Classics, Right On,* with 36 others on *Hitsville USA: The Motown Singles Collection* 1992.

SURE!, AL B.
On 1988 Top Ten Black singles chart for "Nite and Day," album *Private Times . . . and the Whole 9, Sexy Versus, Right Now* 1992.

SURVIVOR
Rock group with Dave Bickler, Marc Droubay, Stephen Ellis, Dennis Keith Johnson, Jim Peternik, R. Gary Smith, & Frankie Sullivan. Hit "Eye of the Tiger" 1982 theme song in *Rocky III.*

SWANDER, DON (1905–   )
b. Marshaltown, Iowa. Composer, with words by his wife June Hershey,* wrote the music for "Deep in the Heart of Texas" 1941.

SWEAT, KEITH
Won 1988 Top Black single for "I Want Her," platinum album

I'll Give All of My Love to You 1990, *Keep It Comin, Make It Last Forever.*

SWEET INSPIRATIONS, THE
Love/soul/gospel quartet with Cissy Drinkard Houston (mother of singer Whitney Houston*), Myrna Smith, Sylvia Shemwell, & Estelle Brown started 1967, later back-up for Elvis Presley. Group had own string of hits 1967–71. Recent album of trio *Estelle, Myrna and Sylvia.*

SWEET, MATTHEW
Singer, garage/pop album *Girlfriend* on best seller lists for 1991.

SWEET, RACHEL (1966–   )
b. Akron, Ohio. Hit single "Baby," album *Fool Around.*

SWEETHEARTS OF THE RODEO
Country duo with singer Janis Gill, wife of guitarist Vince Gill,* & singer Kristine Arnold on albums *Buffalo Zone, One Time One Night, Sweethearts of the Rodeo, Sisters* 1992.

SWING OUT SISTER
English duo with singer Corinne Drewery & keyboardist Andy Connell, albums *It's Better to Travel* 1987, *Kaleidoscope World* 1989, hit single "Am I the Same Girl?" 1992, video *And Why Not?*

SWV
Hit R&B singles "I'm So Into You", "Weak" 1993.

SYLVERS, THE
Rock group with Charmaine, Edmund, Foster, James, Joseph, Leon and Olympia-Ann Sylver.

SYMS, SYLVIA (1919–1992)
Jazz saloon singer, hit "I could have danced all night" 1956, recorded 50 albums during her career, *Then Along Came Bill.* Following a standing ovation after a concert at the Algonquin Hotel in NY City she died of a heart attack on May 10th.

T

TABUCHI, SHOJI (ca. 1947–   )
b. Osaka, Japan. Country singer/violinist, has own very successful theater in Branson, Missouri.

TAIL GATORS
Albums *Mumbo Jumbo, Swamp Rock, Tore Up.*

TAJ MAHAL (1942–   )
b. Henry Sainte Claire Frederick Williams in NY City. Singer. Albums *Giant Step/Ole Folks at Home, Taj, Mulebone, Shake Sugaree, Shake It to the One That You Love the Best* (songs & lullabies in the black musical tradition) 1992.

TAKE 6
Soul/gospel group won 1988 Grammy for "Take 6," 1990 Soul Gospel Album Grammy for *So Much to Say, He is Christmas,* with Ben Tankard* on album *Key to Life,* "I'm Always Chasing Rainbows" track from *Glengarry Glen Ross* Grammy winner 1993.

TAKE THAT
British pop group, debut album *Take That and Party* 1993.

TALK TALK
British group, albums *Colour of Spring, It's My Life, Laughing Stock, The Party's Over,* video *Talk Talk.*

TALKING HEADS, THE
British rock group formed 1977 with leader/composer David Byrne,* Chris Franx, Jerry Harrison, Martina Weymouth. Hits "Burning Down the House" 1983, "Wild, Wild Life," "Once in a Lifetime," video *Stop Making Sense* 1985. Albums *Fear of Music, Naked, Little Creatures,* etc. David Byrne left the group & toured US in 1992. Video *Storytelling Giant.*

TANGERINE DREAM
Electronic jazz group with guitarist Edgar Froese, drummer Klaus

Schultz, and cellist Conrad Schnitzler in 1971. Schultz and Schnitzler were replaced by Peter Bauman and Chris Franke, later Froese, Franke, & Johannes Schmoelling all were on synthesizers and keyboards in San Francisco, 1980/90s. Albums *Canyon Dreams, Force Majeur, Le Parc, Phaedre, Rubycon, Rockvon* Grammy winner 1993.

TANKARD, BEN (1964–)
b. Florida. Pianist/6′ 5″/pop/jazz/gospel singer, album *Key to Life* featuring **Take 6***& the **Winans Sisters** top on Billboard Gospel Chart in October 1992.

TANNAHILL WEAVERS
Albums *Best of Tannahill Weavers '79–'89, Dancing Feet, Passage*, etc.

TASTE OF HONEY
With Janice Marie Johnson & Hazel Payne.

TATUM, ARTHUR "ART" (1910–1956)
b. Toledo, Ohio. Pianist, partially blind, accompanist for Adelaide Hall 1932/33, led trios 1940s/50s. Albums *Complete Tatum Vols. 1 & 2, Tatum Group Masterpieces Vols. 1 to 7*, etc. Suffered with uremia & died in Los Angeles on 11/5.

TAUPIN, BERNIE
Songwriter, with Elton John* wrote "Philadelphia Freedom," "I'm Still Standing," & other songs. On 11/4/92 they signed a $39 million contract with Warner-Chappell Music.

TAYLOR, ARTHUR (1929–)
Drummer/leader of the **Wailers.*** Between 1950s/80s he played on some 300 records including John Coltrane's* *Giant Steps* 1959, solo album *Mr. A. T.* 1992.

TAYLOR, CECIL PERCIVAL (1933–)
b. Long Island, NY. Jazz pianist, played in NY night spots in 1950s, at jazz festivals 70s/80s, *down beat* award as Acoustic Pianist of Year 1980, composed "Pots, Bulbs," & "Mixed." Albums *In Florescence, Jazz Advance, Unit Structures*, etc.

TAYLOR, JAMES VERNON (1948–   )

b. 3/12 Boston, MA. Singer/songwriter, called "Sweet Baby James" after his 1970 album, hit "You've Got a Friend." James, Hugh, Kate, & Livingston Taylor,* all singers, hit on album *Shower the People You Love with Love* 1982. Albums *Dad Loves His Work, Gorilla, Flag, Walking Man, New Moon Shines* 1992. Married singer Carly Simon* in 1972.

TAYLOR, JOHNNY (1937–   )

b. Crawfordville, West Memphis, AK. Singer, traveled with **Michael Jackson*** & the **Soul Stirrers,*** albums *Crazy 'Bout You, Raw Blues, Wanted: One Soul Singer.* etc.

TAYLOR, J. T.

Singer, former front man for **Kool and the Gang,*** album *Feel the Need* 1991.

TAYLOR, KOKO (1930–   )

Blues singer, albums *An Audience with the Queen, Queen of the Blues, From the Heart of a Woman, Jump for Joy: Live,* toured on the Alligator Records 20th Anniversary tour 1992.

TAYLOR, LIVINGSTON (1950–   )

b. 11/21 Boston, MA. Singer, brother of James Taylor.* Hit single "I Will Be in Love with You" 1978.

TAYLOR, TELL (1876–1937)

b. Vanlue, Ohio. Composer, wrote "Down by the Old Mill Stream" 1910 and with Ole Olson and composer Isham Jones* wrote the lyrics for "You're in the Army Now" 1917 popular in World War I.

TAYLOR, WILLIAM "BILLY" (1906–1977)

b. Washington, D.C. Bassist, with Elmer Snowden & others in 1920s, with Duke Ellington* in 30s, with Cootie Williams* & others in 40s, then played in Washington, D.C. where he died on 11/15.

TAYLOR, WILLIAM E. "BILLY" (1921–)

b. 7/24 Greenville, NC. Jazz pianist with Dizzy Gillespie* & others in 1940s, later formed his own trio, with bassist Victor Gaskin in NY City in 1980s.

TEAGARDEN, CHARLES (1913–1984)

b. 7/19 Vernon, TX Trumpeter, brother of Jack.* With Benny Goodman* in 1930s, served with Ferry Command in World War II, with Jimmy Dorsey* & others in 50s, led own bands in Las Vegas 60s/70s.

TEAGARDEN, WELDON L. "JACK" (1905–1964)

b. Vernon, TX. Trombonist/singer with Billy Lustig's **Scranton Sirens** in 1920s, recorded in 30s with Louis Armstrong,* Benny Goodman,* & Paul Whiteman* 1933/38, led own bands 1939/46, with Louis Armstrong* 1947/51, led his own **All Stars** 1951/64. Albums *A Hundred Years from Today, That's a Serious Thing.* Died of pneumonia 1/15 in New Orleans.

TEARS FOR FEARS

British rock group with Roland Orzabal, Curt Smith, hit single "Everybody Wants to Rule the World" 1985, platinum album *Sowing the Seeds of Love, Songs from the Big Chair, Tears Roll Down,* videos *Going to California, Sowing the Seeds.*

TECHNOTRONIC

Platinum single "Pump Up the Jam" 1989, album *Trip on This: The Remixes.*

TEENAGE FANCLUB

Rock quartet from Glasgow, Scotland with singer/guitarist Norman Blake, bassist Gerard Love, drummer Bendan O'Hare, & guitarist Raymond McGinley, album *Bandwagonesque* 1992.

TEENA MARIE (1957–)

b. Mary Christine Brockert in Santa Monica, CA. Singer, called "Lady T," has worked with Rick James,* hits "I Need Your Lovin'," "It Must be Magic."

TEMPLE, SHIRLEY (1928–)
b. Santa Monica, CA. Singer/child actress, in films *Little Miss Marker* 1934, *Heidi* 1937, etc.

TEMPLE OF THE DOG
Rock band on track "Hunger Strike" 1992, album *Temple of the Dog*.

TEMPTATIONS, THE
Alabama rock group formed 1964 with Dennis Edwards (b. 1943), Mel Franklin (b. 1942), lead tenor Eddie Kendrick* (1940–1992), Otis & Paul Williams.* Hits "My Girl," "Just My Imagination." Albums *25th Anniversary, Cloud Nine, Meet the Temptations*, etc.

TEN CC
British rock group with Paul Burgess, Lol Creme, Kevin Godley, Graham Gouldman, Eric Stewart, & Ten CC. Albums *Deceptive Bends, How Dare You*.

TEN CITY
Chicago trio, album *No House Big Enough* 1992.

10,000 MANIACS
Lead singer/songwriter Natalie Merchant (b. 1963), Bob Buck, Dennis Drew, Steve Gustafson, Jerome Augustyniak, albums *Blind Man's Zoo, Hope Chest, The Wishing Chair, Our Time in Eden* 1992, video *Time Capsule 1982–1990*.

TEN YEARS AFTER
British rock group formed 1967, albums *A Space in Time, Cricklewood Green, Positive Vibrations, Ssssh, Universal, Wait*, etc.

TENNILLE, TONI (1943–)
b. 5/8 Montgomery, Ala. Singer with **Captain and Tennille,*** hit song by Neil Sedaka,* "Love Will Keep Us Together" 1975, album *Never Let Me Go*.

TERRY, CLARK (1920–)

b. St. Louis, MO. Trumpeter/vocalist/musician, in All-Star Navy Band 1942–45, with Lionel Hampton* & others in 1940s, with Count Basie* 1948/51, Duke Ellington* 1951/59, toured Europe & Japan in 60s, at jazz festivals 70s/80s. Albums *Memories of Duke, Having Fun, Portraits,* with pianist John Hicks* on album *Friends Old and New* 1992.

TERRY, SONNY (1911–1986)

b. Saunders Teddell in Durham, NC. Singer, blinded at age 13 in an accident, with Brownie McGhee as **Terry & McGhee** in 1950s, with Harry Belafonte* in 60s, at Place des Arts in Montreal, Canada in July 1980. Albums *Sonny & Brownie, Classics/Blowin' the Fuses, The Folkway Years 1944–63.*

TESH, JOHN (1953–)

Pianist, album *A Romantic Christmas* 1992. Host on *Entertainment Tonight.* Married actress Connie Sellecca.

TESLA

Platinum album *The Great Radio Controversy* 1989, *Five Man Acoustical Jam, Mechanical Resonance, Psychotic Supper,* video *Five Man Video Band.*

TEX, JOE (1933–1982)

b. Joseph Arrington, Jr. 8/8 Rogers, TX. His single "Hold On to What You've Got" 1964, albums *Believe I'm Gonna, Best of Joe Tex.*

TEXAS TORNADOS

With Freddy Fender,* Doug Sahm, Flaco Jiminez,* & Augie Meyers, hit "Hey Baby, Que Pasa," albums *Texas Tornados, Zone of Our Own, Hangin' On By a Thread,* group sang at an inaugural ball for President Clinton in January 1993.

THARPE, SISTER ROSETTA (1921–1973)

b. Rosetta Rubin in Cotton Plant, AK. Singer in bands of Cab Calloway* & Lucky Millinder, album *Gospel Train.*

THE THE
Hit "Dusk" 1993.

THEBAUDET, JEAN-YVES
Pianist, over the years a regular at the Spoleto Festival in Charleston, SC., at Daytona Beach, FL in January 1993.

THEY MIGHT BE GIANTS
Brooklyn based duo of John Flansburgh & John Linnell, album *Apollo 18, People* magazine wrote: "The record is totally cool" 1992.

THIELEMANS, TOOTS
Albums, *Do Not Leave Me, Footprints, Only Trust Your Heart.*

THIN LIZZY
Irish rock group founded 1970. They featured comic book hero-ism, with Eric Bell, Brian Downey, Scott Gorham, Phil Lynott, Gary Moore, Brian Robertson, Midge Ure, Darren Wharton, & Snowy White. Albums *Jailbreak* 1976, *Fighting, Johnny the Fox, Thin Lizzy, Nightlife,* video *Live and Dangerous.*

THIRD WORLD
Reggae band with Michael "Ibo" Cooper, Willie "Root" Stew-art, William "Bunny Rugs" Clarke, Stephen "Cat" Coore, & Richard "Richie" Daley. Albums *96 Degrees in the Shade, Hold On to Love, Reggae Greats, Sense of Purpose, Serious Business, Committed* won Grammy 1993.

.38 SPECIAL
Rock band formed 1979 with Don Barnes, Steve Brookius, Jeff Carlisi, Jack Grondin, Larry Junstrom, & Donnie van Zandt. Hit singles "If I'd Been the One" 1983, "Back Where You Belong" 1984, albums *Bone Against Steel, Rock & Roll Strategy, Special Forces, Strength in Numbers, Wild-eyed Southern Boys, Tour de Force,* video *Wide-eyed and Live.*

THOMAS, BILLY JOE "BJ" (1942–)
b. 8/22 Houston, TX. Hits "Raindrops Keep Fallin' on My

Head,'' ''I Just Can't Help Believing.'' Albums *Greatest Hits, Midnight Minute, New Looks.*

THOMAS, GARY
b. Baltimore, MD. Jazz saxist, albums *Code Violations, While the Gate is Open, Till We Have Faces* 1993.

THOMAS, IRMA
Albums *Simply the Best, The New Rules, The Way I Feel.*

THOMAS, JOHN R. (1829–1896)
b. Newport, South Wales, settled in NY City. Songwriter, with lyricist George Cooper* composed ''Rose of Killarney'' 1876.

THOMAS, MICHAEL T. (1944–   )
b. 12/21 Hollywood, CA. Conductor. His grandparents Boris & Bessie Thomashafsky helped found the Yiddish Theater in NY City. Conductor in Los Angeles 1968, Boston, Buffalo 1971, New World Symphony, Miami Beach, FL 1990s.

THOMISON, LAWRENCE
Rev. Lawrence Thomison and the **Music City Mass Choir** (gospel singers) won Grammy 1993 for *Never Let Go of His Hand.*

THOMPSON, HENRY W. ''HANK'' (1925–   )
b. 9/3 Waco, TX. Singer/songwriter/leader, served in Navy in the Pacific Theater in World War II, with Billy Gray wrote ''Yesterday's Girl.'' Wrote ''Rub-A-Dub-Dub'' & ''Wildflower.'' Albums *All Times Greatest Hits, Capitol Collection Series.*

THOMPSON, LINDA
Raised in Memphis, TN. Songwriter, lived with Elvis Presley* for over four years, married producer David Foster. They wrote ''Shining Through'' for Miki Howard* & ''Grown Up Christmas List'' for Amy Grant.* She wrote ''I Have Nothing'' for Whitney Houston* on soundtrack *The Bodyguard* 1992.

THOMPSON, RICHARD
Albums *Amnesia, Daring Adventures, Hand of Kindness, Henry*

the Human Fly, Rumor and Sigh, with Linda Thompson*
Hokey Pokey, Pour Down Like Silver, Shoot Out the Lights.

THOMPSON TWINS
British rock group with Tom Bailey, Alannan Currie, Joe Leway, hits "Hold Me Now" 1984, "King for Just One Day" 1986, album *Best of the Thompson Twins,* video *Live at Liverpool.*

THOMPSON, WILL L. (1847–1909)
b. Liverpool, Ohio. Popular composer, wrote "Softly and Tenderly" about 1900.

THOMSON, VIRGIL G. (1896–1989)
b. 11/25 Kansas City, MO. Composer, composed *Four Saints in Three Acts* (opera 1928), *The Mother of Us All* (opera 1947), *Louisiana Story* (suite for orchestra 1948) Pulitzer Prize winner 1949. Died 9/30 New York, NY.

THORNHILL, CLAUDE (1908–1965)
b. Terre Haute, IN. Pianist/leader, formed his own band 1939, with singer Maxine Sullivan.* Album *Best of the Big Bands.* Died of a heart attack.

THORNTON, JAMES (1861–1938)
b. Liverpool, England. Actor/composer, came to NY City. Wrote the words and music for "When You Were Sweet Sixteen" 1898.

THORNTON, WILLIE MAE (1926–1984)
b. 12/11 Montgomery, AL. Singer, hits "Have Mercy Baby," "Ball and Chain," "Hound Dog." Was known as "Big Mama." Her recording of "Hound Dog" was on the soundtrack of the film *A Few Good Men* 1992. Died 7/25 Los Angeles, CA.

THOROGOOD, GEORGE
George Thorogood and the Destroyers, guitarist/singer, with Jeff Simon and Bill Blough. Albums *Bad to the Bone, Maverick, Live, Move it Over,* video *Born to be Bad.*

THREE DOG NIGHT
Australian rock band organized 1968 with Michael Allsup, James Greenspoon, Daniel Hutton, Skip Konte, Charles Negron, Joseph Schermine, Floyd Sneed, & Cory Wells, hit "Joy to the World" 1971, albums *Best of Three Dog Night, Cyan, Hard Labor.*

3 MUSTAPHAS 3
Albums *Friends, Friends and Fronds, Heart of Uncle, Soup of the Century.*

THREE SUNS, THE
Singers, hit song "Twilight Time."

TIBBETTS, STEVE
Albums *Big Map Idea, Exploded View, Northern Song, Safe Journey.*

TIFFANY (1971–)
b. 10/2 Norwalk, CA. At age 16 she was singing in shopping malls and sold millions of records, on 1988 Top Ten singles list for "Could've Been," albums *Tiffany, Hold On and Old Friend's Hand.* She married Bulmaro Garcia, had a son, and retired temporarily from show business.

TIJUANA BRASS *see* HERB ALPERT

TILLIS, MELVIN "MEL" (1932–)
b. 6/8 Pahokee, FL. Singer/songwriter, named Country Music Award entertainer of the Year 1976, has written over 450 songs. Albums *14 Greatest Hits, American Originals, The Very Best of Mel Tillis,* etc.

TILLIS, PAM (1958–)
Country singer, daughter of Mel Tillis,* hit singles "Shake the Sugar Tree," "Maybe it was Memphis" won 1993 Grammy, album *Homeward Looking Angel* 1992, with others on CBS Special in January 1993.

TIMBUCK 3
Albums *Big Shot in the Dark, Edge of Allegiance, Greetings from Timbuck 3.*

TIME, THE
Twin cities pop/funk group with frontman Morris Day, Terry Lewis, "Jellybean" Johnson, Jesse Johnson, Jimmy "Jam" Harris, Jerome Benton, & Monte Moir. Albums *Ice Cream Castles, The Time, What Time is It, Pandemonium* 1992.

TIN MACHINE
Band of David Bowie,* album *Oy Vey, Baby* 1992.

TINY TIM (1922–)
b. Herbert Buckingham Khaury 4/12 New York, NY. Ukulele player/falsetto singer best known for "Tiptoe through the Tulips" 1968. Tiny Tim criticized Elizabeth Taylor & Magic Johnson for raising money for AIDS research & said AIDS is caused by "the disobeying of God's laws & fornicating" (*Florida Today* newspaper 6/7/92).

TIOMKIN, DIMITRI (1899–1979)
b. St. Petersburg, Russia. Composer came to Hollywood, CA 1930 & wrote musicals for MGM, wrote scores for over 120 screen plays, won Oscars for *High Noon* 1952, *The High and the Mighty* 1954, *The Old Man and the Sea* 1958, & wrote "The Ballad of the Alamo" 1960.

TIPPIN, AARON
Country howler, hit "There Ain't Nothin' Wrong with the Radio" about a junk car radio, & "The Sound of Your Goodbye," albums *You've Got to Stand for Something, Read Between the Lines* 1992.

TIZOL, JUAN (1900–1984)
b. San Juan, Puerto Rico. Trombonist/composer, came to US with Marie Lucas Orchestra in 1920s, with Duke Ellington* 1929/44, with Harry James* 1944/51, with James & Ellington later at

various times. He wrote "Perdido" and "Caravan" recorded by Duke Ellington. Died of a heart attack in Inglewood, CA.

TJADER, CALLEN R., JR. "CAL" (1925–1982)
b. 7/16 St. Louis, MO. Jazz vibist/drummer, album *La Onda Va Bien* Grammy winner 1981, *A Fuego Vivo, Shining Sea, Soul Sauce, Stan Getz/Cal Tjader,* etc. Died 5/5 in the Philippines.

TLC
R & B group with Lisa "Left Eye" Lopez, Tionne "T-Boy" Watkins, & Rozando "Chilli" Thomas, Top Ten Singles "Baby-Baby-Baby" & "What about Your Friends" during 1992, hit album *Oooooohh . . . On the TLC Trip,* on NBC *Jay Leno Show, Showtime at the Apollo,* on *Oprah Winfrey Show,* Dick Clark's *New Year's Rockin' Eve* on ABC 12/21/92.

TOAD THE WET SPROCKET
Santa Barbara group formed 1989, albums *Bread & Circus, Pale, Fear,* 1992, toured US 1992.

TOBIAS, CHARLES (1898–1970)
b. NY City. Songwriter, brother of songwriter Harry Tobias. With Sammy Stept* and Lew Brown,* Charles Tobias wrote "Don't Sit Under the Apple Tree With Anyone Else But Me" 1942 and with Cliff Friend* wrote "Don't Sweetheart Me" 1944, both songs were very popular during World War II.

TOM TOM CLUB
Group with bassist Tina Weymouth, drummer Chris Frantz, Bruce Martin & Mark Roull, albums *Boom Boom Chi Boom Boom, Tom Tom Club,* hit single "Dark Sneak Love Action" 1992.

TOMITA, ISAO
Albums *Back to Earth, The Tomita Planets, Tomita's Greatest Hits,* etc.

TOMMY JAMES & THE SHONDELLS
His single "Crimson and Clover," albums **Anthology, Crimson/ Clover/Cellophane, Very Best of Tommy James & the Shondells.**

TONE LOC
Sold over 2 million albums of *Loc'd After Dark* 1989, Cool Hand Loc, hit single "Funky Cold Medina" 1989.

TOO SHORT
Platinum album *Life Is . . . Too Short, Born to Mack, Short Dogs in the House* (censored), *Short Dogs in the House* (uncensored), *Shorty the Pimp* 1992.

TORME, MELVIN H. "MEL" (1925–)
b. 9/13 Chicago, IL. Singer/songwriter, wrote "The Christmas Song," formed **Mel-Tones** in 1940s, wrote "Stranger in Town," "California Suite," at NY City night clubs 50s/80s. Albums *The Mel Torme Special* 1983 with Mel Lewis* orchestra, *Compact Jazz, Fujitsu Concert Jazz Festival, Songs of New York, Smooth as Velvet,* etc. at Chicago Jazz Festival in September 1992.

TOSH, PETER (1944–)
b. Winston H. MacIntosh 10/9 Westmoreland, Jamaica, West Indies. Singer with Bob Marley* and the **Wailers,** reggae soloist since 1974. Albums *Captured Alive, Equal Rights, Legalize It, No Nuclear War* won 1987 Reggae Grammy, *Wanted Dead or Alive.*

TOTO
Los Angeles rock group with drummer Jeff Porcaro (1954–1992), Mike Porcaro, Steve Porcaro, Bobby Kimball, Steve Lukather, & David Paich, won 1982 Grammy for hit songs "Rosanna," "Africa," albums *Toto IV, Fahrenheit, Hydra, Seventh One,* video *Past to Present,* album *Kingdom of Desire.* Jeff Porcaro died 8/5/92 Hidden Hills, CA from cocaine related hardening of the arteries.

TOUGH, DAVE (1908–1948)
b. Oak Park, IL. Drummer with Mezz Mezzrow & others in 1920s, with Tommy Dorsey* in 30s, Artie Shaw's* naval band 1942/44, toured with **Jazz at the Philharmonic*** 1946. Died in Newark, NJ.

TOWER OF POWER
Albums *Back to Oakland, Direct, Live in Living Color, Tower of Power.*

TOWNER, RALPH
Albums *City of Eyes, ECM Works, Slide Show, Solstice, Trios/ Solos.*

TOWNSHEND, PETE (1945–)
b. 5/19 London, England. Guitarist/singer/composer formerly with **The Who,*** albums *Another Scoop, After the Best Cowboys, Have Chinese Eyes, Deep End, Empty Glass, Who Came First,* video *Deep End Brixton.* Composed the rock opera *Tommy* performed at London's Coliseum 1969 & at Metropolitan Opera 1970, and again on Broadway, NY City in April 1993. Album *Psycho-Derelict* 1993.

TRADITION HALL JAZZ BAND
Led by drummer/vocalist Bob French, son of Papa French, played at Tradition Hall in New Orleans, LA in 1979/80s.

TRAFFIC
British rock group with Jim Capaldi, Dave Mason, Stevie Winwood,* & Chris Wood (1944–1983), hits "Traffic" 1968, "When the Eagle Flies," "Feelin' Alright," albums *John Barleycorn Must Die, Welcome to the Canteen, Traffic,* video *Live at Santa Monica.*

TRANSVISION TRAMP
With rock singer/songwriter Wendy James, she went solo with the help of songwriter Elvis Costello,* first solo album *Now Ain't the Time for Tears* 1993.

TRAVELING WILBURYS
Bob Dylan's* band, on Top Ten albums list for *Traveling Wilburys Vol. 1* 1989. Singer/guitarist Tom Petty* joined the group & with ex-Byrd Roger McGuinn sang "Mr. Tambourine Man" at the concert in honor of Bob Dylan at Madison Square Garden in NY City in October 1992.

TRAVIS, MERLE ROBERT (1917–1983)
b. 11/29 Rosewood, KY. Singer/songwriter, wrote "16 Tons," "Old Mountain Dew," albums *Best of Merle Travis, Merle Travis Story.* Elected to Country Hall of Fame, Nashville 1977.

TRAVIS, RANDY (1959–)
b. 5/4 Marshville, NC. Baritone, hit single "On One Hand" 1985, won 1988 Grammy for "Old 8x10." Hit album *Storms of Life,* won 1987 Grammy for *Always and Forever,* albums *High Lonesome, Storms of Life,* video *Forever and Ever,* won 1993 Grammy for "Better Class of Losers." Married Lib Hatcher.

TRAVOLTA, JOHN (1954–)
b. 2/18 Englewood, NJ. Actor/singer, starred in *Saturday Night Fever, Grease, Welcome Back Kotter* 1975/79.

TRESVANT, RALPH
Singer, album *Ralph Tresvant,* hit R&B single "Money Can't Buy You Love" 1992.

TREVINO, RICKY (1971–)
Country guitarist/singer, hit single "Just Enough Rope."

T. REX
British rock group with Marc Bolan, Steve Currie, Mickey Finn, Jack Green, Bill Legend, Steven Peregrine Took. Albums *Electric Warrior, The Essential Collection, The Slider.*

TRISTANO, LEONARD J. "LENNIE" (1919–1978)
b. 3/19 Chicago, IL. Jazz pianist/clarinetist/saxist, blinded at age nine, played in Chicago clubs in late 1930s, came to New York City 1946. Innovator in the "Cool Jazz" era. Albums *Complete on Keynote, Live at Birdland, Live in Toronto 1952, Manhattan.*

TRITT, TRAVIS (1963–)
From Marietta, GA. Guitarist/singer/actor/songwriter, album *The Whiskey Ain't Workin'* 1991. He wrote "Here's a Quarter, Call Somebody Who Cares," hit "Anymore," toured with Marty

Stuart* 1992, video *It's All About to Change,* hit single "Lord Have Mercy on the Working Man" Grammy winner 1993, hit "Can I Trust You with My Heart?" 1993.

TRIUMPH
Canadian rock group with Rick Elmer, Mike Levine, Gil Moore, albums *Never Surrender, Stages, Thunder 7, Triumph Classics.*

TROCCOLI, KATHY
Singer, hit single "You've Got a Way" 1992.

TROOP
Album *Attitude,* R&B hit single "Sweet November" 1992.

TROWER, ROBIN (1945–)
b. 3/9 London, England. Guitarist/composer, albums *Bridge of Sighs, Essential, Live, Truce, Twice Removed . . . Yesterday.*

TRUDELL, JOHN (1946–)
b. Santee Sioux reservation. Poet/singer/leader, national chairman of the American Indian Movement 1973/79. His poems were set to music by guitarist Jesse Ed Davis, single "Rockin' the Res." Trudell toured with his band in 1992.

TUBB, ERNEST "ERNIE" (1914–1984)
b. 2/9 Crisp, TX. Country singer/songwriter, hit "Walking the Floor Over You" 1941. Wrote over 150 songs, albums *Live 1965, Country Music Hall of Fame,* video *Thanks Troubadour, Thanks.* Died 9/6 Nashville, TN.

TUBES, THE
Rock group with lead singer Fee Waybill (b. 1950 Omaha, Nebraska), singer/dancer Re Styles, bassist Rich Anderson, keyboardists Michael Cotton & Vince Welnick, guitarists Bill Spooner & Roger Steen, drummer Prairie Prince. Albums *Completion Backwards, The Tubes,* group appeared in the film *Xanadu* 1980, video *The Tubes.*

TUCKER, HENRY (1826–1882)
b. 12/26 New York State. Composer, with lyricist Charles Carroll

Sawyer* composed "Weeping Sad and Lonely; or When this Cruel War is Over" 1863 popular during the Civil War; and with lyricist George Cooper* wrote "Sweet Genevieve" 1869. Died 12/26 Brooklyn, NY City.

TUCKER, ORRIN (1911–)

b. 2/17 St. Louis, MO. Singer/leader, organized own band 1936, his singers were Evelyn Nelson "Bonnie" Baker, later Scottee Marsh and Helen Lee.

TUCKER, SOPHIE (1884–1966)

b. Russia. Singer/entertainer, sang in NY City night clubs.

TUCKER, TANYA (1958–)

b. 10/10 Seminole, TX. Singer, hit "Delta Dawn" 1973, a millionaire by age fifteen. Album *Should I Do It* 1982, on Top Ten Country Singles chart 1988 for "Strong Enough to Bend" and "If It Don't Come Easy." 1992 hits "If Your Heart Ain't Busy Tonight" and *What Do I Do With Me?*. She sang the "Star Spangled Banner" at the Republican National Convention in Houston, TX in August 1992, with Delbert McClinton* on "Tell Me About It" from album *Can't Run from Yourself* Grammy winner 1993.

TUCKER, TOMMY (1908–1989)

b. 5/18 Souris, ND. Bandleader with singers Don Brown, Kerwin Sommerville, & Amy Arnell, hit "I Don't Want to Set the World on Fire" 1941. Died 7/11 Sarasota, Florida.

TURNER, "BIG JOE" (1911–1985)

b. 11/3 Baltimore, MD. Pianist/vocalist, with Louis Armstrong* & accompanist for Adelaide Hall in 1930s, in service band at Camp Kilmer, NJ in World War II, popularized "Shake, Rattle and Roll" 1954, at NY City clubs in 1970s. Albums *Blues Train, Rhythm and Blues Years, The Boss of the Blues*, etc.

TURNER, IKE (1931–)

b. 11/5 Clarksdale, MS. Singer/songwriter, hits "A Fool in Love" 1960, "Goodbye, So Long" 1971, albums *Greatest Hits, Proud Mary*. Divorced from Tina Turner.*

TURNER, JOE (1911–)

b. 5/18 Kansas City, MO. Vocalist, sang in clubs in Kansas City in 1930s, with Joe Sullivan & others in 40s/60s, at Monterey Jazz Festivals in California in 1970s.

TURNER, TINA (1938–)

b. Annie Mae Bullock 11/26 Nutbush, TN, graduated from high school in St. Louis, MO. Singer. Hits "Proud Mary" 1972 & "What's Love Got to Do with It?" 1984 Grammy winner, *Tina Live in Europe* won 1988 Rock Vocalist Grammy, albums *Break Every Rule, Private Dancer, Simply the Best,* video *Foreign Affairs,* "The Bitch is Back" track from *Two Rooms* won Grammy 1993. Married Ike Turner,* later divorced.

TURNER, TROY (1969–)

Baton Rouge blues/rock/jazz guitarist/singer, album *Handful of Aces* 1992.

TURPIN, THOMAS M. (1873–1922)

b. Savannah, GA. Pianist/composer, played at the Rosebud in St. Louis, MO. Wrote first ragtime song to be published by a black man, "Harlem Rag" 1917. Known as the "Father of St. Louis Ragtime."

TURRE, STEVE (1949–)

b. California. Trombonist, joined Art Blakey* & the **Jazz Messengers** in 1973, with his wife cellist Akua Dixon Turre & violinist John Blake on album *Right There* 1992.

TURRENTINE, STANLEY

Saxist, albums *Best of Stanley Turrentine, Coming Your Way, La Place, Pieces of Dreams, Straight Ahead,* video *In Concert.* With pianist Cedar Walton, bassist Ron Carter,* & drummer Billy Higgins on *More Than a Mood* 1992.

TURTLES, THE

Los Angeles rock group, originally lead vocalist Howard Kaylan, drummer Johnny Barbata, bassist/singer Mark Volman & Jim Tucker. Albums *20 Greatest Hits, Best of Turtle Wax Vol. 2.*

TWISTED SISTER
Heavy metal group formed 1976 with Jay Jay French, Mark "The Animal" Mendoza, Eddie "Fingers" Ojeda, A. J. Pero, Dee Snider. Hit single "We're Not Gonna Take It" 1984. Albums *Come Out and Play, Stay Hungary, You Can't Stop Rock n Roll.* Dee Snider appeared before a Senate Committee in July 1992 defending rock & roll lyrics and protesting censoring actions of Tipper Gore (Mrs. Al Gore).

TWITTY, CONWAY (1933–1993)
b. Harold Jenkins 9/1 Friars Point, MI. Country singer/songwriter, had over 50 No. 1 hits, "It's Only Make Believe" 1958, "Hello Darlin' " 1970, with Loretta Lynn* "After the Fire is Gone" 1971 Grammy, "Feelin's" 1975, won Country Music vocal Duo awards 1972/75, opened Twitty City near Nashville in 1982. Twitty suffered a ruptured stomach vessel in Springfield, MO. and died 6/5/93.

2 LIVE CREW
Founded by Luther Campbell,* platinum album *Nasty as They Wanna Be* 1989, *Is What We Are, Move Somethin', Sports Weekend* 1992, video *Banned in the USA.*

TYLER, BONNIE
Albums *Faster than Speed of Light, Secret Dreams & Forbidden Dreams.*

TYLER, STEVE (1948–   )
b. 3/26 Boston, MA. Singer with **Aerosmith*** heavy metal band since 1970, platinum album *Toys in the Attic* 1975.

TYMPANY FIVE
Jazz band led by saxist/singer Louis Jordan* in NY City in 1940s, new group toured U.S. & Europe in early 1970s until Jordan's death in 1975.

TYNER, MC COY (1938–   )
b. Philadelphia, PA. Pianist/composer also known as Sulaimon Saud, formed own trio in NY City 1966, accompanist for Ike*

& Tina Turner,* won *down beat* poll for his album *Sahara* 1972, his *Enlightenment* won Diamond prize, *down beat* poll named Jazzman of the Year 1975. Played in the White House for President & Mrs. Carter in June 1978, his group won 1988 Grammy as Jazz Instrumentalists, albums *44th Street Suite, Remembering John, Soleloquy, Uptown Downtown, The Turning Point* won Grammy 1993, video *Harvest Jazz Series.*

TYNER, ROB (1945–1991)
b. Robert Derminer in Detroit, MI. Lead singer for **MCS*** (Motor City Five) group formed 1967, album *Kick Out the Jams* 1968, group dissolved 1972. Tyner continued singing with local groups. Died 9/17 in Detroit, MI.

TYSONS see **IAN AND SYLVIA**

U

UB 40
British reggae group named for British unemployment benefits card formed 1978 with Astro (Terence Wilson), James Brown, Ali Campbell, Robin Campbell, Earl Falconer, Norman Hassan, British Travers, & Michael Virture. Albums *1980–83, Geffery Morgan, Labour of Love, Live from Moscow, Rat in the Kitchen.*

UFO
British rock group with Neil Carter, Paul Chapman, Phil Mogg, Andy Parker, Michael Schenker, & Pete Way, albums *Best of the Rest, Force It, Obsession, Phenomenon,* etc.

UGGAMS, LESLIE (1943–   )
b. 5/25 New York, NY. Singer/actress, sang at the Apollo Theater in NY City, starred in TV mini-series *Roots* & in *Backstairs at The White House.*

UGLY KID JOE
Isla Vista, CA punk/pop/metal band with singer Whitfield Crane, slash guitarist Klaus Eichstadt, rhythm guitarist Dave Fortman (replaced Roger Lahr). Album *As Ugly as They Wanna Be* sold over one million copies, album *America's Least Wanted* 1992, group toured US 1992/93.

UH HUH GIRLS
With Meilani Paul, Darlene Dillinger, & Gretchen Palmer, singers on Ray Charles's* Pepsi ads at the 1991 Super Bowl.

ULTRA VIVID SCENE
Hit single "Rev" 1993.

ULTRAVOX
Albums *Lament, Quartet, Rage in Eden, Vienna,* video *The Collection.*

UNCLE FESTIVE
Albums *Paper Plus The Dog, Say Uncle, That We Do Know, Young People with Faces.*

UNCLE TUPELO
From Belleville, IL. Guitarist Jay Farrar, bassist Jeff Tweedy, & drummer Mike Heidorn, albums *No Depression* 1990 & *Still Feel Gone* 1992.

UNDEAD
Hard core band with lead singer/guitarist Bobby Steele formerly with **The Misfits,*** hit single "Nine Toes Later" about accident which left Steele with a limp. Album *Act Your Rage* 1993.

UNION STATION
Bluegrass group with singer Alison Krauss* on album *Every Time You Say Goodbye* Grammy winner 1993.

UNITED JAZZ & ROCK ENSEMBLE, THE
With trombonist Albert Mangelsdorff, trumpeter/fluegelhorn players Kenny Wheeler, Ian Carr, and Ack Van Rooven, bassist Eberhard Weber, guitarist Volker Kriegel, saxists Charles Mariano, & Barbara Thompson, pianist Wolfgang Dauner, percussionist John Hiseman on album *The Break Even Point* 1980.

UNREST
Punk rock/pop group with singer/bassist Bridget Cross & Mark Robinson, albums *Kustom Karnal Blackxplotat, Imperial f.f.r.r.* one of the best for 1992.

UNTOUCHABLE FACTOR
Jazz band led by vibist Kahn Jamal & drummer Sunny Murray played at Jazzmania in NY City in late 1970s.

UPCHURCH, PHIL (1941–)
b. Chicago, IL. Guitarist/fender bassist/composer recorded with Dizzy Gillespie,* Stan Getz,* Woody Herman,* & others in 1960s, in Army Special Services in Germany 1965/67, with

Ramsay Lewis* & Quincy Jones* in 1970s, toured Japan with Jones 1972.

UPPITY BLUES WOMAN, THE
Group with Koko Taylor* & Lonnie Brooks* on the *Christmas Collection, The Uppity Blues Women,* etc.

URBANICK, MICHAL (1943–)
b. Warsaw, Poland. With the **Wreckers** in Poland and the US 1962/64, formed own group 1965 & **Fusion** in Chicago & New York 70s/80s.

URIAH HEEP
British rock group with Mick Box, David Bryon, Ken Hensley, Al Napier, & Paul Newton. Albums *Uriah Heep, Demons & Wizards, Best of Uriah Heep.*

UTAH SAINTS
Hit album *Utah Saints* 1993.

UTOPIA
Albums *Adventures in Utopia, Anthology 1974–1985, Swing to the Right, Utopia,* video *An Evening with Utopia.*

U2
Irish group with singer Bono Vox (Paul Hewson), bassist Adam Clayton, guitarist The Edge (David H. Evans), & drummer Larry Mullen, Jr. Their album *War* 1983 described violence in Northern Ireland, won 1987 Grammy for *The Joshua Tree* hit single "With or Without You," won 1988 Grammy for "Desire," videos *Rattle & Hum* 1988, *Unforgettable Fire.* Their "Zoo TV" toured USA 1992, won MTV award for video *Even Better Than the Real Thing, Achtung Baby* sold 4 million copies & won Grammy 1993. They have sold 60 million albums. Johnny Cash* sang on their 1994 Grammy-winning album *Zooropa.*

V

VALE, JERRY (1932–)
b. Gerano Louis Vitaliamo 7/8 Bronx, NY City. Singer, hits "Innamorata" 1956, "Dommage, Dommage" 1966, albums *All Time Greatest Hits, Most Requested Songs, The Jerry Vale Italian Album.*

VALENS, RITCHIE (1941–1959)
b. 5/13 Los Angeles, CA. Guitarist/singer/songwriter, wrote "La Bamba" recorded by Trini Lopez. Albums *Ritchie, Ritchie Valens, Concert at Pacoima Jr. High, Best of Ritchie Valens-Golden Archives,* etc. Killed in an airplane crash near Fargo, ND along with Buddy Holly* & "Big Bopper" J. P. Richardson.* A postage stamp was issued in his honor in 1993.

VALENTIN, DAVE
Albums *Fruit Juice, Jungle Garden, Kalahari, Mind Time,* etc.

VALENTINE SALOON
Nashville, TN group with singer William Jewell & drummer Billy Baker.

VALLEE, RUDY (1901–1986)
b. Herbert Prior 7/28 Island Pond, VT. Singer/saxist/actor, appeared in several films, his theme song was "My Time is Your Time." Album *Vagabond Lover.* Died 7/3 Los Angeles, CA.

VALLI, FRANKIE (1937–)
b. Francis Castelluccio 5/3 Newark, NJ. Singer with the **Four Seasons,*** hits "Sherry," "Big Girls Don't Cry," "My Eyes Adored You." Albums *25th Anniversary Set, Motown Superstar Series, Anthology, Greatest Hits,* video *Frankie Valli.*

VAN ALSTYNE, EGBERT (1882–1951)
b. Chicago, IL. Composer, wrote the music for "In the Shade of the Old Apple Tree" 1905, with lyricist Earle C. Jones wrote "That Old Gang of Mine" 1912, with lyricist Gus Kahn*

422 / Van, Bobby

"Memories" 1915, and with lyricist Tony Jackson composed "Pretty Baby." Died in Chicago.

VAN, BOBBY (1935–1980)
b. Robert Van Stein 12/6 New York, NY. Singer/actor/dancer, appeared in *No, No Nanette, On Your Toes*. Died 7/31.

VANCE, KENNY (1943–   )
b. 12/9 Singer with **Jay and the Americans,*** then went solo.

VANDROSS, LUTHER (1951–   )
b. 4/20 New York, NY. Soul/R&B singer, platinum album *Never Too Much* 1971, won 1990 Grammy R&B vocal for "Here and Now," platinum video *Live at Wembly* 1990, *Power of Love* Grammy winner 1991, won 1992 R&B Grammy, with Janet Jackson* "The Best Things in Life are Free" won Grammy 1993. Albums *Any Love, Busy Body, Never Too Much, The Power of Love, Little Miracles* 1993. American Music Soul/R&B New Artist Award 1994.

VANGELIS
b. Vangelis Papathanassiou. Composer/keyboardist, won an Oscar for best score for *Chariots of Fire*, albums *The City, Opera Sauvage, The Mask, Themes: Vangelis*.

VAN HALEN, MICHAEL ANTHONY (1955–   )
b. 1/20 Chicago, IL. Bassist with **Van Halen*** heavy metal/rock band, brothers Alex & guitarist Eddie (b. Netherlands), lead singer David Lee Roth,* singer Sammy Hagar. Hit single "Jump" 1984, Van Halen's Monsters of Rock on 1988 top ten grossing concerts list, music video *Live Without a Net* 1990. Album *For Unlawful Carnal Knowledge* 1991 Grammy winner. Eddie van Halen married actress Valerie Bertinelli & they have a son. Video *Right Here, Right Now* won 1992 MTV music award.

VAN HEUSEN, JIMMY (1913–1990)
b. Edward Chester Babcock 1/26 Syracuse, NY. Composer of "Swinging on a Star" 1944 for Bing Crosby,* "Come Dance

with Me," "Moonlight Becomes You," "All the Way," "Love and Marriage." "High Hopes" 1959 won an Oscar. Died 2/7 at Rancho Mirage, CA.

VANILLA FUDGE
New York rock group formed 1966 with singer Tim Bogart (b. 1944), drummer/vocalist Carmine Appice, bass guitarist Vincent Martell, & organist Mark Stern. Band has backed Rod Stewart.* Albums *Vanilla Fudge, Beat Goes On, While the World Was Eating,* etc.

VANILLA ICE (1967–)
Sold 6 million albums *To the Extreme,* platinum single "Ice Ice Baby" 1990, videos *Ninja Rap, Olay that Funky . . . Whiteboy.* His pictures appeared in Madonna's* book *Sex* 1992.

VANITY
b. Denise Mathews at Niagara Falls, NY. Singer/actress, albums *Nasty Girl* with **Vanity 6,** solo album *Wild Animal* 1985, in film *The Last Dragon* 1985.

VANNELLI, GINO (1952–)
b. 6/16 Montreal, Quebec, Canada. Singer/songwriter, hits "Wheels of Life" 1979, "Living Inside Myself," albums *Big Dreams Never Sleep, Brother to Brother, Nightwalker,* etc.

VAN RONK, DAVID (1936–)
b. Brooklyn, NY City. Songwriter/leader of the **Ragtime Jug Stompers.*** Album *Inside David Van Ronk,* his "Cocaine Blues" on album *Troubadours of the Folk Era, Vol. 1* issued 1992.

VAN SHELTON, RICKY
Country singer, platinum album *Loving Proof* 1989, albums *Rvs LII, Sings Christmas, Wild Eyed Dream,* with Dolly Parton* won TNN vocal video duo 1992, hit single "Backwoods," videos *Honeymoon in Vegas* 1992, *Rvs. . . To be Continued,* disc *Greatest Hits Plus* sold over 500,000 copies. Toured US 1992/93.

VAUGHAN BROTHERS
Musicians, platinum album *Family Style* 1990 Rock Instrumental Grammy winner.

VAUGHAN, JIMMIE
Guitarist/leader, older brother of the late Stevie Ray Vaughan,* played with Eric Clapton* at London's Royal Albert Hall in 1991, and his own band there in 1993.

VAUGHAN, SARAH (1924–1990)
b. 3/27 Newark, NJ. Jazz singer with Earl Hines* & others in 1940s. Won *Esquire* New Star award 1947, *down beat* polls 1947/52. Sang for President & Mrs. Johnson in The White House 1965, at Monterey Jazz Festivals in California in 1970s. Albums *Best of Sarah Vaughan, Crazy & Mixed Up, Jazz Collector Edition,* with pianist Jimmy Jones, bassist Richard Davis, & drummer Ray Haynes on CD *Swinging Easy,* video *Live from Monterey.* Married trumpeter George Treadwell 1947, later divorced.

VAUGHAN, STEVIE RAY (1955–1990)
Blues guitarist, albums *Couldn't Stand the Weather, Double Trouble In Step, Soul to Soul,* videos *Live at the El Mocambo, Pride & Joy with Double Trouble,* "Little Way" track from *Sky is Crying* won Grammy 1993. Vaughan & four band members were killed in a helicopter crash after a concert at East Troy, WI on August 27, 1990.

VAUGHN, BILLY (1919–1991)
b. 4/12 Glasgow, KY. Singer/leader with Jimmy Sacca formed the **Hilltoppers**, wrote "Trying" 1952 & arrangements for Pat Boone* & the Fontaine Sisters. Hit "Melody of Love."

VEDDER, EDDIE
Singer/songwriter with **Pearl Jam.*** With Jeff Ament wrote "Jeremy," Grammy winner 1993.

VEE, BOBBY (1943–)
b. 4/30 Fargo, ND. Singer, hit singles "Please Don't Ask About

Barbara," "Sharing You," "Punish Her." Albums *Meets the Crickets, Legendary Master Series.*

VEGA, SUZANNE (1960–)
b. 7/11 Santa Monica, CA. Pop/folk singer/guitarist, albums *Days of Open Hand, Solitude Standing,* with drummer Jerry Marotta & guitarist Richard Thompson on *99.9 degrees F* 1992.

VELVET UNDERGROUND
New York jazz/rock group with lead guitarist Louis Firbank (1967–70), John Cale, Sterling Morrison, Maureen Tucker, & singer/songwriter Lou Reed.* Reed had a solo album *Walk on the Wild Side* 1973. Group albums *Another View, Best of Velvet Underground, Live With Lou Reed Vols. 1 & 2, White Light/ White Heat.*

VENTURA, CHARLIE (1916–)
b. Charles Venturo 12/2 Philadelphia, PA. Jazz saxist/leader, with Gene Krupa* & others in early 1940s, led own combos 1946/51, then with Gene Krupa 50s/60s, house leader at Sheraton Tobacco Valley Inn in CT. 1972/75.

VENTURES, THE
Rock group formed 1960 with Rob Bogle, Johnny Durrill, Nokie Edwards, Howie Johnson, Jerry McGee, Mel Taylor, & Don Wilson. Hits "Walk, Don't Run" 1960, "Hawaii Five-O" 1969, albums *Legendary Masters Series, Walk Don't Run–the Best of The Ventures.*

VENUTI, GIUSEPPE "JOE" (1899–1978)
b. Lecco, Italy. Jazz violinist, raised in Philadelphia, PA, with Bert Estlow's Quintet & later co-led band at the Slipper in Atlantic City, NJ, joined Paul Whiteman's* band 1929, led own bands 1935/70s with singer Kay Starr* & others. Album *Joe Venuti and Zoot Sims.* * Died of a heart attack 8/14 Seattle, WA.

VERLAINE, TOM (1949–)
b. Tom Miller 12/13 Morris, NJ. New wave guitarist/composer, albums *Little Johnny Jewel* 1975, *Cover* 1984, CDs *Marquee Moon, Adventure, Warm and Cool* 1992.

VERNOR, F. DUDLEIGH (1892–1974)
b. Detroit, MI. Organist/songwriter, with Byron D. Stokes* wrote "The Sweetheart of Sigma Chi" 1912.

VICIOUS, SID (1957–1979)
b. John Simon Ritchie in England. Singer with **The Sex Pistols.*** Died 2/2 Greenwich Village, NY City.

VILLAGE PEOPLE, THE
Rock group formed in late 1970s with Alex Briley, David Hodo, Glenn H. Hughes, Randy Jones, Jeff Olson, Felipe Rose, Ray Simpson, & Victor Willis. Hit single "YMCA" 1979. Album *Greatest Hits.*

VINCENT, GENE (1971–)
b. Vincent Eugene Craddock 12/12 Norfolk, VA. Singer/composer, hit single "Lotta Lovin'," album *Gene Vincent.*

VINSON, EDDIE "CLEANHEAD" (1917–1988)
b, 12/18 Houston, TX. Jazz saxist/singer, with Chester Boone in 1930s, with Cootie Williams* in 1940s/50s, co-led band in 60s, at Montreaux Jazz Festivals in Switzerland 1971 & 74. Albums *Cleanhead/Roomful of Blues, I Want a Little Girl, Kidney Stew.* Died in Los Angeles, CA.

VINTON, STANLEY ROBERT "BOBBY" (1935–)
v. 4/16 Canonsburg, PA. Singer, called the "Polish Prince," hit song "Blue Velvet," sold over 25 million records by 1974, albums *16 Most Requested Songs, Great Songs of Christmas,* with George Burns on album *As Time Goes By* 1992, performed in Las Vegas and Atlantic City in 1980s/90s, toured US 1992.

VIOLENT FEMMES
Albums *Blind Leading the Naked, Hallowed Ground, Violent Femmes, Why Do Birds Sing?*

VOGUES, THE
Rock group with Charles Blasko, William Burkette, Hugh Geyer, & Don Miller, album *Greatest Hits.*

VOLLENWEIDER, ANDREAS
Electric harpist, albums *Behind the Gardens, Book of Roses, Caverna Magica, Dancing with the Lion, Down to the Moon, White Winds.*

VON STADE, FREDERICKA "FLICKA" (1945–)
b. 6/1 Somerville, NJ. Singer. Album *My Funny Valentine,* in concert with Andre Previn* at Carnegie Hall in NY City in December 1991. Married Peter Elkus.

VON TILZER, ALBERT (1878–1958)
b. Albert Gumm, Indianapolis, IN, brother of Harry Von Tilzer.* Composer, wrote "I'll Be With You in Apple Blossom Time," with lyricist Jack Norworth* wrote "Take Me Out to the Ball Game" 1908 and with Junie McCree wrote "Put Your Arms Around Me Honey, Hold Me Tight" 1910.

VON TILZER, HARRY (1872–1946)
b. Harry Gumm, Detroit, MI. Composer, with lyricist A. J. Lamb* wrote "A Bird in a Gilded Cage" 1900, "On a Sunday Afternoon" 1902, "Wait 'till the Sun Shines Nellie" 1905, with Will Dillon* wrote "I Want a Girl Just Like the Girl That Married Dear Old Dad" 1911 and "The Green Grass Grew All Around."

VON TRESS, DON (1948–)
Songwriter, wrote "Achy Breaky Heart" made famous by Billy Ray Cyrus,* Grammy winner 1993.

W

WAGNER, JACK PETER (1959–   )
b, 10/3 Washington, MO. Singer/actor, hit single "All I Need" 1984, appeared on the soap opera *General Hospital,* album *Lighting Up the Night.*

WAGONER, PORTER W. (1927–   )
b. 8/12 West Plains, MO. Country singer, joined Grand Ole Opry Nashville 1957, with Dolly Parton* won three Country Music awards.

WAHLBERG, MARK (1972–   )
b. Boston, MA. Singer, joined brother Donnie Wahlberg's **New Kids on the Block*** then went solo. Album *Music for the People* 1991, appears shirtless on his video *Good Vibrations* 1992.

WAILER, BUNNY
Reggae singer, albums *Blackheart Man, Gumption, Liberation, Protest, Sings the Wailers, Time Will Tell—Marley Tribute* 1990 Reggae Grammy winner.

WAILERS, THE
Founded by Bob Marley* (died in 1981), drummer Carlton Barrett (shot down in 1987), drummer Arthur Taylor,* group toured 1988, current leader/bassist Aston "Family Man" Barrett (brother of Carlton), guitarist/singers Junior Marvin & Al Anderson, keyboardist Earl Lindo, "Carrott" Jarrett, drummer Michael Richards, guitarist Owen Reid, keyboardist Martin Batiste. Albums *Id, Reggae Hits, The Wailers.*

WAILING SOULS
Reggae Album Grammy 1993 for *All Over the World.*

WAINWRIGHT, LOUDON, II
Album *More Love Songs.*

WAINWRIGHT, LOUDON, III (1947–)
b. 9/5 Chapel Hill, NC. Guitarist/singer/songwriter, albums *A Live One, Fame and Wealth, I'm Alright, Therapy.*

WAITS, TOM (1949–)
b. 12/7 Pomona, CA. Pianist/singer/composer, hit albums *Rain Dogs* 1985, *Frank's Wild Years* 1987, *Blue Valentine, Heart Attack & Vine, Nighthawks at the Diner, Small Change,* recorded Depression Era anthem "Brother Can You Spare a Dime?" 1992, hit album *Bone Machine* won Grammy 1993.

WAKELY, JIMMY (1914–1982)
b. 2/16 Mineola, AK. Actor/singer/songwriter, starred in western films, had CBS radio show 1952/57.

WAKEMAN, RICK (1949–)
b. 5/18 London, England. Keyboardist/composer, albums *Journey to the Center of the Earth, Myths and Legends, The Six Wives of Henry VIII.*

WALDMAN, WENDY
Songwriter with Jon Lind and Phil Galdston wrote "Save the Best for Last" popularized by Vanessa Williams,* Grammy winner 1993.

WALES, HOWARD
Album Howard Wales and J. Garcia on *Hooteroll?*

WALKER, AARON "T-BONE" (1910–1975)
b. 5/25 Linden, TX. Guitarist/pianist/singer, called the "Daddy of the Blues," toured with Ida Cox* & Ma Rainey* in 1930s, with Les Hite 1940/45, soloist in 50s/60s, toured Europe, wrote "Stormy Melody" & other songs. Died 3/16 Los Angeles, CA.

WALKER, ALBERTINA
Gospel singer, won Grammy 1993 for *Live.*

WALKER BROTHERS
California rock group with Gary, John, and Scott Walker, hit

singles "Make It Easy on Yourself" & "The Sun Ain't Gonna Shine Anymore."

WALKER, JERRY JEFF (1942–)
b. 3/16 Oneonta, NY. Guitarist/singer/songwriter, albums *Driftin' Way of Life, Navajo Rug, Nolan Ryan (He's a Hero), Viva Terlingua, Great Gongos* 1992.

WALKER, JUNIOR (1942–)
b. Autrey de Witt, Jr. in Blythesville, AK. Singer with **Junior Walker and the All Stars** with James Graves, Vic Thomas, & Willie Woods, hit song "Shotgun." Albums *Gotta Hold Onto This Feelin', Greatest Hits, Motown Superstars Vol. 5.*

WALLACE, SIPPIE (1898–1986)
b. Beulah Thomas in Houston, TX. Pianist/organist/singer, went to Chicago in early 1920s, in Detroit and toured 30s/70s, at Carnegie Hall in NY City in July 1980. Album *Women Be Wise.*

WALLER, THOMAS "FATS" (1904–1943)
b. New York, NY. Pianist/singer/composer, with McKinney's **Cotton Pickers,** Jack Teagarden,* & others in 1920s, toured with own band 30s//40s, with lyricist Andy Razaf* wrote "Honeysuckle Rose," "Ain't Misbehavin'," & other songs. Albums *A Legendary Performer, Jazz Collector's Edition, Joint is Jumpin', Lounging at the Waldorf, Piano Solos: Turn on Heat.* Died of pneumonia on a train near Kansas City, MO.

WALLFLOWER
Group with Jakob Dylan, Son of Bob Dylan.*

WALSH, JOE (1947–)
b. 11/20 Wichita, KS. Guitarist/singer/songwriter, albums *Best of Joe Walsh, But Seriously Folks, Ordinary Average Guy, The Confessor, Barnstorm,* at the Ultimate Guitar Concert in San Francisco in September 1992.

WALT MINK
Minneapolis pop trio with singer/guitarist John Kimbrough,

drummer Joey Waronker, & bassist Candice Belanoff, album *Miss Happiness* 1992.

WALTERS, JAMES (1969–   )
b. Marblehead, MA. Actor/singer, sang "How Do You Talk To an Angel?" in film *The Heights,* planned wedding with actress Drew Barrymore in June 1993 (never occurred).

WANG CHUNG
British jazz/rock group founded 1981 with Darren Costin, Nick Feldman, & Jack Hues. Name is Chinese for "perfect pitch." Albums *Mosaic, Points on the Curve.*

WAR
Formed in San Pedro, CA as a backing band for singer Eric Burdon, with singer/drummer Harold Brown, guitarist Howard Scott, singer/keyboardist Lonnie Jordan, saxist Charles Miller, Lee Oskar, later bassist Luther Rabb, singer Tweed Smith, saxist Pat Rizzo, drummer Ron Hammaon, hit single "Slippin' into Darkness." Albums *All Day Music, Best of War, Rap Declares War,* toured US 1992.

WARD, CHARLES B. (1865–1917)
b. London, England. Popular composer, came to New York. With lyricist J. F. Palmer* he composed "The Band Played On" 1895 which sold over one million copies of sheet music.

WARD, ROBERT (1917–   )
b. Cleveland, Ohio. Composer, his opera *The Crucible* won the 1962 Pulitzer Prize, albums *Fear No Evil, Crucible/Buckley.*

WARD, SAMUEL A. (1848–1903)
b. Newark, NJ. Composer, wrote the tune "Materna" which became the music for the lyrics by Katherine Lee Bates*: "America the Beautiful" 1895.

WARINER, STEVE (1954–   )
b. 12/25 Kentucky. Singer, albums *Christmas Memories, I am Ready, I Got Dreams, Laredo, Life's Highway,* etc.

WARING, FRED (1900–1984)

b. Tyrone, PA. Bandleader, formed the **Pennsylvanians**. The *Fred Waring Show* was popular on radio in the 1940s/50s. Albums *Christmas Time, The Best of Fred Waring*. Died 7/29 Danville, PA.

WARNER, ANNA B. (1820–1915)

b. West Point, NY. Hymnist, with composer W. B. Bradbury* wrote "Jesus Loves Me" 1859, sung by Roy Rogers* & Dale Evans on the *Reader's Digest* album *50 Beloved Songs of Faith* 1992.

WARNES, JENNIFER (1947–)

b. Orange County, CA. Singer, with Joe Cocker* sang "Up Where We Belong" 1983 & won an Oscar. Albums *Best of Jennifer Warnes, Famous Blue Raincoat, The Hunter,* hit single "Rock You Gently."

WARRANT

With lead singer Jani Lane, guitarists Joey Allen & Erik Turner, bassist Jerry Dixon, & drummer Steven Sweet. Double platinum album *Dirty Rotten Filthy Stinking Rich* 1989, double platinum album *Cherry Pie* 1990, *Quality You Can Taste,* video *Dog Eat Dog* 1992.

WARREN, HARRY (1893–1981)

b. Salvatore Guaragna in New York, NY. Songwriter, with Billy Rose wrote "I Found a Million Dollar Baby in a Five and Ten Cent Store" 1931, with Al Dubin* "Shuffle Off to Buffalo" 1932, with Mack Gordon* "The Chattanooga Choo Choo" 1941.

WARWICK, DIONNE (1941–)

b. 12/12 East Orange, NJ. Singer, hits "Alfie," "Heartbreaker," "I'll Never Fall in Love Again," albums *At Her Very Best, Friends, Sings Cole Porter, Friends Can Be Lovers* 1992, videos *Dionne Warwick, The Wall/Live in Berlin.*

WASHBURN, HENRY S. (1813–1903)
b. Providence, RI. Lyricist, with composer G. F. Root* wrote the popular Civil War song "The Vacant Chair" 1862.

WASHINGTON, DINAH (1924–1963)
b. Ruth Jones in Tuscaloosa, AL & raised in Chicago. Singer, known as the "Queen of the Blues," recorded with Lionel Hampton* 1943/46, went solo, in London & Stockholm 1959. Albums *Complete on Mercury Vols. 1 to 7, Dinah '63, Golden Classics, In Love, Mellow Mama.* A postage stamp was issued in her honor in 1993.

WASHINGTON, GROVER, JR (1945–   )
b. 12/12 Buffalo, NY. Jazz/pop clarinetist/pianist, with Bill Withers* had hit "Just the Two of Us" 1981, with **Four Chefs** 1959/63, with various groups 60s/80s. Albums *A Secret Place, Anthology, Come Morning, Feels So Good.* "Summer Chill" track from *Next Exit* Grammy winner 1993. Played in The White House for President & Mrs. Clinton in June 1993.

WATANOBE, KAZUMI
Albums *Mobo Club, Mobo 1 & 2, Spice of Life,* etc.

WATANOBE, SADAO
Albums *Elis, Fill Up the Night, Front Seat, Round Trip, Sweet Deal,* etc.

WATERBOYS, THE
Albums *A Pagan Place, Best of 1981–1990, Fisherman's Blues, The Waterboys, This is the Sea.*

WATERS, ETHEL (1900–1977)
b. 10/31 Chester, PA. Singer, sang in Cotton Club & Plantation Club in NY City in 1920s, in Lew Leslie's *Blackbirds* 1930, hit "Stormy Weather" 1933, sang in the Billy Graham Crusades, sang in The White House for President & Mrs. Nixon in January 1971.

WATERS, MUDDY (1915–1983)
b. McKinley Morganfield 4/4 Rolling Fork, MS. Jazz guitarist/ vocalist, hits "I'm a Man," "I've Got My Mojo Working," "Rollin' Stone." Won five Grammys, toured England 1958, elected to Ebony Hall of Fame 1973, toured Japan 1980. Albums *Folk Singer, King Bee, London Sessions, Best of Muddy Waters,* etc. A postage stamp was issued in his honor 1994.

WATERS, ROGER
Singer, with guest stars Rita Coolidge* & others on album *Amused to Death* 1992, videos *Radio K.A.O.S., The Wall/Live in Berlin, What God Wants* Grammy winner 1993.

WATLEY, JODY (1961–   )
Albums *Affairs of the Heart, Jody Watley, Larger than Life, You Wanna Dance with Me?,* video *Classics I.*

WATSON, BOBBY (1954–   )
Soprano saxist with Art Blakey & the **Jazz Messengers*** 1977/ 81, leader of **Horizon** on *Post-motown Bop* performed with **New York Jazz Giants** 1992, album *Present Tense* 1992.

WATSON, DOC (1923–   )
b. 3/2 Deep Gap, NC. Blind singer/banjoist/guitarist, albums *At Last, Old Timey Music, On Praying Ground* (1990 Grammy for Traditional Folk Songs), *On Stage, Southbound,* with Merle Watson on *Ballads from Deep Gap, Down South, Pickin' the Blues.*

WATSON, GENE (1943–   )
b. 10/11 Palestine, TX. Albums *Back in the Fire, Greatest Hits,* etc.

WAYANS, DAMON (1960–   )
b. New York, NY. Album *Mo' Money* 1992.

WAYNE, BERNIE (1919–1993)
Composer, wrote the music for "Blue Velvet" which was a 1963

hit for Bobby Vinton,* revived in the film *Blue Velvet* 1986. Also wrote "There She Is," the crowning theme for the Miss America Pageant held yearly in Atlantic City, NJ.

WEATHER REPORT
Rock group with Alejandro Acuna, Alphonso Johnson, Jaco Pastorius, Wayne Shorter,* Chester Thompson, Norada Walden, & Josef Zawinul. Instrumental hit "Birdland" 1978. They won 1980 Jazz-fusion Grammy award, voted by *down beat* readers as Top Jazz Group 1980 for ninth straight time. Albums *Evolutionary Spiral* 1984, *Black Market, I Sing the Body Electric, Sportin' Life, Weather Report with Pastorious,* etc.

WEAVERS, THE
Folk singers with singer/musician Erik Darling (b. 1933 Baltimore, MD), Fred Hellerman, Lee Hays, Ernie Krause, & Pete Seeger,* albums *Almanac, Weavers at Carnegie Hall, Vol. 2,* etc.

WEBB, GEORGE J. (1803–1887)
b. Salisbury, Wiltshire, England. Composer, came to Boston in 1830. Composed a song in 1837 whose tune was used for George Duffield's* "Stand Up for Jesus" 1858.

WEBB, JIM (1946–   )
b. 8/15 Elk City, OK. Songwriter, hits "Up, Up, and Away" 1967, "MacArthur Park," "Galveston," "By the Time I Get to Phoenix," etc.

WEBB, WILLIAM "CHICK" (1902–1939)
b. Baltimore, MD. Drummer, was hunchbacked by tuberculosis of the spine, but led his **Harlem Stompers** at the Savoy in NY City 1927, toured 1927/29. Album *Chick Webb & Orchestra 1935–38.* Suffered with pleurisy & while playing on a riverboat was taken ill and rushed to Johns Hopkins Hospital in Baltimore. Seven days later he called out: "I'm sorry, I gotta go" and was gone.

WEBBER, *see* LLOYD WEBBER, ANDREW

WEBSTER, BEN F. (1909–1973)

b. Kansas City, MO. Pianist/tenor saxist, toured with Andy Kirk's **Twelve Clouds of Joy** during the Great Depression of the early 1930s, also with Blanche Calloway* & others, led own combos 50s/70s, toured Europe with Jazz at the Philharmonic, albums *At the Renaissance, Ben Webster and Associates, Ben & Sweets* (Sweets Edison), *Soulmates* (Ben & Joe Zawinul).

WEBSTER, JOSEPH P. (1819–1875)

b. Manchester, NH. Organist/composer, with lyricist S. F. Bennett* composed the music for "In the Sweet Bye and Bye" 1867. Johnny Cash* sang the song on the *Reader's Digest* album *50 Beloved Songs of Faith* issued 1992.

WEBSTER, KATIE

Albums *Swamp Queen Boogie, Two Fisted Mama, No Foolin', The Swamp Boogie Queen.*

WEBSTER, PAUL FRANCIS (1907–1984)

b. 12/20 New York, NY. Lyricist, wrote over 500 songs, hits "Shadow of Your Smile" 1965 won an Oscar, "Love is a Many Splendored Thing." Died 3/22 Beverly Hills, CA.

WEEN

Hit "Pure Guava" 1993.

WEILL, KURT (1900–1950)

b. Dessau, Germany. Composer of *The Three Penny Opera* 1928, *Lady in the Dark* 1941, *One Touch of Venus* 1943, etc. Albums *A Stranger Here Myself, Aufstieg/Bruckner, 3 Penny Opera/ Klemperer, O Moon of Alabama, Street Scene,* etc.

WEINBERG, MAX M. (1951–)

b. 4/13 South Orange, NJ. Drummer, called "The Mighty One," with **E Street Band*** & with Bruce Springsteen* since 1974.

WEIR, BOB (1949–)

b. Robert Hall 10/16 San Francisco, CA. Singer/musician with the

Grateful Dead,* solo albums *Bombs Away* 1978, *Bobby and The Midnights, Heaven Help the Fool.*

WEISGALL, HUGO (1912–)
b. Eibenschultz, Czechoslovakia. Composer, came to USA to live, wrote ballet *Quest* 1942, musicals *The Tenor* 1950, *The Stranger* 1952, *Purgatory* 1959, *Atholick* 1964, *The Gardens of Adonis* performed at Opera Omaha International Fall Festival 1992.

WELCH, KEN (1926–)
b. 2/4 Kansas City, MO. Composed music for *Carol Burnett Show* 1976 & *Linda in Wonderland* 1981 won Emmys.

WELK, LAWRENCE (1903–1992)
b. 3/11 Strasburg, ND. Bandleader, his six-man combo played on radio station WNAX, Yankton, SD 1925, moved to Chicago 1930s. Known as the "King of Champagne Music," hosted the *Lawrence Welk Show* on Public Television for many years. Albums *22 Great Songs for Dancing, 22 Great Songs for Easy Listening, All Time Favorite Waltzes,* etc. Gave his last concert in San Francisco, CA in June 1982 and died on 5/17 at Santa Monica, CA. Welk's birthplace in Strasburg was dedicated in June 1992.

WELL, CYNTHIA (1937–)
Songwriter, with Barry Mann* wrote "You've Lost that Loving Feeling" & "Saturday Night at the Movies."

WELLS, DAWNA KAY (1961–)
Country singer. Dawna won Song of the Year & Video of the Year 1989 from the California Music Association for "Burn One for Me," hit single "The Echo of Mama's Cry." After her father Rusty Morris murdered her mother in Phoenix, AZ in June 1989 she helped solve the mystery. Her father was sentenced to life in prison.

WELLS, JUNIOR (1932–)
b. West Memphis, AK. Harpist/singer, albums *Coming at You/ Buddy, Guy, Hoodoo Man Blues, It's My Life, Baby,* etc.

WELLS, KITTY (1919–   )
b. Muriel Deason 8/30 Nashville, TN. Singer, known as the "Queen of Country Music." Albums *Dust on the Bible,* etc., honored at country music concert Sept. 1992. Married singer Johnny Wright.

WELLS, MARY (1943–1992)
b. 5/13 Detroit, MI. Pop singer, her early 1960s hits were "The One Who Really Loves You," "You Beat Me to the Punch," "Twin Lovers," & "My Guy" co-written with Smokey Robinson.* Wells toured with the **Supremes,* Temptations,* Four Tops,** & the **Beatles.*** Albums *Bye Bye Baby, Greatest Hits, Mr. Guy, Two Lovers.* Died of cancer on 7/26 in Los Angeles, CA.

WELLS, WILLIAM "DICKIE" (1909–1985)
b. Centerville, TN. Jazz trombonist/vocalist, with Count Basie* 1938/46, toured Europe five times in 50s/60s, played at clubs in NY City in 70s/80s.

WELLSTOOD, RICHARD M. "DICK" (1927–1987)
b. Greenwich, CT. Pianist with Gene Krupa,* **Ferryboat Band** in Brielle, NJ, then with **Dukes of Dixieland.*** Led own groups 70s/80s, at Newport Jazz Festival picnic at Stanhope, NJ in June 1980.

WENDLING, PETE (1888–1974)
b. New York, NY. Songwriter, wrote ragtime music, composed "Yacka Hula Hickey Dula" featured by Al Jolson.*

WENRICH, PERCY (1887–1952)
b. Joplin, MO. Composer/vaudeville entertainer with his wife Dolly Connolly. With lyricist Stanley Murphy* wrote "Put on Your Old Gray Bonnet" 1909, "Moonlight Bay," etc.

WEST, DOTTIE (1932–1991)
b. Dorothy Marie Marsh 10/11 McMinnville, TN. Singer. Album *Collectors Series.* Married Alan Winters, then Bill West. Died 9/4 in an auto accident in Nashville, TN.

WEST, HEDDY (1938–)

b. Cartersville, GA. Singer/banjoist, sang in USA & Europe, hit single "500 Miles" on *Troubadours of the Folk Era, Vol. 3* 1992.

WESTENBERG, PAUL

Singer, formerly with **The Replacements,*** hit rock track "Dyslexic Heart" 1992, album *14 Songs* 1992.

WESTENDORF, THOMAS P. (1848–1923)

b. Bowling Green, VA. Popular composer, wrote words & music for "I'll Take You Home Again, Kathleen" 1879.

WESTON, RANDY (1926–)

b. Brooklyn, NY City. Jazz pianist, leader of a 14-member ensemble of Pan-African roots of jazz, albums *Portrait of Duke Ellington, Portrait of Monk, Self Portraits,* etc.

WHAM!

British group formed 1982 with lead singer/bassist George Michael* & guitarist/drummer Andrew Ridgeley, hit singles "Wake Me Up Before You GoGo" 1984, "Careless Whisper" 1984, "Everything She Wants" 1985, albums *Fantastic, Make It Big, Music from the Edge of Heaven,* videos *The Video, Wham, In China-foreign Sky, Wham! The Final.*

WHISPERS, THE

Album *Rock Steady* 1992.

WHITCOMB, IAN

Albums *Happy Days are Here Again, Old Friends, Tango Dreams,* etc.

WHITE, BARRY (1944–)

b. 9/12 Galveston, TX. Singer, hits "Never, Never Gonna Give You Up" 1973, "My First, My Last, My Everything" 1974. Albums *Beware, Greatest Hits Vols. 1 & 2, Put Me in Your Mix, Just for You* 1992.

WHITE, COOL (1821–1891)
b. Philadelphia, PA, Minstrel showman/popular composer, wrote "Lubly Fan" 1844. With lyricist Henry Russell this tune became "Buffalo Girls, Won't You Come Out Tonight?" 1854 & was later used for "Dance with Dolly" 1944.

WHITE HEART
Gospel Singers, won Grammy 1993 for "Tales of Wonder."

WHITE, JOY
Country singer, debut album *Between Midnight & Hindsight* 1992.

WHITE, KARYN (1964–)
b. 10/14 Singer, album *Superwoman* 1992.

WHITE LION
Albums *Big Game, Mane Attraction, Pride.*

WHITE ZOMBIE
Monster music on *La Sexorcisto: Devil Music, Vol. 1.*

WHITEFIELD, GEORGE (1714–1770)
b. Gloucester, England. Methodist preacher/hymnist, came to Savannah, GA in 1738, traveled through the colonies & returned to England. With composer Mendelssohn wrote "Hark the Herald Angels Sing" 1753. Returned to America in 1769 and died in Newburyport, MA.

WHITEMAN, PAUL (1890–1967)
b. Denver, CO. Violinist/leader, known as the "King of Jazz," played in Denver Symphony 1912/15, in U. S. Navy in World War I, led bands in Atlantic City, NJ and in NY City in 1920s/50s. Album *When Day is Done.* Died in Doylestown, PA.

WHITESNAKE
British rock group formed 1978 with belter David Coverdale,* albums *Come an' Get It, Live in the Heart, Love Hunter, Slide*

It On, Trouble, Whitesnake, video *Trilogy.* Coverdale dissolved the group in 1990 & retired to Lake Tahoe, NV. Album *Coverdale/Page* 1993.

WHITESPREAD DEPRESSION ORCHESTRA
New England jazz group formed in 1962 with singer/vibist Jon Holtzman & saxist Michael Hashim in NY City in 1979/80s.

WHITFIELD, MARK
Pop/jazz fusion guitarist, album *Mark Whitfield* 1993.

WHITFIELD, THOMAS (d. 1992)
Gospel choir director/pianist/singer on album *Alive and Satisfied* 1992, winner of male solo performer at the eighth *Stellar* awards show.

WHITING, GEORGE (1884–1943)
b. Chicago, IL. Singer/lyricist, with composer Walter Donaldson* wrote "My Blue Heaven" 1927.

WHITING, MARGARET (1924–   )
b. 7/22 Detroit, MI. Singer, hit "Moonlight in Vermont," album *Collectors Series.*

WHITING, RICHARD A. (1891–1938)
b. Peoria, IL. Popular composer, wrote the music for "Some Sunday Morning," "Till We Meet Again" 1918, "Sleepy Time Gal," with W. F. Harling: "Beyond the Blue Horizon," "One Hour with You," "On the Good Ship Lollipop" for Shirley Temple,* "My Ideal." Died in Beverly Hills, CA.

WHITLEY, CHRIS
Singer, hit single "Kick the Stones" on album *Living with the Law* 1991.

WHITLEY, KEITH
Country singer, top country 1988 single "Don't Close Your Eyes," albums *Greatest Hits, Kentucky Bluebird, L.A. to Miami,* etc. With Earl Thomas Conley* nominated for Country Duo 1992.

WHITSON, BETH SLATER (1879–1930)
b. Goodrich, TN. Lyricist, with composer Leo Friedman* wrote "Let Me Call You Sweetheart" 1910.

WHITTAKER, ROGER
b. Nairobi, Kenya. Singer/guitarist, albums *Best Loved Ballads, Classics Collection, Country Collection, Living and Loving, The Wind Beneath My Wings,* etc. Toured USA 1992. "The Last Farewell" sold eleven million copies.

WHO, THE
British rock group formed in 1960s with singer Roger Daltry,* drummer Kenny Jones, John Entwistle, guitarist Peter Townshend,* & Keith Moon (died of a drug overdose in 1978). Townshend composed the rock opera *Tommy* 1969 & filmed in 1974, & produced again in April 1993. The group performed at the Woodstock Festival in NY State in 1969. Hit "My Generation" on music video *British Rock: The First Wave* 1985, videos *Quadrophenia,* platinum *The Who Live Featuring Tommy* 1990.

WHODINI
Brooklyn group with Ecstacy, Jalil, & Grandmaster Dee, hits "Funky Beat" 1986, "Fugitive" 1986, albums *Open Sesame, Escape,* video *Back in Black.*

WILDE, KIM (1960–   )
b. 11/18 London, England. Singer, hit "Kids in America" 1982.

WILDER, ALEX (1907–1980)
b. Alexander Lafayette Chew 2/17 Rochester, NY. Composer of pop/jazz/classical works, an arranger for Frank Sinatra,* Judy Garland,* Jimmy Dorsey,* & others. Died 12/24 Gainesville, FL.

WILDER, WEBB
b. John McMurray. Singer/guitarist, albums *Hybrid Vigos, Doo Dad* 1992.

WILDSIDE
Five man rock group formerly **Young Guns** 1988, album *Under the Influence* 1992 about life, drugs, and violence on the Sunset Strip in California.

WILEY, LEE (1915–1975)
b. 10/9 Port Gibson, OK. Singer/composer, sang on radio programs 1931/33 with Paul Whiteman,* sang in clubs, co-wrote "Anytime, Anydate, Anywhere," at Newport Jazz Festival in NY City 1972. Albums *As Time Goes By, Night in Manhattan, Sings Gershwin & Porter,* etc. Married Jess Stacy 1943 but separated 1945. Died of cancer in NY City.

WILL TO POWER
Singers, on Top Ten singles list for "Baby, I Love Your Way/Freebird Melody" 1989, albums *Journey Home, Will to Power.*

WILLARD, EMMA C. H. (1787–1870)
b. Berlin, CT. Lyricist, with composer Joseph P. Knight (1812–1887) wrote "Rocked in the Cradle of the Deep" 1839, sung by basso Knight and tenor John Braham (1774–1856) in New York City in 1840. Died in Troy, NY.

WILLIAMS, ALYSON
Singer, duet with Chuck Stanley "Make Your Mine Tonight" 1987, debut album *Raw* 1989, hit R&B single "Just My Luck" 1992, album *Alyson Williams* 1992.

WILLIAMS, CHARLES M. "COOTIE" (1908–1985)
b. 7/24 Mobile, AL. Jazz trumpeter with Duke Ellington* 1929/40, Benny Goodman* 1940/41, formed own band 1941, at Savoy Ballroom when it closed in 1948, toured Europe 1959, with Duke Ellington* 1962/74 then with Mercer Ellington.* Died 9/15 Long Island, NY.

WILLIAMS, CHRISTOPHER
Baritone singer nephew of Ella Fitzgerald,* album *Changes* 1992.

WILLIAMS, DENIECE (1951–)

b. 6/3 Gary, IN. Singer, with Johnny Mathis* had hit song "Too Much, Too Little, Too Late" 1978, hit "Let's Hear It For the Boy" 1984, albums *As Good as It Gets, My Melody, Special Love, This is Niecy,* with others on *'Till Their Eyes Shine* (Lullaby Album) 1992.

WILLIAMS, DON (1939–)

b. 5/27 Floydala, TX. Guitarist/singer/songwriter, albums *Best of Don Williams Vols. 1, 2, & 3, Greatest Country Hits, I Believe in You, True Love,* video *Don Williams Live.*

WILLIAMS, H. ANDREW "ANDY" (1930–)

b. 12/3 Wall Lake, Iowa. Singer, hits "Lonely Street" 1959, "Where Do I Begin?" 1971, albums *Moon River, Unchained Melody, Greatest Hits Vols. 1 & 2.*

WILLIAMS, HANK, JR. (1949–)

b. 5/26 Shreveport, LA. Country/western singer/songwriter, son of Hank Williams, Sr.* Hit single "Texas Women" 1981, platinum album *Greatest Hits III–1989.* Albums *America, Born to Boogie, Five-O, Lone Wolf, Strong Stuff, Maverick* 1992, *Out of Left Field* 1993, videos *A Star Spangled County PA, Full Access.* Married model Mary Jane in July 1990.

WILLIAMS, HANK, SR. (1923–1953)

b. 9/17 Georgiana, AL. Country singer/songwriter, wrote "Cold, Cold Heart" recorded by Tony Bennett* & "Your Cheatin' Heart" 1952. Albums *24 Greatest Hits Vols. 1 & 2, 40 Greatest Hits, Last Highway, Walkin' Around,* etc. Died of a heart attack in the seat of his golf cart on January 1st at age 29. A postage stamp was issued in his honor in 1993.

WILLIAMS, JOE (1903–1982)

b. Crawford, MS. Blues vocalist known as "Mississippi Big Joe," recorded in Chicago 1930, worked with levee gangs during the Great Depression, with Charlie Jordan in late 1940s. Albums *Blues on Highway 49, Nine String Guitar Blues.* Died 12/17.

WILLIAMS, JOE (1918–)

b. Joseph Goreed 12/12 Cordele, GA. Blues/ballad/jazz singer, with Count Basie* 1954/61, hit "Everyday I Have the Blues," regular at Newport Jazz Festivals, won *down beat* critics' award as Male Singer of the Year 1980, at Playboy Jazz Festival in Los Angeles 1992. Albums *A Swinging Night at Birdland, Nothin' But the Blues, That Holiday Feelin'*, etc. Honored with National Endowment for the Arts American Jazz Masters Award 1993.

WILLIAMS, JOHN (1941–)

b. 4/24 Melbourne, Australia. Guitarist, came to America with Sky. Albums *Echoes of London* 1986, *Home Alone, A Portrait, The Guitar is the Song.*

WILLIAMS, JOHN TOWNER (1932–)

b. 2/8 Flushing, NY City. Composer, won Oscars for scores for *Jaws* 1975, *Star Wars* 1977, *Raiders of the Lost Ark, E.T., Home Alone,* with Boston Pops 1980/93, *Hook* score Grammy winner 1993.

WILLIAMS, LUCINDA

Country-rocker/songwriter, sang in clubs in New Orleans, Austin, & Houston, Texas, wrote "The Night's Too Long" popularized by Patty Loveless* & "Passionate Kisses" sung by Mary-Chapin Carpenter,* albums *Sweet Old World* 1992 & *Joe Ely and Lucinda Williams* 1993.

WILLIAMS, MARION (1927–1994)

b. Miami, Florida. Gospel singer. At age three she sang in a church choir, then with the CLARA WARD SINGERS. In 1959 she formed the STARS OF FAITH, then went solo in 1965. Died on July 2nd, 1994 in Philadelphia.

WILLIAMS, MARY LOU (1910–1981)

b. Mary Elfrieda Scruggs 5/8 Atlanta, GA. Pianist/composer, at age four taken to Pittsburgh, PA, toured with **The Synco Jazzers** 1925/26, arranged music for Andy Kirk 1928/42, married John Williams & toured with his band 1927/28, divorced Williams & married Harold Baker 1942, led own trios in 1950s, sang in NY night clubs 60s/70s. Composed "A Fungus Amungus," albums *Live at the Cookery, The Best of Mary Lou Williams.*

WILLIAMS, PATRICK M. (1939–)
b. 4/23 Bonne Terre, MO. Composer, wrote theme songs for TV shows *Lou Grant* 1980, *The Princess and the Cabbie* 1982, won Emmys. Album *Threshold.*

WILLIAMS, PAUL HAMILTON (1940–)
b. 9/19 Omaha, NE. Singer/songwriter, hit "Evergreen" 1976 won an Oscar.

WILLIAMS, ROBIN (1952–)
b. 7/21 Chicago, IL. Singer/comedian won 1988 Grammy for *Good Morning Vietnam,* video *Robin Williams Live.*

WILLIAMS, ROGER (1926–)
b. 10/1 Omaha, NE. Pianist, hits "Autumn Leaves" 1955, "Born Free" 1966, albums *Ivory Impact, Phantom of the Opera, Somewhere in Time, Somewhere My Love,* etc.

WILLIAMS, SOL "TEX" (1917–1985)
b. 8/23 Ramsey, IL. Country singer/songwriter/leader, formed **Western Caravan** band 1946, appeared on radio programs and in films. Died 10/11 in Newhall, CA.

WILLIAMS, SPENCER (1889–1965)
b. New Orleans, LA. Pianist/composer, wrote "Basin Street Blues" 1923.

WILLIAMS, TOM
b. Baltimore, MD. Trumpeter, with pianist Kenny Barron,* bassist Peter Washington, drummer Kenny Washington, & saxman Javon Jackson on *Introducing Tom Williams* 1993.

WILLIAMS, TONY (1924–1992)
Lead singer with the **Platters,*** hits "Only You" & "The Great Pretender." Williams went solo in 1960, albums *Civilization, Emergency, Foreign Intrigue, Native Heart, Spring.*

WILLIAMS, VANESSA (1963–)
b. 3/18 New York, NY. Beauty queen/singer, album *The Right Stuff*, hits "Just for Tonight" 1992, "Love Is," "Save the Best for Last" 1993 Grammy winner, "The Comfort Zone" 1993 Grammy winner.

WILLIAMS, VICTORIA
Songwriter, wrote "Crazy Mary" sung by **Pearl Jam*** & "Frying Pan" sung by Evan Dando of **Lemonheads*** on album *Sweet Relief* 1993 to help pay her medical bills for treatment of multiple sclerosis.

WILLIAMSON, SONNY BOY
b. Willie Rice Miller in Glendora, MS. Harpist, albums *Bummer Road, Down & Out Blues, Keep It to Ourselves, King Biscuit Time, Real Folk Blues,* etc. Married sister of singer "Howlin' Wolf" (Chester A. Burnett*).

WILLIE D
Houston rapper, single "F... Rodney King" 1992 about the Los Angeles riots, the song ends with gunshots directed at King.

WILLIS, BRUCE (1955–)
b. 3/19 West Germany. Actor/singer, albums *If It Don't Kill You, The Return of Bruno.*

WILLIS, CHARLES "SKEETER" (1917–1976)
b. Coalton, OK. Singer/fiddler, joined with Guy and Vic Willis to form the **Willis Brothers.** Died 1/28 Nashville, TN.

WILLIS, RICHARD S. (1819–1900)
b. Boston, MA. Composer, with lyricist E. H. Sears* composed "It Came Upon a Midnight Clear" 1850.

WILLS, ROBERT "BOB" (1906–1975)
b. 3/6 Limestone County, TX. Singer/songwriter, formed **Texas Playboys** in Tulsa, OK in 1930s, albums *24 Greatest Hits, Best*

of Bob Willis, Time Changes Everything, etc. A postage stamp was issued in his honor in 1993.

WILLSON, MEREDITH (1902–1984)
b. 5/18 Mason City, Iowa. Leader/composer, wrote scores for *The Music Man, The Unsinkable Molly Brown,* hit "Seventy-six Trombones," album *The Music Man.* Died 6/15 Santa Monica, CA.

WILSON, ANN (1951–)
b. 6/19 San Diego, CA. Lead singer of **Heart*** from 1972, with Nancy Wilson* on soundtrack *Singles* 1992.

WILSON, BRIAN DOUGLAS (1942–)
b. 6/20 Hawthorne, CA. Singer/songwriter with the **Beach Boys,*** hits "Surfin' USA" 1963, "Help Me, Rhonda" 1965. Album *Brian Wilson.*

WILSON, CARL DEAN (1946–)
b. 12/21 Hawthorne, CA. Singer/guitarist with the **Beach Boys.***

WILSON, CASSANDRA
Jazz singer, albums *Blue Skies, Jumpworld, Live, She Who Weeps, Dance to the Drums Again* 1993.

WILSON, DENNIS (1941–1983)
b. 12/1 Hawthorne, CA. Drummer/keyboardist/singer with the **Beach Boys,*** hit solo album *Pacific Ocean Blue.* Died 12/28 Marina del Rey, CA.

WILSON, JACKIE (1932–1984)
b. 6/9 Detroit, MI. Singer, called "Mr. Excitement," hits "Lonely Teardrops," "Higher and Higher," "Baby Work Out," "That's Why." Died 1/21 Mount Holly, NJ. Album *Mr. Excitement* issued in 1992.

WILSON, JOEMY
Singer, albums *Carolan's Cup, Carolan's Cottage, Celtic Dreams, Gifts Vi Trad X-mas Cards, Gifts V2, Gifts Vol. 3.*

WILSON, KIM
Blues singer with the **Fabulous Thunderbirds,*** debut album *Tiger Man* 1993.

WILSON, NANCY (1937–)
b. 2/20 Chillicothe, Ohio. Singer, with Cannonball Adderley* in 1960s, at London Palladium 1973, hits "Face It Girl it's Over" & "You're Right as Rain," had own show on KNBC-TV in Los Angeles 1974/75. At age 55 she had recorded more than 50 albums, "With My Lover Beside Me" Grammy winner 1993.

WILSON, NANCY (1954–)
b. 3/16 San Francisco, CA. Guitarist/singer, sang at the Apollo Theater in Harlem, NY City 1972. Album *Dreamboat Annie* 1976 sold 2.5 million copies, *Brigade* 1990 sold two million albums, with her sister Ann Wilson* on soundtrack *Singles* 1992. Married drummer Kenny Davis.

WILSON PHILLIPS
Singers Carnie & Wendy daughters of "Beach Boy" Brian Wilson* & Marilyn Wilson (performer with the **Honeys**); and Chynna Phillips daughter of John Phillips* and Michelle Phillips of the **Mamas and the Papas.*** Chynna was an actress on CBS show *Knot's Landing.* Album *Wilson Phillips* 1990 sold 8 million copies, *Shadows & Light* 1992, *The Videos.*

WILSON, SHANICE (1974–)
Singer, raised in Pittsburgh, PA, daughter of guitarist Carl Black & singer Crystal Wilson. Graduated from Pasadena H.S. 1990, CD *Inner Child,* top single "I Love Your Smile," with sister Penni Wilson on *Crystal Penny* 1992.

WILSON, THEODORE "TEDDY" (1912–1986)
b. 11/24 Austin, TX. Jazz pianist with Louis Armstrong* 1933, recorded with Billie Holiday,* with Benny Goodman* 1936/ 39, led own groups 1940s/80s, toured Europe in 50s/60s. Albums 1935–36/ *Jonah Jones,* 1937/ *Cootie Williams,* 1937– 38/ *Harry James,* 1938/ *Bobby Hackett,* 1939/ *Roy Eldridge, With Billie in Mind.*

WINANS, BEBE & CECE
Brother & sister gospel singers, toured USA 1992, album *Bebe and Cece Winans.*

WINANS, DANIEL
Gospel singer, won Gospel Music award as Male Vocalist and Mom & Pop Winans Group of the Year 1992. Mom & Pop Winans album *For the Rest of My Life* won Grammy.

WINANS, THE
Gospel group, Marvin and his three brothers, albums *The Winans at Carnegie Hall* and *Abundant Life* won 1988 Grammy, albums *Let My People Go, Return, Different Life Styles,* (first gospel album to top the R & B charts 1991). *All Out* Contemporary Soul/Gospel album Grammy winner 1994.

WINANS, VICKI
Sang "Blessed, Broken and Given" at Stellar Awards show in January 1993, album *The Lady* won Grammy 1993.

WIND MACHINE
Albums *Portraits of Christmas, Rain Maiden, Voices in the Wind, Wind Machine.*

WINDHAM HALL
Video features Mark Isham, Liz Story & William Ackerman on *Winter;* Liz Story, Shadowfax & Mark Isham on *Western Light.*

WINDING, KAI C. (1922–1983)
b. 5/12 Aarhus, Denmark. Jazz trumpeter/composer, brought to USA at age 12, with Benny Goodman* in 1940s, led own groups 50s//70s, then lived in Europe until 1980. Hit "Vido's Bop," album *With Strings/Green/Johnson.* Died 5/6 in Yonkers, NY.

WINNER, JOSEPH EASTBURN (1837–1918)
b. 4/21 Philadelphia, PA. Younger brother of Septimus Winner.* Music store owner/songwriter, wrote "Little Brown Jug" 1969 & other songs. Died 11/4 in Philadelphia, PA.

WINNER, SEPTIMUS (1827–1902)
b. 5/11 Philadelphia, PA. Composer/songwriter, wrote "Listen to the Mocking Bird" 1855 which sold a record 20 million copies of sheet music *(Guinness Book of Records)*. Also wrote "Oh Where Has My Little Dog Gone?" 1864, "Ten Little Indians" 1868 and "Whispering Hope" 1869. Died 11/22 Philadelphia. **The Browns*** sang "Whispering Hope" on the *Reader's Digest* album *50 Beloved Songs of Faith* 1992.

WINSTON, GEORGE
Pianist, albums *Autumn, December, Summer, Winter into Spring.*

WINTER, EDGAR H. (1946–   )
b. 12/28 Beaumont, TX. Singer/musician, hits "Frankenstein" & "Free Ride" on his album *They Only Come Out at Night* 1973, *Edgar Winter Collection, White Trash.*

WINTER, JOHNNY (1944–   )
b. 1/23 Leland, MS. Guitarist/singer/songwriter, albums *Captured Live, Guitar Slinger, Let Me In, Nothin' But the Blues, Serious Business,* etc.

WINTER, PAUL THEODORE (1939–   )
b. 8/31 Altoona, PA. Saxist, led the **Paul Winter Sextet,** the first jazz group to perform in The White House, played for President & Mrs. Kennedy 1962; led his own groups in 60s/80s. In 1975 off British Columbia he played for whales who gathered in a circle & stuck their heads out of the water and enjoyed the music. His eight-piece group issued an LP *Common Ground* 1978 with choruses with wolves, whales, and even an eagle. Winter said: "All are in the key of D-Flat, that must be the earth's key." Albums *Canyon, Earth Beat, Icarus, Sun Singer, Wolf Eyes,* etc. *Spanish Angel* New Age Album Grammy 1994.

WINTERHALTER, HUGO (1909–1973)
b. Wilkes-Barre, PA. Conductor/arranger, his record "Canadian Sunset" sold 1.5 million discs in the 1950s.

WINWOOD, STEVE (1948–)

b. 5/12 Birmingham, England. With **Blind Faith*** 1969/70s. Won 1986 Grammy for "Higher Love," 1988 Top Ten Pop single for "Roll with It," named 1988 Adult Contemporary Artist of the Year. Albums *Arc of a Diver, Chronicles, Refugees of the Heart, Steve Winwood,* etc.

WITHERS, WILLIAM H. "BILL" (1938–)

b. 7/4 Slab Fork, WV. Guitarist/pianist/singer/songwriter, served in US Navy, hit "Ain't No Sunshine" won Grammy 1971, "Lean on Me" 1972, "Lonely Day" 1976. Albums *Greatest Hits, Just as I Am, Still Bill.*

WOBBLE, JAN

Bassist with **Public Image, Ltd.,*** then **Invaders of the Heart,** album *Rising Above Bedlam* 1992 with singer Sinead O'Connor.*

WOLF, KATE

Albums *Back Roads, Safe at Anchor, The Wind Blows Wild, Gold in California, Poets Heart,* etc.

WOLF, PETER (1946–)

b. 3/7 Boston, MA. Lead singer with **J. Geils Band*** until 1984, solo single "I Need You Tonight" 1984. Albums *Lights Out, Up to No Good.*

WOLFE TONES

Albums *25th Anniversary, Let the People Sing, Profile, Rifles of the I.R.A., Spirit of the Nation.*

WOLFER, BILL

Albums *Caught in the Blue Light, Rained Through the Night.*

WOMEN'S JAZZ ALL-STARS

Led by Jane Fair with trumpeter/fluegelhorn player Stacy Rowles (daughter of jazz pianist Jimmy Rowles), pianist Jill McManus, bassist Louise Davis, drummer Barbara Merjan, & singer Janet Lawson at the third Women's Jazz Festival in Kansas City, MO in March 1980.

WONDER, STEVIE (1951–)

b. Steveland Morris Hardaway 5/13 Saginaw, MI & raised in Detroit. Pianist/vocalist, blind from birth, won 1973 Grammy for *Innervisions* & 1974 for *Fulfullingness, 1st Finale,* 1976 for *Songs in the Key of Life,* composed "You are the Sunhine of My Life," "Signed, Sealed, Delivered," "I'm Yours." Named by *down beat* as Soul/Rhythm & Blues Artist 1980, with Paul McCartney* with "Ebony and Ivory" 1982, on video *We Are the World* 1985, on album *Handel's Messiah: A Soulful Celebration* 1992, video *Stevie Wonder Live.* Received the Songwriters Lifetime Achievement award in December 1992.

WOOD, MARK

World's only heavy-metal violinist/drummer/guitarist, album *Voodoo Violence* 1992.

WOOD, RON (1947–)

b. 6/1 Guitarist, album *Gimme Some Neck.*

WOOD, ROY (1946–)

b. Ulysses Adrian Wood 11/8 Birmingham, England. Musician/ composer, wrote "Make Them Understand" recorded by the **Nightriders;** "Night of Fear" 1967; with **Wizzard** "Ball Park Incident " 1972; "See My Baby" 1973, etc.

WOODS, HARRY M. (1896–1970)

b. N. Chelmsford, MA. Popular composer, wrote words & music for "When the Red, Red Robin Comes Bob, Bob Bobbin' Along" 1926, "I'm Looking Over a Four-leaf Clover," and with lyricist Mort Dixon* wrote "River Stay Away From My Door" 1931; with lyricist H. E. Johnson "When the Moon Comes Over the Mountain" introduced by singer Kate Smith.*

WOODS, PHIL

Saxist formerly with **European Rhythm Machine.*** Albums *At the Vanguard, Bop Stew, Bouquet, Flash, Slash, Woodlore,* etc., video *Phil Woods in Concert.*

WOODSTOCK FESTIVAL

Concert in New York State in 1969 included Joan Baez* singing "Joe Hill," Richie Havens* "Freedom," **Canned Heat** "Going Up the Country," **Crosby, Stills, Nash & Young*** performing "Wooden Ships." Also performing: **The Who,*** **Sha Na Na,*** Joe Cocker,* Country Joe * and the Fish & others; with Jimi Hendrix,* Arlo Guthrie,* **Santana,*** **Sly and the Family Stone,*** & others on tapes *Woodstock.*

WOODWIND QUINTET

Jazz group led by flutist James Newton with tubist Red Callender, clarinetist John Carter, oboist Charles Owens, & bassoonist John Nunez, made their debut in Los Angeles, CA in 1980.

WOODWORTH, SAMUEL (1784–1842)

b. Scituate, MA. Lyricist, with composer George Kiallmark wrote "The Old Wooden Bucket" 1826.

WORK, HENRY CLAY (1832–1884)

b. Middletown, CT. Popular composer, wrote "Marching Through Georgia" 1865 about General Sherman's famous march (hated in the Southern states), and "Grandfather's Clock" 1876.

WORLD SAXOPHONE QUARTET

Jazz group with alto saxists Julius Hephill & Oliver Lake, tenor saxist David Murray, and baritone saxist Hamlet Bluiett in NY City 1979/80s, albums *Metamorphosis, Plays Duke Ellington, Rhythm and Blues.*

WORLD'S GREATEST JAZZ BAND, THE

Led by trumpeter Yank Lawson* & bassist Bob Haggart with soprano saxist/clarinetist Bob Wilbur, tenorman Bud Freeman,* trumpeter Billy Butterfield,* trombonists Benny Horton & Vic Dickenson,* & drummer Gus Johnson in 1970s, with trombonist George Masso, clarinetist/saxist Johnny Mince, drummer Bobby Rosengarden, & Keith Hingham in 1980s. Album *Live.*

WRECK-N-EFFECT

Trio with Markell Riley, Aquil Davidson, & Brandon Mitchell

(killed in 1990), debut album *New Jack Swing* with hit song "Rump Shaker" on album *Hard or Smooth* 1992.

WRIGHT, DANNY
Albums *Black and White, Phantasup, Time Windows,* etc.

WRIGHT, GARY (1943–   )
b. 4/26 Englewood, NJ. Singer with rock band **Spooky Tooth,** left for solo career 1970, hit albums *Dream Weaver* 1976, *Really Wanna Know You* 1981.

WRIGHT, MICHELLE
Country singer, with others on CBS show in January 1993, named New Female Vocalist by Country Music Association in May 1993.

WRIGHT, SYREETA
b. Pittsburgh, PA. Singer/songwriter, married Stevie Wonder,* later divorced, with Billy Preston* had hit "With You I'm Born Again" 1980.

WRUBEL, ALLIE (1905–1973)
b. Middletown, CT. Pianist/composer, with Herb Magidson wrote "Music, Maestro Please" 1938.

WYNETTE, TAMMY (1942–   )
b. Wynette Pugh 5/5 Red Bay, AL. Pianist/guitarist/singer, Country Music Association Female Vocalist of Year 1968/69/70, with Billy Sherrill wrote "Stand By Your Man" 1969. Albums *20 Years of Hits, Heart Over Mind, Next to You, Tears of Five: The 25th Anniversary Collection* 1992, video *Tammy Wynette,* with Randy Travis* nominated for country duo 1992. Married and divorced four times, then married George Richey.

WYNN, STEVE
Singer/songwriter, former leader of **Dream Syndicate,** went solo, albums *Kerosene Man* 1990, *Dazzling Display* 1992, with Matthew Wynn sang "Light of Hope."

WYNONNA *see* WYNONNA JUDD

X

X
Punk rock/heavy metal/country music group formed 1977 with
D. J. Bonebrake, John Doe, Exene (Christine Cervenka), Billy
Zoom. Albums *Los Angeles, More Fun in the New World, See
How We Are, Under the Big Black Sun.*

X-PENSIVE WIVES
Singer/guitarist Keith Richards,* guitarist Waddy Wachtel, &
drummer Steve Jordan. Group later disbanded and Richards
joined the **Rolling Stones.*** Richards, Wachtel, & Jordan
reunited on album *Main Offender* 1992.

XTC
Singer/songwriter Dave Gregory, bassist Andy Partridge, & bas-
sist Colin Moulding, hit "Then She Appeared" 1992, albums
*Black Sea, Drums and Wires, Oranges & Lemons, Rag & Bone
Buffet, The Ballad of Peter Pumpkinhead, Nonsuch* Grammy
winner 1993.

Y

Y & T
Albums *Contagious, In Rock We Trust, Mean Streak, Open Fire,* video *Live at San Francisco Civic Center.*

YANKOVIC, "WEIRD" AL
Rock & roll vocalist, album *Eat It* 1984, video *I'm Fat* won 1988 Grammy, video *The Compleat Al,* albums *Even Worse, Polka Party, Off the Deep End* 1992.

YANNI (CHRYSSOMALLIS) (1955–)
Pianist, albums *Chameleon Davis, In Celebration of Life, Optimystique, Reflections of Passion, In My Time,* album *Dare to Dream* won Grammy 1993, toured USA April/July 1993.

YARBOROUGH, GLENN (1930–)
b. 1/12 Milwaukee, WI. Tenor, served in Korean War, with Lou Gottlieb formed the **Limelighters*** 1959.

YARDBIRDS
British rock group formed 1963 with guitarist Jeff Beck, Eric Clapton,* Chris Dreja, Jame McCarty, Jimmy Page, Keith Relf, Paul Samwell-Smith, Anthony Sopham, hit "For Your Love," albums *Little Games* 1967, *Greatest Hits, VI-Smoke Stack Lightin', VII-Blues, Back Track A.*

YARROW, PETER (1938–)
b. 5/31 New York, NY. Singer/songwriter joined with Noel Paul Stookey* and Mary Ellin Travers* to form the team of **Peter, Paul and Mary.***

YEARWOOD, TRISHA (1965–)
Country singer from Monticello, Georgia, hit "She's in Love with the Boy" 1991, with Don Henley* sang duet "Walkaway Joe" at 1992 Country Music Awards, hit singles "The Woman Before Me" & "Wrong Side of Memphis" 1992, album *Hearts in Armor* 1992 sold over 500,000 copies, sang at Lincoln Memorial in Washington, D.C. in January 1993.

YELLEN, JACK (1892–1991)

b. 7/6 Razcki, Poland. Lyricist, came to New York, with composer Milton Ager* wrote "Happy Days are Here Again" 1929, Franklin D. Roosevelt's 1932 campaign song.

YELLO

Albums *Flag, One Second, You Gotta Say Yes,* etc.

YELLOW BIRD

Reggae/pop with Nardo Ranks,* Frankie Paul, & Junior Demus on album *Turning Point* 1992.

YELLOWJACKETS

With bassist Jimmy Haslip, group won 1988 Jazz Fusion Grammy for "Politics," albums *Four Corners, Greenhouse, Samurai Samba, The Spin, Yellowjackets, Live Wires* 1992, at the Monterey Jazz Festival in California in September 1992.

YELLOWMAN

Yellowman and his band **Sagittarius** toured USA 1992/93, albums *King Yellowman, Nobody Move, Nobody Get Hurt,* Yellowman & Charlie Chapli on *The Negril Chill.*

YES

British rock group formed 1968 with Jon Anderson, Peter Banks, Bill Bruford, Geoff Downes, Trevor Horn, Steve Howe, Tony Kaye, Patrick Moraz, Chris Squire, Rick Wakeman, & Alan White. Group hit singles "Yours is No Disgrace" & "Owner of a Lonely Heart" 1983, albums *Classic Yes, Close to the Edge, 9012 Live—The Solos, Relayer, Tormato, Union,* etc., videos *9012 Live, Greatest Video Hits, Yessongs, Yesyears.* Bassist Squire had solo album *Fish Out of Water* 1975.

YO YO (1971–)

b. Yolanda Whitaker, raised in South Central Los Angeles, hardcore singer. Albums *Make Way for the Motherload, Black Pearl* 1992, sang on Ice Cube's* 1990 solo album *AmeriKKK's Most Wanted, You Better Ask Somebody* 1993.

YO YO MA (1955–   )
b. 10/7 Paris, France. Cellist, came to USA. With Isaac Stern* on 1988 Top Ten Classical albums list for *Braham: Double Concerto,* teamed with Bobby McFerrin* at concerts in San Francisco & Boston, album *Hush* 1992.

YOAKAM, DWIGHT (1956–   )
b. Pikeville, KY & raised in Columbus, Ohio. Country singer/ guitarist, albums *Buenas Noches, Guitars, Cadillacs, Etc., Hillbilly Deluxe, If There Was a Way,* duet with Patty Loveless* on single "Send a Message to My Heart" 1992 sold one million copies, album *This Time* 1993, toured with Suzy Bogguss* 1993. "Ain't That Lovely Yet" 1994 Country Male Vocal Grammy winner.

YOTHU YINDI
Australian aborigine music played on a long wooden flute & clapsticks, band led by Mandawuy Yunupingud, American debut album *Tribal Voice* 1992.

YOUMANS, VINCENT (1898–1946)
Composer, wrote "Two Little Girls in Blue," "Wildflower," "No, No Nanette," "Hit the Deck," "Rainbow," "Smiles," with lyricist Irving Caesar* wrote "Tea for Two" 1924.

YOUNG GUNS *see* WILDSIDE

YOUNG, JAMES O. "TRUMMY" (1912–   )
b. 1/12 Savannah, GA. Trombonist/vocalist with Booker Coleman's Hot Chocolates 1928, with Earl Hines* in Chicago 1933/37, Jimmie Lunceford* 1937/43, then formed his own bands, with Louis Armstrong's **All-Stars*** 1952/64, in Hawaii 1960s/80s, played at various Jazz Festivals in USA.

YOUNG, JOSEPH (1889–1939)
b. New York, NY. Lyricist, with Sam Lewis & composer Walter Donaldson* wrote "How Ya Gonna Keep 'em Down on the Farm?" made famous by Al Jolson;* with composer Harry Akst* "Dinah" 1925; with composer Mabel Wayne "In a

Little Spanish Town"; with composer Ray Henderson* "Five Foot Two, Eyes of Blue"; and with composer Ted Fiorito* "Laugh, Clown, Laugh."

YOUNG, LESTER "PRES" (1909–1959)
b. Woodville, MS. Tenor saxist/clarinetist/composer, brother of drummer Lee Young. Lester toured with W. H. Young's Band (his father) then with Count Basie* 1936/40, recorded with Billie Holiday,* in army 1944/45, led his own groups 40s/50s, toured Europe with Jazz at the Philharmonic and died within 24 hours of his arrival back in NY City. Albums *Best of Lester Young, Master Takes, Young and Piano Giant Jazz*, etc.

YOUNG M. C.
Platinum album *Stone Cold Rhymin'* 1989.

YOUNG, MAUDE J. FULLER (1826–1882)
b. Beaufort, SC. Lyricist known as the "Confederate Lady," married Dr. S. O. Young of Houston, TX 1846. She wrote the lyrics for "The Song of the Texas Rangers."

YOUNG, NEIL (1945–   )
b. 11/12 Toronto, Ontario, Canada. Guitarist/singer/songwriter, moved to Los Angeles in 1966, music videos *Neil Young in Berlin* 1983 & *Solo Trans* 1986. Albums *After the Gold Rush, Comes a Time, Landing on Water, Rust Never Sleeps, Weld, Harvest Moon* 1992, leader of the **Stray Gators** band with Nils Lofgren* 1992. Videos *Ragged Glory, Freedom/Live Concert* 1993.

YOUNG OLYMPIA BRASS BAND
Played at the New Orleans Jazz Heritage Festival in April/May 1993.

YOUNG, PAUL (1955–   )
b. 11/30 Britain. Singer, albums *Between Two Fires, From Time to Time, No Parlez, Other Voices, The Secret of Association*, video *The Video Singles*.

YOUNG, RITA JOHNSON (1869–1926)
b. Baltimore, MD. Lyricist, with composers Ernest R. Ball* & Chauncey Olcott* wrote "Mother Machree" 1910 and with composer Victor Herbert* wrote "Ah, Sweet Mystery of Life" 1910.

YOUNG, VICTOR (1900–1956)
Composer, with lyricist Ned Washington wrote "My Foolish Heart" 1949, with lyricist Harold Adamson* composed "Around the World I've Searched for You" 1956

Z

ZADOR, EUGEN (1894–1977)
b. Batazek, Hungary. Composer, came to Hollywood, CA, wrote operas & suites, then film scores after 1939. Died 4/3 in Los Angeles, CA.

ZADORA, PIA
Singer, album *Pia and Phil,* duet with Jermaine Jackson on video *Jermaine Jackson: Dynamite Videos* 1985.

ZAMFIR, GHEORGHE
Pan flutist, albums *Christmas with Zamfir, Classics by Candlelight, Fantasy, Folk Songs & Dances, Romanian Flute.*

ZAPPA, FRANCIS V., JR. "FRANK" (1940–1993)
b. 12/21 Baltimore, MD, raised in Lancaster, CA. Leader, founded **The Mothers of Invention*** rock group 1964, played at the Palladium in NY City in October 1978, albums *Sheik Yerbouti, Jazz from Hell,* (Rock Grammy winner 1987), *Absolutely Free, Broadway the Hard Way, Hot Rats, One Size Fits All, You Can't Do That on Stage Anymore,* video *Does Humor Belong in Music?.* Appeared before a Senate Committee protesting Tipper Gore's (Mrs. Al Gore) criticism of rock and roll lyrics, July 1992. Due to prostate cancer he had to cancel an appearance in Germany and return to the states in 1992. Died 12/4 in Hollywood Hills, CA.

ZAPPA, MOON UNIT (1967–   )
Singer, daughter of Frank Zappa,* had a hit song written by her father "Valley Girl" 1982.

ZAPPA'S UNIVERSE
Featuring Steve Vi, *Sofa* Rock Instrumental Grammy 1994.

ZEVON, WARREN
b. Chicago, IL. Crooner/guitarist/songwriter, hit single "Werewolves of London" 1978, albums *A Quiet Normal Life, Excitable Boy, Sentimental Hygiene, Transverse City* 1990.

Album *Learning to Flinch* was recorded on his 1992 World Tour, *Dare to Dream* won 1992 Grammy.

ZIMBALIST, EFREM (1889–1985)
b. 4/9 Rostov, Russia. Violinist/composer, came to the USA, composed the opera *Landara*. Father of actors Efrem Zimbalist, Jr. and Stephanie Zimbalist. Died 2/22 Reno, NV.

ZIMMER, NORMA (1921–)
b. Larsen, Idaho. Singer, with the Lawrence Welk* Show, appeared on the Billy Graham Crusades, album *Whispering Hope*.

ZIMMERMAN, CHARLES A. (1861–1916)
b. Rhode Island. Conductor/composer, musical director of the U.S. Naval Academy in Annapolis, MD. With Alfred H. Miles wrote ''Anchors Aweigh'' 1906.

ZION HARMONIZERS
Group at the New Orleans Jazz Festival in April/May 1993.

ZOMBIES, THE
British rock group formed 1963 with Colin Blunstone, Rod Argent, Paul Atkinson, Hugh Grundy, & Chris Taylor White. Hits ''Tell Her No'' 1963, ''Time of the Season'' 1968, albums *Greatest Hits, Odessey and Oracle*. Singer Blunstone had a solo album *Journey* 1974.

ZWILICH, ELLEN TAAFFE (1939–)
b. 4/30 Miami, FL. Composer, first woman to win a Pulitzer prize in music 1983 for *Three Movements for Orchestra*. Albums *Celebration/Prologue/Nelson, Concerto Grosso, Symphony #2*.

ZZ TOP
Texas rock group formed 1970 with Frank Beard, Billy Gibson, & Dusty Hill, toured the states, albums have reached platinum. Albums *Afterburner, Deguello, El Loco, Eliminator, Rio Grande Mud, Tres Hombres, Greatest Hits* 1992.

SOURCES

Claghorn, Charles E. *Battle Hymn: The Story Behind the Battle Hymn of the Republic.* New York, NY: The Hymn Society of America, 1974.

————. *Biographical Dictionary of American Music.* West Nyack, N.Y.: Parker Publishing Company, 1973.

————. *Biographical Dictionary of Jazz.* Englewood Cliffs, N.J.: Prentice-Hall, Inc., 1982.

————. *The Mocking Bird: The Life and Diary of Its Author, Sep. Winner.* Philadelphia: The Magee Press, 1937.

————. *Women Composers and Hymnists: A Concise Biographical Dictionary.* Metuchen, N.J. and London: The Scarecrow Press Inc., 1984.

ABOUT THE AUTHOR

Charles Eugene Claghorn is a retired accountant whose hobby is writing research books on music and on the American Revolution. His interest in music stems from the fact that he is a great-grandson of Septimus Winner, a 19th century Philadelphia composer who wrote "Listen to the Mockingbird" in 1855, "Where, Oh Where Has My Little Dog Gone?" 1864, "Ten Little Indians" 1864, and "Whispering Hope" 1868. His great-granduncle Joseph Eastburn Winner was also a songwriter and wrote "Little Brown Jug" in 1869, later made famous as a jazz rendition by Glenn Miller.

Claghorn also wrote a Christmas carol "While Angels Sang," music by Nancy Ford Currie, first presented on Christmas Eve 1959 at the First Congregational Church, Old Greenwich, Connecticut and repeated there for several years afterwards. It was also presented in December 1983 at the Riverside Presbyterian Church in Cocoa Beach, Florida.

Presently, Gene Claghorn is serving as Historian of the Florida Society Sons of the American Revolution (1988–1994). His direct ancestor William Claghorn was captain of the ship *Virginia* during the Revolutionary War, and his collateral ancestor Colonel George Claghorn built the Frigate Constitution *Old Ironsides* in 1797. The National Society Sons of the American Revolution twice presented Claghorn with the Steven Taylor Award for the best book on the American Revolution: 1989 for his *Naval Officers of the American Revolution* and 1992 for his *Women Patriots of the American Revolution*. Both of these books were published by Scarecrow Press.